BEFORE THE

EAGLES

BEFORE THE BAND

RIK FORGO

TIME PASSAGES

First Edition (4) – December 2019

ISBN, Paperback (978-1-7343653-1-3)
ISBN, Ebook (978-1-7343653-2-0)

Published by Time Passages LLC
timepassages.net

*For my wife Maureen and
daughter, Emily, whose
support for this project
was unwavering.*

*A portion of the proceeds from this book
will be donated to Overcoming Multiple
Sclerosis, whose tireless efforts to inform,
educate and empower people who suffer
from this terrible disease is inspiring. For
more information, visit:
overcomingms.org*

ACKNOWLEDGMENTS

Time Passages started out as an idea for a rock music research project hatched between me and my best friend from childhood, Eric Rumburg, in the front seat of my 1979 MG Midget in 1984. Music was an important part of our lives. His sisters, Amy and Laura, would join us shouting out songs at the top of our lungs. Driving through the streets of La Plata, Maryland, Eric would swap out cassette tapes of various artists from the 1960s, '70s and '80s and we would regurgitate all the stories we had read about our favorite bands. What inspired the songs? Who played on that album? What gave them their big break? When did everything fall apart? The stories were eternal, but the structure was missing.

We thought it would be cool to gather these stories together, organize them chronologically and weave together everything that happened into an ongoing narrative. That little dream is achieved with this book, at least to a minor degree. Eric passed away in 2014 so he sadly never got to see the final product. I suspect he would approve, and he would demand changes because that was his way. I thank him for being my friend and planting the seed in my brain that evolved into *Time Passages.*

Special gratitude goes out to my lovely wife, Maureen, who was my sage advisor and enthusiastic cheerleader for this project. Her extreme patience for the long nights, early mornings and lost weekends needed to finish this book was, frankly, saint-like. Thanks babe, I love you.

We are also grateful for the help provided by Danielle Anderson, who did such a great job copy editing the manuscripts; Bruce Elrond and Sandy Graham, of *Cashbox* and *Record World*, who allowed us access to their company's treasure trove of music history; MJ at Gryphon Publishing Consulting, LLC, who so professionally handled the right clearances for our photos and illustrations; Todd Bates for the brilliantly conceived cover art and the interior design; Shaun Loftus and her team, who managed our marketing and helped us understand the world of social media. This project does not succeed without their assistance, contributions and encouragement. Thank you all!

HOW TO USE THIS BOOK

Time Passages books track a band's history one season at a time. The important moments in a band's origin story appear as an event occurred. Dates are estimated using the best data available, and are nested within a specific season. These events are categorized to give readers a view of milestones and events of different band members that illustrate how origin stories overlap and sometimes co-mingle. Informational graphics help illustrate important milestones in each band member's story, keeping pace with everything from singles releases to collaborations, touring partners and televised appearances. Those informational graphics cover:

Album Milestones

 Charts when the band and its individual band member's albums and singles reach sales milestones, including Recording Industry Association of America designations for Gold (500,000 albums sold or 1 million singles sold), Platinum (1 million albums sold or 2 million singles) and Diamond (10 million album or singles) certifications.

Awards & Honors

 Recognition of awards and honors bestowed on the band and its individual members, including Grammy, Hall of Fame and other music industry awards, as well as pop culture awards. *Sources: various halls of fame, Grammies, television networks.*

Chart Peaks

 Tracks when songs and albums from the band, including its individual members' solo careers, achieve their highest charting position on the Billboard singles or album charts. *Sources: Billboard, Cashbox, Record World*

Collaborations

 Identifies when members of the band participated with other artists in duets/group sessions, or provided studio support for other musicians. These listings are exhaustive, but incomplete as there is no absolute way to capture every collaborative instance. The intent is to show how band members contributed their talents to – and were sought out by – other artists. *Sources: Record labels (Asylum, Warner Brothers, etc.), Discogs.com*

End Notes

 Citations for the source material for stories, briefs and snippets are tagged at the end of each article as an end note. A full listing of citations can be found at the end of the book.

On Screen

 Appearances on television and movies are cited, along with the date of the appearance for the band or individual band members. Citations are based on verifiable sources and are exhaustive, but may not be complete because records for every appearance may not be published.

On the Road With ...

 Tracks who the band toured with or appeared on stage with for a given season. Tours and tour partners are highlighted, and appearances with other artists for one-off televised concerts and rock festivals are also cataloged. The listing is exhaustive, but not complete. *Sources: Setlist.fm, TourDatabase.com, magazine and newspaper references*

Pathways

Tracks important albums and singles completed by the band and band members.

Releases

 Tracks the release of singles and albums from the band, its individual members, and bands they participated in prior to joining the Eagles (e.g., Poco, the Flying Burrito Brothers, Flow, Longbranch Pennywhistle, Shiloh, etc.).

CONTENTS

CHAPTER 1 - INSPIRATIONS

CHAPTER 2 - BEGINNINGS

CHAPTER 3 - LEAVING HOME

CHAPTER 4 - LOS ANGELES

CHAPTER 5 - MEET THE EAGLES

INSPIRATIONS

Elvis, the Beatles and Motown were inspirations that helped propel the Eagles into their musical careers. Electrified folk and bluegrass music were also key components that moved the band into a period of self-discovery and creativity that evolved the California sound.

Before AM radio stations across the nation started playing *Take It Easy* to fans who couldn't get enough of the new country-rock sound coming from Los Angeles, the individual members of the Eagles were spread across the country in very different environments. They were raised in hard-working, regular American families that shared a common theme: they all loved music and passed that love down to their children. Another common inspirational theme among all the Eagles? Their love for **The Beatles** and **Elvis Presley**.

The leader of the Eagles, **Glenn Frey**, had a mother who insisted he learn to play piano. And he grudgingly did. But he also loved Elvis, Motown and, especially, he loved The Beatles. The day his aunt took him to see the Fab Four play live in Detroit's Olympia Hall in 1964 was an inspirational moment for him, and he often cited it as an important moment in his musical career.

Likewise, **Don Henley**'s musicial inspirations emerged from a family who would religiously turn on the radio to listen to the *Louisiana Hayride* on Sunday evenings. From their East Texas home, he and his family would gather to listen to Elvis, **Hank Williams** and a host of country legends perform every week. It kindled an interest in music that his mother, Hughlene, would nurture as he grew older. She, with his father CJ's approval, bought him his first drumset as a teenager. It was a pivitol moment that helped launch an award-winning musical career for Henley. Like Frey, Henley was inspired by The Beatles, and especially by **John Lennon**.

Elvis and The Beatles inspired legions of fans across the world and helped launch a multitude of musical careers, including that of young **Randy Meisner**, who saw Elvis perform live on *The Ed Sullivan Show* as an 12-year old; three years later he was playing bass for a local band in Scottsbluff, Nebraska, and credits that moment he saw Elvis on his black and white television set as the moment he knew he would be in music.

Far away from Nebraska, in the southwestern-most tip of the country, was a curly-haired teenager whose family bounced around the country like a ping-pong ball in the 1960s and 1970s. That teenager, **Bernie Leadon**, found inspiration in a quaint little guitar shop in San Diego, the *Blue Guitar*, where key components of California's folk and bluegrass movement of the late 1960s emerged. He developed strong friendships there with **Larry Murray**, **Ed Douglas**, **Kenny Wertz** and future Byrd **Chris Hillman** and learned to play guitar, banjo and mandolin – skills that would serve him well in the years to come and make him a valuable original member of the Eagles. And while Leadon's love for country and bluegrass music was critical to his origin story, he, like the other Eagles, also had an affinity for British music, particularly The Beatles and **George Harrison**. He even bought a Gretsch Tennesseean guitar, the same model Harrison played.

Joe Walsh had similar affections for John, Paul, George and Ringo. His life in music started with playing the oboe in high school in New Jersey, but he was forever changed when he saw The Beatles play live at Shea Stadium in 1965. He was stunned by the screaming girls and the music, which was so different than what he was accustomed to then. He dropped the oboe, picked up a guitar and found a band.

Nearly 1,000 miles south in Gainesville, Florida, another hot-shot guitar player named **Don Felder** had his interest in music piqued when his father bought him his first guitar. He liked The Beatles' cool presence, but his musical inspirations were driven more by Elvis and rhythm and blues' resident guitar legend, **B.B. King**. Felder connected with and was also inspired by a parade of some of Florida's soon-to-be prominent musical royalty, including the **Allman Brothers**, Duane and Gregg, and his one-time guitar student **Tom Petty**. Also there was future Eagle Leadon, who became friends with Felder when his aerospace engineer father moved his family to Florida.

The only Eagle who was actually born and bred in California, **Timothy B. Schmit**, arrived at music with a folk infleunce, and drew inspiration from artists like the **Kingston Trio**'s **Nick Reynolds** and, like the other Eagles, was amazed by The Beatles. He saw the band perform live twice in San Francisco, which was impressive given their short touring life as a band. He was in attendance in San Francisco at Candlestick Park when the group performed their final concert in the United States.

These inspirations were the drivers for a disparate set of fledgling musical careers for the four original Eagles. It all came together one day in Disneyland on a stage backing up a fast-rising country-rock singer named **Linda Ronstadt**. Their collective backgrounds laid the foundation for one of America's signature rock bands.

The stories that follow help describe the people and organizations that helped inspire and give the band's career gravity, and provided the building blocks for Eagles, before they were a band.

FALL 1894

Billboard Advertiser Publishes Its First-Ever issue

Billboard magazine is widely recognized as the industry standard for measuring record sales and the popularity of music played on "mechanicals" (jukeboxes and other music playing devices), phonographs, radio, tape decks, CDs, and now streaming devices. It got its start in 1894 as the *Billboard Advertiser*, and billed itself as "The World's Foremost Amusement Weekly." It was the go-to monthly black-and-white periodical for the advertising and bill posting industry, which itself evolved into billboards.

The publication turned its focus to recording and playback devices as those machines gained popularity in the early 1900s. Over the years *The Billboard* pages would cover vaudeville, minstrel shows, motion pictures, radio, and recorded music. It eventually backed away from motion picture coverage because *Variety* had become the industry Goliath. *Billboard*, however, would rule the music industry roost. In 1936, it launched its "hit parade" feature, which shone a spotlight on the most popular records being played. That feature evolved into the *Billboard* Hot 100 singles chart and the *Billboard* 200 chart, which tracks album sales. **Casey Kasem**'s syndicated *American Top 40* radio show would base its weekly rankings on Billboard's Hot 100 charts.

Billboard would be challenged over the years by publications like *The Cash Box*, *Record World*, and *New Musical Express*, but would outlast them all despite staring down bankruptcy several times. [1178, 1179]

WINTER 1931

Rickenbacker Produces First Cast Aluminum Guitar

When Joe Walsh and Don Felder unleashed their dueling guitars at the end of *Hotel California*, they may not have been thinking about how that performance was made possible when the album was released in 1976.

Walsh played the classic song with his Fender Telecaster and Felder matched his licks with his Gibson EDS-1275 double neck on the history-making song. It was historic, but the song, and perhaps popular music, may have turned out differently if not for **Adolph Rickenbacker**, **John Dopyera**, and **George Beauchamp**, who created the first cast aluminum

electric guitar in 1931 and, in the process, built the foundation for rock music.

Beauchamp was a vaudeville performer who played violin and acoustic guitar. Often playing alongside an orchestra, he was looking for a way to have his music rise above the pit. He met with Dopyera, a violin-maker and after a few attempts, finally got an early version of the guitar working. Rickenbacker was a production engineer and machinist who had a shop nearby in Santa Anna, California. When Dopyera went solo, Rickenbacker and Beauchamp began working on their version, and by the summer of 1932, they had developed the A25 Hawaiian, an aluminum-bodied guitar with string-driven electro-magnetic pickups that became known by most as the Ro-Pat-In Fry-Pan.

Rickenbacker continued evolving his designs that included wooden solid-body designs, but the business model changed when he sold the business to **F.C. Hall** in 1953. Hall, who owned Radio-Tel, refocused the business away from steel guitars and instead on standard electric and acoustic guitars with "through the neck" construction. These evolved Rickenbackers soon became the favorites of rock and roll heavyweights, including **Roger McGuinn**, **Graham Nash**, **Pete Townshend**, **John Lennon**, **George Harrison**, **Steve Van Zandt**, and **Stevie Ray Vaughn**. Eagles Glenn Frey and Joe Walsh owned them as well. [1421, 1422]

FALL 1931

33-1/3: Columbia Develops The Long-Playing Record

The long-playing record, or LP, changed the recorded sounds industry when The Columbia Company perfected the technology in the late 1930s. Up until then, sounds were captured on cylinders and were limited to two-to-three-minute recordings.

By the early 1920s, Western Electric had perfected a method of synchronizing sound to movies using 16-inch platter discs of hard shellac. By the late 1920s, that technique had further improved with the 78 RPM. In September 1931 a new Columbia design packed an entire symphony or opera, up to 24 minutes of sound, into the same size disc as the existing short-playing records of the day. These short-plays cost buyers 75 cents in 1926, but after the innovation the cost of an entire 24-minute disc was just $1.24. What's more, it allowed listeners to dispense with "albums," which were large sleeve books of discs that were gathered in a bound set of folders. The industry kept the "album" naming convention even after the practical use of the physical albums disappeared.

By 1948, Columbia had refined its design even more, offering 12-inch discs with 260 grooves per side and a sapphire needle (rather than the steel needles used up until then) to extract the sound. The new design allowed the packing of 45 minutes of recorded music on a single disc. It was a game changer. Listeners no longer had to replace a disc after 10 minutes of listening. A disc could play continuously; the new designs for record players even knew when the disc was over and could automatically flip to the other side. [1427, 1428]

SUMMER 1942

The Cash Box Becomes a Music Industry Barometer

Billboard magazine has been considered to be the bellwether for tracking the popularity of recorded music since the early 1930s, but a publishing industry newcomer, *The Cash Box*, became a credible competitor in July 1942 when it published its first issue.

The subscription-based magazine started out as a weekly classified ad for the coin-operated game industry, which was surging at that time. Like *Billboard*, *The Cash Box* expanded its field of business in the mid-to-late 1940s when jukeboxes became the rage in post-World War II America.

Recording companies flocked to the magazine and used it as a barometer for their industry. Soon, ad sales from those music companies was driving revenue and the coin-operated industry began to fade from its core business, although it never did disappear completely.

In its heyday, *Cash Box*'s charts were relied upon by music industry insiders as reliably as *Billboard*'s. Later renamed simply *Cashbox*, the magazine fell on hard times

Nannette Fabray and the cast of *The Bandwagon Year* perform during the live showing for a broadcast during the Louisiana Hayride in 1953. The Hayride was a sensation in the 1950s and was inspirational for a generation country and even rock performers.

LOUISIANA HAYRIDE MAKES ITS DEBUT BROADCAST

SPRING 1948 – When KWKH in Shreveport, Louisiana, decided to broadcast a weekly show at the Shreveport Municipal Memorial Stadium in the spring of 1948, it was not likely aware of the institution it was creating. It may not have foreseen the fan adoration or musical inspirations it generated among the country and folk music faithful either. It fostered both, and the warmth from this weekly program extended far beyond Louisiana.

The three-hour live program made its debut April 3, 1948, at 8 p.m., and in just a few short months, it became a staple among listeners in the American southeast and southwest. KWKH's Horace Logan acted as emcee and guided the show through nationally known performers like the **Bailes Brothers**, **Johnny and Jack and the Tennessee Mountain Boys**, the **Four Deacons**, and **Tex Grimsley** with his **Texas Playboys**.

Still second fiddle to its more well-known cousin, the **Grand Ole Opry** in Nashville, the show's prominence nonetheless grew over the years and even played host to a young, emerging **Elvis Presley** on December 15, 1956. While Presley's performance left adults nonplussed, youngsters were electrified.

The phrase "Elvis has left the building" was coined on that very evening, and Elvis signed a one-year contract with the *Hayride*. The show proved an inspiration to a young Texas-born Don Henley, who told *Billboard* in 2015 that he grew up listening to Elvis, **Johnny Cash**, **George Jones**, and others on the Hayride on Saturday nights with his parents. "We'd hear all that music," Henley told *USA Today*. "It was a part of my growing up."

The Hayride enjoyed a long, successful run until August 1960. Evening radio had lost its audience to television by then, so KWKH scaled back the *Hayride* to bi-weekly, monthly, and then quarterly operations. The station shut the landmark program down entirely in 1969, but not before launching a multitude of musical careers. [468, 469, 470, 1128]

The Cash Box was dedicated to the coin machine industry when it formed in 1942, an industry that included juke boxes that were becoming a force in the music industry. Within a decade Cashbox was primarily covering sales in the music industry and covered artists like Hank Williams in this December 1949 issue.

in the mid-1990s and published its last issue in November 1996. It was resurrected by new owner **Bruce Elrod** in 2006 as an online magazine and began charting singles again in roots music, bluegrass, bluegrass gospel, beach music, roadhouse blues and boogie, country Christian, and southern gospel.

The industry trade magazines were an important tool for musicians, including the Eagles, who used them to learn what other bands and labels were up to. Eagles co-founder Don Henley, disappointed by

the lack of communication between his managers, **David Geffen** and **Elliot Roberts**, told *Rolling Stone* in 1975: "We found out our management company had signed **Poco** and **America** by reading *Melody Maker*, yet another music industry publication. [88, 1175]

SPRING 1949

Sound Quality Boost: RCA Victor Releases 45-RPM Single

Building off the success of the long-playing record perfected by The Columbia Company in 1948, RCA Victor rolled out the 45 RPM record player, which it lauded as superior—if shorter than the LP—in sound quality.

Consumers were not pleased at first. The new 45 record did offer unquestionably better tonal qualities to music and speech, but it required a completely separate turntable to play the discs because its 45 revolutions per minute required a different motor than the 33-1/3 RPM discs that had been popularized.

The 45 RPM discs were also smaller, about seven inches across, and not capable of storing as much sound. But audiophiles of the day loved the sound quality, so turntable manufacturers began making machines that played both speeds. RCA made a successful play for younger buyers as well.

The vinyl being used was much quieter than the previous shellac records that were dominant in the 1930s. The vinyl was more flexible too, and manufacturers even pressed records in different colors for different classifications of music, including ruby red for classical, midnight blue for semi-classical, jet black for popular, lemon drop yellow for children's records, grass green for western music, sky blue for international, and cerise (red) for folk music. By the early 1950s, the era of 78 RPM records had reached an end, and the era of stereo music had emerged. The very first stereo 45 RPM record was released by Bel Canto Records in June 1958 for **Larry Fotine** and his orchestra.

FALL 1950

Fender Telecaster Gains Worldwide Acceptance

Adolph Rickenbacker gave the world the first cast aluminum guitar in 1931, but just a few short years later, the concept was being modified and improved upon by engineers and musicians who were looking for a particular sound. With the help of a war buddy, **Clarence Leo Fender** took guitar manufacturing to another level when he created what would become the Fender Telecaster, one of the most widely used guitars through today.

Oddly enough, the journey that led to rock music's most dependable guitar started in a dark office amongst stacks of corporate accounting ledgers. Fender was studying to be an accountant in 1928, but he always had a fascination with electronics. He was working as a bookkeeper for an ice compa-

ny in his hometown of Fullerton, California, when a local band leader who knew of his interest in electronics asked him if he could build a public address system for dances in Hollywood. Fender then built six of them.

In 1938, he borrowed $600 and started the Fender Radio Service, and he made, rented, sold, and serviced PA systems to musicians and band leaders. During World War II, Fender met **Clayton "Doc" Kaufmann**, who used to build steel guitars for Rickenbacker. They became business partners, formed K&F Manufacturing, and then began building amplified Hawaiian steel guitars. In 1944, Fender and Kaufmann patented a lap steel guitar using an electric pickup that Fender had already patented.

Players had been "wiring up" instruments for greater volume and projection since the late 1920s, and manufacturers like Gibson and Rickenbacker were well known. Fender and Kauffman built a crude wooden guitar as a pickup test rig, and local country players who knew about it kept borrowing it. The guitar was a favorite because it had a bright sound and it was sustaining. Fender knew that he and Kaufmann were onto something, so he built a better version of it as a solid body with a bolt-on neck. It had all the same features that would become the Telecaster.

The first single-pickup version was the Fender Esquire, made of ash and maple, and because it came in just one color, it was called "blonde." The Esquire had issues since there were no trusses in the neck, and most of the first 50 were brought back because the necks would bend. The next iteration, a two-pickup model, was called the Broadcaster, and it had truss rods to keep the neck from bending. The Gretsch Company sold a line of drums called "Broadkaster" that were trademarked, so Fender simply dropped the name "Broadcaster" to avoid a lawsuit. Models without the name then became known to collectors as "Nocasters."

In 1950, Fender came out with its next iteration, the Telecaster, that then dominated the industry. It also rolled its stablemate Precision Bass, which eventually became known as the Telecaster Bass. In 1954, Fender released the next in its line, the hugely successful Stratocaster, but demand for the Telecaster never relented and it remains a guitar player staple today. Many musicians favored the Telecaster because its solid construction allowed guitarists to play loudly with long sustain if needed. Hollow body instruments would sometimes produce uncontrolled whistling or hard feedback.

Fender gave both current-day and wanna-be guitar gods an outlet for their musical ya-yas when he created the Telecaster. He was inducted into the Rock and Roll Hall of Fame in 1992, just one year after he died from complications of Parkinson's Disease. The line of rock musicians who swear (or swore) by the Telecaster is long and distinguished. **James Burton** and his "Pink Paisley" Telecaster and Joe Walsh famously used a classic 1970s Telecaster in his guitar duel with Don Felder on the Eagles' *Hotel California* according to EquipBoard.com.

Bernie Leadon used a 1960s Telecaster on the first two Eagles albums, and Glenn Frey favored a 1966 white Fender Telecaster. Country artist and latter-day Eagle **Vince Gill** keeps a couple Telecasters at the ready as well. Outside the Eagles circle, Telecasters are used by **Slash**, **Jack White**, **Alex Lifeson**, **Pete Townshend**, **Sheryl Crowe**, **David Gilmour**, **Billy Joe Armstrong**, and **Eddie Van Halen**. [1422, 1423, 1477]

WINTER 1950

Fats Domino Records First 'Rock' Record, *The Fat Man*

When asked in the mid-1950s how it felt to be a pioneer in rock and roll, **Fats Domino** stood up from his piano bench, smiled broadly, and said, "What you call rock and roll, I call rhythm and blues, and I've been playing it for 15 years in New Orleans."

Antoine Domino Jr. was born in New Orleans in February 1928, and by the time he was 14, he was playing piano in local bars. He was discovered by **Billy Diamond**, a local bandleader, at a backyard barbecue and he hired him to play clubs for $3 per week. Diamond nicknamed him "Fats" because Domino reminded him of another piano player, **Fats Waller**.

Domino's career took off in 1949 when Imperial Records owner **Lew Chubbs** signed him. Their contract was unique for the day because Domino preferred to be paid royalties based on sales rather than earning a flat fee for each song. Chubbs agreed to those terms. Domino and producer **Dave Bartholomew** then began working on a modified version of *The Junker Blues*, a scurrilous song about drug addiction sung by blues artist **Champion Jack Dupree**. The pair reworked the song's lyrics, and more importantly, they played a more aggressive, boogie-woogie version with "piano-triplet-and-snare-backbeat hits."

Boogie-woogie players of the era had a certain style, and Domino adapted that style by playing a more stripped-down boogie-woogie version. They called their grooves "rocks"—hence the first recognized "rock" record—and Domino elaborated on that style by working his keyboard triplets and integrating swing with rhythm and blues.

The song was released by Imperial in December 1949 and Chubbs claimed it sold 10,000 copies in 10 days. By January 1950, it had rocketed up to #2 on the *Billboard* R&B Singles chart. By 1953, it had sold a jaw-dropping one million copies. Domino went on to place 35 records in the *Billboard* Top 100 over his career, including five gold records before 1955. He had 11 top 10 hits between 1955 and 1960, and over that span, he was the only artist to sell more records than **Elvis Presley**. He sold more than 65 million records over his career and Elvis even proclaimed him as the true "King of Rock and Roll" at a 1969 concert.

Domino had an impact on the Eagles, as well. He has been cited as an inspiration by both Glenn Frey and Don Henley. "There's an old recording artist from New Orleans called Fats Domino and his mantra was, 'just give me a catchy tune,'" Henley told the *New Zealand Herald* in 2017. "As simple as that may sound I think there's a lot of truth in it."

At a June 20, 2018, concert in New Orleans, Henley remembered Domino again during the Eagles' two-and-a-half-hour set. He remembered fondly to how he had tuned in to a broadcast of New Orleans' WNOE at his boyhood home in Linden, Texas. They were playing Domino's *Walkin' To New Orleans*, and the drummer remembered the moment fondly before the Eagles broke into their own rendition of the blues classic. [1431, 1432, 1433]

SUMMER 1951

Dominoes' *Sixty Minute Man* Banned, But Record Sales Surge

Songs laced with sexual innuendo were nothing new in the early 1950s, but they only occasionally made it onto popular radio. That changed in 1951 when Philadelphia-born **Billy Ward** and his band, the **Dominoes**, released *Sixty Minute Man* and it caught on with radio stations nationwide.

Ward, an educated African-American man who went to the Juilliard School of Music in New York, struck up a business partnership with agent **Rose Marks**. The two wanted to form a group that would rival famous groups of the day, like the **Ink Spots** or the **Orioles**. In 1950, they pulled together the pieces that formed the Dominoes: **Clyde McPhatter**, **Bill Brown**, **Charlie White**, and **Joe Lamont**.

Marks suggested Ward and the Dominoes to future Rock and Roll Hall of Fame inductee **Ralph Bass**, who then ran Federal Records.

Bass signed the group and had them record *Do Something for Me*, a single that did reasonably well. But it was their second song that created a stir. *Sixty Minute Man* was written by both Ward and Marks, and spoke from the singer's perspective of his sexual prowess. "*There'll be fifteen minutes of kissin'/Then you'll holler 'Please don't stop'/There'll be fifteen minutes of teasin'/And fifteen minutes of blowin' my top.*"

Ward opted to use Brown's deep bass vocals for the song rather than McPhatter's tenor voice, and the results were immediately successful, but also controversial. Many conservative radio stations labeled the song too risqué and banned the song from their playlists. But the old axiom "there's no such thing as bad publicity" rang true for **Billy Ward and his Dominoes**. While some radio stations forbade the song, the music-buying public was pushing the single up the charts. When Federal released the song in 1951, it quickly ascended to #1 on the *Billboard* R&B Singles chart and stayed there for 14 solid weeks.

The Eagles would have their own encounter with the concept of scrutinized lyrics in the late 1970s and early 1980s when their epic album *Hotel California* came under scrutiny for lyrics that some interpreted as cultish and satanic. More recently a radio station in Alabama opted to remove *Life in the Fast Lane* from its 2009 playlists because of the band's use of "Goddamn" in the song's lyrics. [1434, 1435, 1436, 1474]

WINTER 1952

Alan Freed Organizes First-Ever Rock Concert in Cleveland

Few people in the early days of rock and roll had a more tangible impact on the genre than **Alan Freed**. As a disc jockey at Cleveland's WJW-AM, he embraced the rising popularity of R&B-infused "race" music in the early 1950s and tied it to the sexually laced term "rock 'n roll," a phrase he coined as part of his late-night radio show the *Moondog Rock 'n Roll Party*.

Freed was born in Windber, Pennsylvania, December 21, 1921, but his family moved to Salem, Ohio, when he was 12. He attended Ohio State University and then served a brief stint in the Army. He then opted to study broadcasting in Youngstown, Ohio. He became a sports announcer on WKAR in Akron, and by 1950, he had landed a job as a disc jockey at WJW.

Freed was passionate about his work and would often visit local record stores to learn what local teenagers were buying. He watched with amazement as white teens from urban Ohio communities were buying up R&B records by black artists, which were then referred to as "race" records. Quick to take advantage of the trend, he worked those songs into his nightly program—he was the first white deejay to air rhythm and blues records on Ohio's north coast. His ratings soared. Emboldened, Freed then took the trend to the next level. He worked with local record store owners to promote his Moondog Coronation Ball, which became the first-ever rock and roll concert. It was simultaneously a raging success and an absolute disaster.

The concert was held March 21, 1952, at the Cleveland Arena. It featured **Billy Ward and his Dominoes**, **Paul Williams and the Hucklebuckers**, **Tony Grimes and the Rocking Highlanders**, **Danny Cobb**, **Varetta Dillard**, and a host of others artists. Freed and his promoters ran into logistical problems that night. It was the first rock and roll concert, so there wasn't a blueprint for how to manage the night. The arena could seat 10,000 people, but more than 25,000 showed up to attend, thanks mostly to advertisements that failed to differentiate between that show and another planned for the following week. The hall filled up so quickly that people who bought tickets in advance couldn't get in, and they weren't happy. Police and firefighters showed up and, in a manner that seems befitting of a rock and roll concert, rioting ensued. Firefighters hosed down the crowd, which dissipated soon after. Undaunted, Freed began scheduling more and learned from the mistakes of the first. [1438, 1439]

SUMMER 1953

Birthday Gift: Elvis Presley Wanders In To Sun Records

Recent high school graduate **Elvis Aaron Presley** wanted to give his mother an "extra" birthday gift in the summer of 1953. Studying to become an electrician, Presley had some exposure to the gospel music that enriched Memphis, Tennessee, where his family had just moved to from his hometown of Tupelo, Mississippi.

Sam Phillips had just recently opened his Sun Records studio in Memphis, and Presley wanted to surprise his mother with an acetate recording of the songs *My Happiness* and *That's When Your Heartaches Begin*. He cut the tracks and paid $4 for the recordings. Sun's secretary, **Marion Keisker**, was impressed by his talent, and one year later when Presley returned to make another recording, Phillips asked him to try out a few other songs. The recording sessions were hit and miss—mostly miss—but Phillips believed there was something special about the young singer.

Phillips invited Presley back for more sessions and added backing musicians **Scotty Moore** and **Bill Black**. He also found songs that better fit Presley's impressive vocal range and finally settled on **Arthur "Big Boy" Crudup**'s *That's All Right, Mama*. Phillips recorded and it was an immediate sensation. Presley's electrician studies came to an end and Phillips began recording more and scheduling live shows. One poor performance at *The Grand Ole Opry* devastated the young singer's confidence, but he picked himself up and found favor with the Opry's main competitor, the *Louisiana Hayride*, which signed him to a string of well-received performances. It would be the launchpad for an illustrious musical career. [1440, 1441]

FALL 1954

Music Vendor Joins *Billboard*, *Cashbox* as Music Biz Scribes

Billboard and *Cashbox* ruled the world music industry trade magazines from the 1930s through the early 1960s, but these venerable magazines got competition when a young, flashy upstart came into the industry and began to take market share: *Music Vendor*.

The publication, which has its main of-

Music Vendor was the third publication dedicated to the business side of the music industry. It was founded in 1954, but underwent a transformation in the late 1960s. It then became *Record World* and began used cutting edge technology and modern design. Its journalistic approach to music made it a favorite among musicians and agents.

fices across the street from the Ed Sullivan Theater in New York, was founded in 1954 and foundered along as the third wheel in the music trade press for nearly a decade. But when the music industry surged in the late 1960s as the music industry began undergoing huge changes the publication changed its name to *Record World*, and rolled with those changes along with the industry.

Solid reporting and a welcoming attitude that was more attractive to musical acts than *Cashbox* and *Billboard*, which artists often viewed as older, stodgier and even arrogant, *Record World* was "hipper" and "lively" by comparison. For industry executives, *Record World* served an important, unserved niche. Even though all three trade magazines charted songs similarly, *Billboard*'s charts, for example, would not measure "rack jobbers," who were the middle men who supplied records to non-record store retail outlets and department stores like K-Mart, which were a huge and growing part of the industry. Record executives needed *Record World* to get a clear picture of that missing segment of the industry.

Artists generally believed *Record World* was the best of the three journalistically. It took a journalistic approach that was somewhere between *Billboard* and *Rolling Stone*, and recognized that the industry needed to understand the artists view on the business side of the recording industry. They towed that line better than the others, but all that came to an end in 1982

Elvis Presley signs autographs early in 1956 after the release of Heartbreak Hotel, the single that catapulted the Tupelo, Mississippi-born singer. Presley was an inspiration for a multitude of rock and roll artists, including Eagles leader Glenn Frey and guitarist Don Felder.

ELVIS, RCA RELEASE CHART-TOPPING *HEARTBREAK HOTEL*

WINTER 1956 – Elvis Aaron Presley was an emerging rockabilly sensation in the winter of 1956. After working with Sun Records producer **Sam Phillips**, Presley had begun to develop a following. He had recorded a hit with *That's All Right, Mama* and his star was rising quickly. After two years with Sun, the young crooner was lured away by music promoter Colonel **Tom Parker** to the *RCA Victor* label. Presley, then just 21 years old, released his first RCA single, *Heartbreak Hotel*, which rocketed to #1 on the *Billboard* charts.

Heartbreak Hotel raised Elvis' stature. Colonel Parker was attentive in the studio and collected a group of top-shelf supporting musicians like **The Blue Moon Boys**, pianist **Floyd Cramer** and legendary guitarist **Chet Atkins** for Elvis's RCA debut. The single was unlike any other on the radio in the mid-1950s, and it crossed over from the pop charts to the country charts, as well. It stayed perched atop the *Billboard* charts for seven straight weeks in January and February 1956.

Heartbreak, and to a larger degree Elvis and his mystique, served as an inspiration for a parade of future rockers, including former Eagles guitarist Don Felder. In his 2008 book *Heaven and Hell: My Life in the Eagles*, Felder cited Presley as huge inspiration for him. Shortly after hearing *Hotel* for the first time, he remembered, a flood of music called "rock and roll" followed, and he knew right away it was for him. "Something about it really made the hairs stand up on the back of my neck."

Two years later, Felder rode that inspiration to form *The Continentals*, his first real rock band, along with fellow Rock and Roll Hall of Famer **Stephen Stills**. Felder also said former bandmate, the late Glenn Frey, was a huge Elvis fan as well. While Elvis was known as "The King," during Frey's early days as an Eagle, he was known as the "Teen King" in homage to Presley. Don Henley also said that the very first rock and roll record he ever bought was by Elvis Presley. [218, 1129]

when corporate financial troubles, as well as a downturn in the music industry, sent *Record World* into bankruptcy. It never recovered and folded. [1176, 1177]

FALL 1955

James Dean Appears in *Rebel Without a Cause*

Moody, rebellious, and full of angst. **James Dean**'s character, Jim Stark, was a teenage delinquent who exuded these qualities in *Rebel Without a Cause*, a film that spoke volumes to America's youth when it was released in October 1955.

Dean, as Stark, gets in knife fights, steals cars, and runs away from home. He doesn't want to become his father. In the second of three films that made up his short movie career, Dean became a vibrant anti-hero symbol for his generation.

These rebellious qualities also happened to align well with rock and roll's emerging place in society. Dean's aloof, restless demeanor emitted a similar angsty vibe given off by Holden Caulfield, the cynical central character in **J.D. Salinger**'s 1951 novel *Catcher in the Rye*. It wasn't just the characters he was playing; Dean seemed to be playing himself. America was changing, and Dean became a poster boy for that evolution. In his role as Jim Stark, he finds himself at a crossroad between childhood and becoming an adult. He has a coarse exterior but a kind heart. He wants his father to stand up to his controlling mother. He seeks

out daredevil challenges to satiate his need for peer approval and he struggles with his place in school, love, and with the guilt that comes with knowing he had some perceived culpability in a rival's death. These types of themes are played out in the lyrics of rock songs across generations, and for many, Dean was the inspiration.

David Essex provided the first tribute in song to "Jimmy" Dean in 1973 with *Rock On*, which remains a staple on classic rock playlists. The song paid homage to early rock and roll and its subculture, with a specific callout to Dean and his anti-hero influence. At roughly the same time as Essex's release, the Eagles were gathering material for their second album. They were looking for desperado types and considered songs about people like Dean and famed depression-era outlaw **John Dillinger**. But when the decision was made to steer the album to a Western concept, their song *James Dean* was shelved until work started on their third album, *On the Border*.

Dean was a hero to the committee who wrote the song: Glenn Frey, **Jackson Browne**, **J.D. Souther**, and, to a lesser extent, Don Henley all contributed. Henley told *Rolling Stone*'s **Cameron Crowe** that Dean's mystique didn't quite reach him in his East Texas childhood. "I sat there and listened to the guys talk about James Dean," he said in 2003. "They had evidently studied him and knew much more about him than I did. I had seen most of Dean's movies, but I somehow missed the whole icon thing. The mythology never quite reached my part of East Texas, but I pitched in and ended up with a writing credit—although the song was mostly Jackson's, I think."

The image of Dean within the Eagles had just one representative. On Frey's passing in 2016, Don Felder called Frey the "James Dean of the Eagles." [209, 602, 1443]

SUMMER 1956

Music Television: Dick Clark Hosts First *American Bandstand*

Dick Clark was working as a deejay at Philadelphia's WFIL when he was called to fill in on *Bob Horn's Bandstand* in the summer of 1956. Clark, who would go on to become one of the most well-known television hosts in the world, stepped into the Bandstand role and never let it go.

Clark began his career in radio in 1945 working in the mailroom at WRUN in Rome, New York, a station that was owned and managed by his family. He bounced around in disc jockey jobs, and even kept up with the family business by buying two radio stations in Riverside and Santa Barbara, California, KTMS and KTYD, respectively, all the while serving as a deejay at various New York radio stations. He took a deejay job at WFIL in 1952 in Drexel Hill, Pennsylvania, a suburb of Philadelphia, and was slowly given more responsibility.

Bob Horn was the host of WFIL's television affiliate in Philadelphia, WPVI, and hosted his own afternoon dance show, *Bob Horn's Bandstand*. Clark hosted the radio version of the show and would often guest host when Horn was on vacation.

Horn was arrested for drunk driving in the summer of 1956 and was dismissed. The popular show needed a new host and Clark got the call. His accessible nature and strong rapport with the live teenage audience boosted the show's ratings and it got picked up nationally in August 1957 by the ABC television network, which renamed the show *American Bandstand*. A year later, ABC dropped its gruelling five-days-a-week schedule and gave the show a permanent place on Saturday afternoons. By the end of the year, it had more than 20 million viewers. It became the favorite spot for up-and-coming artists who would perform semi-live with lip-synced performances that would nearly always assure a record sales boost after appearing. **Fats Domino**, **Buddy Holly**, **Jerry Lee Lewis**, **Sam Cooke**, and **Fabian** were some his early guests.

ABC moved the show from Philadelphia to Los Angeles in 1964, and Clark remained a fixture. As the country's musical tastes changed, Clark adapted. In the 1960s, he played host to **Ike and Tina Turner**, **Stevie Wonder**, **Simon and Garfunkel**, **The Beach Boys**, **Smokey Robinson and the Miracles**, and **Michael Jackson**.

Kenny Rogers appeared on Bandstand on June 19, 1971, and brought with him a band he discovered in Dallas, Texas, called **Shiloh**, which was led by **Richard Bowden** and future Eagle Don Henley. Shiloh performed *Down on the Farm*, and *Simple Little Down Home Rock and Roll Love*

Berry Gordy and Motown Records became a formidable player in the record industry in the late 1950s. With hit after hit Motown carried its momentum through to the 1980s. The company's was motivational to millions of music fans, including a young future Eagle, Glenn Frey.

GORDY BORROWS $800, STARTS TAMLA-MOTOWN RECORDS

WINTER 1957 – **Berry Gordy** got his first taste of success in the winter of 1957 when **Jackie Wilson** recorded his song, *Reed Petite*, and watched it climb to #62 on the *Billboard* singles chart.

Encouraged by the charting performance, Gordy offered his songwriting skills to other artists and experienced some success, including **Etta James**, who recorded his *All I Could Do was Cry*. But Gordy had bigger plans than just writing songs for others. He and his friend, **Smokey Robinson**, worked together on recordings including the single *Got A Job,* with his band, **The Miracles**, which was released by The End Records in the spring of 1958. Gordy produced the single, which got airplay nationally, but the recording earned him a paltry $3.19.

With that disappointing return, Robinson encouraged Gordy to remove the middleman and form his own label. Gordy took his advice and invested his songwriting earnings, along with an $800 loan from his parents, and he started Tamla Records in 1959; by 1960 Tamla Records and Anna Records, a label started by Gordy's sister Gwen, had merged to form Motown Records. Fronted by Robinson, The Miracles became a hit machine for Gordy. *Shop Around* became the label's first million-selling single, and was quickly followed by high-charting singles like *You've Really Got a Hold on Me*, *Mickey's Monkey*, *What's So Good About Goodbye*, and *I'll Try Something New*. The label gained traction in December 1961 when **The Marvellettes**' *Please Mr. Postman* gave Motown its first #1 single.

The success of The Miracles, along with all-girl bands like the Marvellettes and the **Supremes**, opened the door for a parade of musicians that were discovered and nurtured by Gordy and Motown. Artists like **Marvin Gaye**, **The Temptations**, **Jimmy Ruffin**, **The Four Tops**, **Gladys Knight & the Pips**, the **Commodores**, **Martha and the Vandellas**, **Stevie Wonder** and, in the mid-1960s, bands like the **Jackson 5** were brought into the fold.

Gordy guided Motown's success for nearly three decades, and brought in new talents in the 1970s and 1980s, including the **Jacksons**, **Rick James** and **Lionel Richie**. But the recording industry had changed dramatically by the late 1980s and Motown fell upon hard times. Gordy sold his interest in the label in 1988 to MCA Records for $61 million.

Motown's imprint on popular music was significant. The label had a lasting impact on millions of fans worldwide, including Eagles co-founder Randy Meisner.

"I loved R&B, Smokey Robinson and the Miracles, Mary Wells, the Temptations, Marvin Gaye," Meisner told the *San Francisco Weekly* in 1998. "The bass players on the Motown stuff were great. They really inspired me."

Likewise, Eagles leader Glenn Frey drew a lifelong inspiration from the music of Motown. A Detroit native, Frey was enamored of Motown's R&B stylings. He, along with fellow rock and roll hall of famer and friend **Bob Seger**, got an up-close look at how the label produced records and was amazed by their work. He said he and Seger visited with Motown's artist and reportoire man **Mickey Stevenson** in 1976 and Seger played his recently completed single *Heavy Music*.

"Mickey went into a rant. 'Here's how we would have cut this record if we'd done it at Motown!'" Frey recounted. "He [Stevenson] proceeded to stand up in front of us. 'Here's what we do! The backbeat is the most important thing. We put everything on it: hand claps, snare drums, another snare drum, this, that.' My mouth was wide open. This revelation!"

Frey, Seger and **J.D. Souther** would find some of that rhythm years later when they co-wrote *Heartache Tonight* for the Eagles' *The Long Run* album. Inspirationally, Gordy and Motown resonated with Frey for the rest of his life.

Smokey Robinson (right) and his band, The Miracles, were Motown's first hit group and delivered Berry Gordy's very first million-selling single for Motown Records.

"He named his last kid Otis!" Seger told the *Detroit News* in 2016 after Frey's passing. "He loved **Michael Jackson**'s *Off the Wall* album when that came out, he drove me crazy playing that. He really was a closet soul guy in a country-rock band. You can hear it burst through a bit in *One of These Nights* and later, in *The Long Run*, that soul thing he loved."

In a 2016 interview with *Rolling Stone*, J.D. Souther said "Glenn had two things in spades. He had an incredible sense of humor — a wild, almost infantile love of a really great joke. And he had this Motor City groove. He knew every note Motown ever released. He brought the beat." [392, 462, 1226, 1410, 1411, 1412]

Song for Rosie on the show, which they had recorded earlier that summer for their new label, Amos Records.

Clark would host the show for 33 years until it was cancelled by ABC in 1989. It was picked up for a year by the USA Network with Clark no longer hosting, but finally ended in October 1989 after a 26-week run. [1454, 1455, 1456]

FALL 1956

Elvis Draws Huge Ratings On *The Ed Sullivan Show*

Elvis Presley made his first appearance on *The Ed Sullivan Show* on CBS on September 9, 1956. It was by all counts a landmark performance viewed by more than 60 million people and landed a 43.7 rating—an astonishing 82.6 percent of America's entire viewing audience.

The night, and the two subsequent performances by Presley on the show, changed modern American music and paved the way for rock and roll as a musical genre. Sullivan, who was recovering from an auto accident, didn't host the show; CBS installed actor **Charles Laughton** as his stand-in host. It was a bit of a capitulation on Sullivan's part since he had vowed never to have Presley on the show because he believed his act was not suited for families.But the show was nevertheless a huge hit and it had a resonating impact on future musicians. A then-ten-year-old Randy Meisner, a founding member of the Eagles, watched Presley perform on Sullivan's show and was inspired. "[Elvis] actually started me off," Meisner told the *Associated Press*. "Now I see that it's really hard to become somebody that special. He broke a lot of openings for everybody."

Likewise, former Eagles guitarist Don Felder was awed by Presley's presence in a later performance on that same show. "I remember seeing Elvis Presley on *The Ed Sullivan Show* one Sunday night in 1957 and going wild," Felder said in his 2008 book. "He sang *Hound Dog*, *Heartbreak Hotel*, and *Love Me Tender*, and I was completely blown away." [218, 463, 1133]

WINTER 1956-57

Jackie Wilson Records Berry's *Reed Petite*; Motown Launches

Jackie Wilson got his rock-and-roll hall of fame start with *Reed Peitite*, a frolicking be-bopping song co-written by a then-unknown **Berry Gordy**. Wilson, then just a budding 23-year-old singer from Detroit, signed a recording deal with the venerable Brunswick Records, a old-line company that began recording in 1916. It was a gamble for Wilson, who had some security backing **Billy Ward and the Dominoes**. But Wilson thought he could do more.

Brunswick tapped Wilson's friend Gordy, and he and his sister **Gwen Gordy** and his cousin, **Roquel "Billy" Davis**, set out to write songs for Wilson's debut album. They authored six songs for Wilson's debut, and Brunswick worked the phones at radio stations across the country to get airplay. It worked and *Reed Petite* reached #62 on the *Billboard* singles chart in September 1957. It launched Wilson's hall of fame career that spawned huge hit singles like *Lonely Teardrops* and *(Your Love Keeps Lifting Me) Higher and Higher*, but the success of *Petite* had another lasting, though less immediately apparent impact. It gave Gordy the funding he needed to start Motown Records, which would go on to become an iconic institution in the recording industry and set the bar for rhythm and blues artists for the next six decades. [392, 1226, 1410, 1411, 1412]

Lennon Creates Popular Skiffle Group, The Quarrymen

Motivated by rock and roll music coming from America, high schooler **John Lennon** formed his own band in November 1956, the Quarrymen. At the time, popular radio was dominated by the likes of **Buddy Holly**, **Fats Domino**, and **Elvis Presley**. Lennon learned to play the banjo from his mother, **Julia Lennon**. From there, it wasn't a far leap to learn guitar, and he and school friend **Eric Griffiths** decided to form a "skiffle" band, which was a fusion of improvisational jazz and blues that many credit as the root form of rock and roll. Lennon and Griffiths learned to play songs like *Ain't That a Shame*, *Alabamy Bound*, and *That's All Right, Mama* and began adding band members. They played at local dance halls, parties, and social events. In July 1957, Lennon was introduced to **Paul McCartney**, who had watched the band perform during

a church event. By October, McCartney was in the band and the group's repertoire grew to include more complex songs, like **The Everly Brothers**' *Bye Bye Love* and Elvis's *All Shook Up*. McCartney suggested adding his friend **George Harrison** in February 1958 and Lennon agreed, though reluctantly because Harrison was just 14 at the time.

McCartney and Harrison's musical skills far surpassed the other Quarrymen, and Lennon's skills had improved greatly as well. The group ventured further from skiffle and more toward mainstream rock and roll, and some members left the band as a result, leaving the group with just Lennon, McCartney, and Harrison. By 1960, they renamed themselves **The Beatles**. **Ringo Starr** was brought in as drummer, and the group began to get noticed. By 1962, they had taken the world by storm and, with more than 800 million records sold, became the most successful rock band in history.

Lennon and The Beatles had a lasting impact on members of the Eagles. "John Lennon is still a great influence on my life, and my career," Don Henley told **Uncle Joe Benson** on his radio program. "The first song I ever tried to sing in public was one of his songs; it was called *She's a Woman*. He was my biggest hero, even bigger than Elvis.

"I loved his voice, I loved his sense of humor—his dry wit. I loved the songs he wrote, the lyrics he wrote. I loved what he stood for, what he believed in, everything about him, really. He was a great influence on me. He's certainly been one of our role models." [562, 1158, 1418, 1419]

WESTON OPENS THE TROUBADOUR CLUB IN HOLLYWOOD

WINTER 1957 – As an incubator for top emerging musical acts in the late 1960s and through the 1970s, the Troubadour club in West Hollywood had many rivals, but few real peers. It was a musical and cultural mecca, but started out as an inconspicuous little coffeehouse on La Cienega Boulevard in 1957. The business operated as primarily a jazz club, but in 1961, its wily owner, **Doug Weston**, had moved it to nearby Santa Monica Boulevard and it gradually evolved into the epicenter of the music industry. That progression was accelerated during the winter of 1966 when Los Angeles police and music-hungry, club-hopping youths clashed on Sunset Strip.

A window was broken, and youths skirmished with police. Local politicians were livid, so new rules on established clubs like the Whiskey a Go Go, Gazzarri's, and Pandora's Box were imposed to appease businesses fearing a rise in drugs, sex, and violence. For a while the Strip suffered, and Weston saw opportunity. He knew his West Hollywood-based Troubadour was unzoned and unrestricted, offering an advantage over the clubs on Strip. He opened his doors to the **Buffalo Springfield** and their electrified instruments, and the Troubadour became the nexus of the music world.

The club would often strain its 350-person capacity and became the go-to venue for music executives looking for talent. It was also a valuable stage for artists hoping to be discovered. Weston seeded the club's growth by building a brand to attract artists. He catered to the hippies and flower children. "There's been a gradual drift to meaningful music," Weston told *Billboard* in 1972. "It's the increasing awareness of college-educated and media-oriented young people, who through their use of drugs, etc., have expanded their consciousness to realize that life itself is the most important thing. All the rest ain't nothin' at all."

The free-love early 1960s and the emergence of Bob Dylan-inspired folk rock altered the rock and roll landscape. Many of those seismic changes occurred at "The Troub." **Roger McGuinn** found **Gene Clark** and **David Crosby** there, and they became **The Byrds**. The Eagles' Don Henley and Glenn Frey found each other in the Troubadour too, along with **Jackson Browne**, **David Blue**, **Linda Ronstadt** and a host of other performers, all of whom would have varying and overlapping impacts on each other's careers. [164, 206, 538]

❝❝ THE TROUBADOUR

The Eagles' Glenn Frey and Don Henley were already habitués of the Troubadour club in 1970 when Frey recruited the young drummer to play with him in **Linda Ronstadt**'s backup band. **Rick Nelson** watched Randy Meisner play with **Poco** there, and that planted the seeds for him to join Nelson's **Stone Canyon Band**. Bernie Leadon was on-stage there during **Dillard & Clark**'s famous meltdown that helped him decide to leave that band. And **David Geffen** plucked talent from the iconic club to stock his Aslylum Records stable. The Troubadour was, in a sense, the incubator for the Eagles.

The Troubadour, man, was and always will be full of tragic fucking characters. Has-beens and hopefuls. Sure, it's brought a lot of music to people but it's also infested with spiritual parasites who will rob you of your precious artistic energy. I was always worried about going down there because I thought people would think I had nothing better to do. Which was true.
– *Glenn Frey, Rolling Stone, September 1975*

The Troubadour was the first place I went when I got to LA. The first night I walked in, I saw **Graham Nash** and **Neil Young** and **Linda Ronstadt** was standing there in a little Daisy Mae kind of dress. She was barefooted and scratching her ass. I thought "I've made it. I'm here. I'm in heaven."
– *Don Henley, The Troubadour Club: A History, January 1997*

On Hoot Night at the Troubadour they had a cattle call to get up and play. Maybe fifteen or twenty acts would get up, and see what the crowd reaction was. We went over really well. One of the songs we did was a cover version of **Linda Ronstadt**'s *Silver Threads And Golden Needles*. That was something that always went over great. Linda happened to be there and she really liked us and liked Henley, because he had such a strong voice.
– *Michael Bowden of Shiloh, Desperados: The Roots of Country Rock, 2001*

We drank a lot of beer there (laughs). **Randy Newman**, **Steve Martin**, **Jim Morrison**, all these people that we'd know hung out here. We'd go down there and have a few beers. That's how I started *Take It To The Limit*. I went back to my house one night from the Troubadour. It was real late at night. I was by myself and started singing and playing (sings) "*All alone at the end of the evening.*" That's where it started.
– *Randy Meisner, San Francisco Weekly, April 1998*

The Troubadour was like a café society. Everyone was in transition. No one was getting married, no one was having families, no one was having a particular connection ... so our connection was the Troubadour. It was where everyone met, where everyone got to hear everyone else's act. It was where I made all my musical contacts, and found people who were sympathetic to the musical styles I wanted to explore. We used to sit in a corner of the Troubadour and dream.
– *Linda Ronstadt, The Troubadour Club: A History, January 1997*

[The Troubadour] was the big place to play. They'd put a big picture of you in the window. In those days, if you sold out the Troubadour, that was it. At the Troubadour, they announced your name and picked you up with a spotlight at the cigarette machine, and they'd walk you to the stage with the light. It was the coolest thing.
– *Tom Waits, MOJO, April 1999*

The Sad Cafe was inspired by the Troubadour and Dan Tana's restaurant. We could feel an era passing. The crowd that hung out in the Troubadour and the bands that were performing there were changing. The train tracks that had run down the middle of Santa Monica Boulevard had been ripped out. The train no longer came through – the same train that **Steve Martin** had once led an entire Troubadour audience to hop aboard and ride up to La Cienega Boulevard, then walk back to the club. Those remarkable freewheeling times were receding into the distance.
– *Don Henley, Rolling Stone, june 2016*

McCabe's Guitar Shop in Santa Monica started out as a furniture repair and restoration shop, but Gerald McCabe soon learned that his customers needed someone who could repair violins and guitars. So he did, and then they started selling instruments. The rest is history.

McCABE'S GUITAR SHOP OPENS IN SANTA MONICA

FALL 1958 – Gerald McCabe was a talented furniture designer in Los Angeles in 1958 when he opened a little shop at 3015 Pico Boulevard in Santa Monica dedicated to building and restoring couches, dressers, chairs, and tables. The opening of his shop coincided with the blossoming of folk music in L.A.

One day, a friend of McCabe's came into the shop with a broken guitar and asked him if he could fix it. McCabe's job was, after all, working with wooden furniture. Soon they started getting more requests and decided to modify the business a bit. McCabe and his partner, **Walter Camp**, made repairs a regular part of the business, and even began offering new instruments. Soon they were selling guitars, banjos, mandolins, dulcimers, fiddles, ukuleles, psalteries, bouzoukis, and sitars. The shop became a hangout for 1960s-era beatniks, folkies, and acoustic instrument aficionados. Former employee **Dave Zeitland** told *LA Weekly* in 2008 that a 16-year-old **Ry Cooder**, who would go on to become a slide guitar legend, practically lived there.

The quaint little shop turned into a folk mecca in 1969 when late folk-blues guitarist **Elizabeth "Libba" Cotton** needed bus fare home after an L.A. gig was unexpectedly canceled. The shop's staff put blankets up over the windows and moved guitars out of the way. Then, even with no sound system, she played and earned her bus fare home. It was the first unofficial concert there.

Jackson Browne performed the first official concert at McCabe's later that year, and that show was followed by a different show hosted by McCabe's every week ever since. In one performance there in 1973 Browne told the crowd in attendance that he preferred playing at McCabe's over playing at the famed Troubadour club in West Hollywood.

In writing about the legendary shop, **Richard Cromelin**, of the industry tabloid *Phonograph Record*, likened going to McCabe's to navigating a wrinkle in time. "[A time warp] is exactly what it is," he said. "And there's no insult intended. The folk people of Southern California are like a band of visionary pioneers whose happy trek toward their Earthly paradise was rudely clashed by circumstances, but who huddle resolutely in their bypassed valley and cling tenaciously to their way of life. You can't knock integrity, and I love time warps. The music is pretty good too."

The parade of folk, country, blues, pop, and rock artists to perform there since is long and distinguished, including **The Dillards**, **Hoyt Axton**, **Graham Parker**, **Steve Earle**, **Nicolette Larson**, **Fairport Convention**, **David Lindley**, **Roseanne Cash**, **Loudon Wainwright**, **Rickie Lee Jones**, **Linda Ronstadt & Country Gazette**, and Glenn Frey with **J.D. Souther**, then performing as **Longbranch/Pennywhistle**.

McCabe's was an incubator for young talent. **Robert Kimmel**, stage director for McCabe's from 1969 to 1975, remembered Frey and Souther's session in the main room. "I remember J.D. playing with Glenn Frey in Longbranch/Pennywhistle," Kimmel told the *Los Angeles Times* in 2008. "In the early days I discovered a lot of really talented musicians who played there through other musicians. Longbranch was an example of that. Somebody told me about them and said, 'You haven't heard of those guys?' The next thing I knew they both had their own record deals."

McCabe's needed more space in 1972, so it moved to its now-familiar location of 3103 Pico Boulevard (pictured below) and expanded to 3105 shortly after. The live shows continue, and in 2018, Browne returned to the main room to help the shop celebrate its 60th anniversary, including an encore performance of *Take It Easy*, the song he famously co-wrote with Frey. [1230, 1231, 1276, 1278, 1279, 1420]

McCabe's became an impromptu concert hall in 1969 when Elizabeth "Libba" Cotton sang for cab fare home. Jackson Browne then led off the official live performances later that year and McCabe's has had weekly concerts scheduled ever since in its cozy confines on Pico

BEGINNINGS

The Eagles got their individual starts playing in lowly dive bars, sparkling teen clubs and dusty dance halls. These were small stages for meager dollars, but they honed their skills and they paid their dues. Years later it paid off handsomely.

FALL 1958

Felder Forms The Continentals; Recruits Stills, Leadon

Inspired by the pelvis twirling **Elvis Presley**, a 14-year-old future Eagles guitarist **Don Felder** cobbled together a group of Gainesville, Florida kids his age and met in his parents' garage in late 1959 to begin rehearsing.

Felder was the leader and, with greased back hair and a cheap Fender Musicmaster guitar his dad bought him, began jamming with his new band. After some generous name-making back and forth, the group became *The Continentals*. They were on their way—business cards were printed and bookings started coming in.

His bandmates would come and go over the years, but one newcomer made a strong impression on Felder, and, a few years later, on rock music as a whole; a rhythm guitar player with a military haircut named **Stephen Stills**. Shy and with a rebellious streak, Stills played several gigs with The Continentals and fit in well, Felder said in his book *Heaven and Hell: My Life in The Eagles*.

Stills left the band when his family moved to Tampa and Latin America, and he started a winding journey that would eventually lead him to the iconic **Buffalo Springfield**. When Stills left the band, Felder recruited another guitar player who would become a significant player in the Eagles' lore, Bernie Leadon. The two musician's paths would cross in Gainesville, Florida and Leadon would play with Felder into the band's next metamorphosis.

When **The Beatles** arrived in America in 1964, Felder loved their "cool." Leadon was a big British Invasion fan too, and was particularly taken with the Fab Four and **George Harrison**. Felder, along with Leadon, formed the British-inspired **Maundy Quintet** and started playing songs to match their distinctly English name. Soon he traded in his low-budget Fender for a $300 Les Paul and began taking lessons from another new friend, the yet-undiscovered **Duane Allman**, who introduced him to the wonder of playing slide guitar. The Maundy Quintet would work gigs from New York to Miami for several years, and then they'd take an aggressive next step in their careers. [218, 1130]

WINTER 1960-61

The Decibels, Bob Seger Record First Single, *The Lonely One*

Bob Seger was just a sophomore at Ann Arbor High School in Michigan when he and two of his classmates, **Pete Stanger** and **H.B. Hunter**, recorded an acetate demo of a Seger-penned song called *The Lonely One*. Seger led the group, the **Decibels**, and played piano, keyboards, guitar and sang vocals with Stanger on guitar and Hunter playing drums.

"I started writing when I was 16 or 17 and that really helped," Seger told *The Atlanta*

DON FELDER

Don **Felder** was inspired by **Elvis Presley**'s moves and mystique, and his father fueled that interest when he bought him his first Fender Musicmaster guitar. Felder harnessed that inspiration and created his first band, **The Continentals**, in 1958. He recruited several musicians as band members in the early 1960s, including a young, brooding **Stephen Stills**. When Stills moved on, future Eagle **Bernie Leadon** took his place. The Continentals evolved into the **Maundy Quintet** when the band decided to try to capture some of the British Invasion vibes overtaking the country. When Leadon left the Quintet, Felder joined up with an improv jazz band called **Flow** and moved to New York.

Felder and Leadon reconnected a few years later. Now an Eagle, Leadon invited Felder to help the Eagles in the studio in 1975, which led to a full-time gig shortly after. He brought a harder edge to the Eagles' music and earned writing credits for *Visions*, *Victim of Love*, and *Hotel California*. After the band broke up in 1980 he released his discarded song from the Eagles' *The Long Run* sessions called *Heavy Metal (Takin' A Ride)*, on the soundtrack for the film *Heavy Metal*; it climbed to #43 on the *Billboard* Hot 100 chart and became his most successful solo single.

The Eagles reformed in 1994 and he joined the band's *Hell Freezes Over* tour. He was inducted with the Eagles to the Rock and Roll Hall of Fame in 1998, but was fired from the band in 2001 over a profits dispute. Later that year he released his autobiography, *Heaven and Hell: My Life In The Eagles*, a *New York Times* Bestseller. It sold well, but upped tensions with his former bandmates.

He returned to the studio in 2012 and 2019 and produced the albums *Road to Forever* and *American Rock 'n' Roll*, respectively, featuring an all-star cast of rock musicians including **Sammy Hagar**, **Slash**, **Mick Fleetwood**, **Richie Sambora** and **Peter Frampton**.

His home state of Florida recognized his accomplishments as an artist when it inducted him into the Florida Artists Hall of Fame in 2017. [209, 218, 229, 309, 414, 1130, 1265]

Constitution in 1986. "It especially helped when **The Beatles** came in and songwriting became an in-house thing. I was writing songs for **Del Shannon** and **Bobby Vee** and other people and I was getting interest from those people. They were saying, 'Send us more.' They weren't hits, but they were close."

The group's demo, which was cut in Del Shannon's studio, made it to the airwaves just once when Seger persuaded an Ann Arbor disc jockey to play it. It was never played on the air again, but by then Seger had already built some musical credibility. Still, it would be another four years before another Seger song was cut on vinyl under his name. Shortly after that he started a lifelong friendship with a wise-ass musician from nearby Royal Oak, Michigan, future Eagle leader Glenn Frey. [1141, 1142]

Meisner Brings High Notes, Bass to The Dynamics

Long before **Randy Meisner** was plucking bass strings for the Eagles, he was reaching for high notes for *The Drivin' Dynamics* in Scottsbluff, Nebraska. Known originally as just *The Dynamics*, the band got its start playing a private party in 1961 with a 15-year-old Meisner on bass guitar and lead vocals.

Founder **Larry Soto** formed the band with **Richard Rohnke**, **John Ankeny**, and Meisner. The band's first paid performance was at a dance hall at Little Moon Lake near Henry, Nebraska, in December 1961, and they earned regular return engagements there

through 1962. The band played a mix of the popular songs of the day, some rhythm and blues, and were among the first bands to play rock music in western Nebraska.

Their crowds grew with every performance, and they began to fill the 800-person hall. Meisner displayed "showmanship and had a knack for feeding off large crowds," according to his biography in the *Nebraska Music Hall of Fame*, into which he was inducted in 2000. The band would take its next step, making a single, at the end of 1961. [486, 1133, 1202]

SUMMER 1961

Geffen Drops Out of University of Texas-Austin, Heads to L.A.

David Geffen was a critical early cog in the machine that became the Eagles. Known as a billionaire philanthropist, music, movie, and theatrical producer, and frequent foil to Eagles co-founder **Don Henley**, he crafted a compelling rags-to-riches story that was built largely on guile and moxie, according to **Tom King**'s biography on Geffen, *The Operator*.

He got his first exposure to the glitz of production in his high school's drama club. He helped organize and stage one of the school's most successful productions, and that shining moment left him starry-eyed. He wanted to produce more and knew where he needed to go. At his mother's behest, he grudgingly agreed that he would need a college degree to be successful. After graduating high school in Brooklyn, Geffen desperately wanted to

RANDY MEISNER

When Randy Meisner found himself onstage in Disneyland with **Linda Ronstadt**, Glenn Frey, and Don Henley in the summer of 1970, it was just an opportunity to earn some money backing another rising artist. He might not have known it was the start of something so huge.

A veteran of several bands by that time, including two nationally known acts, Meisner was arguably the most seasoned performer of the four original Eagles, and the high-singing bass player had, along with co-founder Bernie Leadon, the strongest resume in the group when they formed in 1971.

Hailing from Scottsbluff, Nebraska, Meisner was born March 8, 1946, and began his musical career playing bass and singing for **The Drivin' Dynamics**, a dance hall band that developed a strong following across Nebraska, Wyoming, and Colorado. In 1966, Meisner joined a new group, the **Soul Survivors**, and moved to Los Angeles, but didn't find much success; the group later changed their name to **The Poor**, which described their current state, but the name change didn't help pay the bills.

Meisner got his big break when he learned about an opening for a bass player in a new band formed by ex-**Buffalo Springfield** guitarist **Richie Furay** called **Pogo** (later renamed **Poco**). Meisner auditioned for the spot, and won out over future Eagles bassist Timothy B. Schmit on the same day. He toured with the band for a year while they gathered material for their first album. But Meisner quit the band in a dispute with Furay, and joined **Rick Nelson's Stone Canyon Band**. He joined Ronstadt's backing band in 1970, along with future Eagles bandmates Frey and Henley.

Meisner played with the Eagles from 1971 through 1977. He co-wrote and sang lead on *Take It To The Limit*, the band's first million-selling single. He quit the Eagles in 1977 and recorded his first solo album a year later; it reached #7 nationally. He recorded four more albums through 1991, and one album each in 2001, 2002, and 2005. He was inducted into the Rock and Roll Hall of Fame with the Eagles in 1998. He reunited with The Drivin' Dynamics in 2000 to celebrate the band's induction into the Nebraska Music Hall of Fame. [48, 49, 463, 486, 1143]

THE BEACH BOYS RECORD FIRST SINGLE, *SURFIN'*

WINTER 1961 – The Beach Boys jumped into the rock and roll world in the early 1960s with a unique and groundbreaking sound. A flood of copycat acts followed, but none matched the band's creativity and beautifully crafted songs. Led by **Brian Wilson** and his two brothers, **Carl** and **Dennis**, the band also included their cousin **Mike Love** and high school friend **Al Jardine**.

In September 1961, the band recorded a demo of *Surfin'* that employed guitar licks and 1950s-style harmonies. Brian's father, **Murray Wilson**, arranged a meeting with a local music publisher and soon after the band had a recording deal with the short-lived Candix label. The band started out as the **Pendletons**, but their label ditched that name in favor of The Beach Boys. In December, Candix released *Surfin'*, an instant regional hit and that made its way to #75 on Billboard's Hot 100 chart. Capitol Records picked up the band by 1962 and released *Surfin' Safari*, which rose to #14 nationally. In all, the band would place 80-plus songs on the charts worldwide between the 1960s and 2010s, including 36 in the Top 40 and four reaching #1 overall.

The Beach Boys and their signature "California sound" harmonies had a profound effect on the Eagles. Glenn Frey said the Eagles crafted their songs with a goal of creating their own signature sound.

"We were looking for a vocal stamp," Frey told *Q* in 1996, "so that when an Eagles song comes on the radio, you know it's the Eagles. The same way you know it's The Beach Boys, **The Beatles** or the **[Rolling] Stones**."

In his book *I Am Brian Wilson*, Wilson recalled **Don Henley** visiting him backstage after a concert and bringing copy of *Pet Sounds*. "I knew the Eagles, of course," Wilson said. "If the Beach Boys were California in the '60s, the Eagles and **Fleetwood Mac** were California in the '70s. [He] sat down next to me and started telling me everything about his history with Beach Boys music. He said that we inspired him so much when he was growing up. He told me that he listened to the harmonies of the group but also to the way we put songs together." Wilson signed the album, thanking Henley for all the "great" songs, which Wilson playfully changed to "good," drawing a chuckle from Henley.

At a January concert at the Forum in Los Angeles in 2014, Frey said in appreciation: "The Beach Boys were pioneers. The Eagles were settlers. We carved our place in the musical landscape, but they were one of the great harmony bands and we loved their work." [138, 1137, 1138, 1374]

BOB SEGER

Bob Seger and Eagles leader Glenn Frey were good friends in Michigan long before Frey ever became an Eagle. The two met through gigs they would play in and around Detroit in the mid-1960s. An older-brother figure, Seger tutored Frey on the music business and encouraged his to keep working at singing and songwriting. Frey even sang backup on Seger's first hit single *Ramblin' Gamblin' Man* in 1968.

Seger was born May 6, 1945, in Detroit, and in high school, he was fronting bands that played local clubs, including **The Decibels**, **Doug Brown & The Omens**, and **The Last Heard**. He signed a recording deal with Capitol in 1968 and found initial success, but later struggled to get airplay. That would change. As the Eagles were finding success in the mid-1970s, so was Seger. His *Stranger in Town* album produced #4 single *Still the Same*, *Hollywood Nights* (#12), and *We've Got Tonight* (#13).

Seger earned a co-writing credit for his contributions to the Eagles' #1 single *Heartache Tonight*. That collaboration was about Frey and Seger's early days in Detroit, and Seger contributed the well-known chorus over the phone as the band tried to close production on *The Long Run* in 1979. Frey and his Eagles bandmates returned the favor to Seger by playing and singing backing vocals on his #1 *Against the Wind* album in 1980. He continued writing and touring relentlessly through the 1980s.

Seger and Frey's paths crossed often as the years passed. In 1987, Frey was set to record *Shakedown* as a follow-up to his #2 hit single *The Heat Is On*, which he recorded for the *Beverly Hills Cop* soundtrack in 1984. With the *Cop* sequel set to be released, producers looked to Frey to provide a follow-up song. But fate intervened. Frey, who wasn't fond of the song's original lyrics, lost his voice just prior to the recording session. Frey recommended Seger, who rewrote the words and rode the rearranged *Shakedown* to #1, the only chart-topping single of his career. After the song reached the top of the charts, Frey called Seger to congratulate him, saying, "At least we kept the money in Michigan."

When Frey passed away in 2016, Seger took the loss hard. He wrote *Glenn Song* for Frey, and dedicated his 2017 album *I Knew You When* to his lifelong friend. Seger was enshrined in the Rock and Roll Hall of Fame in 2004. [50, 51, 433, 1205, 1206, 1224]

attend UCLA, but his poor grades haunted him and he was rejected.

His brother, Mitchell, had gone to the University of Texas-Austin. At that time, the school had a reputation for accepting students with spotty academic records, so Geffen applied there and was accepted. But his short attention span proved his undoing, and after just one semester he dropped out. His brother, now living in Los Angeles, invited him out and he became an usher in the CBS television studios for *The Judy Garland Show*. His Hollywood fascination would continue to grow, and in the winter of 1963, he would get a personal peek at how the music world operated. [1, 2, 3]

WINTER 1962

Schmit, Friends Form Sacramento Folk Trio, Tim, Tom & Ron

One of the great regional folk bands of the 1960s was created when three young Sacramento, California teenagers took to harmonizing behind a ukulele.

The ensemble, **Ron Floegel**, **Tom Phillips**, and future Eagles bassist **Timothy B. Schmit** would become a favorite at Encina High School. The trio called themselves **Tim, Tom & Ron**, and they began playing folk music for local church groups, high school rallies, and class breakfasts in 1961.

Floegel told the Sacramento Rock & Radio Museum that he knew Schmit from little league baseball and had been best friends until he transferred from Dyer Kelly to the Howe Avenue School. Schmit and his brother Greg sang harmonies behind Floegel's ukulele playing when he would spend the night with them at their home on Auburn Boulevard. He suggested to Phillips that Schmit join them one afternoon and liked their sound, so the group was born.

Floegel said they set out to perfect some folk songs of the day with the goal of performing in public. As high school progressed, they found themselves playing after-game events, open dances, and had a regular summer gig at the Fairhaven Apartment complex. Schmit, who would later go on to join country-rock stalwarts **Poco** and the Eagles, would also enjoy a prolific career as a studio musician, got his start on guitar, but later switched to bass when it became clear what the other band members' strengths were. Phillips took lead guitar and Floegel played rhythm guitar. They were later joined by drummer **George Hullin**.

Inspired by the surf music gaining popularity—and no longer a trio—they changed their name to **The Contenders**. Their singer-songwriter credentials would continue to grow, and by the winter of 1965, the band evolved and changed their name yet again to **The New Breed**. They would soon become a regional hit complete with an international fan club. [347, 348, 349, 403, 1140]

Geffen Gets Indirect Peek at Record Industry via Phil Spector

Long before **David Geffen** became a titan in the entertainment industry, he got a brief yet inspirational look at how the record in-

TIMOTHY B. SCHMIT

When Timothy B. Schmit joined the Eagles in 1979, he had solid credentials in the country-rock world after spending nearly a decade with **Poco**. The Eagles were pioneers in the country-rock world, but by the time Schmit joined the band, they had become an edgier rock band. They still played *Peaceful Easy Feelin'* and *Lyin' Eyes* at concerts, but the country-rock vibe had faded from their new original music. When it was time for him to contribute to the new album, Glenn Frey and Don Henley suggested he take an R&B approach, and the result, *I Can't Tell You Why*, was a top 10 hit.

Schmit got his start in a Sacramento folk trio **Tim, Tom & Ron**, which eventually grew into larger bands, **The New Breed** and **Glad**, that became regionally popular. These bands were better promoted than similar bands of their time and stature, and they performed alongside nationally prominent bands like the **Buffalo Springfield**, **Jefferson Airplane**, and **The Yardbirds**. It gave them credibility, but neither iteration of the band caught on outside California.

Although Schmit's early bands didn't find fame, he did get noticed. As a talented bass player with a high-vocal register, he had sought-after skills. Former Buffalo Springfielder **Richie Furay** was a fan and invited him to audition for his new band, **Pogo** (later renamed **Poco**). Although he lost out to future original Eagle Randy Meisner, he joined Poco a year later after Meisner left the group. This time Schmit stayed nearly a decade. In an ironic twist, Schmit got another call after Meisner left the Eagles in 1978, and once again, he replaced Meisner, this time as a full-time Eagle.

Schmit played on just one Eagles studio album before they broke up in 1980, but he blossomed in his post-Eagles life, becoming an in-demand session musician, supporting artists like **Toto**, **Crosby, Stills & Nash**, **Dan Fogelberg**, and **Elton John**. He released five solo albums since 1987 and toured frequently with **Jimmy Buffett** and **Ringo Starr**. He was inducted into the Rock and Roll Hall of Fame with the Eagles in 1998. [6, 350, 1140, 1199, 1414]

dustry operates via the erratic but influential **Phil Spector**.

After Geffen had given up on college, he accepted an invitation from his then more successful brother, Mitchell, to visit him in Los Angeles. Mitchell was dating **Renee Merar**, a UCLA law school graduate whose sister, Annette, also happened to be dating Spector. The youngest-ever owner of a record label at the time, Spector was already a music industry icon by 1960, when he was just 21 years old.

Over his career, he wrote, co-wrote, or produced records for acts like the **Ronettes**, the **Crystals**, **John Lennon**, **George Harrison**, and **The Righteous Brothers**. Annette invited Mitchell and Renee to a recording session with the Ronettes, and asked David to come along.

Geffen, now 20, watched in awe as Spector engineered songs for the Ronettes (including backup singer **Cherilyn LaPiere**, who went on to become better known as **Cher**) and the Crystals. Spector treated Geffen like a flunky during that and other sessions he attended. But it didn't matter; a determined Geffen decided he'd learn from Spector rather than be run off. In the spring of 1963, he would also borrow from Spector's reputation to enhance his own. [1, 2, 3, 393]

FALL 1962

RELEASES
The Drivin' Dynamics, with Randy Meisner, *Sidewinder* (single)

Drivin' Dynamics, Meisner Release 4-Song EP Single

Future-founding Eagle Randy Meisner was fronting his band, **The Dynamics**, and the group was packing the halls in western Nebraska by the end of 1962. The group expanded its repertoire by adding the saxophone-playing **Paul Asmus**, and they officially changed their name to the **Drivin' Dynamics** to better punctuate the faster rock beats in their music.

Encouraged by their success, the band decided to cut a record, a 45-RPM extended play single featuring an original instrumental, *Sidewinder*, and covers of **Sam Cooke**'s *You Send Me*, **Booker T and the MG's**' *Green Onions*, and the **Ventures**' *Walk, Don't Run*. The self-published single only had a small original press run of 500, but they were gobbled up by local fans.

Primarily a western Nebraska band, the group began to expand by taking gigs in Colorado, Wyoming, and Kansas, and their fan base grew, which got them some unexpected but welcomed attention from an Oklahoma record company in the summer of 1965. [486]

DAVID GEFFEN

David Geffen was arguably the most important person in the early evolution of the Eagles, where he acted as the group's manager and his label, Asylum Records, marketed the band. That relationship dynamic would spawn a lawsuit years later, but at the outset of their pairing, he quickly recognized the group's talent and put them in a position to succeed. He determinedly pursued a top-rated producer, **Glyn Johns**, and successfully marketed their first self-titled album. The band and Geffen were rewarded with three *Billboard* Top 25 singles within a year.

Geffen was born in 1943 and rose from middle-class beginnings in Brooklyn, New York, to become one of the most influential men in the music and film industries. He started his ascent as a college dropout in the mailroom at the William Morris Agency (WMA) in 1964. In 1969, he and his WMA colleague **Elliot Roberts** formed Geffen-Roberts Management. They signed artists like **Joni Mitchell** and **Crosby, Stills, Nash & Young**, and a year later they formed Asylum Records with the backing of Atlantic Records chairman **Ahmet Ertegun**. Within six months, he had added, among many others, **Jackson Browne**, **J.D. Souther**, the Eagles, and **Judee Sill**.

Under Geffen's leadership, Asylum became one of the most powerful labels in the music industry. Warner Brothers bought Asylum and merged it with Elektra Records in 1972, and made Geffen vice chairman of Warner Brothers Pictures. He left Warner in 1976 amid legal troubles, but emerged in the 1980s with Geffen Records and made immediate splashes by signing Mitchell, **Donna Summer**, **Cher**, **Elton John**, **John Lennon**, and even a reluctant Don Henley. The sale of Geffen Records to MCA in 1990 made him a billionaire, and he ran the company through 1995. He joined **Steven Spielberg** and **Jeffrey Katzenberg** to create DreamWorks SKG in 1994.

His philanthropic efforts over the years have been sizable, including donations to help research with AIDS, as well as the arts and theater. He was inducted into the Rock and Roll Hall of Fame in 2010 for his contributions to the music industry. [1, 3, 569, 1288]

WINTER 1962-63

ON THE ROAD WITH ...
Scottsville Squirrel Barkers, with Bernie Leadon: Hedy West

Leadon 'Fills In' with the Scottsville Squirrel Barkers

San Diego's bluegrass roots were born during the folk music surge that overtook Southern California in the early 1960s. Much of this Kentucky-imbued music emerged partly due to a quartet of banjo-playing, guitar-picking men called the **Scottsville Squirrel Barkers**.

The group was the official house band of the Blue Guitar, a small music store and repair shop on San Diego's Midway Drive. In 1962, **Ed Douglas**, **Kenny Wertz**, **Larry Murray**, **Gary Carr**, and future Byrd and Flying Burrito Brother **Chris Hillman** formed the first iteration of the band and began playing hootenannies around Southern California.

Later in 1963, when Wertz and Carr left the band to join the Air Force, guitarist **Doug Jeffords** joined and future-founding Eagle Bernie Leadon "filled in" with the band.

"I saw the Squirrel Barkers at a weekend hootenanny down at a local church hall near where I lived," Leadon told **Mike Fleming**, owner of the Bluegrass website *The North Georgia Bluegrass Chronicles* in 2007. "I think I was 15. Kenny's [Wertz]'s banjo ripped my head off. I went up to them after the show and found out that they had the Blue Guitar and basically, I started ditching school and going to the shop every day. Ed [Douglas], Larry [Murray and **Yuris Zeltins**] were at the shop every day making banjos, selling instruments and hosting bluegrass, folk and flamenco lessons. There was always folk or bluegrass music either being played or flamenco on the sound system. They had a little stage area and on the weekends would have shows, so it was a great scene."

Leadon, though, never considered himself a true Barker. "Two of the [Barkers] had been drafted," Leadon said. "And they had a couple of gigs, so I filled in. But I was never a *member* of the Squirrel Barkers. It was wonderful because I got to step in and play with my heroes."

Hillman nonetheless considered Leadon an "honorary member" of the Barkers because he filled in 1963 after other members had departed. But Leadon had been a friend of the band from the group's inception and was inspired to pick banjo by Wertz. Leadon's time with the Barkers created in-roads he may not have anticipated, but helped his career, most notably the exposure to **Linda Ronstadt**, who attended Barker performances during the early-to-mid-1960s in southern California and remembered Leadon's talents. By the early 1970s, he would be backing her band, which led him to the Eagles. [218, 264, 534, 750, 1131, 1186, 1256]

BERNIE LEADON

The jangly sounds of country-rock introduced by the **Byrds** and **Buffalo Springfield** matured and evolved in the late 1960s and early 1970s. No band captured that movement more successfully than the Eagles, thanks largely to the bluegrass and country picking skills of Bernie Leadon.

Leadon was born in Minneapolis, and his family moved frequently in support of his father's career. One stop was in San Diego, which was pivotal in Leadon's musical development. As a teenager, he loved bluegrass music and discovered the Blue Guitar, a small music store on San Diego's Midland Drive. Musically, he learned from a band there called the **Scottsville Squirrel Barkers**.

When his family moved to Florida, Leadon met future Eagle Don Felder. They teamed up in a couple of bands, but Leadon moved back to Southern California looking for better musical opportunities. He caught on with the group **Hearts and Flowers**, but it broke up a year later. He then joined **Dillard & Clark** and later joined **The Flying Burrito Brothers**. None of them found commercial success, so Leadon made ends meet by backing **Linda Ronstadt** with his own band, **The Corvettes**.

Ronstadt's manager, **John Boylan**, was working with two young artists who were backing Ronstadt on her tour, Glenn Frey and Don Henley; they wanted to form a band. One day at McCabe's Guitar Shop, Leadon learned that they were looking for another guitarist. Boylan connected them and shortly after, Leadon joined the soon-to-be Eagles and famously spoke for the group with Asylum Records founder **David Geffen**, giving him a "do you want us or not" ultimatum. Geffen took them.

Leadon had a strong resume in the country-rock world, and that helped the band through their first three southwestern-themed albums. The band's musical direction changed in the mid-1970s, and by their fourth album, *One of These Nights*, it was a different group. With dwindling songwriting credits and unhappy about the direction the band was heading, Leadon left in December 1975.

In the years following his departure, he became one of the music industry's most sought-after session guitarists and banjo players, backing artists like Ronstadt, **Alabama**, **Travis Tritt**, **Nanci Griffith**, **Stephen Stills**, **Kenny Rogers**, **Emmylou Harris**, and the **Nitty Gritty Dirt Band**. He was inducted into the Rock and Roll Hall of Fame with the Eagles in 1994. [218, 739, 1221, 1256]

SUMMER 1963

Bowden, Henley Become Friends, Create The Four Speeds

Don Henley and childhood friend **Richard Bowden** both grew up in Linden, Texas and were drawn to each other through a mutual interest in music. Polar opposites, the flamboyant Bowden encouraged Henley to come out of his shell by giving him an opportunity to perform.

Henley would spend time in the classroom at high school beating out cadences on his books and desks, and eventually Bowden came out and said, "Why don't you just play the drums?" Henley recalled.

Bowden was helping his friend find an outlet for his musical expression, but he was recruiting too. He played guitar in his dad's Dixieland band and invited Henley to join the group in the summer of 1962. Bowden's dad, Elmer, would drive the boys to jobs in a multicolored van called the "Spotted Pup." They would play at American Legion Hall dances where they were so popular they would draw 200 to 300 every Saturday night.

When Elmer dropped out, the band's Dixieland vibe gave way to guitar-driven instrumentals, country ballads, and Top 40 hits. Joined by friends **Jerry Surratt** and **Freddie Neese**, the band began picking up gigs throughout the area, usually frat parties and clubs in Austin and Dallas. They finally settled on a name: **The Four Speeds**, a name drawn from the gear shifter in a car.

Talent set the band apart from other groups in the area. Henley was a great drummer with a golden singing voice. Surratt had a unique ability to play the trumpet with one hand, while playing keyboards with the other. The flexible Bowden could play lead, rhythm, or bass guitar, and Neese added licks as the band's lead guitarist.

Bowden, Neese, and Surratt already had their instruments, but Henley didn't own a drum set. That presented a problem for the band when gigs came along. Bowden told the *Texarkana Gazette* in 2014. They remedied that problem by secretly raiding their school's band room on weekends. On Fridays, they would unlock a window in the band room at Linden Kildare High School. On Saturdays, they'd sneak the band's drums out the windows, play their gigs, and then return them on Sundays.

Henley's mother, Hughlene, would eliminate the need to heist drums for good when she and Henley, then just 15 years old, took an hour-and-a-half drive to the McKay Music Company in Sulphur Springs, Texas, where she bought him a Red Sparkle Slingerland drum kit that he still owns. She owed him that favor after the mischievous teenager destroyed her black cauldron wringer washing machine with a cherry bomb, forcing his dad, C.J., to buy a new automated one.

The core of the group stayed together, even as high school gave way to college. The band would take the next step in their progression when they recorded a single for Hartlyn Records in the spring of 1964. [412, 471, 1145, 1147, 1152, 1377]

DON HENLEY

David Geffen suspected he had a talented singer-songwriter in Don Henley when he rescued him from the purgatory of an Amos Records contract in 1970. But Henley was so demure in his approach to recording the Eagles first album that Geffen feared listeners wouldn't know he was there. So, Geffen added **Jackson Browne**'s *Nightingale* to the LP so the quiet drummer would have more than just one singing credit on the Eagles' debut album. Henley took a progressively more prominent role in Eagles albums as the band matured.

Raised in the small east Texas town of Linden, Henley was inspired by early rock and roll and country music he heard while listening to the *Louisiana Hayride* during his childhood. **Elvis Presley** and **The Beatles** were particular inspirations. He joined the band of his friend **Richard Bowden** and they were discovered by country singer **Kenny Rogers**. Their group **Shiloh** recorded an album, but the group was disappointed when it went nowhere. Still, Henley didn't go unnoticed.**Linda Ronstadt**'s manager **John Boylan**, tapped him for her backing band and that's where he met the other three original Eagles.

Over the next decade, the Eagles took their place among the top-selling bands in history, securing gold records with each of their six original albums released between 1972 and 1979, along with a greatest hits album in 1976 that went platinum a jaw-dropping 38 times. The Eagles broke up in 1980 and its members embarked on solo careers; Henley enjoyed the greatest success. His first three albums, *I Can't Stand Still*, *Building the Perfect Beast*, and *The End of the Innocence*, ascended to #24, #13, and #8 on *Billboard*'s album chart, respectively. The band mended fences in 1994, got back together and embarked on the *Hell Freezes Over* tour the following year. Two new albums followed.

In 1998 Henley and the Eagles were inducted into the Rock and Roll Hall of Fame by longtime touring partner **Jimmy Buffett**; all six Eagles participated. Henley was honored as MusiCares Person of the Year in 2007 by the Recording Academy for his philanthropic causes from environmental issues to artists' rights concerns. [5, 6, 15, 140, 209, 301, 312, 412, 534, 1404]

FALL 1963

 ON THE ROAD WITH …
Scottsville Squirrel Barkers, with Bernie Leadon: Knob Hill Singers, Oak Knoll Singers, The Yachtsmen, Cherry Creek Singers

WINTER 1963-64

Whiskey a Go Go Opens On Sunset Boulevard

One-time nightclub operator for the mob, **Elmer Valentine**, ventured into a club while traveling in Paris in 1963 when he was struck by the novelty of the establishment. It was a discothèque, with women dancing on platforms and frenzied crowds dancing shoulder to shoulder on the floor to music being spun by DJs. It was the Whisky à Go-Go in Paris, the world's first discothèque.

Enticed by the concept, he decided to re-create the club in Los Angeles, but with a twist: live music. The result was the Whiskey a Go Go on West Hollywood's Sunset Boulevard, an iconic landmark where both huge and obscure rock and roll acts jammed and cultivated their images.

Valentine took the idea to the next level. When live bands weren't playing, short-skirted female DJs in calf-high go-go boots would spin records from suspended cages near the stage. The DJs kept the crowds pulsating, but it was the live music that drew people in. Rock legends like **The Doors** and **Janis Joplin** would take to the stage there regularly to standing-room only crowds. True to its name, the Whiskey helped popularize go-go dancing and spawned the birth of Whiskey a Go Go franchises across the country, the first appearing in Washington D.C. in 1966. It became a cultural phenomenon that not only showcased the artists, but the theme became woven into the fabric of the music as well.

The Miracles recorded *Going to a Go Go* in 1966, and it was re-recorded by the **Rolling Stones** in 1982. **Nancy Sinatra**'s *These Boots Are Made for Walkin'* furthered the iconic image. Soon after the Whiskey opened, "go-go" outfits became fashionable and the look became a staple in teen movies and television. Airlines even outfitted their flight attendants in short skirts and go-go boots to appeal to youths.

The Whiskey was also at the epicenter of the Los Angeles riots of 1968, where local businesses and politicians imposed curfews in an attempt to keep teenagers, drugs, and sexuality off the Strip; the riots spawned the **Buffalo Springfield**'s protest anthem *For What It's Worth*, and widened the notoriety of the Strip in the process. Whiskey owner Valentine decried the new anti-teens laws, calling the new measures "stupid" and "insane." "These laws don't just affect the Strip," he said, "but under certain conditions they now make dancing illegal in the entire county." Those laws were eventually rolled back.

Although the Whiskey was just one of many clubs on Sunset Strip, from the start it was a different breed. It catered to a more raw, bluesy rock sound than others hosting

THE BEATLES PERFORM ON *THE ED SULLIVAN SHOW*

WINTER 1964 – The British Invasion of American airwaves was launched when AM radio station WWDC in Washington, D.C. got an illicit copy of **The Beatles**' *I Want to Hold Your Hand* and started playing it in December 1963. It started a phenomena that was unrivaled in American pop culture before or since: Beatlemania.

The Beatles were thriving in late 1964 and American teenagers could not get enough of them. An American tour was scheduled. American television hosts, knowing they would be landing in New York in February, scrambled for the television rights. **Ed Sullivan**, whose viewership had faded out of the Top 10 by 1963, won the sweepstakes and booked the band to perform live on his show February 9, 1964, drawing a then-record 73.7 million viewers. The Beatles performed *All My Loving* and *Till There Was You, I Saw Her Standing There* and *I Want to Hold Your Hand.* The band's music had significant impact on future Eagles' band members.

Eagles' drummer Don Henley told English newspaper *The Daily Express* that he remembered The Beatles' debut well. "It was a black-and-white TV and you had to rotate the antenna on the roof to pick up the station," Henley said. "I was just smitten by the Beatles as were millions of other kids. They were so new and different and they brought that whole European culture, that sense of style and fashion."

Glenn Frey told the *Detroit Free Press* that on September 6, 1964, his aunt, Virginia, took him to see the band perform at the now-demolished Detroit Olympia stadium. "I was just blown away," he said. "The audience was delirious, screaming at top of their lungs, shouting out the guys' names. It was pandemonium and spectacle. And I was very, very impressed. So I started thinking about playing the guitar. I got a tenor guitar—a four-string—and started playing with a couple of my friends in tenth grade."

Joe Walsh told *Rolling Stone* in 1975 that he never got serious about music until The Beatles broke in 1964. "I took one look on *The Ed Sullivan Show* and it was, 'Fuck school. This makes it!' I memorized every Beatles song and went to Shea Stadium and screamed right along with all those chicks." Later, Walsh told **John Tobler** of the *BBC* in 1982 that "I was a dumb kid going to high school in New Jersey in a band ... but I still have a really clear image of watching them, and my parents shaking their heads left and right and me shaking my head up and down, and that hit a spark inside me and I knew that was what I wanted to do. I thought, 'Those guys are cool', and I'd like to do that, and that stayed dominant in my thinking." [135, 363, 392, 551]

Frank Zappa and the Mothers of Invention, **Led Zeppelin**, **The Who**, and **Otis Redding**. By contrast, its older Santa Monica cousin, **Doug Weston**'s Troubadour, typically hosted the more folk- and country rock-oriented bands in the late 1960s and 1970s.

The Whiskey could shuffle its repertoire easily, and still played host to its share of those musicians as well. **The Byrds** and Buffalo Springfield played the Whiskey, as did Randy Meisner's **The Poor**. Ex-Byrd **Gene Clark**, **Linda Ronstadt**, and the **Nitty Gritty Dirt Band** brought their brand of country rock to the Strip, and so did **Bernie Leadon** and his band, **The Flying Burrito Brothers**. Glenn Frey and **J.D. Souther**'s band, **Longbranch/Pennywhistle**, played the Whiskey on December 30, 1970, opening for the Burritos. Joe Walsh played there too, with his post-**James Gang** band, **Barnstorm**, in September 1973. The Whiskey was designated as a landmark by the Rock and Roll Hall of Fame and Museum in 2006, and 50-plus years after its creation, the nightclub remains a thriving institution along Sunset Strip playing host to bands like **Metallica**, **Soundgarden**, and **System of a Down**. [1272, 1273, 1274]

Linda Ronstadt Signs First Recording Deal in Arizona

Long before she became the most popular female artist in America in the 1970s and 1980s, **Linda Ronstadt** was a singing teenager trying hard to keep to traditional folk singing in her hometown of Tucson, Arizona.

With a mixed heritage of German, Mexican, and English origins, Ronstadt explored most of those musical styles during her illustrious career, and she played a pivotal role in collecting members of the Eagles into her supporting band before they struck out on their own. Without that key assist, the Eagles, as millions of fans know the group, may not have formed.

As a senior at Catalina High School in Tucson, Ronstadt and two of her siblings, Peter and Suzy, formed the **New Union Ramblers**; the group began singing at local events and coffeehouses. They were quickly noticed. By January 1964, the group had been signed to a seven-year recording contract with the Copper State Recording Company. That contract required the group to cut three singles and one album of folk songs per year, along with one Christmas album of folk songs. Still very focused on her art, she admitted she had signed the contract reluctantly.

"It's all the personal appearances, night club stands and TV work that may go with the contract that I'm adverse to," she told the *Arizona Daily Star* at the time. "I'm an ethnic folk singer, and very much against all the commercialism in folk music today. You can preserve a genuine ethnic quality on records, but most of the faddists who fill the concert halls for a hootenanny like the jazzed-up folk sound, which I despise."

Her views on music softened a bit as she began to feel restricted by the poorly attended folk shows in Tucson, which was accompanied by an indifference for classes at Arizona State. Encouraged by friends to

LINDA RONSTADT

The Eagles might have looked very different if not for **Linda Ronstadt**. The band and Ronstadt's paths crossed often over their performing years in the 1970s and 1980s, but they first found each other when her manager **John Boylan** started gathering musicians to serve as her backup band for her 1970 summer tour. He hired Glenn Frey after his band, a duo with **J.D. Souther** called **Longbranch/Pennywhistle**, began to shut down. Boylan also hired Don Henley, whose band **Shiloh**, was in similar straits. They both agreed to work for $250 a week. Randy Meisner was looking for work after leaving **Rick Nelson's Stone Canyon Band**, and he joined too. Bernie Leadon, who already had a history with Ronstadt, played with the others one day in Disneyland. Although she didn't know it at the time, she brought together the four original Eagles.

But Ronstadt's accidental creation of a supergroup was just a small footnote on a resume filled with chart-breaking accomplishments. She started out as a folk singer in Tucson, Arizona, and moved to Los Angeles in 1964 to find better musical opportunities. She and her band, the **Stone Poneys**, reached #12 on the Billboard chart with their single *Different Drum*. Capitol Records dropped the Poneys but kept Ronstadt. She recorded three albums for Capitol, *Hand Sown… Home Grown*, *Silk Purse*, and the self-titled *Linda Ronstadt*, but none charted higher than #103 nationally.

That changed when she signed on with **David Geffen**'s Asylum Records in 1973. Her first Asylum LP, *Don't Cry Now*, was co-produced by Eagles contemporary **J.D. Souther** and backed by, among others, all four Eagles. It was a commercial and critical success and set the stage for the next decade in her career, which was arguably the most successful period of many females in rock history. She has earned three #1 pop albums on *Billboard*'s Top 10 pop albums and 38 charting pop albums.

During the 1970s and the early 1980s, she was the highest paid female in the rock industry, and she toured relentlessly. She expanded her skillset by starring on Broadway and fearlessly recording albums outside of the traditional pop-rock genre. She was inducted into the Rock and Roll Hall of Fame in 2014, and in 2019, she was a Kennedy Center Honoree. [167, 340, 534, 587, 731, 1195, 1400]

visit Los Angeles, where folk venues had enthusiastic crowds, Ronstadt followed friend **Bobby Kimmel** to the California coast. She and Kimmel would become bandmates in a new group called the **Stone Poneys** recording with Capitol Records; in 1974 they would crack the Billboard Hot 100 with *Different Drum*. [530, 531, 534]

McGuinn, Clark, Crosby Form Landmark Group,The Byrds

The country-rock credentials that the Eagles developed over the years can be traced back to a few seminal bands in the 1960s and 1970s, and acts like **Buffalo Springfield**, the **Flying Burrito Brothers**, and **Poco** stand tall among them. But few bands set the example for them better than **The Byrds**.

The band leaped into the music scene in the summer of 1965 with their debut album *Mr. Tambourine Man*, and that jangly single helped set a standard for folk rock's progression into the musical mainstream. The group, whose members would go on to significant careers with other bands and solo, included **Roger McGuinn**, **Gene Clark**, **David Crosby**, **Chris Hillman**, and **Michael Clarke**. They would churn out 12 important albums in eight years and received critical acclaim for nearly all of them. Songs like *Eight Miles High*, *Turn! Turn! Turn* and *So You Want to Be a Rock 'n' Roll Star* remain staples on classic rock stations today.

The band sowed the seeds of country rock when it released the landmark album, *Sweetheart of the Rodeo*, widely considered the bible for fusing of country and rock music today. Disagreements over the band's musical path forward and unresolved personnel issues would eventually lead to The Byrds' demise.

Fighting depression and anxiety, Clark left the band in 1966. Crosby and Michael Clarke left in 1967. McGuinn and Hillman did a good job of recruiting replacements, bringing in **Gram Parsons** and later **Clarence White,** but infighting continued and the group disbanded in March 1973.

The group left in its wake the fusing of thought-provoking lyrics with a mesmerizing, instantly recognizable sound that set it apart from most music of the era. Their example was received strongly by the Eagles.

"Those sixties groups opened the way for a lot of what we're doing," **Don Henley** told *Sounds* magazine in 1976. "We are a product of the sixties. Nothing in the seventies has influenced me at all. All our influences come from the sixties—**Beatles**, Byrds, Buffalo Springfield – bands who just got up there and played. It's just the songs with us; no gimmicks, flashy clothes, glitter or bullshit."

Even though there was evolutionary distance between The Byrds and the Eagles, there was still a mutual feeling of respect between the groups.

"The Eagles? To me they're more of an extension [of The Byrds] than an innovation," **Gene Clark** told *Sounds* in 1976. "They're very Byrds sounding. They're a growth of that sound, but their patterns are very similar to what The Byrds would be doing if The Byrds were still together."

Chris Hillman agreed. "I always felt The Byrds and the [**Flying Burrito Brothers**] drew the game plan and the Eagles picked up the ball and made a lot of touchdowns, deservedly so. Don Henley's a fabulous singer and writer. So, they were good."

The Byrds in their entirety would reunite one last time in 1991 when they were inducted into the Rock and Roll Hall of Fame. Henley gave their induction speech and waxed nostalgic over his first concert to see them at Hirsch Memorial Coliseum in Shreveport, Louisiana. [1157, 1158]

SPRING 1964

Weston Starts Monday 'Hoot Nights' at the Troubadour Club

Doug Weston created a cultural phenomenon in the spring of 1964 when his soon-to-be-famous establishment, the Troubadour club, tried to enliven otherwise slow Monday nights with an open-mic night concept that would catapult a multitude of talented acts into stardom.

The Troubadour, located on Santa Monica Boulevard in the West Hollywood neighborhood of Los Angeles just outside of Beverly Hills, began "Hoot Nights" with 13 young entertainers that Weston simply called **The Men**. He embellished their vocals with amplified acoustic instruments, which was a novelty at the time. Folk and bluegrass music acts were growing increas-

ingly popular during the early 1960s across California, and Weston began experimenting with hootenannies in May 1963 when Troubadour introduced leading folk singers and guitarists in a open mic setting at the La Mirada Festival in La Mirada, California.

Hootenanny shows were being scheduled by rival clubs and arenas across Los Angeles by the fall of 1963, including the venerable Hollywood Bowl on North Highland Avenue. But none matched the shear folk magnetism that the Troubadour created. And Weston did his part to make the musicians feel welcomed.

"Folk-rock music has contributed something of value because it has generated the idea that a popular song can have a meaning and still be groovy," a 39-year-old Weston told the *Los Angeles Times*. "Up until a couple of years ago the folk music people were only singing to themselves. I wanted to move more meaningful songs—not liberal necessarily, but songs with something of value—out into the mass audience."

Weston, who a few years later would reveal a more profit-driven attitude, managed to capture the hearts and minds of the folk music movement. "Hoot Nights" served as a focal point for aspiring folk acts and singer-songwriters, including the Eagles and their associates.

J.D. Souther, a frequent Eagles contributor and source of inspiration, told the *Gaffney (S.C.) Ledger* in 1980 that the club was important to the band's emergence. "We were all hanging around on Hoot Night at the Troubadour, comisserating about our lack of recognition in the music world, and Glenn and Don got together and started writing."

"As the [1960s] was kicking in, the place was always jammed on Monday nights," said Henry Diltz, who photographed the Eagles's album cover and promotional material. "That was the night of the weekly Hootenanny session, where a parade of future folk stars like **Judy Collins** or **Phil Ochs** would perform a couple songs each free of charge simply to get a foot on the ladder. You'd see ten to fifteen acts on Monday nights. The place would be packed with agents, managers and record company people."

By the early 1970s Hoot Nights had become big business. Artist and Reportoire (A&R) men from the major labels would descend upon the Troubadour in search of new talent. It was a haunt for record execs like **David Geffen**, **Lou Adler** and **Albert Grossman**, who would look for talent on Hoot Nights. And they weren't alone in that search.

"**Linda** [**Ronstadt**] would go down to the Troubadour and hang out in the bar and meet songwriters and get songs," Ronstadt's manager **Peter Asher** told **John Einarson** in his book *Desperados: The Roots of Country Rock*. Asher said the Los Angeles, and the Troubadour specifically, felt like the center of the musicial universe at that time.

As the 1970s evolved so did the Troubadour. Glenn Frey waxed about "tragic and hopeful stories" being a fact of life. Though unforgiving to some, the club did bring the Eagles into each other's orbit some eight years after Weston began his Hoot Nights. [164, 206, 285, 1159, 1186]

LEAVING HOME

Spreading their collective wings, the artists who
would become the Eagles packed up their beat
up cars, trucks and vans and left home. They
picked up paying gigs and began learning how
tough a musician's life could be.

SPRING 1964

Geffen Fibs, Gets Mailroom Job At the William Morris Agency

After landing an usher job with CBS Television Studios in Los Angeles, **David Geffen** spent months guiding people to their seats for programs like *The Judy Garland Show*, *The Red Skelton Show*, *The Danny Kaye Show*, and *The Art Linkletter Show*. Geffen was performing his usher duties for Linkletter's show on the afternoon of November 22, 1963, when Linkletter interrupted the show and announced that President **John F. Kennedy** had been assassinated.

Someone in the crowd cheered inappropriately and Geffen, a loyal Kennedy devotee, lost his composure and took a swing at the man in anger. CBS fired him. With few other options, Geffen found himself on a plane back to his mother's house in Brooklyn's Borough Park.

Undaunted, he applied for a low-level job at the prestigious Ashley Famous talent agency, hoping to keep close to the entertainment elite. He filled out his application truthfully, including not being a college graduate and bouncing from job to job, but he was not hired. That truthfulness, he thought, cost him his opportunity, so he wouldn't let it happen again. His next target was the William Morris Agency (WMA), the top talent agency in the world at the time, in Manhattan. He placed a call to the man who hired mailroom trainees and Geffen brazenly claimed to be Phil Spector's cousin.

His WMA employment application also showed that he had graduated from UCLA, another blatant lie. The hiring manager warned that the job would be a slog—long hours, low pay, and menial work. But there was also an expectation that mailroom workers would move up to work as assistants to agents, and that's where many successful agents got their starts.

Geffen assured the manager he was up to the task and was hired on June 22, 1964. The deceptions didn't stop there, however. Geffen, now 21, was surprised to learn that WMA did background and education checks for all hires and heard that another recent trainee had been fired for lying on his application. Now he took to coming in four hours early every day to intercept a letter that was surely coming from UCLA.

The letter came, and Geffen intercepted it. He pulled his brother Mitchell into the ruse by asking him to obtain UCLA Admissions Office letterhead and writing a letter stating that David had graduated from UCLA with an undergraduate degree in theater arts. Mitchell obliged, and then sent the letter from Los Angeles so the postmark would appear correct. It all worked and Geffen remained at WMA. Geffen would continue doing what he needed to succeed, and in December of 1966, he would land his first successful rock act. [1, 2, 3, 393, 1164]

JOE WALSH

Joe Walsh already had a rock career some musicians would have died for by the time he decided to join the Eagles in 1975. With his breakout band, the **James Gang**, and as a solo act, Walsh had as many gold records, four, as the Eagles when he joined them in the studio in 1976 as they recorded their landmark album *Hotel California*.

Walsh started his career playing dive bars and hard rock clubs in Ohio. His first bands, the **G-Clefts** and **The Measles**, introduced him to rock music, but he didn't get his real initiation into rock and roll until he joined the James Gang in 1968. Within a year the band had its first hit, *Funk #48*. They followed that up with *Funk #49* in 1970. Along the way the James Gang completed four charting albums, including two certified as gold. But Walsh felt increasingly pressured to produce hits. Further, his band was reluctant to evolve outside of its hard-rock comfort zone, so he quit in 1973 and headed to Colorado with his producer, **Bill Szymczyk**. Once there he started a new band, **Barnstorm**. The group was slow out of the gate, eventually giving way to Walsh's inevitable solo career. Along the way, he churned out more hits, including *Turn To Stone* and his signature hit *Rocky Mountain Way*, his first-ever top 25 hit.

Life took a different turn for Walsh when he met **Irving Azoff** at Sunset Strip's Whiskey a Go Go in the winter of 1972. Azoff and Walsh had met before at Lake Geneva in Wisconsin in 1970, and Joe was unhappy with his manager. He wasn't getting any paying gigs and didn't seem to care much about Walsh's career. Azoff offered to help, and immediately began landing gigs for the then-needy artist. After that, Walsh hired Azoff to manage everything for him, including his career.

Azoff was also managing the Eagles in 1975 when Bernie Leadon left the band, and helped nudge Walsh and the band together, with mutually beneficial results. Walsh has been an Eagle ever since and rejoined the band in 1994 when it came out of its 14-year hiatus. Eagles work aside, he still maintained a successful solo career. He has released 11 solo albums and has been the most prolific go-to studio performer among his Eagles bandmates.

Walsh was inducted into the Rock and Roll Hall of Fame with the Eagles in 1998, and was inducted into the Colorado Rock Hall of Fame in 2017. [82, 135, 223, 361, 1326]

The Four Speeds, Henley Cut Two Singles, Become Felicity

The Four Speeds, the Linden, Texas-based band led by **Don Henley** and **Richard Bowden**, continued to gather a strong fan following through early 1964. High school proms, bars, frat parties, and clubs were the band's usual gigs, but boredom was beginning to set in for the group.

Singing from behind his drum set, Henley had become adept at imitating other singers like **James Brown**, **Wilson Pickett**, and **Otis Redding** to appease ticket buyers who wanted to hear songs they knew. Little by little, the band started working original material into their sets. Songs like *I'm Gone* and *God Is Where You Find Him* were written by Henley and Surratt and played at gigs, but they weren't what the crowds wanted to hear. The band signed on with a small local label, Hartlyn Records, and released two singles, *Why Did You Leave Me* and *Variety*. Seemingly channeling **Eric Burdon**, Henley sang vocals on both cuts. Neither garnered much airplay and the band was disappointed it didn't fare better.

Feeling stagnated, the group changed its name to **Felicity** and kept working on original music. They would soon have a chance encounter with a visiting recording star that would prove helpful to their careers. [6, 1145, 1146]

WINTER 1965

Walsh Drops Oboe, Forms High School Bands G-Clefts, Nomads

Joe Walsh got his start as a as a bashful oboe player at Montclair High School in Montclair, New Jersey.

A gifted, versatile musician, Walsh learned to play guitar, bass guitar, steel pedal guitar, piano, and clarinet too. But Walsh would become best known as a guitar virtuoso and has earned professional praise from guitar legends like **Jimmy Page**, **Pete Townshend**, and **Eric Clapton**.

Walsh and his family moved to New Jersey from New York when he was 12 years old, and he proved to be musically adept, but personally shy. "I was the All-American boy," Walsh told *Rolling Stone* in 1975, "a child of the silent majority, a third-chair clarinet in my junior high school band."

School band aside, Walsh developed a love for guitar during those high school years and formed a duo with a school friend, **Bob Edwards**. They called themselves the **G-Clefts**. "Even though we could hardly play anything, we had plans to be the next **Ventures**," Walsh said. "All those instrumentals like *Wipe Out*, *Wild Weekend* and *Walk, Don't Run*, were coming out and we learned them all. We were terrible; but it was cool. I never got any shit 'cause I only played rhythm." It was a start for him.

Walsh was born November 20, 1947, in Wichita, Kansas, and his mother was a classically trained pianist. His birth father was a pilot in the U.S. Air Force, **1st Lt. Robert N. Fidler**, and died in 1949 when his Lockheed F-80 Shooting Star collided with another F-80 over Irisuma Island near Okinawa, Japan.

His mother remarried and when he was formally adopted, he took his stepfather's last name, but kept his birthfather's last name as his middle name. The family lived in Columbus, Ohio, for a few years before moving to New York and then New Jersey. Walsh dissolved the G-Clefts and soon found another: **The Nomads**.

"They had just dumped their bass player and asked me if I could play. I said 'sure.' I never played bass in my life, but I figured it couldn't be too hard with only four strings. I ended up playing bass for the Nomads most of my senior year. My parents still have a picture of me all slicked up, with a collarless **Beatles** jacket and Beatles boots, playing at the prom."

Walsh would return to Ohio for college and major in English at Kent State University. It was a stunted experience that lasted just one quarter. Walsh, disinterested in studies, ended up with a 1.8 grade point average, but developed a reputation among local musicians and bars. Rather than returning to New Jersey, he hung around Kent State looking for pickup work with local bands and found some with a garage band called **The Measles**.

The band would become legendary in northern Ohio and Walsh, now 18, settled into a condemned farmhouse near the Kent city limits and spent three years polishing his skills. Their reputation growing, The Measles would record a few singles in 1966 and were approached by the management team for the **Ohio Express** to record three Measles songs, including Walsh's own *I Find I Think of You*. That summer those singles would make it onto the Express's album. [25, 223, 358, 363, 364, 1160]

SPRING 1965

 ON THE ROAD WITH …
The New Breed, with Timothy B. Schmit: The Riptides

SUMMER 1965

 RELEASES
The Drivin' Dynamics, with Randy Meisner: *One of These Days* (single)

 ON SCREEN
The New Breed, with Timothy B. Schmit appeared on Los Angeles' KLAC-TV's teen afternoon show *Hollywood Discotheque*.

Drivin' Dynamics, Meisner Sign Record Deal with Sully Records

The **Drivin' Dynamics** and their lead singer, **Randy Meisner**, developed a reputation as a flexible band, capable of rocking and laying down a smooth ballad too.

Near the end of the summer of 1965, their reputation drew attention from Sully Records, an Oklahoma City, Oklahoma-based label with a history that led back to **Buddy Holly**. The Sully label was started by **Gene Sullivan** in 1959, but by 1965 it was owned by **Ray Ruff**, a colleague of Holly, moved the studio to Amarillo, Texas.

Ruff would drive those same highways from Scottsbluff, Nebraska to Minot, South Dakota that Sullivan traveled in search of talent at local bars and clubs and that is where he stumbled upon Meisner and the Drivin' Dynamics. Ruff liked what he heard and signed the band. They cut three singles for him. Meisner sang *One of These Days* and *So Fine*. The singles charted well regionally, and the band's reputation continued to blossom. But that attention would soon put the spotlight on Meisner, and not in a way that was helpful for the Dynamics. [486, 1161]

FALL 1965

RELEASES
▶ **The Drivin' Dynamics**, with Randy Meisner: *So Fine* (single)
▶ **The New Breed**, with Timothy B. Schmit: *Green Eye'd Woman* (single)
▶ **The Four Speeds**, with Don Henley: *Why Did You Leave Me* (single)

ON SCREEN
The New Breed, with Timothy B. Schmit appeared on KHJ-TV television show 9th Street West. Appeared with Sam the Sham and The Motleys.

ON THE ROAD WITH ...
▶ **The Drivin' Dynamics**, with Randy Meisner: Boenzee Cryque
▶ **The New Breed**, with Timothy B. Schmit: Sam the Sham, The Motleys

Henley Drops Out at SF Austin, Enrolls at North Texas State

Don Henley, **Richard Bowen**, and the rest of the band **Felicity** graduated high school and started looking to extend their lives beyond the borders of their hometown of Linden, Texas.

Henley followed his high school girlfriend to Stephen F. Austin University, in Nacogdoches, Texas. The school was two hours south of Linden, but, he explained to **Marc Eliot** in his book *To the Limit: The Untold Story of the Eagles*, he was frustrated and isolated at SFA. Perpetually ridden by jocks who incessantly flirted with his girlfriend, and bored with the campus, he became increasingly disenchanted. Meanwhile, he and the band had been taking gigs around Dallas, which had more opportunities to play and many more serious musicians.

In the fall of 1967, he broke up with his girlfriend and headed just north of Dallas where he enrolled at North Texas State. When he settled into the dorms there, he met another student who would become an enduring friend. "I was in my dorm room blasting some hard rock—I think it was **Led Zeppelin**—and **Jim Ed Norman** ... knocked on the door and introduced himself by giving me a copy of *Wheatstraw Suite* by the **Dillards**.

"After I heard that record it was over." Henley would invite Norman, who played keyboards and guitar, to become a member of **Felicity**, where he helped the band record an album. But he had further reach-

GLENN FREY

A frustrated Glenn Frey was in the Troubadour Club one night shortly after agreeing to join **Linda Ronstadt**'s backing band in the fall of 1970. Don Henley was also in the club that night, and Frey, knowing that Ronstadt still needed a drummer for her tour, struck up a conversation. He was persuasive. Henley joined her band and on the first night of the tour, the two in-need-of-a-break musicians agreed they would start a band together. It was the beginning of the Eagles.

A half-decade before Frey set foot in the Troubadour, he was a long-haired teenager trying to become a rock musician in Detroit's suburbs. Inspired by **The Beatles** and **Elvis Presley**, he played in high school bands that taught him a little about how the music world worked. He sang lead and played some rhythm guitar for **The Mushrooms**, the most meaningful of those bands. The group got gigs in local teen clubs called "Hideouts," which were operated by **Bob Seger**'s managers. Seger took a liking to Frey, so he took him under his wing and taught him the importance of songwriting.

Frey followed his girlfriend to Los Angeles in the summer of 1968 and met **J.D. Souther**, with whom he joined to form the L.A. duo **Longbranch/Pennywhistle**. They produced one album, but it went nowhere. Playing around L.A., however, got him noticed and invited to Ronstadt's band, which then led to the Eagles. It took a couple of albums and a producer switch for the band to find its feet, but the Eagles eventually became one of the most successful rock groups in history. Frey and the Eagles were together through six studio albums, one live album, and one record-breaking greatest hits album—before calling it quits in 1981.

Frey released four solo studio albums after the Eagles broke up, with *No Fun Aloud* and *The Allnighter*, both earning gold record certifications and producing top 15 hits, including *You Belong to the City*, which reached #2. He rejoined the band when hell froze over in 1994 and contributed to two new Eagles albums.

Frey was inducted into the Rock and Roll Hall of Fame with his Eagles bandmates in 1998 and became a member of the Songwriters Hall of Fame in 2000. He passed away at 67 in January 2016. [209, 263, 327, 331, 340, 433, 479, 1226]

ing input later for Henley and the Eagles when he handled the string arrangements for the Eagles *Desperado* and *Hotel California* albums. [6, 29, 1144]

High Schooler Frey Joins First Band, the *Subterraneans*

One cool night in the fall of 1965, future Eagle co-founder Glenn Frey, then just a high school junior, heard a freshman band playing at a party in the Detroit suburbs and boldly asked them if he could sing with them. Soon he was belting out a song with the group and they were so impressed they asked him to join the band.

Frey became the *de facto* leader of the group, which dubbed itself the **Subterraneans**, after the **Jack Kerouac** book. Unlike so many other garage or party bands of the day, the Subterraneans had, in Frey, someone who actually understood music.

Frey's mother, Nellie, force-marched him through eight years of piano lessons, so he knew how to read music and had a solid understanding of musical composition. They carved a niche quickly and cultivated a following. Dances they played would draw upwards of 600 students.

Eventually the band grew beyond high school dances and parties. They started playing at a chain of local teen clubs around Detroit called "Hideouts." The Subterraneans never evolved beyond playing at local clubs, but the experience got Frey noticed by Hideout operators **Dave Leone** and **Punch Andrews**. The connection with Leone and Andrews was important, since they were

also managers to emerging Detroit phenom **Bob Seger**.

"These were the happening teen clubs in Detroit," Frey told the *Detroit Free Press* in 2003. "We set our goals for auditioning and getting a gig. We changed drummers, and ultimately, we got hired. We got a gig. We played at the Southfield Hideout. I remember the key song in our set was [the Who's] *My Generation*. Our drummer **Lenny Mintz** from Southfield—could play all the **Keith Moon** fills, so we thought that was pretty cool. We got good enough, and I think I may have even started playing bass or rhythm guitar."

Frey's time with the Subterraneans was fleeting. Another band that drew inspiration from the burgeoning British and California harmonizing sounds, **Four of Us**, would soon recruit Frey and give him a lesson that he carried with him to Los Angeles and the Eagles. [345, 392]

WINTER 1965-66

RELEASES
The Four Speeds, with Don Henley: *Variety* (single)

ON THE ROAD WITH …
The Drivin' Dynamics, with Randy Meisner: The Soul Survivors

The New Breed, Schmit Hit Charts with *Green Eye'd Woman*

The New Breed, with future Eagle **Timothy B. Schmit**, was an often-headlining act in northern California through the early 1960s. The band had been managed by a neighborhood friend, **Roy Yano**, but Yano dropped his management of the band to attend UC-Berkley in the fall of 1964, according to the Sacramento Rock & Radio Museum in 2007.

The group recruited **Gary Shiro**, who was friends with **Johnny Hyde**, the program director at Sacramento's KXOA. That relationship would quickly prove beneficial. In the summer after high school, the band began trying out original material.

Floegel had written a song about his high school girlfriend. Hyde thought that the song could be commercially successful with the right arrangement. Soon the reorganized song became *Green Eye'd Woman.*

By the winter of 1965, the cut would be getting occasional airplay nationally, but was a huge regional hit, reaching #1 for several weeks on the West Coast. During the band's Christmas break, it did a 14-city tour up and down the California in **George Hullin**'s 1959 Chevrolet Impala, pulling their gear in a U-Haul trailer. The band's stature began to grow even more, and by the winter of 1968, a record deal—and another name change—was on the way. [348, 350, 351, 1140]

Frey Leaves Subterraneans, Joins Folk-Rock Band, Four of Us

Eagles co-founder **Glenn Frey** had established his role as the leader of his high school band, the **Subterraneans**, by the winter of 1966. The group was now playing at various Hideout teen clubs around Detroit and he had a budding relationship with the club's operators, **Punch Andrews** and **Dave Leone**, who also happened to manage emerging Detroit singer-songwriter **Bob Seger**.

Frey, now a senior, had expanded his musical repertoire by taking on rhythm guitar and bass with the Subterraneans, in addition to singing. Around that time, Frey and another band started to take notice of each other. "The best band in Birmingham was **The Four of Us**," Frey told the *Detroit Free Press* in 2003. "They were the only band I saw going around the clubs in Detroit that really had all the vocals."

Every young band in Detroit was patterning themselves after **Mitch Rider and the Detroit Wheels**, or what he called "the greaser soul-band vein," or **The Rolling Stones** or **The Animals**. **Gary Burrows**, the leader of The Four of Us, was looking for someone to replace the band's rhythm guitar player and took note of Frey's singing skills.

Frey auditioned as a rhythm guitar player and got the job, leaving the Subterraneans behind. His new band brought new challenges. "Before I met Gary Burrows, I didn't think too much about harmonies and that kind of thing," Frey said. "But that's what he was into, and we spent a lot of time working on vocals. I joined the only surf band in Detroit. There was no other band in the suburbs that had the kind of set list we had. We wore those white boat-neck surfer shirts, white jeans and socks."

Burrows pushed the band to the new West Coast sounds of **The Beach Boys** and the **Hollies**. "**Jeff Alborell**, Glenn Frey, and I practiced harmony parts every day," Burrows said. "That was something our band had that a lotta bands weren't doing." Frey's time with The Four of Us was short, and he began another band called the **Mushrooms**. With that band. Frey got Andrews to bring him closer to Seger, who allowed him to attend studio sessions. That connection would lead the Mushrooms, and Frey, to their first single. [345, 392]

Azoff Becomes Manager for School Band, Shades of Blue

Irving Azoff's father was a respected pharmacist in his hometown of Danville, Illinois, and Azoff had enrolled in the University of Illinois Urbana-Champaign to follow in his footsteps. But on August 12, 1966, Azoff saw the **Yardbirds** playing at Indiana Beach, an amusement park in Monticello, Indiana, and, he explained to *Rolling Stone*'s Cameron Crowe in 1978, that after that there was no looking back.

The Yardbirds may have given Azoff the existential motivation he needed to pursue a career in music, but he had done plenty of research before **Jimmy Page** and **Jeff Beck**

went on stage that night. Breaking into the music industry is challenging when you can't sing or play an instrument, but Azoff had a different approach: he'd manage the bands.

Earlier in 1966, a group of friends from Danville High School formed a band called **Shades of Blue**. The band included **Tim Frazier** on an upside-down Hoffner bass, **Chuck Olmstead** on lead guitar and trumpet, **Cloyd Shank** on rhythm guitar, **Rick Miller** on drums, and **Mike Supp** on keyboards. The group had gotten extremely popular in Danville, and Azoff, just 19 at the time, wanted in. He started booking the band in teen clubs in the Danville area and then moved up into bigger clubs.

"Irving was our first manager and a childhood friend," Frazier told *60sGarageBands.com in 2004*. "I believe he wanted to play, but couldn't sing or [play an instrument] so we made him our manager." It proved to be a perfect marriage as Azoff scheduled the band's gigs through high school and he learned the ropes as a booking agent.

Along the way, he booked Shades of Blue in clubs being played by bands he would get close to later, like **One-Eyed Jacks**, **The Regiments**, an as-yet unknown **REO Speedwagon**, and an unflinching folk singer, **Dan Fogelberg**. His entrepreneurial spirit was never in doubt. **John Baruck**, twice a business partner with Azoff in life, remembered his early days managing gigs. "In high school in Danville ... he would sit at one of those folding card tables and

IRVING AZOFF

Irving Azoff began working for Asylum Records CEO **David Geffen** in the spring of 1973, and about that time, the Geffen-managed Eagles were unhappy with their contractual arrangement with the label. It was an opportune time for Azoff, who had been working in the trenches for artists since he started booking bands in Danville, Illinois, in the mid-1960s. Geffen and his partner, **Elliot Roberts**, had a growing stable of artists that needed attention, and he gave the day-to-day management responsibilities for the Eagles to Azoff. It would be the start of a five-decade relationship.

Azoff grew up in Danville, Illinois, and managed a band made up of high school friends, **Shades of Blue**, in 1966. He enrolled in the University of Illinois at Urbana-Champaign and began working as a booking agent on the band circuit there. Blytham Limited was the biggest booking agency in the area and was owned and operated by **Bob Nutt**. Azoff and Nutt partnered and controlled rock band bookings from Wisconsin to Ohio. Azoff would manage bookings for acts like **REO Speedwagon**, **Michael McDonald**, **Dan Fogelberg**, **The Finchley Boys**, **One-Eyed Jacks**, and many others.

In 1971, Azoff headed to Los Angeles and began managing Fogelberg and, eventually, Joe Walsh. He took a job working for his idol, Geffen, in 1973, and soon he was managing the Eagles for Geffen/ Roberts Management. By 1974, Azoff left to form Front Line Management and took the disgruntled Eagles with him. He also initiated, and helped win, a legal fight to recover the Eagles publishing rights from Warner Brothers.

Azoff and Front Line's stable of artists grew, and he developed a reputation for putting their interests first. Along the way, his stature and wealth in the music industry grew. He created his own label, Full Moon Records, in 1975, branched out into producing movies, rescued a failing MCA Records in the 1980s, and formed his own Giant Records in the 1990s. In the 2000s, he became CEO of Ticketmaster and led the merger with LiveNation. In 2012, *Billboard* named him the most powerful man in music. [200, 481, 597, 1318, 1359, 1465]

break up $100 [among a few bands], then collect two dollars at the door," Baruck told *Billboard* in 2017. "That's how he paid for college."

Azoff also showed a willingness to bend the rules in support of his band. Shades of Blue entered themselves in a Battle of the Bands competition at the Eastern Illinois Fair, and Azoff made sure the band had an edge.

"I can't remember who we played against," Frazier said. "But it could have been the Stones and we still would have won. We found out later that Irving paid the judges off." In fairness, the band had a sympathetic audience that night after their drummer, Rick Miller, fell thirty feet off his drum riser, Frazier said, dusted himself off and finished the show.

It wouldn't be the last time Azoff extended himself for the benefit of an artist he represented. The lessons he learned with Shades of Blue would soon be applied in other ways, especially as his connections with local venues became better established. [481, 1317, 1318, 1319, 1333, 1351]

Drivin' Dynamics Lose Bands' Battle, and Meisner Too

By the winter of 1966, the **Drivin' Dynamics** had put a stamp on their sound and fans were eagerly buying tickets to see them in Nebraska, the Dakotas, Kansas, and Colorado. In February, the band signed up to compete in a Battle of the Bands competition in Denver at an arena called The Cow Palace.

The Dynamics did well, but didn't win over the judges. **Randy Meisner**'s pristine vocals and thumping bass drew the attention of the competition's winning band, the Denver-based **Soul Survivors**. The band had plans to go to Los Angeles to record, but their bass player didn't want to go.

Like Meisner, he played bass and sang the high notes well, and the Soul Survivors saw an opportunity to patch a gaping hole. They told Meisner they would be heading to L.A. soon to open for another Denver band and ask him to join them. It seemed like the next logical step for Meisner, who was eager for a bigger stage. His decision came as disappointing news for the Dynamics, who were forced to continue on without him.

Meanwhile, the Soul Survivors began making plans for California and played another month of shows in Colorado to finance the trip. Had they known the hard times they would face in Los Angeles, they might have considered playing a few more, as their money ran out quickly. [6, 1107, 1331]

SPRING 1966

RELEASES
The Poor, with Randy Meisner: *Once Again* (single)

Stills, Young, Furay form the Iconic Buffalo Springfield

Few bands captured the angst and anti-war sentiment that permeated the country in the late 1960s better than the **Buffalo Springfield**. The band lasted just over two years, but produced three important albums and, along with **The Byrds**, help set the table for the folk- and country-rock trends that would surge to popularity through the 1970s.

The Springfield, like so many iconic bands of that era, blossomed out of the musical collective in Laurel Canyon in Hollywood. Guitarist **Neil Young** and bass player **Bruce Palmer** migrated to Los Angeles from Canada, while **Stephen Stills** and **Richie Furay**, also guitarists, arrived via Florida and Ohio, respectively.

The group played their first gig at **Doug Weston**'s Troubadour Club on April 11, 1966, and found immediate success. Before long, they had become the house band for the Whiskey a Go Go on Sunset Strip. Captivated by their unique sound and, moreover, the appeal that they had with youths of the day, record companies were clamoring to sign them.

Their first single, the Young-penned *Nowadays Clancy Can't Dance*, became a minor hit, bubbling up to 110 on *Billboard*'s singles chart. By August, they had been booked on television shows like *Hollywood Parlance* and the *Milton Berle TV Spectacular*. And by December, they released *For What It's Worth (Stop, Hey What's That Sound)* which rocketed to #7 on *Billboard*'s Hot 100 list and became a protest anthem for the anti-war movement.

The mixture of personalities in the band was responsible for some of the most creative songwriting and live performances of the late 1960s, but it was also difficult for those personalities to maintain an equilibrium. Stills had issues with Young's dedication and overall dependability. Palmer was deported twice for drug possession. Trying to keep things operational, Furay brought in **Jim Messina** to play bass for the absent Palmer, and the two began to mull starting another band that would eventually become **Poco**.

By the summer of 1968, the wheels had completely fallen off. In the early summer of 1968, the band met with record company executives to discuss the orderly breakup of the band and where the contractually obligated band members would land. Stills would join former Byrds guitarist **David Crosby** and former **Hollies** singer **Graham Nash** to form **Crosby, Stills and Nash**.

Young would break off solo, but shortly after would agree to split time between his solo career with his band, **Crazy Horse**, and a newly constituted **Crosby, Stills, Nash & Young**. Furay and Messina followed through on their plans to create Poco. In their new groups, and solo, the members would continue to make their mark on music.

Those marks resonated with the Eagles, who admired the Springfield. "Those sixties groups opened the way for a lot of what we're doing. We are a product of the sixties," **Don Henley** told **Cameron Crowe** in a 1975 *Rolling Stone* interview. "All our influences come from the sixties—**Beatles**,

The Buffalo Springfield's *single For What It's Worth* spoke to the anti-war sentiment in America's youths, but it also helped establish the emerging genre of country-rock music that was blossoming in Southern California at the time.

WHAT'S THAT SOUND? THE CLASH ON THE SUNSET STRIP

WINTER 1966 – The haunting, understated tremolo notes that echoed off **Neil Young**'s guitar strings on **Buffalo Springfield**'s *For What It's Worth (Stop, Hey What's That Sound)* helped vividly capture the growing anti-war sentiment among the nation's youths in the winter of 1966. Those haunting notes and its foreboding lyrics became a rallying cry against the Vietnam War, but it was actually written as a protest song over the riots on Sunset Strip in Los Angeles that November. Police along L.A.'s famous strip were unprepared for the hordes of teenagers that descended on the area's clubs on Friday, November 11.

Local businesses had grown increasingly wary about teenagers, hippies and drug use at and near popular venues like Pandora's Box and the Whiskey a Go Go. Business owners on the strip and local politicians imposed curfews for teenagers and got Pandora's Box shut down. Hundreds of disquieted teenagers showed up for a mock funeral for the popular club, and their presence intimidated the far-outnumbered Los Angeles police.

Mostly it was throngs of people milling about aimlessly, upset over the rules governing the Strip. No one was hurt and nothing was damaged. But it didn't go away. The next night over 1,000 poorly organized protesters showed up to demonstrate and the police, overly cautious from the night before, increased their presence with more than 200 officers and sheriffs in riot gear. In an apartment above the Strip, **Dickie Davis**, a friend of **Stephen Stills**, described what was unfolding in L.A. to Stills over the phone. The Springfield was in San Francisco that night playing The Fillmore. After returning to L.A., Stills emerged a day later with the as-yet untitled song. Within a week it was arranged, recorded to an acetate single, and on the air on L.A.'s KHJ-AM. As legend holds, Springfield manager **Charlie Greene** named the song after Stills told him, "I have this song for what it's worth." It was untitled, so Greene dubbed it *For What It's Worth*.

The song galvanized a movement. It also helped evolve the California sound created by **The Beach Boys** and moved it in the direction of **The Byrds**. The Eagles would take that sound, country-rock, and refine it more. The Springfield's single flew up the charts and peaked at #7 on April 1, 1967. Though the album was finished, Ertegun rereleased it immediately to include the now-iconic song. [1208, 1209, 1210, 1211, 1212, 1213]

Byrds, Buffalo Springfield—bands who just got up there and played."

The Eagles earned some mutual respect from some members of the Springfield too. "If only for perfectly capturing the feel of L.A., the Eagles are the one band that's carried on the spirit of the Buffalo Springfield," Young told Crowe in that same interview. [247, 1158, 1165, 1166, 1167, 1168]

Jackson Browne Joins the Nitty Gritty Dirt Band

McCabe's Guitar Shop was the home for many bluegrass-enthused musicians in Southern California. **J.D. Souther** and Glenn Frey would play gigs there as **Longbranch/Pennywhistle**, and it was a favorite haunt for **Linda Ronstadt** during her early days in Los Angeles. More importantly, it also served as an incubator for talent, and it was in this legendary guitar shop with a stage that **Jackson Browne** became friends with Long Beach's **Nitty Gritty Dirt Band**.

Browne was an introspective writer and, at least in his formative years as a performer, was shy and withdrawn. His joining with the extroverted and irreverent Dirt Band seemed like an odd pairing. But Browne had been friends with the nucleus of the band for years, and it was growing experience. **Jeff Hanna**, the leader of the Dirt Band, said it was a good pairing since they were already familiar with each other, and there was a desire to play more folk and jug band music as opposed to the surf music that was filling the airwaves. "He had an incredible sense of humor," Han-

na said of Browne. "He was definitely as whacked out as the rest of us."

Rick Wiseman, in his book *Jackson Browne: The Story of a Hold Out*, said Browne may have viewed the band, which was becoming the rage on the hootenanny circuit at local clubs, as a more direct route to success in the music business. Browne joined, played guitar and gut bucket bass, and was there when the group won a talent contest at the Paradox Club. That achievement gave them rights to open at the well-known Golden Bear Club in Huntington Beach opening for the **Sir Douglas Quintet**. That gig went so well that that they were held over to open for **The Lovin' Spoonful**.

Browne penned his landmark song *These Days* around the time he was a member of the Dirt Band, and it had a lasting impact on **John McEuen**, another local musician who often played the Paradox Club. "That's a really nice song. Where did you get it?" McEuen asked Browne. "Oh, I just wrote it," Browne replied. "Oh, where did you get the melody?" McEuen asked further. "I just kind of made it up," he replied.

The irreverence of the Dirt Band didn't quite align with Browne's demeanor. They were good together, but it was clear that Browne's more introspective approach to writing and performing were different, so he dropped out of the band in the summer of 1966. McEuen would replace him.

Although he was no longer in the group, he was not forgotten, When the Dirt Band released their debut album in 1967, they

JACKSON BROWNE

One summer day in 1969 Jackson Browne strode up to Glenn Frey and **J.D. Souther** at a Free Clinic benefit show in Santa Monica and he started singing his new song, *Jamaica Say You Will* to them. They were already familiar with each other since they hung out at the same clubs while they tried to make it in the music industry, but they had never formally met. The typically shy Browne fixed that by approaching them, and started a musical procession that paid dividends for themselves and fans for years to come. Indeed, his path has crossed with the Eagles several times and he co-wrote many of their enduring classics, including *Take It Easy, Doolin-Dalton* and *James Dean*.

Browne was born in Germany, where his father, Clyde, worked for *Stars and Stripes*. His family moved to the Highland Park district of Los Angeles in the early 1950s, and he developed an appreciation for music. As a teenager he began singing at local clubs like the Ash Grove and the Troubadour. After graduating high school he briefly joined the **Nitty Gritty Dirt Band** and experienced the folk scene in Greenwich Village in the early 1960s, but came home to L.A. to find a recording deal. He was signed briefly by Elektra Records, but was released without recording a solo album.

He got his break when he recorded an acetate single of *Jamaica* and *Song for Adam* with backing help from Frey, Souther and **Ned Doheny**. That recording got the attention of **David Geffen**, who signed Browne to an Asylum Records deal that launched his musical career.

Browne has recorded two Top 10 singles in his career, including *Somebody's Baby* (#7), *Doctor My Eyes* (#8). He has had four albums in *Billboard*'s Top 200 chart, including *Hold Out* (#1), *Running On Empty* (#3), *The Pretender* (#5) and *Lawyers in Love* (#8).

Browne was inducted into the Rock and Roll Hall of Fame in 2004, and joined the Songwriters Hall of Fame in 2007. In 2016, after the passing of Eagles leader Glenn Frey, he joined the remaining Eagles onstage at the 58th Annual Grammy Awards and performed *Take It Easy*, which he and Frey co-wrote. [15, 209, 416, 1109, 1226]

covered two of his songs, *Melissa* and *Holding.* They also sometimes appeared together at gigs as Browne continued searching for a recording contract. He would eventually land one with an odd label that served as an Elektra Records incubator, but that deal went nowhere. It wasn't until his stature grew enough at the local hoots that an impressed **David Crosby** recommended he seek out Asylum Records' **David Geffen**.

Shortly after, two of his new friends, Glenn Frey and **J.D. Souther**, helped him prepare a demo tape that was delivered to Geffen's office on Sunset Boulevard. It was initially thrown out by Geffen, but rescued by his secretary who thought Browne was cute and talented. Browne and Geffen would, indeed, meet and Browne became a *de facto* talent scout for Asylum that helped build Geffen Records, and ultimately connected Geffen with the four original Eagles.

Fifty years after they formed, the Dirt Band regrouped in Los Angeles in September 2016 to celebrate their golden anniversary. And Browne joined them onstage where he sang lead on the song that McEuen first heard, *These Days.* (1109, 1413]

SUMMER 1966

Ohio Express Borrows Walsh, Measles' *I Find I Think of You*

Ohio Express was a popular band of studio musicians managed by a music agency called Super K Productions in the mid-1960s, and they got there with a little help from future Eagles guitarist **Joe Walsh**.

The Express was only a "band" in the loosest sense of the word. The agency recorded singles and distributed them to radio stations, and sometimes they'd get airplay. One single, *Beg, Borrow and Steal*, a *Louie, Louie* derivative, was originally recorded by a band Super K had under contract called **The Rare Breed**. But the band had a dispute with them and left the agency.

Super K now had songs, but no band to play them, so it hired a Mansfield, Ohio, band called **Sir Timothy and the Royals** and renamed them Ohio Express. Super K pressed an LP and a tour was planned. But the album was a couple songs short, so Super K took two singles recorded by Walsh and his 1967 band, **The Measles**, and put them on the album virtually untouched. The songs were *And It's True* and the Walsh-penned *I Find I Think of You.* Ohio Express did find some fame, though not with Walsh's songs. After moving to the Buddah label in 1968, the band, now with **Joey Levine** on vocals, released the bubble gum hit *Yummy, Yummy, Yummy* and watched it soar to #4 on the Billboard charts, where it earned a Gold record certification.

The Measles provided a launchpad for Walsh, and other more established bands were taking note. One Cleveland band, the **James Gang**, had lost their lead guitarist to a rival band, and took a long look at the "hotshot" from Kent. [363, 367, 1106]

John David and the Cinders Score a Hit in the Southwest

An understated studio in Clovis, New Mexico, served as the starting line of sorts for one of the best singer-songwriters of the country-rock era. **J.D. Souther** and two of his high school friends, **Charlie Bates** and **Steve Dodge**, known then as **John David and the Cinders**, cut a single for Norman Petty Studios in 1964 that became a regional hit in the southwest in 1966.

The A side of the single was *Day Before Tomorrow*, written by **Eddie Reeves**, but the B side, *No, Not My Heart*, was notable because it was co-written by Souther and Bates. Souther would later score Top 10 hits individually and as a frequent collaborator with the Eagles and others. The single was picked up by Warner Brothers Music, a significant coup for such a young band.

The Cinders' producer for their hit single was the legendary **Norman Petty**, who gained fame producing **Buddy Holly** and **Roy Orbison** in that same Clovis studio; he had a keen eye for talent. He produced Holly when Decca Records declined to record him, and his innovative recording style helped launch Orbison's career into the rock stratosphere as well.

Fame for Souther and the band was fleeting though. While the Cinders didn't find success after their initial single, Souther, a Detroit native who called Amarillo, Texas, home, would soon head to Los Angeles with his guitar and become fast friends with another Detroit-born artist, Glenn Frey. In the winter of 1969, these two aspiring singer-songwriters would take the next step in their rock and roll careers becoming equal halves of the country-rock duo **Longbranch/Pennywhistle.** [285, 1153, 1154]

FALL 1966

RELEASES
The New Breed, with Timothy B. Schmit: *Want Ad Reader* (single)

ON THE ROAD WITH …
▶ **The New Breed**, with Timothy B. Schmit: The Pullice
▶ **The Poor**, with Randy Meisner: Buffalo Springfield

WINTER 1966-67

RELEASES
▶ **The Maundy Quintet**, with Don Felder and Bernie Leadon: *2's Better Than 3* (single)
▶ **Felicity**, with Don Henley: *Hurtin'* (single)
▶ **The Measles**, with Joe Walsh: *I Find I Think of You* (single)
▶ **The Poor**, with Randy Meisner: *She's Got the Time (She's Got the Changes)* (single)

ON SCREEN
Glenn and the Mushrooms, with Glenn Frey, appeared on the ABC TV show *Swingin' Time*. Frey and his band made the first of two appearances on Robin Seymour's weekday CKLW-TV show. They performed two Bob Seger-written songs.

J.D. SOUTHER

Eagles manager **David Geffen** wanted singer-songwriter **J.D. Souther** to be an Eagle. Souther was half of the duo **Longbranch/Pennywhistle**, along with his friend and future Eagle Glenn Frey. Geffen usually got what he wanted, but Souther had other plans.

Like Frey, Souther was born in Detroit, but he was raised in Amarillo, Texas. After graduating high school, he bounced between New York and Los Angeles looking for steady work as a musician. New York wasn't for him, though he did try. The climate in Los Angeles was more hospitable for an aspiring singer-songwriter, and he caught on as a drummer with **Norman Greenbaum** (*Spirit in the Sky*) and met Frey through his then-girlfriend **Joan Sliwin**. He and Frey became friends and songwriting partners. They signed with Amos Records as Longbranch/Pennywhistle, but couldn't find success.

Their mutual friend **Jackson Browne** introduced them to Geffen, who was amassing a growing stable of singer-songwriters at Asylum Records. Geffen was convinced the pair had talent and freed them from their Amos contracts. He had four singer-songwriters in the Eagles already, and figured five would be great. He tried in vain to get Souther to join the Eagles—and even got him to play a few sets with them at the Troubadour Club—but Souther just wanted to stay home with his then-girlfriend **Linda Ronstadt** and write songs. The Eagles moved on without him, but he was a constant contributor to their albums, writing or co-writing some of their biggest hits, including *Best of My Love*, *Victim of Love*, *Heartache Tonight*, *New Kid in Town* and *How Long*.

On his own, Souther focused on songwriting and released four solo albums between 1972 and 1984. The title cut from 1979's *You're Only Lonely* was his best solo effort, reaching #7 nationally. He wrote or co-wrote charting hits for Ronstadt, **James Taylor**, and Don Henley. He was inducted into the Songwriters Hall of Fame in 2017. [326, 415, 534, 575, 733, 735, 1236, 1246]

ON THE ROAD WITH …
▶ **Hearts and Flowers**, with Bernie Leadon: The Standells
▶ **The New Breed**, with Timothy B. Schmit: Oxford Circle, Butch Engel & The Styx

Geffen Concentrates on Music at WMA; Signs Youngbloods

Though drawn to the theater, nightclub, and television side of the William Morris Agency's vast business, **David Geffen** got some advice from **Jerry Brandt**, a Brooklyn-born WMA executive who also started in the mailroom.

Brandt, who had remarkably signed **The Rolling Stones** to the stodgy WMA, told Geffen that trying to climb the WMA ladder to the music department would give him more room to grow and succeed.

Gross receipts in long tours for rock concerts far outstripped the comparative pennies that agents pulled in for nightclub and theater acts.

Geffen took the advice. By the end of 1966, he had settled in at WMA's New York headquarters and began scanning the horizon for rock acts. He leveraged his relationship with **Herb Gart**, who managed a variety of rock and comedian acts. Gart had one act from Greenwich Village that he thought was ready to record, and he brought them to WMA. Geffen was assigned as the lead agent and signed the group to RCA Records. He immediately started a publicity blitz for the band, taking out full-page ads in *Billboard* and *Cashbox* pushing their debut RCA record **The Youngbloods**.

Led by lead singer **Jesse Colin Young**, the band hit the charts with *Grizzly Bear* in December 1966, and the song peaked at #52 on *Billboard*'s Hot 100 chart. RCA queued up their next single, *Come Together*, which became a bona fide hit, surging to #5 on Billboard's chart and earning a gold record.

It was a solid start for Geffen in music, and soon a friendly recommendation from a client connects him with a performer who would change his life. [1, 393, 569]

Seger Pens Debut Songs for Glenn and the Mushrooms

Glenn Frey's second band, **Four of Us**, introduced him to harmonies. By the fall of 1966, he learned that he was not accepted into his first-choice school, Michigan State, and admittedly had little interest in the education he was supposed to be getting at Oakland Community College, where he was enrolled.

"I ended up going to junior college and did three things: went to the parking lot and got high, went to the lunchroom and looked at girls, and went to folk club meetings," Frey told the *Detroit Free Press* in 2003. "I basically wasted my parents' money."

While he was not laser-focused on school, his love for rock music had not diminished. The band broke up in late 1966 and Frey started a new band called **Glenn and the Mushrooms**. The band included **Jeff Burrows**, the brother of former Four of Us bandmate **Gary Burrows**, **Bill Barnes**, **Doug Gunch**, and **Larry Mintz**. Playing the local teen Hideout clubs, Frey got to know the clubs' operators, **Dave Leone** and **Punch Andrews**, who also managed Detroit rocker **Bob Seger**. Andrews was impressed with Frey and the Mushrooms and wanted to record them.

The problem was that that band hadn't written any original material. Andrews suggested that Seger write a couple singles for the band and produce them. The Mushrooms recorded Seger's *Such a Lovely Child* with *Burned* on the flip side.

"The most important thing that happened to me in Detroit was meeting Bob [Seger] and getting to know him," Frey said. "He took me under his wing. He produced those sessions. Nothing much came out of it, and it didn't get much play."

Seger and Andrews' were instrumental in getting the band some fleeting attention. The band twice played on a *Robin Seymour's Swingin' Time* television show in the winter of 1967, a weekday afternoon Detroit version of *American Bandstand*. They also played on the *Hy Lit* show in Cleveland. Even those appearances couldn't move the needle for The Mushrooms, who had broken up by the end of 1967.

Frey and a collection of friends from his former bands then created a new band called **Heavy Metal Kids**. Jeff Burrows from the Mushrooms and **Jeff Alborell** from Four of Us joined newcomers **Paul Kelcourse** and **Lance Dickerson** to complete the band. Their stay together was short, and Frey kicked around with another band, **Doug Brown & the Omens**, shortly after. But his

musical future wouldn't be furthered in the clubs of Detroit. He began to sense that he would need to go elsewhere. But before that happened, he would get some much-needed experience from his Detroit mentor. [344, 345, 392, 472]

Azoff Takes Job at Rising Booking Agency, Blytham Ltd.

Irving Azoff spent most of 1966 as a student by day at the University of Illinois at Urbana-Champaign and by night booking gigs for **Shades of Blue**, a band made up of friends from Danville High School.

Through those gigs, Azoff turned up on the radar of **Bob Nutt**, the aggressive owner of Blytham Limited, a prolific booking firm that targeted college campuses and that was a favorite agency among well-known halls, clubs, and arenas from Ohio to Wisconsin.

Nutt is often credited with creating the rock 'n roll movement on campuses across the Midwest, and after Azoff joined his agency, he quickly ascended to become Nutt's second in command. Together they managed a stable of nearly 100 different acts, including high-profile national acts like **Wilson Pickett, Fuse** (who would later become **Cheap Trick**), then-unknown **REO Speedwagon**, as well as many well-known local bands like **The Regiment** and **One-Eyed Jacks**.

Blytham was "incredibly aggressive and used a 'take-no-prisoners' approach to [signing bands] on their roster," **Gregg Philbin** told *IllinoisAlumni.org* in 2012. Philbin, who played bass guitar for REO Speedwagon from 1968 to 1977, was in a position to know.

"They changed the Champaign music scene forever by getting the Big Three clubs [Chances R, the Red Lion, and the Brown Jug] into bidding wars, driving prices up. The bands began to make a lot of money." **Ralph Senn**, who played for the Azoff-managed Regiments, said that Blytham helped the band earn $69,000 in its second year, which would equal $533,000 in 2019 dollars. The driving force was Nutt, according to **Larry Fredrickson**, who played with the band **Ginger** in 1967. "Bob was almost—not mystical, but he had that kind of aura," Fredrickson said, adding that with his long hair and wild clothes, Nutt was the guru, while Azoff was the frenetic workaholic.

Success came quickly as Azoff learned the system. Within a year of joining Blytham, he had started his own sub-agency called Irv Azoff & Associates, and maintained a small office behind the Red Lion, one of the Big Three clubs in Champaign.

Rich Hazdra, the leader of a Champaign band called **Fawn**, recalled that his band would always outdraw another local band, the Azoff-managed REO Speedwagon, when they played at the Chances R club.

"[Fawn] used to be regulars at Chances R," Hazdra said. "We were loved by all the frats and sororities playing many of them in 1971 and '72." Azoff was upset that whenever Fawn played the same night as REO Speedwagon at a rival club, Fawn would have a bigger turnout. So, he said, Azoff in-vited the band to his office and offered to sign them.

"He plain out said if he couldn't beat us he wanted to sign us and made arrangements to have the contracts drawn up within two days. The main thing he demanded was that we never play Chances R again."

They agreed and planned to sign with Azoff as soon as the contracts were drawn up. But that very day, Chances R had a band cancellation and literally begged Fawn to fill in. After a lot of grousing they finally agreed.

"The next day driving in our van down the main drag I heard a car beeping from my left," Hazdra said. "I looked over and it was Irving Azoff sitting in his little two-seater giving me the finger! That was one bad move on our part."

Azoff's reputation as a booking agent would eventually precede him. He approached the job like no other, seeming to have innate foresight into what promoters stood to pocket from their shows, **Cameron Crowe** told the *Los Angeles Times* in 2010. But it wasn't so much innate as it was investigative. Crowe said Azoff would send employees into the parking lot to count the number of cars paying parking fees and call the venue's food concession managers and ask for sales figures. What he couldn't sleuth out on his own, he would tease out from the promoter's staff. Promoters in that era didn't employ those guerrilla tactics.

"He'd come out of Urbana-Champaign with a knowledge of where the bodies were buried because he was a booking agent in

Irving Azoff (left, striped shirt) and Bobb Nutt (center) discuss a deal between Students for Democratic Society and University of Illinois students in 1966. The pair were the one-two punch for Blytham Limited, a dominant 1960s Midwest booking agency.

THE NAME GAME: NUTT FORMS BLYTHAM LIMITED

FALL 1966 – Long before future Eagles manager **Irving Azoff** became a media mogul, he cut his teeth booking bands in Champaign, Illinois. The fiery Azoff forged a partnership with a rising promoter named **Bob Nutt** and together they what would run the dominant Midwest booking agency of the late 1960s, Blytham Limited. It was a name that bands in the mid-to-late 1960s were drawn to, but it would have been far more drab if it weren't for **Jim Cole**, the recalcitrant lead singer of Champaign, Illinois's **Finchley Boys**.

In the fall of 1966, the band was approached by Nutt, who was busy gathering up bands as a booking agent. Nutt would book acts in parking lots, local halls, bars, amusement parks, festivals, and later, as his business grew, into local clubs like Champaign's Red Lion, Chances R, and the Brown Jug. Blytham developed enviable connections to deejays at WLS-AM, the megastation in Chicago and other radio stations across the region. But Nutt, then just a student at the University of Illinois, was still pinching pennies trying to develop a viable business. He was open to suggestion too, even if it was delivered in a puckish manner. Cole said Nutt was giving him a lift to school one day when he showed him his new business card.

"[Nutt] just had cards printed up that said *Robert Nutt Enterprises*," which Cole, thought was especially prosaic, and brashly told Nutt so from the passenger seat. "'This is really a lame name. It's dull and unimaginative to me." Nutt defensively agreed, but snapped back at Cole, "Why? You got a better name?" And he did.

Cole had grown up in England and knew that the Finchley Boys, who were Nutt's *only* act at the time, and were always playing **Yardbirds**, **Beatles**, **Kinks**, and other popular British Invasion music of the day, thought a British name would be more in keeping with the times and relevant. "Blytham Limited," he shot back.

Nutt griped about the change, but agreed and scrapped his planned name and had new cards printed. When Nutt was getting started, Cole said, every penny counted so he wasn't excited about paying for new cards. "I mean, at the time he was crashing at other people's houses" for lack of somewhere to stay.

As it turns out, the name change was distinctive and the business worked. Blytham became well-known in the entertainment industry in the Midwest. It booked and managed acts across six states in the Midwest. Shortly after the name change, Nutt took on a partner that helped grow the business exponentially, a young and roguish Azoff. [1387]

his previous life, and he'd buried them," Crowe said. "At the time, there was a lot of mystery about promoting concerts and a lot of promoters had a wonderful ride until Irving came to town." [481, 521, 1341, 1342, 1343, 1354, 1355]

The Poor, Meisner Sign Record Deal with Loma Records

Following a loss in a Battle of the Bands competition in Denver in February 1966, the winning band, the **Soul Survivors**, won again after luring the talented **Randy Meisner** to replace their outgoing bass player. The band had a month's worth of saved-up gig money in their pockets when they made their trek from Denver to Los Angeles in search of a record deal.

There wasn't much of plan beyond that, but the group found a place to store their bags when another Denver band, the **Back Porch Majority**, let them stay in their Encino home. They found their own run-down house in East Hollywood and began rehearsing with a goal of landing a recording contract. Both of Meisner's bands—the Soul Survivors and the **Drivin' Dynamics**—had already succeeded in landing recording deals for singles. The Survivors' single had already received strong airplay in Denver, but they hoped that with Meisner in tow, they'd parlay that small regional success into a bigger album deal.

But L.A. was already teeming with starry-eyed bands and they all wanted the same thing. It proved a daunting task for the band, and they didn't have much success.

Eventually, the group found managers in the fast-buck team of **Charlie Greene** and **Brian Stone**, who originally managed **Buffalo Springfield** and were managing **Sonny & Cher**. Greene and Stone set the band up with regular, albeit low-paying, gigs in L.A. clubs like the Whiskey a Go Go opening for the Springfield and other better-known bands. But by that stage, the Survivors weren't creating any buzz and weren't finding any meaningful work. They began to realize their prospects were nonexistent.

Meisner told **John Einarson** in his book *Desperados: The Roots of Country Rock* that the band ended up the way they arrived: with nothing. "We lost all our money and the house, then briefly struggled under the name of **The North Serrano Blues Band**," Meisner said. "I had to sell my car, because I was basically down to nothing." Now the *de facto* band leader, Meisner changed the name of the band to **The Poor**, since that's what they were. Greene and Stone helped the newly dubbed band get the band a contract with Loma Records, a subsidiary of Warner Brothers Records. After a year of obscurity, Meisner and his bandmates were finally going into the studio again. [6, 1107, 1185, 1186]

Ronstadt Heads for Los Angeles, Joins The Stone Poneys

Playing in folk festivals and coffeehouses around her native Tucson, Arizona, was a bit deflating for the 20-year-old musically precocious **Linda Ronstadt**. While folk music was flourishing in California in 1967, small-town Arizona had not yet caught the fever.

Ronstadt performed at the venues with her siblings, Peter and Suzy, but the usually sparse crowds were dispiriting. She also had a decided disinterest in her studies at Arizona State University, and the allure of an exploding folk music movement in California had her considering a change. So, when her friend **Bobby Kimmel** decided to move to Los Angeles to find the folk music wellspring, she decided to go along. Once they arrived in L.A., they, along with friend **Malcom Terrence**, who was a young reporter for the *Los Angeles Times*, set up housekeeping in a clapboard bungalow on Hart Street in Ocean Park, a neighborhood situated between Santa Monica and Venice Piers. Ronstadt, Kimmel, and his friend, Los Angeles native **Kenny Edwards**, practiced in the bungalow and began performing at local clubs and coffeehouses. They got their big break performing on an open-mic Monday night "hoot" at the Troubadour club in West Hollywood, about 20 minutes from their house in Santa Monica.

Hoot nights were regularly attended by record executives, managers, and agents looking for talent. Ronstadt and her troupe, calling themselves the **Stone Poneys** (after the **Charlie Patton** blues song), played and after were quickly offered the opportunity to open for folk music legend **Odetta Holmes**, which they accepted. Soon after, the group was approached by soon-to-be-manager **Herb Cohen**, a one-time drug and gun runner from Cuba, who got them a recording deal with Capitol Records. They would be produced by **Nik Venet**, who had also produced records for Capitol's flagship American band **The Beach Boys**.

By February 1967, Capitol had released the Stone Poneys' first album, a collection of non-commercial folk songs that did not get airplay. The band would briefly break up, then get back together, and with Venet's encouragement, they tried again a year later—this time with a more folk-rock theme and with Ronstadt and her silky vocals clearly leading.

Their second album, *Evergreen, Vol. 2*, was released in June 1967, but wasn't earth-shaking either, though it did contain a hit single that would crack the national top 20. But cracks were already forming in the band, largely because Capitol saw a future that only involved Ronstadt. It would force changes, strain friendships, and give the group a view of just how brutal the music business could be. [531, 532, 533, 534, 1189]

SPRING 1967

 RELEASES
▶ **The Mushrooms**, with Glenn Frey: *Such a Lovely Child* (single)
▶ **The New Breed**, with Timothy B. Schmit: *Fine With Me* (single)

 ON THE ROAD WITH …
The New Breed, with Timothy B. Schmit: The Pullice; Oxford Circle, The Animals, Universal Joint, The Acme Jugs Band

Maundy Quintet: Leadon, Felder Write Single, *2's Better Than 3*

Don Felder had moved away from his family home by the spring of 1967, and he had gained considerable experience as a musician. Along with future Eagles co-founder **Bernie Leadon**, Felder and the rest of the **Maundy Quintet** were now working club dates up and down the East Coast and earning upwards of $1,000 per gig, which was beyond respectable for a late-1960s Florida cover band. **The Young Rascals** came to play at the University of Florida in their hometown of Gainesville and the Quintet opened for them. That show led to a gig at a New York club that summer, which proved an eye-opening experience.

"Before we came to New York we were doing covers, we were on the circuit, playing the fraternities in town, and [our manager] would get us gigs down in Miami at The World, a club with four stages. We'd play with **The Byrds**, **The Turtles**, pretty good bands. We were getting some good bucks," said **Tom Laughlon**, the band's lead singer.

But when the band got to New York, they learned that those bands played their own material or their own interpretations of hits of the day. That's when bass player **Barry Scurran**, Leadon, and Felder decided they needed to begin writing original material or resign themselves to simply being a cover band.

"Bernie and Don said, 'We need to record a single,'" Laughlon said, and Leadon quickly wrote two singles: *2's Better Than 3* and *I'm Not Alone*, with some riff help from Felder.

"We went down to H&H Productions [Gil Cabot Enterprises] in Tampa and recorded them," Laughlon said. "They came out on a vanity label called Paris Tower, so there was no label promotion of the record. It was four-track, it was a little studio, the studio's whole mission in life was to get bands like ours to come and pay for a session, they made you feel like they could help promote your record, but they had no connections, so it was just ordering your minimum amount of records, and good luck and God speed." Leadon and Felder worked with the engineer to polish the mix. Fortunately one member of the band was moonlighting as a DJ at local radio station WGGG, so the single received more airplay attention than it might have otherwise; for a short time, *2's Better Than 3* was the most requested single at the station.

Roughly a year later, Leadon decided that the musical fortunes of Florida were not good and quit the Maundy Quintet. He tried in vain to convince Felder to join him on the trip to California, but Felder wasn't ready to leave yet. The two musicians' paths would cross again years later with the Eagles, but with one going through the "in" door and one going through the "out." [218, 229]

The Poor, Meisner Release First Single, *She's Got the Time*

Randy Meisner's band, the **Soul Survivors**, had dissolved by the winter of 1966. Unwilling to give up on his musical dreams in Los Angeles, Meisner formed a new band stitching together the remaining players from the Survivors with a few new additions that had connections to **Buffalo Springfield**.

In a desperate moment, they opted to keep the Survivors' present-but-inattentive management team of **Charlie Greene** and **Brian Stone** to lead them to a record deal. The new band, aptly named **The Poor**, which best described their current state, signed a recording deal with Atlantic Records subsidiary Loma Records to cut some singles. The first single, *She's Got the Time (She's Got the Changes)* was a classic late 1960s thumper played in the spirit of **Eric Burden and The Animals**. It was written by **Tom Shipley**, who would later go on to become half of the folk-rock duo **Brewer & Shipley**. The song was released under the York Records label and gained significant airplay in Pittsburgh, Miami, Hartford, and New Orleans, and, despite the band's new name, it still reached #2 in the **Soul Survivors'** hometown of Denver. It never reached higher than #133 on the *Billboard* singles chart.

There was some bad luck associated with timing of the single's release, as well. Greene and Stone initially pushed *She's Got the Time* hard in the music trade magazines. "There was a big ad in *Billboard* for the song and it goes shooting up the charts and I'm thinking, 'Okay, now it's my turn, I've made it'" said Shipley, the song's writer. "And about that time just when it looked like it was going to peak, the DJs go on strike. It just went right down. Right there I learned everything I ever needed to know about Hollywood and show business."

As dejecting as it was for Shipley, then a song writer for A&M Records, it was more profoundly so for The Poor, who's money-starved, hand-to-mouth lifestyle continued. "We lived in a dive in East Hollywood," said **Pat Shanahan**, the band's drummer who joined Meisner on the trek from Denver. "We had no food. The clothes we had brought from Colorado wouldn't even fit us. We were living on rice. There was no money."

The hard scrabble lifestyle wore thin for Meisner, who started looking for other opportunities. Shanahan and guitarist **Allen Kemp**, the last remaining members of the band, started taking on studio session work to get by. The band would get one last single included on a soundtrack for a new **Jack Nicholson** movie, *Hells Angels on Wheels*, in the summer of 1967, but it didn't help.

Meisner got a break in the summer of 1968 when his friend **Miles Thomas** relayed the news that Buffalo Springfield co-founder **Richie Furay** was auditioning for a bass player. Thomas, who came with the band from Denver, had grown close to members of the Springfield. It would be a move that helped him start one of the seminal bands in country-rock history, **Poco**. [1183, 1184, 1186, 1187, 1188, 1200]

SUMMER 1967

RELEASES
The Poor, with Randy Meisner:
My Mind Goes High (single)

COLLABORATIONS
Bernie Leadon plays guitar for the track
Different Drum on the **Stone Poneys** album
Evergreen Vol. 2 (with **Linda Ronstadt**).
It hits #12 on *Billboard*'s Hot 100 chart in
winter 1968.

ON THE ROAD WITH …
▶ **The New Breed**, with
Timothy B. Schmit: The Yardbirds
▶ **James Gang**, with Joe Walsh: The
Association
▶ **Hearts and Flowers**, with Bernie
Leadon: Bob Lind, The Humane Society,
Buffalo Springfield, Chad & Jeremy

Roberts Finds Gold in Laurel Canyon with Mitchell, Young

David Geffen and **Elliot Roberts** were an inseparable pair at the William Morris Agency in the summer of 1967. They both came up through the WMA mailroom eventually and both took jobs as secretaries at roughly the same time.

The next step in the evolutionary chain for a secretary—business parlance for an agent's go-fer—was to become an actual agent. Geffen had unabashed ambitions and rose to agent first, and once there he would help his friend. Roberts was offered a job at the personal management firm of Manhattan-based Chartoff-Winkler on Geffen's recommenda-

tion, and one of his clients, Native American singer-songwriter **Buffy Sainte-Marie**, dragged him to see a 24-year-old Canadian coffeehouse folk singer named **Joni Mitchell** in October 1967.

The two hit it off so well that he joined her the very next day on a Michigan tour and became her manager before the tour ended. Roberts was soon working on deals to get her recorded in New York. Pitches to Columbia and RCA failed, largely because folk music had withered in the Big Apple by then. Reprise Records, however, was listening. On the strength of Mitchell's then-boyfriend **David Crosby**'s pledge to produce an album for her, she believed she was ready. But she needed to come to California to record.

Roberts left Chartoff-Winkler and he and his solitary client headed for Los Angeles. Roberts' run of luck continued in L.A., as **Buffalo Springfield** was in the studio across the hall from Mitchell's. Mitchell introduced Roberts to her friend **Neil Young**, and Roberts rented a room in his house in Laurel Canyon, essentially an artist's village in the Hollywood Hills. In short order, he became manager for Young, Buffalo Springfield, and for Mitchell's boyfriend, Crosby. It all happened incredibly fast. Excitedly, he told Geffen about the energy and opportunities in the city. Geffen started making trips to the West Coast more frequently. The connections that Roberts was making would soon give rise to he and Geffen's ascension as managers in the nascent country-rock arena, and, be-

HENDRIX BURNS OUT CLUB DATE FOR MEISNER, THE POOR

SUMMER 1967 –Randy Meisner and his new band, **The Poor**, were working hard to get a recording deal in the spring of 1966. They believed their managers, **Charlie Greene** and **Brian Stone**, who first signed **Buffalo Springfield** and managed **Sonny & Cher**, would have the drive and connections to get them contacts too. It didn't happen quickly, and, Meisner said, the pair was getting weary of the band's constant questioning regarding the slow progress toward a deal. So, Greene and Stone dispatched The Poor on a road trip to New York to gain some exposure.

Some New York developers had opened a new venue in Greenwich Village called The Salvation Club, and they had booked **The Jimi Hendrix Experience** for the inaugural show. They needed a house band for two weeks and The Poor fit the bill. It was a disaster from the start. Meisner told *Rock Cellar Magazine* in 2016 that when the band arrived, the club renovations were not even finished. Greene and Stone had gotten them some nice outfits for the gig, complete with bell-bottom pants, but they also put them up in the run-down, poorly maintained Earl Hotel, where the entire band stayed in one bug-infested room with no air conditioning and sweltering 100-degree heat.

"We all had cots and there were cockroaches all over and we couldn't breathe," Meisner said. On opening night, the club chose to start the night off with Hendrix, who didn't show until 1:30 a.m. When he finished playing, he did his well-known pyrotechnics routine, Meisner said, and burned his guitar on stage. The stunt also flamed out the public address system, he said, meaning that The Poor would not perform that night.

"The [club] guy comes back, 'You lucked out, you don't even have to play,'" Meisner said. For a band looking to get noticed, it was hardly a relief. And the troubled New York visit continued for another two weeks. To cap it all, at the end of their two-week run, the band couldn't find anyone to pay them for the gig. They found out where the manager lived and, quite literally, threatened his life. That got them airline tickets back to Los Angeles, but not back to solvency. The Poor was just about out of patience, and Meisner was staring at failure. But while things seemed quite dark for him, a close friend in L.A. had just received news that would offer an opportunity to turn the corner. [6, 231, 1200, 1201]

fore long, the music industry altogether. [1, 1283, 1284]

Murray Recruits Leadon to New Folk Group, Hearts & Flowers

When **Bernie Leadon** left Gainesville, Florida, late in the summer of 1967, he had grown frustrated with his musical prospects in the Sunshine State. In California, his ex-**Scottsville Squirrel Barker** friend **Chris Hillman** had hit it big with **The Byrds**, and his attempts to gain musical recognition in Florida were going nowhere.

He had made lifelong friends in San Diego, the previous stop on his parents' cross-country travels in support of his father's aerospace career. While he enjoyed playing alongside another future Eagle, **Don Felder**, in **The Maundy Quintet**, his frustrations were palpable. After he completed a short active duty stint in the U.S. Army Reserves, he decided to head back to California. He had been getting recruited by two California bands, and he opted to join his friend **Larry Murray**'s band, **Hearts and Flowers**, because the group had a recording deal with Capitol Records and "that was the label of **The Beatles**, **The Beach Boys**, and the **Kingston Trio**," he told Marty Jourard in his book about Gainesville, Florida's rock history, *Music Everywhere: The Rock and Roll Roots of a Southern Town*.

But Leadon didn't want to go alone. He tried in vain to coax Felder, so he set out solo. When he landed in Southern California, he touched base with Murray, his old friend from San Diego's Scottsville Squirrel Barkers. Hearts and Flowers emerged from several bluegrass-infused jam sessions at the Troubadour club in West Hollywood. Murray took lead on guitar, and **Dave Dawson** handled vocals, guitar, and autoharp. **Rick Cunha** provided vocals and another guitar. This lineup recorded an album for Capitol Records called *Now Is the Time for Hearts and Flowers*. It had a unique sound, Murray told John Einarson in his book *Desperados: The Roots of Country Rock*. It was a mashup akin to "**Merle Haggard**-meets-Sgt. Pepper." The uniqueness may have emanated from the band's indecisive direction. The country sound was pervasive in the album, but some members thought the newer folk-rock and country-rock sounds were more marketable. In the end, those differences led to Cunha leaving the band, which opened the door for Leadon in the summer of 1967.

Hearts and Flowers, with Leadon now on banjo and guitar, recorded a second album for Capitol, *Of Horses, Kids and Forgotten Women*. The label assigned well-known **Nik Venet**, who had engineered albums for top Capitol acts like **The Beach Boys** and **Jim Croce**, to produce them. They were noticed, even venerated by some artists and the trade press, and soon were opening for the likes of **The Doors**, **Gordon Lightfoot**, **Arlo Guthrie**, **Buffalo Springfield**, and **Judy Collins**. They played all the major clubs on Sunset Strip and Santa Monica Boulevard, including Ledbetter's, the Troubadour, the Whiskey a Go Go, and Ash Grove. The band's musical direction changed subtlety with the second album, with more of a lean toward coun-

UC-Berkely dropout Jann Wenner (above) and San Francisco Examiner jazz critic Ralph Gleason forged out on their own in 1967 and started a pop culture icon in the then-weekly music and magazine Rolling Stone to provide an artist-centric look at the music industry.

WENNER, GLEASON BEGIN PUBLISHING *ROLLING STONE*

FALL 1967 – Professional journalism about the burgeoning rock and roll industry didn't truly exist until 1967. Before those "make love not war days" of the late 1960s, the music industry news was covered mostly by sales-oriented publications like *Billboard*, *Cashbox*, and *Record World*.

The focus of these weekly magazines was geared decidedly toward record sales and associated company news, new industry products, and the comings and goings of the executives who ran the industry. Sometimes they'd devote some general news about rising artists and offer advice to radio program directors about possible new hit records, but feature stories about the bands or the issues that inspired them were not their domain.

Magazines like *Tiger Beat*, which rolled out in 1965, and its sister publication, *Teen Beat*, arrived to fill the editorial void for fans, but they lacked cutting edge journalism. *Circus* and *Crawdaddy!* did a better job when they came out in 1966, but it wasn't until 1967 when UC-Berkley dropout **Jann Wenner** and *San Francisco Examiner* jazz critic **Ralph Gleason** cobbled together $7,500 to create *Rolling Stone*, a San Francisco-based weekly magazine that would go on to become a bellwether publication for the hippie counterculture, artists, fans, and the music industry as a whole.

Named for the saying "a rolling stone gathers no moss," which was also the inspiration for **Muddy Waters'** *Rollin' Stone* and **Bob Dylan**'s *Like a Rolling Stone*, the weekly gave an artist- and industry-centric look at music, but didn't stop there. The magazine looked closely at the issues that were behind social change and driving musical inspiration. In its premiere November 9, 1967 issue, Wenner, in his role as editor, told readers that "the trade papers have become so inaccurate and irrelevant, and because fan magazines have become an anachronism, fashioned in the mold of myth and nonsense, we hope that we have something here for the artists and industry, and every person who "'believes in magic that can set you free.'"

The magazine's first weekly edition went straight at the issues of the day, with an anti-war cover featuring **John Lennon** wearing an infantryman's uniform for his role in **Richard Lester**'s protest film *How I Won the War*. A short front-page story lamented over the **Jefferson Airplane**'s five weeks in the studio without producing an album, and the inside pages passed along the bittersweet news that **The Byrds** had kicked **David Crosby** out of the band.

Wenner, Gleason, and their growing team of writers and editors would cover the world in a way no other magazine quite had. Over the years, they broke ground on Woodstock, the Vietnam and Gulf Wars, AIDS, and the financial meltdowns of the 1970s and 2000s. Along the way the magazine helped launch the careers of, among many others, writer and director **Cameron Crowe**, gonzo journalist and author **Hunter S. Thompson**, and political satirist **P.J. O'Rourke**. The magazine also famously got under the skin of the Eagles, who believed that the magazine, which moved its headquarters to New York in 1977, and other New York publications harbored an East Coast bias against the band. In the summer of 1978, *Rolling Stone* and the Eagles settled their differences on a softball field in a grudge match that helped bury the hatchet between them, at least to some degree. [1192, 1193, 1194]

Rolling Stone – September 25, 1975

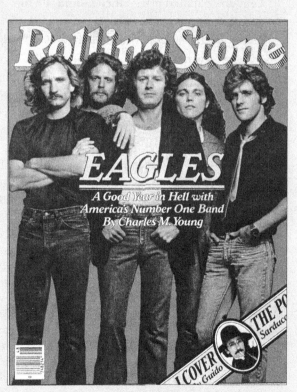

Rolling Stone – November 29, 1979

PATHWAY ALBUM | BERNIE LEADON

HEARTS AND FLOWERS
Of Horses, Kids and Forgotten Women
Capitol Records, January 1968

Hearts and Flowers' founder **Larry Murray** was looking to improve on his group's year-old first LP, *Now Is The Time of Hearts and Flowers*. That album got strong reviews, but wasn't commercially successful. The biggest change on the second album was Murray inviting his friend, **Bernie Leadon**. Leadon replaced **Rick Cuhna** and the curly haired guitarist was beginning to find himself as a songwriter. Leadon's improving songwriting skills coincided well with the band's new focus on original material. Seven of the LP's 10 tracks were original (compared to just one of 12 on the first), and Leadon was the lead writer on four. *Of Horses* was more mature, and cuts like *She Sang Songs Out of Tune* and Leadon's *Legend of Ol' Tenbrookes* shined. It reviewed well, but even with Capitol Records' **Nik Venet** producing it couldn't get it airplay. The fusion of country, bluegrass and rock was just emerging as a music trend, but Capitol had not yet figured out how to market it.

....

Record World
March 9, 1968

These fellows lead off with their theme song, *Now Is the Time for Hearts and Flowers*, and follow it up with *Highway in the Wind*, **Arlo Guthrie**'s tune, and then move on other haunting, thoughtful songs like *Extra, Extra*. The best single might be **Jesse Lee Kincaid**'s *She Sang Hymns Out of Tune*. It's not likely programming for alternative radio, but good signs that a fine writer is about to get recognition.

Honolulu Advertiser
June 20, 1968

Of Horses, Kids and Forgotten Women has a special interest for Hawaii. **Dave Dawson**, former Honolulan, is the leader of this folk-rock trio, whose inviting vocal blends (*When I Was a Cowboy*, *Second-Hand Sundown Queen* and *Highway in the Wind*) have a fresh country sound, nice guitar phrasing and are augmented by explanatory notes on the back of the LP jacket.
– *Wayne Harada*

St. Louis Post-Dispatch
July 26, 1968

The ghost of **Hank Williams** lurks somewhere in the background in *Of Horses, Kids and Forgotten Women* by **Hearts and Flowers**. This group has done its homework and treats country music with awareness and honesty. The LP is gritty, but soft where it needs to be. It also has its sad and uplifting moments. The only thing phony about them is their name.
– *Harper Barnes*

try-rock. The personnel change from Cunha to Leadon was, however, more noticeable.

"Bernie was probably a little bit more adept musically than Rick," Murray said in the liner notes of *The Complete Hearts and Flowers Collection*. "Rick's music was focused in Rick's style, so everything we got from Rick was pretty much linear from what he did. Bernie was a very broad-stroke musician. We were starting to kind of get a handle on what we were capable of doing, and where that niche was out there that wasn't being filled. It was going very much toward the Byrds and Eagles—more singable songs, that broad wall-of-vocal stuff we were working on. We were trying to write songs in that area."

But the complete vision was never realized, and the group disbanded in the late summer of 1968. "We just got tired," Murray said. "We got frustrated with it. We'd reached a plateau. We didn't feel like we were advancing fast enough on our own terms. The stuff that we did have to show, people weren't doing back flips over it. We kind of got depressed at the same time that nobody else was interested. And all of a sudden you wake up, and there's no group anymore."

Being in the headwaters of the Los Angeles country-rock movement proved beneficial to Leadon, even if Hearts and Flowers never caught on. The band's haunts included some of the trendiest coffeehouses and clubs in the movement, particularly **Doug Weston**'s Troubadour, where Leadon became friends with another bluegrass aficionado, **Doug Dillard**. That connection gave

him a bridge to his next expedition. [231, 750, 1222, 1223, 1265]

FALL 1967

 RELEASES
The Poor, with Randy Meisner: *Knowing You, Loving You* (single)

 ON SCREEN
The New Breed, with Timothy B. Schmit, appeared on the ABC TV show Malibu U., with **Dionne Warwick** and **Peter and Gordon**.

 ON THE ROAD WITH …
▶ **The New Breed**, with Timothy B. Schmit: Captain Beefheart & His Magic Band, Hour Glass, Jefferson Airplane, Nitty Gritty Dirt Band, Spirit, The Sunshine Company
▶ **James Gang**, with Joe Walsh: The Up, The Stuart Avery Assemblage
▶ **Hearts and Flowers**, with Bernie Leadon: Hoyt Axton
▶ **The Poor**, with Randy Meisner: Kaleidoscope, W.C. Fields, Spirit

Geffen Pursues Laura Nyro; Lands Deal with Davis, Columbia

While now-independent manager **Elliot Roberts** was busy courting, signing and getting high with many of Laurel Canyon's elite musicians in the fall of 1967, his future business partner, **David Geffen**, was in New York—in Hell's Kitchen to be precise—wooing a lonely artist that had been disgraced after an abysmal performance on one of rock's biggest stages.

Laura Nyro was an aspiring Bronx-born singer-songwriter when she was signed by

THE DILLARDS RELEASE LANDMARK *WHEATSTRAW SUITE*

SUMMER 1968 – **The Dillards** were an established bluegrass band by the time they got national attention by appearing as *The Darlings* on *The Andy Griffith Show*, a top-five television show in 1963. Remembered widely for those six appearances through 1966, the fame they earned doesn't begin to speak to the indelible impact the band had on progressive bluegrass, folk rock, and country-rock music in the 1960s and 1970s.

The band started out in traditional bluegrass, but changed the musical landscape by becoming one of the first bluegrass bands to electrify their instruments with their fourth album *Wheatstraw Suite*. The move away from traditional bluegrass proved groundbreaking as many folk-rock acts began tweaking their musical direction. Bands like **The Byrds** and **The Flying Burrito Brothers** were borne out of that movement. The album was unique in the way it creatively integrated harmonizing, orchestral strings, and even radio broadcast overdubs.

"*Wheatstraw Suite* was a beautiful album," **Bernie Leadon** told John Einarson in his book *Desperados: The Roots of Country Rock*. "The three-part harmonies were meticulous. That influenced the sound of the Eagles. Henley and Frey were big Dillard fans." That creative growth shown by the Dillards was adventurous for the 1960s, and it had a memorable impact on Eagles co-founder Don Henley.

"I was in my dorm room [at North Texas State in Denton, Texas, in 1967] blasting some hard rock—I think it was **Led Zeppelin**—when **Jim Ed Norman** … knocked on the door and introduced himself by giving me a copy of *Wheatstraw Suite* by The Dillards," Henley told the *Dallas Morning News* in 1994. "After I heard that record it was over."

That gift from Norman, who went on to join Henley in the band **Shiloh** and conduct strings for the Eagles' *Desperado* album, apparently had a lasting impact on Henley. "[*Wheatstraw Suite*] was a very influential album in my life," Henley told *CMT* in 2015. "I was a big fan of the Dillards. In fact, I drove through a snowstorm to hear them play in Fort Worth back in 1968." That influence had a lasting impact on Henley and the Eagles, and bluegrass elements appeared in their earlier works. **Glyn Johns**, who produced the Eagles first album and part of their second, insisted on Leadon playing double-time banjo on *Take It Easy*, and the band recorded **Paul Craft**'s bluegrass-infused *Midnight Flyer* in the *On the Border* album in 1974.

"I was happy to do something in that vein [*Midnight Flyer*], because I was a big bluegrass fan," Henley said. "The Dillards, in particular, had an enormous impact on me. Along with **Doug Dillard** and **Herb Pedersen**, Bernie Leadon was one of the top banjo players in the country, so I was proud to do a bluegrass tune—thought it lent a certain amount of authenticity and credibility to our band. It showed versatility. Even now the Eagles are thought of as a country-rock band. The music industry and the media saddled us with that label at the very beginning, and, no matter how diverse our musical palate, it has been impossible to shake that stereotype. At the end of the day, we're an American band. We're a musical mutt with influences from every genre of American popular music. It's all in there, and it's fairly obvious." [209, 231, 470, 473, 1144]

music manager **Artie Mogull** as a teenager. Mogull saw something marketable in Nyro and decided to take a chance on her, signed the then-minor singer-songwriter to a five-year management contract, and got her signed to the Verve-Folkways label. She released her debut album, *More Than a New Discovery*, and it had a minor impact, though it didn't chart. But her song *And When I Die* was recorded by **Blood, Sweat & Tears** and rocketed to #2 nationally. In late 1966, Geffen's friends suggested he listen to Nyro's album, and he soon realized why Mogull signed her. Her songs were expressive, touching, and expertly crafted pieces.

Mogull, more of a hustler than a true manager, was neither hands-on nor empathetic. He booked her for the Monterey Pop Festival and let the fledgling artist manage her own set and choreography, and the result was an overproduced, disjointed performance that left her depressed, questioning her abilities, and unwilling to ever perform live again. After that, she retreated to her small apartment in Hell's Kitchen and wasn't heard from again until Geffen, eager to sign her, knocked on her door.

Geffen spoke glowingly of her songwriting skills, and slowly built her up. He touched her on an emotional level, and she agreed to let him manage her career, which took a lawsuit to free her from Mogull. Geffen, still an impressively rising agent at the William Morris Agency, was also acting as Nyro's manager, which was against WMA's policy. An agent and a manager serve dif-ferent functions for the performer, and one person serving both roles could be construed as a conflict of interest.

In **Tom King**'s book *The Operator*, he said that Geffen kept this fact hidden from WMA. It was a questionable practice he would continue with other acts he represented later in his career, including the Eagles. And it would cause problems when it was exposed. With her, he also formed Tuna Fish Music, a music publishing company that the two shared a 50-50 interest.

To lift Nyro, Geffen worked the phones, and by the end of 1967 he had gotten her a personal audition with Columbia Records President **Clive Davis**.

After an intimate performance, Davis signed her on the spot. The audition was a revelation on two levels. First, it resurrected Nyro's career and her psyche. But it also moved Geffen's relationship with Davis, a giant in the industry, to a more personal level. That relationship would come in handy in 1968, when he, Davis, and Atlantic Records President **Amhet Ertegun** sat down to negotiate the contractual mess that arrived with the breakup of **Buffalo Springfield**. And that deal would make him a music industry legend. [1, 393, 1285]

WINTER 1967-68

RELEASES
▶ **Hearts and Flowers**, with Bernie Leadon: *Of Horses, Kids and Forgotten Women* (album)
▶ **The New Breed**, with Timothy B. Schmit: *Fine With Me* (single)

🚌 **ON THE ROAD WITH …**
Hearts and Flowers, with Bernie Leadon: Arlo Guthrie

Azoff Works WLS Deejays To Secure More Airplay

Working every conceivable angle to better position the artists he represented was part of **Irving Azoff**'s business model. And in the early days of his career when he was working alongside promoter **Bob Nutt** under Blytham Limited, he found a way to give his acts a leg up by working closely with radio deejays, including megastation WLS-AM in Chicago.

John Rook, who became director of programming at WLS, an ABC affiliate, in 1967, was a little more than a year into his job when he was approached by his bosses at ABC about the relationship between his deejays and the record companies.

Networks and radio stations were being watched closely by federal regulators at the time. There had been congressional payola hearings in the early 1960s, and even a whiff of impropriety might put a radio station's license at risk. At the time, WLS was not playing the top song in the nation, **Aretha Franklin**'s *Respect*, which was on Atlantic

Records. Strangely, the popular Chicago station was playing all the Franklin songs from her previous label, Columbia, and, Rook said, WLS happened to employed a deejay with a brother who worked at Columbia.

WLS kept a close watch on the record company relationships forged by their deejays. One day, future ABC Radio President **Hal Neal**, Rook's supervisor at WLS, glanced at a pad of scribbles on his desk and asked, "Do you know someone named Irving Azoff?" "Never heard of him," Rook replied. "He's got the station wrapped up in some kind of deal he has with the jocks and I want that ended." Rook said that Azoff would book acts into the vast WLS listening area, then hire a station disc jockey to front it and get free mentions on the air during the disc jockey's show, all without paying for commercials. Azoff reportedly had tight relationships with WLS jocks like **Art Roberts** and **Larry Lujack**.

Barry Fasman, who played keyboards for the **One-Eyed Jacks**, one of the bands championed by Blytham, was aware of the approach.

"Our managers and booking agents, Nutt and Azoff, were the key for us," Fasman said. "They knew that courting disc jockeys would be helpful so that we could get airplay for our records. Hence, [they] would pay disc jockeys to MC our shows."

The practice came under closer scrutiny at WLS, however. "Someone who wanted to do the same thing had complained to ABC, after getting nowhere when they brought it up to [Station Manager] **Gene Taylor**," Neal told Rook. "Find out what's going on and clean that damn station out, John, just clean it out, before we lose our damn license." Rook said Neal's suspicions were correct; Azoff had created solid relationships with the WLS jocks, and "he would also become a good friend of mine for all the years ahead. Who would have thought the diminutive Mr. Azoff would become one of the biggest wheeler dealers in the music business? Always returning every call to me, opening any doors I wanted to enter, even forty years later." [1354, 1385, 1388]

Ronstadt, Leadon Hit Charts With Nesmith's *Different Drum*

Linda Ronstadt and her band, the **Stone Poneys**, were back in the studio of Capitol Records in the spring of 1967 recording songs for their second album, *Evergreen, Vol. 2*. But a wedge was being placed between Ronstadt and the other Poneys, **Bobby Kimmel** and **Kenny Edwards**. Ronstadt was unhappy with the songs that Kimmel was writing for the album, feeling that they didn't give her the opportunity to stretch her vocals.

While Kimmel and Edwards worked on new material, Ronstadt found a song by the **Greenbriar Boys**, a bluegrass band that used to open for **Joan Baez**, on an album they released in 1966. The song, *Different Drum*, was written by **Michael Nesmith**, a folk- and country-rock singer-songwriter who would later become one of **The Monkees**. Ronstadt and the Poneys recorded

the song, but their producer **Nik Venet** did not like the arrangement and wasn't fond of Kimmel and Edwards' talent either.

Unknown to the band, Venet wanted to bring in a new arranger and a team of session musicians to rerecord the track. "A few days later I walked into the studio and was surprised to see it filled with musicians I didn't know," Ronstadt said in her book *Simple Dreams*. While she didn't know them, Venet had brought in a solid team of musicians to back the song, including **Don Randi** (harpsichord), **Jimmy Gordon** (drums), **Jimmy Bond** (bass), **Al Viola** and future Eagles co-founder **Bernie Leadon** on guitars. It would be the first time Leadon would back Ronstadt, but not the last.

Venet also incorporated an orchestra, and finished the job after just two cuts. Tensions reached a high point when Kimmel and Edwards were told and showed up outside the recording session. By then, Capital had already planned to bill the band as "Linda Ronstadt and the Stone Poneys."

Ronstadt doubted and protested Venet's new arrangement in the recording session. "I didn't think we could use it because it was so different from the way I had imagined it," she wrote. "Also, it didn't include Bobby or Ken. [Venet] ignored me. It was a hit." The song shot up the charts, rising to #12 on the *Billboard* Hot 100 chart. It would also send Ronstadt's career into the stratosphere. [534, 1195, 1196]

PATHWAY SINGLE | BERNIE LEADON

LINDA RONSTADT
Different Drum
Capitol Records, September 1967

Different Drum was groundbreaking song for **Linda Ronstadt**, but it was also harsh lesson in how cold the record business could be. Ronstadt followed her friend **Bobby Kimmel** from Tucson, Arizona to Los Angeles in search of a recording contract. Along with **Ken Edwards** the trio formed the **Stone Poneys** and were signed by Capitol Records. Their first album went nowhere, but producer **Nik Venet** knew Ronstadt would be a star. She found the **Michael Nesmith**-penned song on an album by the **Greenbriar Boys**, and told Venet it could be a hit. He agreed. The Poneys worked on acoustic arrangements for the song, but Kimmel and Edwards couldn't get in the studio. Venet brought in musicians he believed would improve the song, including **Hearts and Flowers** guitarist and future Eagle **Bernie Leadon**, who played lead guitar. Ronstadt protested, but Venet was resolute. The song soared to #13 nationally and made Ronstadt a star. Her rising stature in the rock industry brought Leadon and the future Eagles together.

....

Cashbox
September 30, 1967

Things are looking good for the **Stone Poneys** with *Different Drum*, which is penned by Monkee **Michael Nesmith**. Cross the vocal styles of **Cher** and **Joan Baez**, add fire and you've got a semblance of the sound on this overwhelming deck. The light-hearted orking, a catchy instrumental break and the smashing vocal make a side that should come on very strongly.

Paterson (N.J.) News
December 1, 1967

Nothing could keep this one down. The vocal is what really does it, although *Different Drum* is really distinctive. The female vocal lead, **Linda Ronstadt**, asserts herself in a strong, assured manner. The song has a smooth country feeling and sensitive lyrics add to an overall perfection of the disc. This is a certified hit record and we will see much more of the **Stone Poneys** to come.

Chicago Tribune
May 5, 1968

The [**Stone Poneys**] received general recognition with a strong hit single *Different Drum*, a manifesto of the free-floating entity written by Monkee **Michael Nesmith**. The first Poney is **Linda Ronstadt**, and the others are mere background. Her voice is high, crystal clear, with good range and with considerable drive for upbeat numbers and has just the right amount of ache for the blues.

SPRING 1968

 RELEASES
▶ **Hearts and Flowers**, with Bernie Leadon, *She Sang Hymns Out of Tune* (single)
▶ **Glad**, with Timothy B. Schmit, *Glad* (album)
▶ **Glad**, with Timothy B. Schmit, *Let's Play Make Believe* (single)

 COLLABORATIONS
Bernie Leadon plays guitar on the **Nitty Gritty Dirt Band** album *Rare Junk*.

 ON THE ROAD WITH ...
▶ **James Gang**, with Joe Walsh: The Youngbloods, The Stooges, The Human Beinz
▶ **Hearts and Flowers**, with Bernie Leadon: Jackson Browne, Mark Levine, Tom Tutt and the Bluegrassers

The New Breed Signs Deal with ABC Records; Becomes Glad

Fresh off the regional triumph of their first successful single, *Green Eye'd Woman*, **The New Breed**, including future Eagle *Timothy B. Schmit*, signed a recording contract with ABC Records, which was a prolific mid-level record company in the 1960s with acts that included then-up-and-coming artists **Ray Charles**, **Steely Dan**, and **Joe Walsh**'s first breakthrough band, the **James Gang**.

In 1966 they had created their own World United label and released the single *Fine With Me* that did well regionally. They followed that up with *Want Ad Reader*, which was eerily reminiscent of their heroes, **The Beatles**' recent hit, *Paperback Writer*.

By the spring of 1968, the band also had moved around a bit signing singles contracts with a few different labels, and issued releases for *I've Been Wrong Before* on Diplomacy Records (distributed by Mercury). The band remained popular in California, but had not developed a following outside of the Golden State. ABC Records hoped to change that. It started by changing the band's name to **Glad**, and then brought the group to Los Angeles to start recording what would be their first album in January of 1968.

The songs were written almost entirely by band leader **Ron Floegel,** with Schmit getting one co-writer credit on *Sweet Melinda*. ABC rolled out the first single, *Say What You Mean*, in March 1968, but it couldn't get airplay. ABC released the album in March along with a new single *Let's Play Make Believe*, but it didn't chart either. The label released two new singles, *A New Tomorrow* and *Johnny Silver's Ride* in July and December, respectively, including a publicity push for "Johnny" late in the year; neither managed to gain traction. The band's prospects were becoming clearer, and Schmit was getting noticed by other artists. A few months after cutting the Glad album, he would get invited to audition for a new country-rock band that was emerging from the ashes of **Buffalo Springfield**. Glad's other band members would push on, and eventually signed a five-record deal with Fantasy Records under the new name, **Redwing**. [350, 351, 1240, 1241, 1242, 1243]

PATHWAY ALBUM | TIMOTHY B. SCHMIT

GLAD
Feelin' Glad
ABC Records, April 1968

Timothy B. Schmit got his start in music playing bass and singing for the Sacramento folk group, **Tim, Tom & Ron**, which later evolved into a regionally popular group, **The New Breed**. In 1968 they were signed by ABC Records, who then changed the band's name to **Glad**. They previously had local success with two songs, *Green Eye'd Woman* and *Want Ad Reader*, and producer **Erik Wangberg** hoped they could continue that success. The band's leader, **Ron Floegel**, wrote or co-wrote most of the songs for *Feelin' Glad*; Schmit sang lead and received one co-writing credit for *Sweet Melinda*. The cuts were slickly produced and offered a flavor that was a cross between early **Jefferson Airplane** and **The Grass Roots**. ABC included Glad in its marketing package that put the band alongside **Ray Charles** and a collection of other up-and-coming bands in *Cashbox* and *Record World*, but the album never took off. Later in 1968 Schmit was invited to audition for **Richie Furay**'s post-**Buffalo Springfield** band, **Pogo**. He lost out to future Eagles founder and kept playing with Glad, but joined Furay a year later when Meisner abruptly quit the band, which had been since-renamed **Poco**. Schmit would become a fixture with Poco for the next nine years. Ironically, would replace Meisner once again when he quit the Eagles in 1977.

Santa Rosa Press-Democrat
December 16, 1968

Glad spent most of the past summer in Los Angeles working on an album. The LP, *Feelin' Glad*, and a single, *Johnny's Silver Ride*, a cut about **John Lennon** in his early days when he was known as **Johnny Silver and the Silver Beatles**. The new album offers a new country-rock sound.

Paterson (N.J.) Times
May 16, 1969

A foursome calling itself The Glad Group (sic) let's the listener know it's *Feeling Glad*. Of the dozen selections that are contained on this album all but two are compositions of **Ron Flegal** (sic), one of the quartet. The group is on ABC Records.
– *Henry C. Schwartz*

Meisner, Schmit Audition to Play Bass for Furay's *Pogo*

Randy Meisner's band, **The Poor**, was trying desperately to get noticed in the winter of 1967. Their managers, **Charlie Greene** and **Brian Stone**, had some industry credibility having discovered **Buffalo Springfield** and managed **Sonny & Cher**, but the duo was not having luck getting The Poor recognized.

The group had a rising single in the spring of 1967 with *She's Got the Time*, but it never got beyond regional airplay. It got off to a good start, but a radio DJ strike early that year helped derail it just as it was getting noticed. Now, just after a two-week run at a new Greenwich Village club failed to raise their stature among New York deejays, the band was at a crossroads.

Individual band members started taking on session work to make ends meet. Others went their own way. On a personal level, Meisner wasn't ready to give up, but he needed a helpful break. He got one when his friend, **Miles Thomas**, a Buffalo Springfield roadie, informed him that the Springfield co-founder **Richie Furay** was auditioning bassists to replace the outgoing **Jim Messina**. Meanwhile, future Eagle **Timothy B. Schmit**, who had spent the last two-and-a-half years with **The New Breed**, was invited to the same audition by Furay. Schmit and the New Breed had become well known across California; the band's stature outside the Golden State was muted.

On a fateful afternoon on May 1968, their paths would unexpectedly cross. Meisner, Schmit, and a host of other auditioners thought they were trying out for Buffalo Springfield's vacant bass job, but Furay and Messina were already turning the gears on their next project: **Poco**. Although Furay personally invited Schmit to audition, according to *Rolling Stone*'s **Charles Young**, the young bass player suffered some guilt over the notion of leaving his boyhood friends from The New Breed. Perhaps the timing wasn't right, or it may have been that Meisner's experience won out.

"When I arrived at [Furay's] house for an audition Tim Schmit was playing. So, I auditioned right after him. A couple of days later, they called me back and said, 'We want you.'" Furay, Meisner, **Rusty Young**, and the rest of the new Poco – the name changed from Pogo after **Walt Kelly**, creator of the famous daily comic strip *Pogo*, whom the band was named for, threatened legal action if they continued to use it. With a new name, the band spent the next six months working on their first album. Their effort would become one of the seminal albums in the country-rock movement, but it would mark another turning point for Meisner, and for Schmit, as well. [343, 486, 1140, 1293]

Felder's New Jazz Band, Flow Signed by Creed Taylor

Since high school, the musical evolution of Don Felder was built on experiences he gained from the two bands he founded, **The Continentals** and **The Maundy Quintet**. He had also worked with and taught some of Gainesville, Florida's best rock musicians, including **Duane** and **Gregg Allman**, **Tom Petty**, and his bandmate in the Quintet, **Bernie Leadon**. By the early summer of 1968, however, the Quintet had disbanded.

Leadon left after hearing the siren call of the country and bluegrass music movement in Southern California. His departure didn't kill the Quintet, but the group finally dissolved permanently when lead singer **Tom Laughlon** left for college. For the first time in years, Felder was without a band, and he felt directionless.

That feeling didn't last long. An Ocala, Florida, three-piece band called **Gingerbread** (later renamed **Flow**) asked him to join them. They needed a guitarist, and they were impressed with Felder's performance with the Quintet. It was an attractive offer because they were also connected to the management team for the **Young Rascals**, the chart-topping group who reached #1 with *Good Lovin'* in 1966. Faced with either returning to school or playing with a band that had a reasonable chance to get a record deal, he chose the latter. It wasn't a perfect fit since the band played an eclectic mix of rock and jazz, and Felder didn't have that musical background. But soon he was immersing himself in jazz, listening and learning from artists like **Sonny Rollins** and **Django Reinhardt**. In his book *Heaven and Hell: My Life in the Eagles*, Felder said the experience with Flow was educational.

"We'd start off singing a couple of verses and a chorus and then have a free-form section in the middle that could be anywhere from a minute to five minutes long," he said.

"It was really quite innovative for its time, and the best part was that every time you played, you were thrown naked out on the floor, figuratively speaking."

By the fall of 1968, the Young Rascals' road managers, **John Calagna** and **Andy Leo**, had set up a coming-out gig for the band, now officially known as Flow, at the Fillmore East in Manhattan. The band traveled up from Florida, but it wasn't well prepared. Felder said their set was mechanical and that they played uptight, but the performance was good enough to impress jazz producer **Creed Taylor**, who came there to hear them. He offered them a $5,000 recording contract on the spot, which they immediately signed.

Taylor's studio was in New Jersey, so it meant the band would leave the warm confines of Florida. They would settle into a run-down apartment in New York and begin preparing material for their first album. In some ways it was a dream come true for Felder, but the realities of living in New York and depending on less-than-reliable bandmates would bring more challenges. [218, 1198, 1265]

Farewell WMA: Geffen Leaves Morris, Joins Ashley Famous

David Geffen was a rising star in the spring of 1968. Working both the television and music sides of the business for the William Morris Agency, he had a growing stable of clients and was attracting the attention of rival talent firms.

Before Geffen applied to work in the

mailroom at WMA, he had applied at its rival New York talent firm, Ashley Famous. Openly admitting he had no degree, he was laughed out of Ashley's offices. It was a valuable lesson for him. He famously lied about his lack of college credentials to WMA, and parlayed his career from the mailroom to an executive in less than four years.

With his reputation growing, Ashley Famous was now wooing Geffen, and he loved it. Making a little less than $500 a week for WMA, Ashley offered to double his salary. WMA couldn't match the offer, so just six weeks shy of his fourth anniversary, Geffen moved to the rival company. His role was exclusively within the music business with Ashley, so he set out to bring in new talent. He first started by trying to woo folk artist impresario **Albert Grossman** and his large stable of talent that included **Bob Dylan**, **Janis Joplin**, and **Peter, Paul & Mary**.

Grossman's artists were stabled at the Agency for Performing Artists, an Ashley rival, and Grossman was happy with the work APA was doing for his performers. Geffen took note of a young APA manager who came up during the conversation. **Todd Schiffman** was overseeing the accounts for Grossman, including the management of all concert tours with a meager staff of three.

Geffen saw an opportunity. He and Ashley's president, **Ted Ashley**, pitched to Schiffman hard. They offered him Ashley's West Coast division, with a staff of 25, plus

hooks for his artists into Ashley's TV and film operations. Like Geffen, Schiffman also was working a questionable artist-management arrangement with one of his most successful bands, **Iron Butterfly**. Geffen, now the head of the Ashley division that would care about the arrangement, looked the other way. Schiffman signed, and Goldman followed him to Ashley along with virtually all of their acts. The move instantly transformed Ashley Famous into the upper stratosphere of New York's talent management elite. Geffen's reputation as an elite negotiator was again ascending, and that cache put him in a solid negotiating position when the biggest band on the West Coast, **Buffalo Springfield**, decided to break up at the end of 1968. [1, 3, 1286, 1287]

SUMMER 1968

 RELEASES
Glad, with Timothy B. Schmit, *A New Tomorrow* (single)

 COLLABORATIONS
▶ **Glenn Frey** produced **The Bottle Company**'s single *Lives for No One* on their album, *Lives for No One*.
▶ **Glenn Frey** played acoustic guitar and provided backing vocals on **The Bob Seger System**'s single *Ramblin Gamblin' Man*, on the album *Ramblin' Gamblin' Man*.

> **ON THE ROAD WITH …**
> **James Gang**, with Joe Walsh: Cream, Blue Cheer, MC5, Spirit, Fever Tree

Frey Adds Backing Vocals to Seger's *Ramblin' Gamblin' Man*

Glenn Frey's friendship with Detroit rocker **Bob Seger** began when Seger's manager, **Punch Andrews**, offered to produce Frey's then-band **The Mushrooms**. The eventual Eagles co-founder was certainly aware of Seger, who by the mid-1960s had become a well-known artist in Michigan.

At Andrew's behest, Seger wrote two songs for The Mushrooms, and even though they didn't get any significant airplay on Detroit AM radio, it lit a fuse of sorts. It gave the aspiring Frey a start. After that, he and Seger started hanging out. "We'd drive around all night and smoke dope and listen to the radio," Frey told the *Detroit Free Press* in 2003. "We'd drive to Ann Arbor and hang with [musician] **Scott Richardson** at his house, go to the Fifth Dimension club and see **The Who** and **Jimi Hendrix** there. We were all trying to scratch the puzzle: how to make it in the music business."

Another benefit of the friendship was that Seger invited Frey into the recording studio. It started small, with Frey working in percussion overdubs on Seger's *Heavy Music*, and eventually he was playing acoustic guitar and singing background vocals for Seger's breakthrough hit *Ramblin' Gamblin' Man*.

Seger remembered the session fondly. "I knew Glenn was going to be something.

We recorded [the song and] his voice on the first chorus—that says it all. He blurts out above everybody, just wailing. 'Ramblin' man!'—it's louder than shit." Frey remembered the session fondly as well. "It was my first professional recording experience, where things were miked and rehearsed," he said. "I was impressed. He was like my big brother for those couple of years before I left for California."

By the winter of 1968, the song was surging up the charts; it crested at #17 on *Billboard*'s Hot 100 and made it as high as #16 on *Record World*'s Top 100 in February 1969. Things slowed down for Seger after that landmark first single, and he wouldn't see another Top 40 hit for seven long years. Meanwhile, Seger and Frey's girlfriends were in a band, the **Mama Cats**, and by the end of 1968, they had gone to Los Angeles is search of a recording deal. Seger stayed in Michigan nurturing his renamed band, **The Bob Seger System**, but Frey would follow the girl west and his first day in L.A. would change his fortunes forever. [345, 392, 1204, 1205, 1224]

Springfield Ashes: Geffen Works Deal for Crosby, Stills & Nash

In the ruins of the short-lived steamroller that was **Buffalo Springfield**, the players of the now-defunct band were left with record label obligations that didn't quite align with the musicians' creative directions.

Neil Young wanted a solo career. **Stephen Stills** found an unexpected vocal harmony with ex-Byrd **David Crosby** and soon-to-be

THE BOB SEGER SYSTEM
Ramblin' Gamblin Man
Capitol Records, February 1968

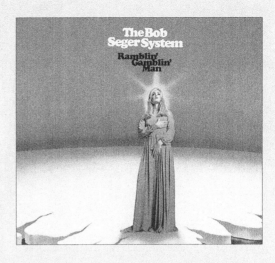

By January of 1968 **Bob Seger** and his band had been through a couple of name changes, and had developed a strong following in and around Detroit. But the band had not had a national hit yet. That changed when he went into the studio to record his first album, *Ramblin Gamblin' Man*. In the mid-1960s the term "Ramblin' Gamblin' Man" had become synonymous with Tennessee singer **Jim Reeves**, but Seger recast that term. His manager, **Punch Andrews**, brought Seger into the studio and they gave another aspiring musician, Glenn Frey, his first-ever role in the a studio. Frey would start with some simple percussion, and provided backing vocals for the song along with he and Seger's girlfriends, **Joan** and **Alexandra Sliwin**. Those same sisters would become the **Mama Cats** and, later **Honey Ltd.**, and sign recording deals in Los Angeles. Frey followed Alexandra to California, but he cut his teeth in the studio with Seger, and *Ramblin' Gamblin' Man*. The song was released in Februry 1968, but didn't find an audience until that fall. It cracked the *Billboard* Hot 100 singles chart in September, and by October it had climbed to #17 nationally, making it Seger's first real hit. Seger remembered the session fondly. "I knew Glenn was going to be something. We recorded [the song and] his voice on the first chorus—that says it all. He blurts out above everybody, just wailing. 'Ramblin' man!'—it's louder than shit." Frey remembered the session fondly as well. "It was my first professional recording experience, where things were miked and rehearsed," he said. "I was impressed. He was like my big brother for those couple of years before I left for California."

Cashbox
October 5, 1968

Bob Seger started to happen the hard way with a progressive hit, but the *2+2=?* single fell just a bit short of the final break. Now, Seger drives back with rhythmic session aimed at establishing his reputation. Pulsing bass and drumming highlights the dance appeal of this new outing and Seger's power should do the rest. Exciting teen track.

Newark (Ohio) Advocate
October 10, 1968

Ramblin' Gamblin' Man is a new song by **Bob Seger**, and it is great. He is a singer way ahead of his time. He has a talent of recording a trend in music before anyone else starts groovin' on it. His "sound" is evident in this new one, but it is also original. I want him to come to Newark. I'm working on it.
–Johnny Buck

Patinson (N.J.) News
January 17, 1969

Here's a disc that's been around a while. It has probably been some months now that it has been getting attention and public acceptance in one area after another. Finally, it is climbing the national hit ladder, and Bob's driving, energetic vocal will keep it moving for sure.
– Charles Schreiber

Randy Meisner (center, with the rest of the original Pogo) won an audition over future Eagles bassist Timothy B. Schmit, and toured with Pogo/Poco for a year while the band gathered material for its debut album.

MEISNER LEAVES POCO AFTER STUDIO DISPUTE WITH FURAY

After struggling with marginally successful bands for years, future Eagle Randy Meisner had finally caught a break. A friend from his days with **The Poor** had tipped him off to an opportunity for a bass player with **Poco**, a band formed from the ashes of the **Buffalo Springfield**. The band's leaders, former Springfielders **Richie Furay** and **Jim Messina**, were looking for complementary pieces for a band that would stretch the electrified country movement in a way it had not been explored before. The composition of the band wasn't cut and dried. While the two leaders agreed on adding **Rusty Young** and **George Grantham**, both congenial Coloradans and former alums of the respected band **Boenzee Cryque**, there was some division over who should play bass.

Many bass players were auditioned. Furay had personally invited **Timothy B. Schmit**, a young musician with crystal falsetto vocals for the well-known California band **Glad**, to audition. Meanwhile, **Miles Thomas**, road manager for Poco—and who had recommended Young—thought his friend with Colorado roots Randy Meisner was a solid fit. Another experienced bass player with impeccable high vocals, Thomas thought he would be perfect for the part. Meisner and Schmit auditioned on the same day at Furay's house in Laurel Canyon. Furay said in his book *Pickin' Up the Pieces* that both musicians aced their auditions, and he felt that the band couldn't go wrong with either. When it came time to decide, Furay said the key issue was keeping a "family feeling within the band," and with Young advocating for Meisner—and with Furay and Messina not having strong feelings either way—the band chose Meisner.

The decision was made largely to placate Young, who had lobbied hard for Meisner. But even after selecting Meisner, Furay said he still didn't feel at ease, adding that Randy's personality didn't mesh well with the other four members of the band. "Not that Randy's personality entirely disrupted the family feeling I was seeking," Furay said in his book. "From the beginning the camaraderie we achieved in the new band was much more comfortable than it had been in the Springfield."

With Meisner now on bass and singing his trademark high notes, the band spent the next year touring, perfecting their sound and writing songs for their debut album. Underlying tensions surfaced once all the recording was finished and the engineering began. Furay and Messina had forged a tight bond in the Springfield, and they planned to pull together the debut album together alone. Meisner believed that because he was involved in making the music, he should be able to listen to the mixes. Furay flatly refused, and an insulted Meisner quit.

"All I needed was for someone to explain it all to me but at that point I just felt like I wasn't a member, just a sideman," Meisner told **John Einarson** in his book *Desperados*. Much of the drama surrounding the incident stemmed from miscommunications and the stress of getting the album out.

During a Poco reunion in 1989, Meisner said Messina told him that he was unaware of Furay's refusal, and said had he known, he would have let him attend. In his book, Furay said his recollection of the episode was fuzzy, but that Messina, who had a background as a sound engineer, was doing much of the physical work and didn't want the long process hindered unnecessarily.

Further, he said the band was dealing with union engineers and weren't even allowed to touch the sound board. "Maybe Randy caught us at a moment when we weren't as patient or understanding as we should have been," he said. "But it still seems a little strange that an incident as seemingly minor as this would have caused him to leave the band."

> **Maybe Randy caught us at a moment when we weren't as patient or understanding as we should have been. But it still seems a little strange that an incident as seemingly minor as this would have caused him to leave the band.**
>
> *—Richie Furay, Poco co-founder*

Regardless, for Meisner, it was the final straw. Meisner's lead vocals were replaced with Grantham re-recordings, but his backing vocals and bass work remained, according to the album's credits. The final indignity was when Furay removed Meisner's likeness from the painting on the album cover and replaced it with a dog, a move that might have lost the band points with the legendary **Clive Davis**, the Epic Records producer who grudgingly paid the bill for the last-minute production changes.

Meisner still played some sets in Poco's live appearances after the breakup, but he had left the band completely by April 1969. Messina took over on bass for live shows after Meisner left, but Furay wanted Messina's skills on guitar, so another bass player was needed. Later that summer, Furay attended a Glad concert and afterward invited the previously passed-over Schmit to the band. He accepted and joined Poco in May, though he didn't actually perform live with the band until September.

Meisner wasn't out of work long after leaving. **Dickie Davis**, the well-connected stage manager for the Troubadour club, had told **John Boylan**, producer for **Linda Ronstadt** and **Rick Nelson**, that Meisner had quit. "When Rick heard I was leaving, John Boylan, his producer, asked if I wanted to put a band together with Rick," Meisner told **Sheree Homer** in her book *Rick Nelson: Rock 'n' Roll Pioneer*. He agreed and soon Boylan had Meisner playing bass behind Nelson, as **The Stone Canyon Band**, and he tapped his former bandmates from **The Poor** to join him. [231, 463, 781, 1169, 1269] ex-Hollie **Graham Nash**. **Richie Furay** and **Jim Messina** were planning out their musical futures for a band that would become **Poco**. It was a tangled mess, and some of the artists were looking for help from their manager, **Elliot Roberts**. In Tom King's book *The Operator*, Elliot was on the hook for setting up a recording deal for Stills, Nash and Crosby, but didn't feel up to the challenge. The three all had separate deals with different recording companies, and unwinding those contractual obligations would be complicated.

He turned to his new partner, **David Geffen**, to help untangle the presumptive mess. Roberts explained to Geffen that through his association with **Joni Mitchell**, who Roberts managed, he had gotten involved with the three. They were all signed to different record companies, but they wanted to be in a band together. "[Elliot] needed my help," Geffen said in the *PBS American Masters* series on his life. "He needed me to get them out of their contracts so they could get together and make a record deal."

Crosby specifically wanted Geffen because of the reputation he had developed over the last year in the recording industry. He sensed that Geffen would fight for the best money deal available, and he felt that he had a necessary level of ruthlessness needed to land the best deal. He was right, and when Roberts brought him in, Geffen set right to work.

Crosby and Nash had contracts with Columbia, and Stills was obligated to Atlantic. Geffen knew Columbia legend **Clive Davis** well from his negotiations representing **Laura Nyro**, so he felt like he had strong inroads there. He didn't have those same contacts at Atlantic though, but worked out a deal with Atlantic Chairman **Ahmet Ertegun**. In the deal, Atlantic would surrender the rights to Furay and Messina's Poco project, and Columbia would give Atlantic both Crosby and Nash and would keep Stills. Davis believed that Poco, who was already developing a strong following, would mature into a profitable act. Crosby and Stills, perceived as more mercurial, posed more risk for Atlantic, so those involved believed the trade as equitable.

In the end the arrangement served Ertegun best, as Crosby, Stills & Nash became country-rock legends. Poco also achieved recognition, but never achieved the level of fame as CSN, and certainly not the profitability. And perhaps the biggest winner in the deal was David Geffen, who rescued eventual partner Roberts and built valuable credibility for orchestrating the deal. Geffen's next challenge would put him back into negotiations with Ertegun, and on the path to Asylum. [1, 231, 393]

Joe Vitale: Walsh Meets Rival and Eventual Sideman in Ohio

Joe Walsh was still finding his way as a musician in the summer of 1968. After working the club circuits in Cleveland and Kent, Ohio, he had joined the a new band, the **James Gang**. On August 4, 1968, at Meyers Lake Park, a small amusement park in Canton, Ohio, a young high school drummer,

Joe Vitale, attended a concert there and took note of the flamboyant Walsh.

Vitale would go from band to band over the next year, including the **Echoes** and **The Chylds**. In a twist, even though Vitale and Walsh weren't yet friends, they had already played for the same band, **The Measles**. Vitale, an Ohio native, was kicking around with an Akron band called **The Lime**, but left them to join The Measles when he moved to Kent in the summer of 1969. Walsh had already left The Measles to join James Gang, but the two would see each other around the clubs.

"I knew Joey because he was in a rival band in Ohio in pre-James Gang days," Walsh said. "We hadn't paid a whole lot of attention to each other, but we'd been kinda friendly all the time." Walsh followed Vitale's progress and invited him to join his new band, **Barnstorm**, when he decided to leave James Gang in 1971. Vitale, then playing a tour with **Ted Nugent and the Amboy Dukes**, politely asked and received permission from Nugent to leave and took off for Boulder, Colorado, to join Walsh.

Over the years, Vitale became to Walsh what **David Lindley** has been to **Jackson Browne**, more than a just a versatile sideman, he was a talented collaborator and close personal friend. Together they collaborated on Walsh and Eagles songs like *Pretty Maids All in a Row* and *In the City*. Long before Walsh left for Colorado, he still had growing to do with James Gang. And because that personal growth included new friendships with **The Who**'s **Keith Moon** and **Pete Townshend**, it meant hotel rooms would be perpetually in danger. [1308, 1309, 1310, 1344, 1364]

Jimmy Bowen (above) helped resurrect the careers of performers like Bing Crosby, Frank Sinatra and Dean Martin, and was so successful that he started his own label, Amos Records. He had a knack for finding talent and signed Glenn Frey, Don Henley and J.D. Souther.

BOWEN LAUNCHES AMOS RECORDS; RECORDS FREY, HENLEY

SUMMER 1968 – Amos Records is a bit of an afterthought as a foundational element of the country-rock movement of the late 1960s and early 1970s. The company knew talent and had the foresight to sign the early bands of both Glenn Frey and Don Henley, but it was never able to tap the creativity that would eventually blossom into the machine that became the Eagles. But by the spring of 1969, James Albert Bowen, better known in the recording industry as **Jimmy Bowen**, had already established his name as a record producer who could reclaim careers.

Born in Santa Rita, New Mexico, in 1937, he got his first guitar in junior high school and started a band with his boyhood friend **Donnie "Dirt" Lanier** called **The Orchids**. After graduation in 1956, Bowen and Lanier enrolled in college at West Texas State in Canyon, Texas, where they met another musician, **Buddy Knox**, a graduation-averse, folk-singing student who was four years older than them.

Knox had an appealing twangy voice and a gift for writing songs, so he was invited to join The Orchids. The three eventually cut a few acetate records with Bowen playing a stand-up bass, Lanier on electric guitar, and Knox playing rhythm with an acoustic guitar. **Elvis Presley** and **Roy Orbison** had taken the country by storm in the late 1950s. A fan or Orbison's, Bowen had heard that the crooner had recorded his songs like *Ooby Dooby* with **Norman Petty** in his Clovis, New Mexico, studio. With that landmark studio just two short hours from West Texas State, Bowen took a chance and reached out to Petty and he agreed to book the group studio time.

In his book *Rough Mix*, Bowen remembered the studio as "warm" and "tight." The tiny one-room box had a studio and control room set up at one end of an apartment complex, and if a big train or truck rolled by, it would blow a take. Likewise, if Norman's mechanic father was banging on cars outside, they would have to stop recording. Despite these distractions the group spent an entire day recording an up-tempo Knox-authored, too-long-for-radio song called *Party Doll* and *I'm Stickin' With You*, a shorter, more radio-friendly cut. "It took a day or so and we were done," Bowen said. "I handed Norman $300 cash for studio time and for his extraordinary patience as engineer and producer. He had needed eight hours to get a two-and-a-half-minute A-side out of four half-assed musicians. And we walked out of Clovis with our master tapes—probably the last group to ever leave Clovis with their masters."

That was likely true, since Petty also later recorded **Buddy Holly and the Crickets** in Clovis and he owned all the band's records and publishing rights. The experience with The Orchids introduced Bowen to the music industry, but he knew he would be a better fit on the management side of the business. He soon built a career as a producer and engineer and guided artists to the studio. In 1963, a mutual friend connected him with **Frank Sinatra**, who was looking to elevate his label, Reprise Records, with an infusion of youth.

Bowen got the job. Reprise was a struggling subsidiary of Warner Records majority owned by Sinatra, and with Bowen producing, he helped return the label to profitability and resurrected the careers of Sinatra, **Dean Martin**, and even briefly put **Bing Crosby** back on the map with talented engineers and songwriters like **Mike Post**.

With a grateful Sinatra backing him, Bowen was able to work an independent label deal with Warner in 1967 where he hoped to work the same magic with his own researched acts. In mid-1968, he turned the wheels on that dream by creating Amos Records, which immediately began working on new material for **Sammy Davis Jr.** The new label also found an aspiring new band, the First Edition, which later became **Kenny Rogers and the First Edition**. It was an important find for the Eagles faithful, though not necessarily for Bowen.

Rogers would later run into band members of the Linden, Texas-based **Shiloh** (then called **Felicity**) while clothes shopping in Dallas, and later accepted an invitation to see them perform. He and Bowen liked the band enough to sign them. Shiloh included **Richard Bowden** (who would later form the country comedian duo **Pinkard & Bowden**) and future Eagles co-founder Don Henley. Meanwhile, in Los Angeles, Bowen's team had found another two musicians paired as an act, future Eagles co-founder Glenn Frey and frequent Eagles contributor **J.D. Souther**, going by the name of **Longbranch/Pennywhistle**.

Lacking hits, Bowen's label adventure ended in 1971 when he shut down Amos and all its associated businesses. Bowen found himself in a "what-if-we-get-a-hit" conundrum. The label had already been faring poorly trying to get its bands to chart, but Bowen said a deal he brokered with Ampex, makers of eight-track and cassette tapes, put the company at huge risk. In the early 1970s, many larger labels were moving to producing their own cassettes or securing huge deals with companies like Sony and TDK, so Ampex began buying smaller labels and recruiting independent producers, including Bowen and Amos, to keep the production lines moving.

Amos soon found itself as a distributor for a new label, **Lee Hazlewood**'s LHI Records, and Bowen said it was then that he realized the company had become stretched too thin.

"We had already spent most of our startup money on salaries for a dozen staffers and recording budgets," he said. "Now, with a major hit, I'd have to pay the trucking lines within 15 or 30 days and the pressing plant within 30 days. The independent distributors I was working with sometimes didn't pay you for six months. Some of them didn't pay you *at all* unless you came up with another hit; then, at least, they had to buy that from you, so they'd finally settle up. A big hit then I'd go under. I decided to fold the Amos tent."

Amos would make headlines again in the fall of 1983 when then-MCA CEO **Irving Azoff** (and manager of the Eagles) offered Bowen a job and paid $1 million for the entire catalog of Amos Records, Amos Productions, and the masters, which included all of the master of Kenny Rogers, Shiloh and Longbranch/Pennywhistle recordings. [1217, 1218, 1219]

LOS ANGELES

The paths to Los Angeles were different for each individual member of the Eagles, but they shared a common goal: get a recording deal. They each succeeded, but learned that recording contracts aren't always a blessing.

FALL 1968

 RELEASES
▶ **Dillard & Clark**, with Bernie Leadon, *The Fantastic Expedition of Dillard & Clark*
▶ **Dillard & Clark**, with Bernie Leadon, *Train Leaves Here This Mornin'*

 ON SCREEN
The Poor, with Randy Meisner, appeared on the NBC TV show *Ironside*, in *Price Tag: Death*. Meisner appeared alongside his bandmates in the role of a band in the show.

 ON THE ROAD WITH ...
▶ **James Gang**, with Joe Walsh: Spooky Tooth, The McCoys
▶ **Poco** (and occasionally performing as **RFD**), with Randy Meisner: Three Dog Night, Hoyt Axton, Bob Lind, Biff Rose

Leadon Joins Dillard & Clark; *Fantastic Expedition* Released

A well-known **Doug Dillard** was looking to expand beyond the bluegrass roots of his family's band in the fall of 1968, **The Dillards**. He found a willing partner in the country-rock world in **Gene Clark**, the former guitarist of **The Byrds**. Together, the were **Dillard & Clark**. Dillard had also befriended a green, but multi-talented Bernie Leadon through various Troubadour club encounters and offered him a job.

Leadon, then just 21, had kicked around the musical world for the previous five years in San Diego and Gainesville, Florida, with increasingly frustrating results. Fed up, he

left Florida in the summer of 1967 in favor of California and joined up with former **Scottsville Squirrel Barker Larry Murray** in his new band, **Hearts and Flowers**. Murray's group had a Capitol recording contract and a growing taste for country-rock. The band seemed to be going places. But despite two albums well received by music critics, the group never really caught on and disbanded by that fall.

For Leadon, it was a breakthrough experience. He had already earned some musical respect subbing in with the bluegrass-themed Squirrel Barkers, and he wrote two songs that became singles for **The Maundy Quintet**. But Hearts and Flowers gave him the opportunity to record on a major label, and he certainly made the most of it. He wrote four of the five songs on the B side of the band's second album, *Of Horses, Kids and Forgotten Women*, and was growing as a songwriter and instrumentalist. People took notice. So when Dillard came knocking, Leadon was ready. By the middle of 1968, he was living at Dillard's house and playing regularly with him and Clark. The duo tapped friendly resources to support the band, including **David Jackson** (bass), **Don Beck** (mandolin, resonator guitar), two former Byrds in **Chris Hillman** (mandolin) and **Michael Clarke** (drums), **Byron Berline** (fiddle), and, of course, Leadon, who would have a prominent role with vocals, lead guitar, bass, and banjo.

Leadon picked up where he left off with Hearts and Flowers, by co-authoring six of the nine songs on the band's debut album *The Fantastic Expedition of Dillard and Clark*. *Rolling Stone* gave strong marks to the cut *The Train Leaves Here This Mornin'*, penned by Leadon and Clark—and which the Eagles would include on their debut album four years later—but the magazine only offered lukewarm praise for the overall album, crediting it for being "palatable to someone who can't take straight country," but suggesting that the band's direction was too compromising. Others had appreciation for it, however. **Mick Houghton**, rock critic for *Let It Rock*, in 1973 called it "one of the most underrated records of the past few years."

In the end, it may have been too country for rock fans, and too rock for country fans. The lack of focus left A&M's marketers confused about where to slot the album, and as a result, it didn't get noticed and didn't chart. The label likely wondered about the group's long-term fortunes. Undaunted, Dillard, Clark, and Leadon readied another album that would be released in the fall of 1969. But there were unexpected troubles ahead. [529, 1237, 1238, 1239, 1281]

Kelly Threatens Pogo Lawsuit, Furay Changes Name to Poco

Poco was an important band in the country-rock movement. Formed in the spring of 1968 by two-fifths of the now-defunct **Buffalo Springfield**—**Richie Furay** and **Jim Messina**—the band was generating lots of media buzz and was developing its own material, but it was still without a

name by October 1968. They, along with new bassist **Randy Meisner**, kicked around several—White Lightning, Fool's Gold, Pop Corn, Buttermilk, and Pepper Box, but none seemed right. The band played a Hoot Night at the Troubadour club in Los Angeles as **Pogo** on October 14. Again, at the Troubadour two weeks later the band performed as **R.F.D.**, which Furay said was inspired by the popular *Andy Griffith Show* television spinoff *Mayberry R.F.D.* When it returned to the Troubadour in November, it was "Pogo" again.

The name Pogo was suggested by the band's manager, **Dickie Davis**, who was also the stage manager for the Troubadour. "Pogo" was a hat-wearing opossum cartoon character by artist **Walt Kelly** that appeared in syndicated newspapers across the country. Davis was a fan of how Kelly would work politics into the stories of Pogo and his swampland friends. He thought associating the band with Pogo would tell people that the band was cool, smart, and with a country edge.

But Kelly was not a fan of the band using the name of his famous cartoon. He threatened to sue if the they continued. Kelly's threat caught Furay and the band off guard. The Buffalo Springfield Roller Company, a New York-based maker of heavy machinery, had actually supported the Springfield's use of their mark. The good press the band had been receiving as Pogo was overwhelmingly positive and the public had grown accustomed to the name, so they were reluctant to change. But facing off in court

PATHWAY ALBUM | BERNIE LEADON

DILLARD & CLARK
The Fantastic Expedition of Dillard & Clark
A&M Records, October 1968

The fusion of bluegrass, country and rock music was still in its formative stages by mid-1968, but **Dillard & Clark** were looking to push the evolution of the genre more. **Doug Dillard**, with his famous bluegrass family lineage, often collaborated with his friend **Gene Clark**, a co-founder of country-rock icons **The Byrds**. The pair pulled former **Hearts and Flowers** guitarist **Bernie Leadon**, along with **Don Beck** (mandolin, dobro) and **David Jackson** (string bass) together and recorded one of the important albums of the country-rock movement. Dillard and Clark wrote or co-wrote all but one of the songs. Leadon was a substantial contributor as well, earning co-writing credits on six of the nine tracks; his *Train Leaves Here This Morning* also made it onto the Eagles debut album in 1971. It was well received by the music press, and country-rock faithful compare it favorably with the Flying Burrito Brothers landmark album, *Gilded Palace of Sin*. Though considered significant, it was not commercially successful.

Cashbox
December 7, 1968

Dillard & Clark have come up with a striking album that should do good things for them. The style of the LP can be described as folk-country, but the appeal is wider than that. Both Dillard and Clark do vocals, and one or the other or both had a hand in writing all but one of the songs on this set. In addition, Dillard plays banjo, guitar and violin, and Clark plays guitar and harmonica. Keep an eye on this album.

Rolling Stone
February 15, 1969

This album has the kind of country music you get when you mix a rock producer (**Larry Marks**) and artists with various realms of experience. With just nine songs, it provides 28 minutes of better than average music. Affected just enough by contemporary influences, it's palatable to someone dislikes straight country, but that's also one of its flaws. Perhaps it's too compromising, and therefore too slick.

Emporia (Kan.) Gazette
April 3, 1969

Bluegrass purist **Doug Dillard** plays fiddle, and former Byrd **Gene Clark** plays rhythm guitar and is a country music fan. The band has a hard, firm country sound with careful vocal harmony and good feeling. They wrote all the songs themselves with the exception of one **Lester Flatt** song, *Get It on Brother*. Their bluegrass basics bring them close to old-style rock and roll.

against Kelly, who had been using "Pogo" in his comics for decades, seemed like a loser as well. And nobody was buying that the band named itself after a pogo stick. So the band resolved to drop the "g" and replace it with a "c" and Pogo became Poco. "From the start I liked the new name better than the old one," Furay said. [231, 1269]

WINTER 1968-69

RELEASES
Glad, with Timothy B. Schmit, *Johnny's Silver Ride* (single)

ON SCREEN
Poco, with Randy Meisner, appeared live in concert on the CBS TV show *Southern Comfort*. Show aired from the Anaheim Convention Center with Poco opening for headliner **Canned Heat**. Local DJ *Sam Riddle* promoted the show.

ON THE ROAD WITH …
▶ **Dillard & Clark**, with Bernie Leadon: Illinois Speed Pass
▶ **Poco**, with Randy Meisner: Biff Rose, Nitty Gritty Dirt Band, Canned Heat, Steve Miller Band, Black Pearly, Love Amy, Linda Ronstadt, Ralph Plummer, Steve Gillette, Taj Mahal, West
▶ **James Gang**, with Joe Walsh: Frost, Lee Michaels, The Red, White and Blues, The Third Power

Frey, Souther Form *Longbranch/Pennywhistle*; Sign with Amos

Glenn Frey and **J.D. Souther** became fast friends at the end of 1968, starting nearly 50 years of friendship and songwriting

collaboration. With the Eagles and others, they forged some of the most recognizable songs of the 1970s and 1980s, including *Best of My Love*, *Heartache Tonight*, and the Grammy-winning *New Kid in Town*. But during the early country-rock days in Los Angeles, the two budding songwriters didn't have a nickel and stumbled about finding their way.

Souther was the first to come to L.A., having arrived several months earlier with his Amarillo, Texas, band, the **Kitchen Cinq**, in search of a recording contract. By day he labored doing construction and roofing, and by night he and his band got familiar with local clubs, managers, agents, and other musicians. He earned a few dollars playing drums for **Bo Diddley** and **Norman Greenbaum** (of *Spirit in the Sky* fame).

Meanwhile, Frey arrived in town late in 1968 and moved in with his girlfriend, **Joan Sliwin**. Sliwin and her sister, **Alex**, were members of an all-girl band called **Honey Ltd.**, a group that already had a recording contract and was appearing in local clubs and on television. They were working on an album and had contacts in the music industry. Souther was also developing contacts and one exec, **Tom Thacker**, would set him up with occasional session work. Thacker was general manager at Amos Records, a label with Texas roots that also had a distribution agreement with Honey Ltd.'s label, Lee Hazlewood Industries. That connection put Souther and Alex Sliwin in close quarters, and they became involved romantically. So, Glenn and Joan and J.D. and Alex all moved in together.

Frey and Souther immediately connected. "We were flat broke and moved in with our girlfriends," Souther told *Rolling Stone* in 2016, "who were actually doing better than us. We started writing songs day and night. We talked about what we wanted to do and we said, 'Let's write songs and play music, just the two of us.'" The two would hang out at the Troubadour club, which had become a mecca of sorts for musicians looking to be discovered. Troubadour owner **Doug Weston** took an interest in the two budding songwriters and agreed to represent them under his management company, Doug Weston and Associates.

Souther said when they started, they were just called "John David and Glenn," and Weston suggested they change the band's name. "I liked the Penny Whistle and Glenn liked Longbranch, since he liked cowboys," Souther said, and Weston said, "Great—**Longbranch/Pennywhistle**." Within hours, a tiny ad had been taken out in the Los Angeles Free Press and they had their first paying gig on December 16, 1969. "We opened for Poco for a week and the second gig we opened for **The Flying Burrito Brothers**." Thacker had an eye for talent and eventually brought the duo to Amos Records owner **Jimmy Bowen**, a Texan guitarist, engineer, and, most recently, manager who had turned around the flagging musical careers of **Frank Sinatra**, **Dean Martin**, and **Sammy Davis Jr.** The two made a solid impression on him.

"J.D., who was from Amarillo, was bit on the surly, rebellious side," Bowen recalled in his book *Rough Mix*, adding that Frey as an "easygoing sweetheart."

"Their songs were squarely in that acoustic folk-country groove and it was fresh and upbeat, with just enough country to make me think of the early Everly Brothers. I really dug their stuff. They had no money, but I thought I'd give them a shot." The duo started writing songs, and by the fall of 1969, they were in the studio working on their debut album. [534, 1217, 1226, 1236, 1246, 1247, 1249, 1250, 1251, 1267]

Azoff Becomes Booking Agent for REO Speedwagon

REO Speedwagon was solid, if as-yet unremarkable, Midwest rock group that had found solace in 1969 in being the house band for the go-to concert venue in Champaign, Illinois, the venerable Red Lion club. Then one day, future Eagles manager **Irving Azoff** noticed them and asked them if they had a booking agent. They didn't, and shortly after, he had remedied that problem.

He said the first date booked for them "was for beer and pizza and $10 a man." So it started slow, and it got better over time. Before Azoff, REO played at Illinois frat parties and small clubs, and even once shuffled off to Connecticut to cut an album and ended up making a pimple-cream jingle for $100.

Azoff and his partner **Bob Nutt** brought them stability, but not instant fame. Not long after taking over, he was able to slate the band as the opening act on a number of Midwestern tours, including **Bob Seger**. By September 1971, he had guided them to their first album, which didn't have any hits. Along the way Azoff tapped **John Baruck**, who eventually became the band's day-to-day manager.

"When we started out, I was the agent and John was the tour manager for **One-Eyed Jacks** and REO, and we both got a real good feel for the business," Azoff said. "John was ... really good with budgets and numbers and accounting. I was more the schmoozer and he was the bones of the operation," an arrangement that continued until Azoff dropped the band in 1976. "The only training back then was trial by fire. We both survived trial by fire." [1333, 1334, 1336, 1338, 1352, 1358]

Ex-Byrds Hillman, Parsons Form the Flying Burrito Brothers

The Flying Burrito Brothers were formed by ex-Byrds **Gram Parsons** and **Chris Hillman** after they left the group in the summer of 1968. **The Byrds** had just completed their *Sweethearts of the Rodeo* album, which helped pave the way for the country-rock movement, but also alienated many Byrds fans who were fond of the band's folk rock and psychedelia creations.

But "Sweetheart," which band leader **Roger McGuinn** had to be convinced to try, was the band's least-commercial album. It couldn't convince Byrds fans to follow them into another stylistic change, and certainly couldn't bring any of the conservative Nashville country faithful to open up to their country-rock synthesis.

So Parsons and Hillman decided to try again in another form; they left The Byrds and the Burritos were born. They jumped fast out of the gate with a critically acclaimed debut album, *The Gilded Palace of Sin*, and Parsons was clearly at his artistic best. *Hot Burrito #1* and *Hot Burrito #2* delivered a fine mix of country and rock that would lay the foundation for the genre, and give the Eagles some inspiration a few years later.

The country-rock genre still hadn't fully arrived by 1969—and wouldn't, really, until the Eagles debuted in 1972. But A&M Records, which didn't have the foothold there like rival labels Columbia or Atlantic, swooped in and signed the Burritos quickly. A&M's catalog was rooted in Latin-influenced jazz with bankable stars like **Herb Albert** and **Sergio Mendez**, so it was a solid progressive move as the label looked to grow and diversify its artist and repertoire.

Said A&M President **Jerry Moss**: "We didn't have any other country artists, and I didn't want to get stuck in a genre that I was a bit of a neophyte in. I don't recall thinking the Burritos were a country band. We saw them as contemporary music and a great new concept. I related to them as rock artists."

Getting such strong support from a major label was encouraging for Hillman and Parsons, but A&M was still a poor match for the Burritos. The label would struggle in vain to find a marketing strategy that worked for the band. One year later, bass player **Chris Ethridge** left the band, and

Hillman slid over to assume that role. To take his position as lead guitarist, he reached out to his former "fill in" player with the **Scottsville Squirrel Barkers** and future Eagle, **Bernie Leadon**, who was now beginning to experience dysfunction in his latest band, **Dillard & Clark**. [534, 739, 1158]

The Corvettes: Leadon Takes Side Gig Backing Linda Ronstadt

Between gigs and sessions with **Dillard & Clark** in the winter of 1969, **Bernie Leadon** would jam with friends in Los Angeles and occasionally take backing band gigs with other artists to help pay the bills.

Likewise, Leadon's friend **Jeff Hanna**, a Detroit guitarist who co-founded jug band-turned-country rock group, the **Nitty Gritty Dirt Band**, created a new side group with **Chris Darrow** (guitar) and **John Ware** (drums) called the **Corvettes**.

The Corvettes were good enough to record, and **Mike Nesmith**, who had a Top 20 hit with **Linda Ronstadt** singing his own *Different Drum* two years earlier, produced two singles for Dot Records for the Corvettes. The singles didn't chart, however, and when Hanna heard the engines of the Dirt Band revving up again, he left the band and was replaced quickly by Leadon.

Darrow wore many hats in the late 1960s, and in addition to playing with the Corvettes, he also served as Ronstadt's road manager. Ronstadt was planning an East Coast tour beginning with sets in New York, so Darrow and Ronstadt tapped the Corvettes as her backing band. Ronstadt

and Leadon were already familiar with each other. Leadon played guitar on Ronstadt's version of *Different Drum* and they had worked in many of the same clubs. Ronstadt specifically remembered his talents when he subbed in for the Scottsville Squirrel Barkers. The extra work was helpful, but Leadon was still focused on writing material for Dillard & Clark's next album, *Through the Morning, Through the Night*, scheduled for release in the fall of 1969. Leadon's work with Ronstadt would pay dividends later, especially as Dillard & Clark began to unravel as a band. [534, 739, 1263, 1264]

After Less Than a Year, Geffen Leaves Ashley Famous for CMA

Less than a year after leaving the William Morris Agency, and after famously stocking the Ashley Famous music department with bankable talent, **David Geffen** was on the move again.

With his reputation as a music industry executive skyrocketing, it was no surprise when Ashley offered Geffen a larger salary and more authority. The company must have known that others were looking to land Geffen, but when Creative Management Associates (CMA) poached Geffen in the winter of 1969, the Ashley team was caught flat-footed.

Geffen had actually been drawn to exclusively manage artists' careers, like **Laura Nyro**, with whom he had cultivated and brought stature, **Stephen Singular** wrote in his book *The Rise and Rise of David Geffen*. He wanted to be released from his contract to pursue it, and even broached the idea with Ashley's leadership. But they needed his relationships and understanding of rock music, which was still foreign to them.

Sandy Gallin was a high-profile agent at CMA. Geffen thought highly of him, as he had managed the careers of **Richard Pryor** and **Cass Elliot**, and even asked him to form their own management agency before he joined Ashley. Gallin turned him down, but continued to press Geffen on the upside of joining CMA. One particularly attractive feature was CMA's representation in motion pictures. **Freddie Fields** was CMA's chairman, and Geffen thought he could use that relationship to springboard him into what he always desired, feature films.

Geffen finally made the move and joined CMA in the winter of 1969. Although he was a music executive, he was placed on the floor with all the movie execs, as he requested. As he had when he moved from WMA to Ashley, he brought all his talent with him to CMA, who now represented Laura Nyro, **Joni Mitchell**, and **Crosby, Stills & Nash**. Ashley fumed. Geffen began building CMA's stable of artists, as he had done before at WMA and Ashley Famous. But he also started building relationships with the other executives in the film side of the business. Geffen's focus would remain in music, but in a few years, he would return to his first love. [1, 3]

SPRING 1969

 RELEASES
- ▶ **James Gang**, with Joe Walsh, *Yer' Album* (album)
- ▶ **James Gang**, with Joe Walsh, *Stop* (single)
- ▶ **Poco**, with Randy Meisner, *Pickin' Up the Pieces* (album)

 ON THE ROAD WITH ...
- ▶ **James Gang**, with Joe Walsh: Caste, MC5, Three Dog Night, East Wind, Pacific Gas & Electric, The Red, White and Blues Band, Teegarden, Van Winkle, The Warlocks, Joe Cocker, Savage Grace, Chuck Berry, Johnny Winter, Sun Ra, Amboy Dukes, The Little
- ▶ **The Flying Burrito Brothers**, with Bernie Leadon: Betty Carter, The Ansley Dunbar Retaliation, John Mayall, Paul Butterfield Blues Band, Lee Michaels, Procol Harum, The Grateful Dead, Young Flowers, Bobby Doyle
- ▶ **Poco**, with Randy Meisner: Steve Gillette, Lee Michaels, Black Pearl
- ▶ **Rick Nelson's Stone Canyon Band**, with Randy Meisner: The Times Square Two, Buck Owens & His Buckaroos, Diana Trask, Dillard & Clark, Gordon Lightfoot, Gordon Terry, The Dillards
- ▶ **Longbranch/Pennywhistle**, with Glenn Frey: Hamilton Camp

James Gang Signs with ABC; Debut *Yer' Album* Released

One night in a Warren, Ohio club, **James Gang** was playing their standard set, and an in-house producer for ABC Records wandered into the audience to see the show. The producer, eventual Eagles producer **Bill Szymczyk**, liked what he heard and introduced himself to the band. He made an im-

THE JAMES GANG
Yer' Album
Bluesway Records, March 1969

Yer' Album was a coming out party for **Joe Walsh**. He and his **James Gang** bandmates, **Jim Fox** and **Tom Kriss**, were discovered by ABC Records producer (and future Eagles producer) **Bill Szymczyk** in a club in Warren, Ohio. He signed them, brought them into the studio and indulged their desires and whims for long jams. Critics were mixed on the final product, but fans of the James Gang were enthused by their bluesy, hard-driving rock style. While the band's covers of the **Yardbirds** and **Buffalo Springfield** got noticed in the rock press, it was *Funk #48* that became the hit single. Not to be confused with *Funk #49*, which came later, the song gained favor with DJs nationwide and became a minor hit, climbing to #126 on *Billboard's* singles chart. The album rose to #88 on the *Billboard* album chart. Walsh also showed a bit of his famous tongue-in-cheek personality on the disc. In the LP's locked groove at the end of Side 1, Walsh inserted the spoken phrase "turn me over." At the end of Side 2, he says "Play me again."

Record World
October 11, 1969

The boys from Ohio roll out their debut album here and they play the blues, but with a soft edge. There are strings and things – keyboards and flutes among them – behind them on the album. They write their own material and do it masterfully. The best of the pretty lot is *Collage*, which might work as a single. The long jam *Stop* will give grateful deejays that much-needed break from two-minute singles.

Cincinnati Enquirer
October 12, 1969

Yer' Album was made to be played at high volume. It's an incredibly vibrant display of raw energy coming mainly from the drums, lead guitar, bass and, secondarily, from vibes, flute and keyboard. They have the heavy power of funky blues. There's strong original material and some old favorites from the **Yardbirds** and **Buffalo Springfield**. It's a good indication of where a large portion of the rock world, and Cincinnati especially, is today.

Green Bay Press-Gazette
April 26, 1970

The **James Gang** looks like it's a white blues trio, but it's mainly a rock scene with confused directions. They hit some fairly good instrumental moments in *Take a Look Around*, but moments later they mangle **Stephen Stills**' sensitive *Bluebird*. More up their alley is the **Yardbirds'** *Lost Woman*. The title of the long track is *Stop* and it's 12 minutes long. With as few ideas as they have, sustaining five minutes was probably a challenge.

BILL SZYMCZYK

The Eagles were looking for more freedom in the studio when they began recording their third album, *On the Border*. Frustrated by the musical direction current producer **Glyn Johns** was taking the band, they decided to make a change. So they turned to engineer and producer **Bill Szymczyk**, who had already produced three albums with the **James Gang**, a power trio led by eventual Eagle **Joe Walsh**. Szymczyk had a reputation as a creative sound man who wasn't a tyrant in the studio, and that was a perfect fit for the band.

Szymczyk was born in Muskegon, Michigan and he began his career in sound as a sonar engineer in the U.S. Navy. After his Navy tour ended in 1964 he took a job as an engineer with Screen Gems Records, where he worked with artists like **Carol King** and producer **Quincy Jones**. By 1968 Otis Smith of ABC Records offered him a job as house producer for their Bluesway label. Shortly after he helped B.B. King produce his *Live and Well* album, which included the top 10 single *The Thrill is Gone*. Bluesway soon allowed him to begin fishing for his own talent, and while scouting in Ohio he found the James Gang and Joe Walsh. Szymczyk would produce their first four albums, which included three gold records and two Top 100 singles.

With a reputation as an innovative, easy-going engineer, Szymczyk joined the Eagles in the studio in 1974 where he helped them finish *On the Border*. They navigated away from their country-rock roots with his help and he produced *One of These Nights* , *Hotel California* and *The Long Run*, which were all critical and commercial hits.

Outside the Eagles he produced the the **J. Geils Band**, **Edgar Winter**, **Rick Derringer**, **The Who**, **Santana**, **REO Speedwagon**, and the **Outlaws**. He was behind the boards with **Bob Seger and the Silver Bullet Band**, and with various members of the Eagles when they helped him record *Against the Wind* in 1980. Szymczyk worked less in the 1980s and 1990s, but rejoined the Eagles in the studio for their *Long Road Out of Eden* album in 2007. [1373, 1407]

mediate impression on guitarist Joe Walsh.

"He showed up one night and really liked [us], and he and I became very good friends and related to each other," Walsh said during a BBC interview in 1982. The relationship only grew stronger from there. Walsh said in the late 1960s the Cleveland, Detroit, and Cincinnati areas were hotbeds for club-based rock talent, but no one from there had really made it big. That changed when Szymczyk saw them in Warren.

As the go-to producer for **B.B. King**, Szymczyk had industry credibility before meeting Walsh, but had not yet recorded a rock album. He quickly signed James Gang to Bluesway Records, a subsidiary of ABC, and got the band into the studio. The result was *Yer' Album*, a reflection to the English accents the band was trying to adopt after opening for **The Who** in Ohio, and also a nod to what Walsh called the unusual dialect of northern Ohio.

Yer' Album was a fan and critic favorite, and was, quite literally, a mashup of different styles that incorporated orchestral string work and long, jamming solos. Not put off by the length of pieces, Szymczyk allowed indulgences that included long covers of Stephen Stills's *Bluebird*, and **The Yardbird**'s *Lost Woman* and *Stop*, a single with a run time of just 3:55, but the LP version was a never-ending, if melodious, jam that Szymczyk mercifully faded out after 10 minutes with Walsh still axe grinding.

The album rose to #83 on *Billboard*'s Top 200 chart and the single *Funk #48* (not to be confused with its more successful cousin, the entirely different *Funk #49*) peaked at #126. It was a solid start for James Gang, and Szymczyk would have them in the studio again soon. Their next album would put them on the map. [135, 366, 1255]

Meisner Joins Rick Nelson's Stone Canyon Band

Poco co-founder **Richie Furay** told Randy Meisner he couldn't join in the final mixing sessions for **Poco**'s debut album *Pickin' Up the Pieces* in June 1969, so Meisner abruptly quit the band, just a year after he had been welcomed to the group. But it was a fortuitous breakup for then-journeyman bass player, whose availability a year later allowed him to become a co-founder of the Eagles. But at the time, it was an unpleasant ending with a band he had hoped to be with for a while. Luckily, his gigs with Poco gave him great exposure to people searching for talent, including comeback artist **Ricky Nelson**.

Nelson had a clean-cut image from his television show *The Adventures of Ozzie and Harriet*, and he launched a gold-record singing career styled after **Carl Perkins** and **Elvis Presley** that was a huge success in the mid- to late-1950s. He hit #6 on the *Billboard* charts again in 1963 with *For You*, but the arrival of **The Beatles** in 1964 changed the musical landscape dramatically. With his career flagging by the mid-1960s, Nelson reinvented himself as one of the first country-rock artists and became an early influence for the California sound that raged in the late 1960s and early 1970s.

By the spring of 1969 Nelson had charted

a comeback path. Now he needed a backing band. One night at the Troubadour, **Miles Thomas**, who was a close friend of Meisner's, spotted an incognito Nelson curled up in a parka and chain-smoking menthol cigarettes. He struck up a conversation with him about his band and Meisner's name came up. Meisner had a rare combination of excellent bass skills and high harmony vocals that would complement Nelson's singing well.

"Boy, I'd like to have that guy in my band," Nelson told him. Thomas replied, "I can do that for you." But Thomas wasn't the only person with connections eyeing Meisner's talents. **John Boylan**, who was Nelson's manager, remembered Poco's much-lauded debut performance at the Troubadour. When Poco's manager, **Dickie Davis**, told Boylan about Meisner's sudden departure, it didn't take him long to make a move. "Twenty minutes after I spoke with Dickie, I ran into Randy," Boylan told **Sheree Homer** in her book *Rick Nelson: Rock 'n' Roll Pioneer*. "I said, 'You wanna come work for Ricky?' He said, 'You bet.'"

At that time, Meisner was living with his former bandmates from his previous band, **The Poor**. He suggested to drummer **Pat Shanahan** and guitarist **Allen Kemp** that they audition. Both were doing session work to make ends meet, so he recommended them to Nelson, who, in turn, invited them into the band and brought everyone together at his house at Mount Olympus in Laurel Canyon to get better acquainted and map out the plan. Shanahan and Kemp both shared a house in Sherman Oaks on Stone

Canyon Drive, so the Stone Canyon Band was born that night, and rehearsals started soon after. "We had a house in Van Nuys with a room we rehearsed in that we had soundproofed with egg cartons," Shanahan said. "We rehearsed with Rick the first time in that little room."

By April 1969, Nelson had scheduled the band for a week of shows at the Troubadour club. It was a phenomenal success with ticket lines wrapping around the building and a sellout every night. Nelson worked a blend of **Bob Dylan** and **Jim Hardin** songs, and even worked in some John Boylan songs in the sets. The next month they performed at the Country Pop Festival in Acton, California, and appeared with **Gordon Lightfoot**, **Dillard & Clark**, and **Buck Owens**. Nelson had engineered a successful comeback, and the band started a long tour that would take them to the Midwest, the East Coast, and to entertain troops serving in Europe. But the grind of the tour would start to wear on Meisner, who had been apart from his family for a long time, and that would force a change in the months ahead. [6, 486, 781, 1386]

Poco Releases Seminal Album, *Pickin' Up the Pieces*

In the wake of the breakup of **Buffalo Springfield**, former Springfielders **Richie Furay** and **Jim Messina**, along with former **Boenzee Cryque** guitarist **Rusty Young**, and, to some degree, former Springfield road manager **Miles Thomas**, formed what they hoped would be the foundation of a country-rock supergroup: **Poco**. The group

PATHWAY ALBUM | RANDY MEISNER

POCO
Pickin' Up the Pieces
Epic Records, May 1969

Despite leaving **Poco** before its debut album was officially released, Randy Meisner still made it onto the band's debut album. Meisner and Poco leader **Richie Furay** argued over whether he could attend the album's final studio sessions, which led to Meisner's departure. In the aftermath Furay had some of Meisner's work removed, including the cover art where his likeness replaced with a dog. Furay had drummer **George Grantham** re-record Meisner's lead vocals, but his backing vocals and bass work remained. Rock critics received the album well, but the record-buying public was less enthused. Furay and **Jim Messina** included several country-rock songs from the Springfield sessions like *What a Day* and *Nobody's Fool*. Epic Records' **Clive Davis** marketed it heavily, but the LP sputtered to #63 on *Billboard*'s album chart. *Pieces* is still considered a landmark country-rock album, but the lack of marketable songs kept it from becoming a hit. The Eagles would crack the country-rock code three years later.

Record World
May 31, 1969

A few Buffalo Springfielders pick up their pieces and start all over again, and they are one of the tightest groups around. **Jim Messina** and **Richie Furay** sing happy new songs that seem to have no other intent than pop entertainment. The title cut, *Pickin' Up the Pieces*, is an infectious and fun-filled country-rock ditty. The vibes are tops. *First Love* and *What a Day* are possible singles too.

Atlanta Journal-Constitution
June 7, 1969

Pickin' Up the Pieces is another in the seemingly interminable series of country-rock albums. **Poco** features two ex-**Buffalo Springfield** members. The only good cuts on this album are *Consequently, So Long* and a catchy country instrumental, *Grand Junction*. In accordance with the title, it is heartily recommended you smash this album on the floor.

Chicago Sun-Times
June 14, 1969

Former **Buffalo Springfield** members **Richie Furay** and **Jim Messina** have formed a new group, **Poco**, and they have picked up where the Springfield left off. They played country before they broke up, but Poco's music isn't country. The pedal steel twang and the dropped Gs aren't enough. Poco is too original to fit into a country bag. It has a country flavor, but the seasonings don't make the meal.

added drummer **George Grantham**, another Boenzee Cryque alum, and future Eagle Randy Meisner, who beat out another future Eagle, Timothy B. Schmit, for the role of bass player.

The band began rehearsing and recording material for what would become their debut album, *Pickin' Up the Pieces*, in the spring of 1969. It would become an important album in the country-rock movement, and helped lay the foundation for the Eagles and other country-rock bands that blossomed in the early 1970s.

Furay and Messina already had several songs that had not made it onto a Springfield LP yet and they were queued up for recording first, including *What A Day* and *Nobody's Fool*. In his book *Pickin' Up the Pieces*, Furay said debut album's sessions were a bonding period for the band, adding that the group played as a unit, "which is why the songs give off such a warm glow." That glow was felt by rock music critics, who heaped praise on the album when it was released in June 1969.

"The wait has been worthwhile," wrote **Al Rudis**, rock music writer for the *Chicago Sun-Times*, of the post-Springfield album, "because Furay and Messina ... have picked up where the Springfield left off."

Though highly rated by music critics, many of whom believed the effort was on-par with any Buffalo Springfield album, the music-buying public proved less enthused. The album, released by Columbia's Epic Records, peaked at #63 on the *Billboard* album chart and couldn't find airtime on AM radio. But before the album was released, troubles had surfaced in the studio, where Furay and Messina were mixing the album. Meisner wanted to hear the mixes, but was banned from the studio by Furay. Feeling slighted, Meisner abruptly quit the band, which caused some short-term issues for Poco as it segued from the studio to touring. [1269, 1270]

Chance Meeting with Rogers Nets Henley's Felicity a Contract

Country music star **Kenny Rogers** got fatefully recognized one fall afternoon in 1968 while shopping in a boutique clothing store in Dallas. In an important chance encounter, Don Henley's band, then called **Felicity**, had wandered into the same store when their keyboard player, **Jerry Surratt**, spotted Rogers and eagerly struck up a conversation.

"I was looking at a rack of shirts, spinning them around," Rogers told the *Dallas Morning News* in 2007, "and Jerry Surratt says, 'Aren't you Kenny Rogers? I really want you to come hear our band.'" As Henley and his band founder, **Richard Bowden**, looked on hopefully, Rogers smiled and politely declined. Surratt, however, persisted and within minutes, Rogers had agreed to see them perform at the Studio Club in Dallas. "They were really, really good that night," Rogers said. "Once I got back to L.A., I told **Jimmy Bowen** how much I liked them." Bowen, who owned Amos Records and had partnered with Rogers, suggested he bring the band to Los Angeles to record.

Rogers told them to work on original

material, rehearse, and, when the time was right, he would bring them out. In the meantime, the band rehearsed in an abandoned church in Linden, Texas, listened to **Dillard & Clark**, and road dirt bikes to pass the time while they waited. They also added two new band members. Guitarist **Jim Ed Norman**, who was Henley's North Texas State college buddy that introduced him to the Dillards, joined the band. So too did steel pedal guitarist **Al Perkins**, who would later become a highly sought-after session player.

About two months later, Rogers called, as he promised he would, and said that Amos was ready. He financed the group's trip to L.A. and they arrived in the fall of 1969. Rogers and his wife let them stay at their home while he searched for an apartment for them. "[Kenny Rogers] was sort of looking for groups to produce," Henley said. "He's from Crockett, Texas, near Houston. He was sympathetic to the problems of making it from Texas."

Getting to a recording studio in L.A. was the culmination of a dream for the band. They recorded their debut album and Amos charted a plan for its release. Optimism ran high. They had come a long way since Surratt found Rogers in that Dallas boutique. But the band couldn't have known that in the midst of those efforts, Bowen and Amos Records were having financial problems that would cripple its ability to market the records they produced. By the spring of 1970, those problems would be evident. [5, 6, 1146, 1214, 1366]

SUMMER 1969

 RELEASES
▶ **Poco**, with Randy Meisner, *Pick' Up the Pieces* (album)
▶ **Dillard & Clark**, with Bernie Leadon, *Through the Morning, Through the Night* (album)

 ON THE ROAD WITH …
▶ **The Flying Burrito Brothers**, with Bernie Leadon: The Dillards, Linda Tillery
▶ **James Gang**, with Joe Walsh: Led Zeppelin, Creedence Clearwater Revival, The Box Tops, Jethro Tull, Savage Grace, Grand Funk Railroad, The Sacred Mushroom, Regals
▶ **Rick Nelson's Stone Canyon Band**, with Randy Meisner: Nannette Natal

Frey, Souther Connect with Browne at Free Clinic Benefit

On the very day he arrived in Los Angeles, **Glenn Frey** met and instantly connected with **J.D. Souther**, a talented singer-songwriter who became Frey's writing partner.

The two emerging performers had something in common: girlfriends who were sisters. The pair decided to leave the "band" life behind and tried to make it as a duo in the burgeoning country-rock world that was overtaking California. They called themselves **Longbranch/Pennywhistle** and were signed by low-rent label Amos Records, who had a knack for finding good, raw talent. But the label was also often unable or unwilling to nurture or market their acts enough to get them noticed, so the

MOSS IN THE TREES: YOUNG CONJURES *SEVEN BRIDGES ROAD*

SUMMER 1969 – As the opening credits roll for the Eagles documentary *The History of the Eagles* the band – Randy Meisner, Glenn Frey, Don Henley, Joe Walsh and Don Felder – huddle closely in the locker room of the now-demolished Capital Center in Landover, Maryland in 1977. Like a boxer shaking off nerves before a fight, they begin harmonizing the opening verse to their vocal warm-up song, *Seven Bridges Road*. Before *Hotel California* became the band's concert lead-off song they would sometimes start shows with *Seven Bridges*. Fans loved the way the band's blend of voices harmonized the inspiring southern song.

The song was written by **Steve Young**, a gifted song scribe who worked the folk and country singer-songwriter circuit in the 1970s and 1980s, and helped originate the "outlaw country" movement, a sub-genre of country music that wove together rock and folk rhythms, country instrumentation and introspective lyrics. "Outlaw country" broke traditional country music norms and helped lay the foundation for today's modern country music. Young was one of the movement's first purveyors, and it was further popularized by the likes of **Waylon Jennings**, **Willie Nelson**, **Tanya Tucker**, **Hank Williams Jr.**, **Charlie Daniels** and **Steve Earle**.

Young was moved to write *Seven Bridges* on a starry night in Montgomery, Alabama, said **Jimmy Evans**, Alabama's former Attorney General, a friend of Young's in 1969.

"That night there was a full moon. We were in my Oldsmobile, and when I stopped Steve got out on the right-side fender," Evans told *The Birmingham News* in 2018. "We sat there a while, and he started writing down words." Evans and Young had just finished a jam session with bluesman **C.P. Austin** in the nearby town of Orion, and they were driving home along the highway that became the inspiration for the song, Woodley Road, a long stretch of dirt road lined with trees filled with Spanish moss. And it crossed over seven bridges. "I thought it was the most beautiful place around Montgomery that I'd ever seen," Evans added. "That road was a cavern of moss; it looked like a tunnel."

Young put *7 Bridges Road* on his debut album, *Rock Salt and Nails*, which was one of his three original songs. His producer, **Tommy LiPuma**, didn't even want the song on the LP, instead having Young focus on folk and country music covers. He was a known commodity in folk and country-rock circles and had developed a cadre of support that showed up for the album. Legendary session guitarist **James Burton** backed Young on the record, along with **The Byrds**' **Gram Parsons** and **Gene Clark** and the **Flying Burrito Brothers**' **Chris Etheridge** and **Don Beck**.

"One day we ran out of songs to record in the studio," Young told music journalist **Dave Dawson** in 1999. "Burton and [bass player **Dave Jackson**] were there and everything was up and rolling, so I started performing *Seven Bridges* because I didn't have anything else to play. After it was recorded LiPuma, had to admit that, original or not, it was good."

Even with the all-star backing musicians A&M Records could not get the single or the album album airplay. But *Seven Bridges* was remembered. Four years after it was originally recorded former **Fairport Convention** and **Southern Comfort** singer **Ian Matthews** and his producer, former Monkee **Michael Nesmith**, worked up a version of the song for Matthews' new LP, *Valley Hi*. "Ian and I put it together and [we] sang about six- or seven-part harmony on the thing, and I played acoustic. It turned out to be a beautiful record," Nesmith said. The Eagles and Matthews would sometimes cross paths in Los Angeles, and he said he remembered Don Henley having a copy of *Valley Hi*, so it wasn't a total surprise when the Eagles recorded it.

The band used *Seven Bridges* as its opening song occasionally, but *Hotel California* supplanted it as the concert opener in 1976. It was also the B side of *The Long Run* single in 1980. When the band was quietly breaking up in 1980 Asylum Records and Warner Brothers were desperate for a single, so they released the live version and watched it soar to #21 on the *Billboard* singles chart.

> One day we ran out of songs to record in the studio. [James] Burton and [Dave Jackson] were there and everything was up and running, so I started performing *Seven Bridges* because I didn't have anything else to play. After it was recorded [Tommy] LiPuma had to admit that, original or not, it was good.
> —*Steve Young, writer of Seven Bridges Road*

Glenn Frey would look back fondly on the song in a 2003 interview with *Rolling Stone*. "We listened to [Ian Matthews] version and then modified our arrangement from that. Sometimes we start our show with it," Frey said. "It's something we do well — four voices, a cappella. I think the bottom line is, that's a style that comes very easily and naturally to us. It's also something that our fans really love. It's Americana."

Young was born in Georgia and was raised around Gasden, Alabama. He traveled all over exercising his "outlaw country" musical craft. He recorded 14 albums over the years, and his work was in-demand. Waylon Jennings recorded a country hit with Young's *Lonesome On'ry and Mean* and Hank Williams Jr. recorded *Montgomery in the Rain* too.

Young passed away at 73 in Nashville, Tennessee in 2016. Reflecting back on his signature song, Young told *The Gasden (Ala.) Times*, "Consciously, when I wrote it, it was just a song about a girl and a road in south Alabama. Now I think there's almost a mystical thing about it." [209, 474, 1152, 1449, 1450, 1451, 1452, 1453, 1460, 1461, 1470, 1471, 1472]

business was perpetually unsuccessful.

In a clear effort to get more notice, Frey and Souther would schedule appearances wherever they could perform, including coffeehouses and guitar shops like McCabe's in Santa Monica. One such event was a benefit concert for the Long Beach Free Clinic on an early summer day in 1969. On that day, a young singer-songwriter named **Jackson Browne** was trying to get noticed at the same event. He told *Rolling Stone* in 1974 that he had seen Frey and Souther perform before, and wanted to try out a new song for them.

Frey had never met Browne before, but was impressed. "[Jackson] walked up to me and John David with an acoustic guitar and started singing *Jamaica Say You Will*," Frey said, "and me an John David started singing with him." It was a chance meeting that would pay dividends for all three musicians. A few weeks later, Browne would record an acetate demo of *Jamaica* with his new friends, Frey (guitar and vocals) and Souther (drums), and that demo would end up on the desk of **David Geffen**, whose guidance would elevate all their careers. [1207, 1214, 1216]

James Gang, Walsh Land First Hit As *Funk #48* Peaks at #126

When producer-engineer **Bill Szymczyk** walked into a little club in Warren, Ohio, to hear Joe Walsh and the **James Gang**, he was taken by the high-energy show that the group put on. It was the spring of 1968 and Walsh took an immediate liking to Szymczyk, who had already produced blues icon **B.B. King** in his young career.

A relatively new producer, Szymczyk wanted to record a rock album and, having earned the trust of the company brass, was tasked with finding a band, signing them, and recording a hit. An old roommate suggested he come to Cleveland, which was generating lots of acts in the late 1960s. He arrived in Ohio and watched **The Tree Stumps**, who had promise and a talented guitarist named **Michael Stanley**. He signed them, changed their name to **Silk**, and produced them, but they didn't sell. He also found an energetic bar band with a searing guitar player called the James Gang. In them, he found a winner. He brought them into the studio and tried to capture their on-stage energy.

Szymczyk discovered that Walsh was an electrifying guitarist, but was not yet a seasoned songwriter. Nonetheless, he earned writing credits for seven of the 11 songs on the LP, including credits on all three singles that were released. AM radio ignored the first two releases, but the third one finally got airplay. The blues-driven *Funk #48* (not to be confused with its more-popular cousin, *Funk #49*) peaked at #126 on *Billboard*'s singles chart. Album sales were solid for the first-timers, with their first effort, entitled *Yer' Album* peaking at #85 on *Cashbox*'s Top 100 Albums chart. It wasn't great, but their label, ABC-Bluesway, thought that if they pushed the next album hard enough, it might catch fire. Walsh one-upped himself on the next album, and gave James Gang their first bona fide hit. [363, 1197]

PATHWAY ALBUM | BERNIE LEADON

DILLARD & CLARK
Through the Morning, Through the Night
A&M Records, August 1969

Through the Morning, Through the Night was Bernie Leadon's last album with **Dillard & Clark**. Leadon left the band while the recording sessions for the album were underway, and his absence was noticeable. Where the group's first album was an important LP that adventurishly fused country and rock, their second effort was more of a country and bluegrass vehicle. In that regard it succeeded, and cuts like *Rocky Top* and *No Longer a Sweetheart of Mine* were solid in that country-bluegrass vein. Leadon's country-rock presence was missed, though he did earn credit for playing guitar and bass. Where he had six writing credits on the first album, he had none on the second. **Donna Washburn**, **Doug Dillard**'s girlfriend, became a member of the band and assumed the singing roles that Leadon handled in the first album. Without Leadon's influences the album drifted away from country-rock. *Through the Morning* failed to chart as an album, and no singles charted either. Meanwhile Leadon was already backing up **Linda Ronstadt** and had been invited to join the **Flying Burrito Brothers**.

Record World
July 19, 1969

Dillard & Clark are leading proponents of modern, electrified country. They echo the days of **Elvis Presley**'s *Don't Be Cruel* and early [**Johnny**] **Cash**. They do it their way. Check out their cover of **The Beatles**' *Don't Let Me Down*, where the fiddle break is a total melodic departure. One of the few examples of an *altered* arrangement of a Beatle tune. And *Why Not Your Baby* is a beauty that will go far.

The Indianapolis News
November 5, 1969

Through the Morning, Through the Night is basically a country-western album influenced by California studio pop and Ozark hills music. *Roll in My Sweet Baby's Arms* is a country cut with a snappy bluegrass banjo. While not the best in the new country records line, this LP points to a fresh direction that should produce some exciting new sounds in the months to come.
– Bob Basler

Cashbox
November 29, 1969

Country, bluegrass, gospel: take your choice. There's something for everyone on this package from **Dillard & Clark**, as the group effectively displays their vocal and instrumental talents. Worthwhile songs on this set includes *No Longer a Sweetheart of Mine*, *Rocky Top, I Bowed My Head and Cried Holy, Kansas City Southern, Roll In My Sweet Baby's Arms* and the title track. There's good listening throughout.

Geffen-Roberts Management Becomes the Elite Stable

Fresh off cementing a deal that would parse the remaining pieces of the now-defunct **Buffalo Springfield**—including the creation and migration of **Crosby, Stills & Nash** to Atlantic Records and the newly formed **Poco** to Columbia Records—**David Geffen** was still building a rock powerhouse at his new agency, Creative Management Associates (CMA). He had already added **James Taylor** and **Van Morrison** and was trying to find a contract for his newest find, a young singer-songwriter named **Jackson Browne**.

While meeting **Elliot Roberts** in Los Angeles in the fall of 1969, Geffen made Roberts an offer to form a management company. He made similar bold requests in the past year when he tried to convince both **Clive Davis** and CMA's **Sandy Gallin** to partner with him to create a management firm and a label, but neither agreed.

Roberts, close friends with Geffen since their days at the William Morris Agency, was already managing **Joni Mitchell**, **Neil Young**, and **Crosby, Stills & Nash**, and frequently sought Geffen's advice. Roberts said the two were cruising through Los Angeles one day when Geffen stopped the car and told him he wanted to partner. Elliot's response was, "Why would I want to partner? Can't we keep it the way it is?" reasoning that he already had great acts and was doing fine. "He said, 'Elliot, think about it for 30 seconds, if we're together am I going to make you a lot of money? Are we going to do great things?' And by the time we went into the house we had hugged, shook hands, and the next morning we started Geffen-Roberts."

The pair decided they would take a different approach to representing artists, Roberts said, adding that in the late 1960s, artist management contracts were very against the artists. Those firms typically paid small rates and kept the recording masters and the publishing rights. Roberts said Geffen-Roberts would do it a different way. Geffen said the pair didn't want to have contracts with the artists. With Geffen-Roberts in business, Geffen quit CMA and started mapping out his next project: creating a new label. [1, 3, 569, 1287, 1288]

FALL 1969

 RELEASES
▶ **Longbranch/Pennywhistle**, with Glenn Frey, *Rebecca* (single)
▶ **Rick Nelson's Stone Canyon Band**, with Randy Meisner, *She Belongs To Me* (single)

 CHART PEAKS
Poco's album Pickin' Up the Pieces (with Randy Meisner) peaks at #63 on the *Billboard* 200 album chart.

 COLLABORATIONS
▶ **Bernie Leadon** played electric and acoustic guitar on **Denny Brooks**'s singles *Tremble If You Must, Light the Light Within You and Rose of the Mountain* on Brooks's album, *Denny Brooks*.
▶ **Bernie Leadon** played resonator guitar on **Buzz Clifford**'s album *See Your Way Clear*.

ON SCREEN
▶ **Rick Nelson's Stone Canyon Band**, with Randy Meisner, appeared as a musical guest on the syndicated TV show *The Mike Douglas Show*.
▶ **Poco**, with Timothy B. Schmit, appeared as a musical guest on the syndicated TV show *The Della Reese Show*. Also appearing were Wally Cox and Deloras Hall.
▶ **Rick Nelson's Stone Canyon Band**, with Randy Meisner, appeared as a musical guest on the syndicated TV show *The Della Reese Show* and The Joey Bishop Show

ON THE ROAD WITH ...
▶ **James Gang**, with Joe Walsh: Joe Cocker, The Kinks, The Liverpool Scene, The Who, Led Zeppelin, Sly & The Family Stone, Manifest Destiny, Syria Mosque
▶ **The Flying Burrito Brothers**, with Bernie Leadon: Crosby, Stills, Nasy & Young, Dorothy Morrison, Joan Baez, John Sebastian, Joni Mitchell, Mimi Farina, Ruthann Friedman, Sal Valentino, The Incedible String Band, The Holy Modal Rounders, The Byrds, Zephyr
▶ **Poco**, with Timothy B. Schmit: The Sunshine Company, Creedence Clearwater Revival, Smoke, Chicago, Country Joe and the Fish, Hedge & Donna, The Liverpool Scene, Iron Butterfly, King Crimson, The Glass Family, Three Dog Night, Sweetbread, New Atlantis, Water Brothers, Jefferson Airplane, The Grateful Dead, The Byrds, Stonehenge, Merryweather, Nitty Gritty Dirt Band, Jamul City, Roxy, Matchbox, C.K. Strong
▶ **Rick Nelson's Stone Canyon Band**, with Randy Meisner: Ten Years After, The Stooges, Steve Martin, The Sons of Champlin, The Lemon Pipers, Nannette Natal, NRBQ, John Bassette
▶ **Longbranch/Pennywhistle**, with Glenn Frey: Albert Collins

James Gang, Walsh Break New Ground By Opening for The Who

The Who was on its U.S. tour supporting the *Tommy* album when they played the Syria Mosque in Pittsburgh on October 26, 1969. Although **Roger Daltrey** was the English group's frontman, **Pete Townshend** was its undisputed leader, and **Keith Moon** was their mischievous drummer.

Opening for The Who in Pittsburgh that night was the **James Gang**, led by American rock and roll's own class clown, Joe Walsh. Both groups were high-energy performers with electric stage presences, so they naturally became friends.

A year later, they connected as The Who toured through the U.S., with James Gang opening for them again, this time in Cleveland.

"We were the local support band and The Who came to Cleveland, and Pete [Townshend] arrived early and said he enjoyed our show," Walsh said. He said Townshend told him, "You're doing pretty good kid," and took him under his wing, offered advice, and gave him confidence. "He told me I was going about being the only melodic instrument in the band very well, which was obviously very encouraging." The *Tommy* tour would be heading to Europe that fall, and the band invited James Gang to tour with them.

"We would never have come over here if it hadn't been for him," Walsh told *Sounds* magazine in 1970. "England has a kind of aura about it, y'know. Americans expect everyone to be a **Jimmy Page**. And [Town-

David Geffen (second from right) labored to find Jackson Browne (second from left) a record deal after listening to a demo tape of the young singer-songwriter in the summer of 1969. After failing, Geffen then created his own label, Asylum Records, and signed Browne himself.

GEFFEN, BROWNE SEARCH FOR A DEAL, AND FIND ASYLUM

SUMMER 1969 – As **David Geffen** was ascending the music industry ladder through the mid-to-late-1960s, artists took note of his growing presence. Ex-Byrd **David Crosby** had a front row seat as Geffen masterfully helped guide Crosby, along with ex-Buffalo Springfielders **Neil Young** and **Stephen Stills** through a contractual morass that led to the creation of **Crosby, Still & Nash** (and later **CSN&Y**), and many artist-friendly deals for emerging musicians like **Joni Mitchell** and **James Taylor**. Crosby viewed Geffen as a shark, but, in his view, he was a shark on the side of the artists. **Jackson Browne** had become a favorite at the Troubadour club by the fall of 1969. Dark haired and lanky, but with the good looks of a model, he had become well known as one of the up-and-coming singer-songwriters in Los Angeles.

Crosby was drawn to him after seeing him at one of his Troubadour performances, and even offered to produce his debut album, an offer that never materialized. Browne had been writing songs since he was in high school and now, all of 21, he hoped to get a recording deal that would allow him to put his songs on vinyl. His first manager, **Billy James**, had gotten him a contract with Elektra Records in September 1966, but Browne hadn't quite learned to sing yet. After a year without recording an album, the label released him.

Crosby, fresh off having his "shark," Geffen, negotiate a complex deal for CSN, suggested that Browne approach him. "He's an agent," Crosby told him. "But he's one of us." And so he did. He collected his new friends, **Glenn Frey** and **J.D. Souther**, who were recording for Amos Records as the duo **Longbranch/Pennywhistle**, and brought along another friend, **Ned Doheny**, and they recorded an acetate demo. Browne packaged the demo along with a polite cover letter asking for advice on seeking a manager, and tucked in an 8x10 glossy of himself and sent it to Geffen's Sunset Boulevard office.

Geffen, who had been dealing with Crosby, Neil Young, and deeply admired **Bob Dylan**, looked at the glossy photo, and reasoned that someone who looked like a model could not be the next Bob Dylan. He threw the whole package in the trash can. Later that day, his secretary, who had listened to Browne's demo, retrieved it from the trash and asked him to reconsider. Geffen did, and in playing the demo, the tune *Song for Adam* resonated with him. But he was simply observing what many others had already seen.

"There's no wasted words or filler in [Jackson Browne's] tunes," Frey told *Rolling Stone* in 1974. "That kid's a monster. Jackson's trip is multidimensional. It's there musically and lyrically. It makes it a little harder to gain commercial acceptance, but when you do get it, it's longer lasting. To get right down to it, I'm in awe of him. I've seen audiences go through changes during *Song for Adam* that were unbelievable."

For his part, Geffen was a believer. Despite nearly passing on Browne entirely, he knew that he had a performer with enormous potential. He and Roberts were actively cultivating acts capable of creating and performing their own material, and they believed Browne was a veritable fountain of marketable music. Geffen started scheduling auditions for Browne in search of that deal.

He went for his heavy hitter in New York first, Columbia President **Clive Davis**. They set up in his office, and as Browne started playing his new song, *Doctor, My Eyes*, an apologetic Davis excused himself as he was pulled away by a call from his boss, **Goddard Leiberson**. Insulted, Geffen had Browne pack up his guitar and they abruptly left with Davis in pursuit. Davis, musing over artists "that got away," recounted the Geffen scene step-for-step his 2013 book *Clive Davis: The Soundtrack of My Life*. Davis resolved that he hadn't really lost a client because Geffen was already formulating other plans.

Geffen's next stop was at Atlantic Records, where he again went straight to the top: **Ahmet Ertegun**, Atlantic's revered president. But Ertegun wasn't interested in signing Browne either. "Ahmet, look, I'm trying to do you a favor by giving you Jackson Browne," Geffen pleaded. "You'll make a lot of money." Ertegun famously replied, "You know what, David, I have a lot of money. Why don't you start a record company and then you'll have a lot of money, too."

For Geffen, those words were a revelation. And with encouragement from Ertegun, Geffen started down the path of creating Asylum Records, and the tectonic plates of the music industry were about to shift and rumble. [1, 540, 1109, 1207, 1287, 1292, 1473]

> **There's no wasted words or filler in Jackson Browne's tunes. That kid's a monster. Jackson's trip is multidimensional. It's there musically and lyrically. It makes it a little harder to gain commercial acceptance, but when you do get it, it's longer lasting. To get right down to it, I'm in awe of him.**
>
> *—Glenn Frey, Eagles co-founder*

shend] helped us a hell of a lot in the States. Okay, we were getting along but he got us attention and since then The Who has really taken us under their wing. I don't honestly understand what they see in us. I still can't believe we're where we are and what's happened to us. I think, especially playing with them, that we've picked up an awful lot of energy from them on stage. We don't hop about and present ourselves the way they do, but then they must be one of the greatest groups in the world today. But we've picked up that energy just from being around them."

Moon took a particular liking to Walsh and began tutoring him in the ways of destroying hotel rooms for fun, a practice that Walsh would continue for years, including some legendary shenanigans with the Eagles. But he also took a liking to Townshend on a musical level. "Pete and I are in the same zip code in terms of writing music and playing guitar," Walsh told *Sounds* in 1970. "He had taken me under his wing as kind of a mentor. But during Tommy, he'd locked into a certain amp/guitar setup for touring, and he got stuck there. It was time for him to move on and I sensed that."

Walsh's affection for The Who was clear when he decided to send Townshend a guitar, specifically a 1957 Gretsh 6120 with a Bigsby vibrato, the same model that **Neil Young** used with **Buffalo Springfield**. Townshend told *Guitar Player* magazine in 1972 that he was surprised by the gift, but was initially turned off. "I opened the case and it was bright orange and I thought,

'Ugh! It's horrible, I hate it.' I went home and went into my studio and plugged it in and it totally wrecked me out, it's the best guitar I've got now. It's the **Chet Atkins** model, with double pickups, f-holes and single cut-away." The gift kept on giving, as Townshend said he used it on every song recorded on the band's 1971 album *Who's Next*.

The Who's European tour was a huge success for the James Gang, who raised their rock credibility with the connection. Their managers worked up a promotion where the band recorded three-to-four-minute daily reports for Cleveland's WNCR-FM during the tour, and even pulled Townshend into one taping. At the end of the tour's three-week run, the station brought the band into the studio and aired a three-hour recap. **Jim Fox**, James Gang drummer, told *Record World* that money was not the reason for going to England, but rather it was about developing recognition. [766, 770, 1301, 1302]

Leadon Leaves Dillard & Clark, Joins the Flying Burrito Brothers

Bernie Leadon's tenure with **Dillard & Clark** was a great experience in his musical evolution. He was writing songs, playing gigs, and recording the music he enjoyed playing most. But sometimes progress can be hindered by environment, and such was the case with Leadon, and the leaders of his band, **Doug Dillard** and **Gene Clark**. Both band leaders had significant roles in folk rock and country-rock origin stories, but the band was hindered by a lack of commercially viable songs, the inability to rehearse, and, to some degree, Clark's flying anxiety.

While the songs Dillard & Clark produced were important in the country-rock movement, there wasn't a solid radio market for them either on pop- and rock-oriented AM or on country music stations. For a band with limited radio appeal to survive, it would need to compensate by touring, but Clark's flight phobia kept Dillard & Clark grounded in California. Their problems weren't just regional either.

When they did pick up gigs, Leadon said they sounded terrible because the band was unorganized and unrehearsed. In the studio, they were dynamic and creative, often picking and playing off each other. On stage, they were a mess. The band would walk on stage without any prepared set list, without knowing how songs would begin or end, without harmony rehearsals, leading to a performance that was just "noise and confusion."

By the summer of 1969, the band was a bit adrift. **Michael Clarke** had already left to join **The Flying Burrito Brothers**. Leadon had agreed to join **Linda Ronstadt** on her summer tour with his band, the **Corvettes**, and it was becoming clear that Dillard & Clark might be nearing its natural conclusion, even as they worked on their second (and last) album.

Then, one day the Burritos "just came and asked me if I wanted to join their band," Leadon told **John Einarson** in his book *Hot Burritos: The True Story of The Flying Burrito Brothers*. Leadon said had seen the Burritos perform live and was not impressed, but he also knew that ex-Byrd **Chris Hillman** was a great musician, so he figured the ship would be righted at some point. Leadon brought maturity and professionalism to the group, Hillman said, which was something the band needed then, calling him "the perfect guy at the right time." The band needed his guitar playing, but it also needed his harmony vocals, which were superb. Moreover, when Leadon came on board, **Gram Parsons**, the enigmatic frontman for the band, took an immediate liking to him.

Hillman's hope that Leadon would bring stability to the group was realized quickly. **Jim Dickson**, an independent producer with Elektra Records, told Einarson that Leadon was the driving force that finally pulled the band together. Leadon gave notice to Ronstadt and the Corvettes and finished out his commitment, then joined the Burritos in September 1969. But it wouldn't be the last time he and Ronstadt's paths would cross. In the meantime, Leadon and his new Burrito bandmates focused on completing their second album, *Burrito Deluxe*. [739, 1253]

Don Felder (left) and his bandmates in Flow were signed by jazz producer Creed Taylor after an audition in New York.

FELDER, FLOW RELEASE DEBUT JAZZ-INFUSED DEBUT ALBUM

WINTER 1969-70 – Guitarist Don Felder and his new bandmates in the improvisational band **Flow** had secured a $5,000 recording contract from jazz producer **Creed Taylor** in the early summer of 1969. The contract was earned largely on the merits of the band's uneven performance at the Fillmore East in Manhattan a few weeks earlier, but also partly through connections the band had with the chart-topping **Young Rascals**, whose management team was vouching for Flow.

Landing the deal with Creed gave the band a huge lift, and the $5,000 was the most money they had ever earned. It didn't go far and disappeared fast. The band put down a deposit on a large delivery van. Because he was the only one with a solid enough credit report to get a loan, Felder was on the hook for the payments. After that expense, they each bought a warm coat, microphones for their PA system, grass, food, rolled cigarettes, and Jack Daniel's, and they rented a run-down apartment on the Lower West Side on Horatio Street. The neighborhood was bad and they were beaten and robbed a couple times, but Felder stayed focused, even if his bandmates to him seemed far less motivated and frequently stoned.

The band began writing material with the help of the Young Rascals' road managers, **John Calagna** and **Andy Leo**, and by the time they arrived at the Van Gelder Studios in Englewood Cliffs, New Jersey, they had nine songs ready to record. Lead singer and bass player **Chuck Newcomb** wrote four songs, while keyboard player **John Winter** got six songwriting credits. Felder got his only songwriting credit on a track that he and Newcomb collaborated on, the first song on the album's B side called *No Lack of Room*.

When they finally settled into the studio, Felder watched on curiously as sound engineer **Rudy Van Gelder** (credited as the engineer behind the signature Blue Note jazz sound) and Creed, the album's producer, took their places behind the console and waited. And waited. It was Felder's—and the band's—first time in a major studio, but they received little guidance from Van Gelder or Creed, and he began to realize that the huge successes borne out of the New Jersey studio may have had more to do with each band's self-motivation to create the music, rather than the producer's insightful guidance.

Van Gelder applied the same engineering magic he did with **Thelonius Monk**, **Quincy Jones**, **John Coltrane**, and **Miles Davis**, but the result in this instance, Felder said, was a "very forced performance." He said he would later come to recognize the session as a "train wreck," though he was quite proud of the effort at the time.

Given that Flow was a rock band with heavy jazz influences, it was difficult for them to find a market for its music. The group had a small, but devoted following of jazz fans and would still pick up an occasional gig, Felder said. But it was usually playing another artist's material. Stung by the high cost of living in New York City, the band rented a well-worn 20-room house in Dover Plains, New York, a little more than two hours outside of Manhattan. Long haired and deemed suspicious by local police, they were once arrested there for walking on the wrong side of the road. They traveled from Dover Plains into New York City and other locations when gigs were available, and they waited for the promotional push on their album.

Creed was a well-known jazz producer with A&M Records, but was striking out on his own. His new label, CTI, was barely formed when it released Flow's jazz-heavy debut album in January 1970. The band began picking up errant gigs to support the album, including

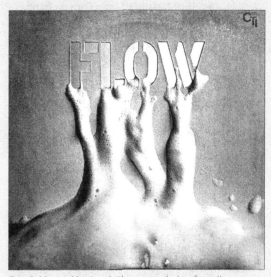

Don Felder and his band, Flow, recorded its first album under the CTI label in the winter of 1970. The album was a mixture of rock and jazz and was released that spring.

sets at the Emergency Club in Washington, D.C., and at the Tompkins Square Park Spring Festival. But there were no real tour plans set up to support the LP. Taylor didn't start the promotional effort until April 1970, and the album got token recognition in *Cashbox*, *Record World*, and *Billboard*. While the trade magazines were generally supportive, the music critics were brutal. The *Asbury Park Press*, one of the few newspapers to review the LP, recognized good musicians in John Winter and Don Felder, but ravaged Newcomb's vocals and lyrics as "horrendous." Ultimately, CTI released just one single, *Mr. Invisible*, and it failed to chart.

Eighteen months after they moved into the house in Dover Plains, and finally convinced that Flow was done, Felder quit the band. Taylor offered to get him an instructor's job at the Berklee School of Music in Boston, but he wasn't ready to give up on his musician's dream just yet. His Florida girlfriend, Susan, had moved back home to Boston and suggested that he could find session work there, so Felder headed to Beantown. He would find menial work there, but he would soon get a call from an old friend in California who had struck it rich with the Eagles. Bernie Leadon was an important part of Felder's early musician journey, and he would play an important role again shortly. [1198, 1296, 1311, 1312, 1313, 1314, 1315, 1316]

WINTER 1969-70

RELEASES
- **Longbranch/Pennywhistle**, with Glenn Frey, *Jubilee Ann* (single)
- **Longbranch/Pennywhistle**, with Glenn Frey, *Longbranch/Pennywhistle* (album)
- **Rick Nelson's Stone Canyon Band**, with Randy Meisner, *In Concert at the Troubadour, 1969* (album)
- **Flow**, with Don Felder, *Flow* (album)
- **Shiloh**, with Don Henley, *Jennifer* (single)
- **Longbranch/Pennywhistle**, with Glenn Frey, *Bring Back Funky Women* (single)

CHART PEAKS
Rick Nelson's Stone Canyon Band single She Belongs To Me (with Randy Meisner) peaks at #33 on the Billboard Hot 100 singles chart.

COLLABORATIONS
- **Randy Meisner** co-produced, played bass guitar and provided backing vocals on **Rick Nelson**'s album *In Concert at the Troubadour, 1969*.
- **Bernie Leadon** played guitar on **Doug Dillard**'s album *The Banjo Album*.

ON SCREEN
- **Rick Nelson's Stone Canyon Band**, with Randy Meisner, appeared as a musical guest on the syndicated TV show *The Glen Campbell Goodtime Hour*.
- **Rick Nelson's Stone Canyon Band**, with Randy Meisner, appeared as a guest on the ABC TV show *The Joey Bishop Show*.

ON THE ROAD WITH ...
- **The Flying Burrito Brothers**, with Bernie Leadon: The Grateful Dead, Seals & Crofts, The Dillards, Steppenwolf, Taj Mahal, The Doors, Rick Nelson & the Stone Canyon Band, Longbranch/Pennywhistle
- **Longbranch/Pennywhistle**, with Glenn Frey: The Flying Burrito Brothers, Penny Nichols, Poco
- **James Gang**, with Joe Walsh:B.B. King, Fleetwood Mac, Jack Bruce, Seigal-Schwall, Soft, Truth, Catfish, Canned Heat
- **Poco**, with Timothy B. Schmit: Lee Michaels, Zephyr, Longbranch/Pennywhistle
- **Rick Nelson's Stone Canyon Band**, with Randy Meisner: The Flying Burrito Brothers, Steve Martin, Morning Reign, Looking Glass, The Glass Family

Poco, Furay Draft Schmit to Replace Meisner on Bass

When Randy Meisner abruptly left **Poco** after being locked out of the final mixing of the band's debut album in the summer of 1969, **Jim Messina** took over on bass for the group's live shows. Messina was a well-rounded musician, an excellent engineer, and a talented bass player too, but the band's leader, **Richie Furay**, wanted his guitar skills, so they went to a familiar source.

During the original auditions when they chose Meisner, it had been a very close decision. Furay and Messina ultimately sided with bandmate **Rusty Young**'s preference for Meisner. But with Meisner gone, Furay planned to reach out again to the bassist not chosen, Timothy B. Schmit.

Schmit was still with his band, **Glad**, and Furay attended one of their shows later that summer. After the show, they invited him to join Poco. He accepted and joined the group in May, though he didn't actually perform live with them until September.

Meisner wasn't out of work long after leaving. **Dickie Davis**, the well-connected stage manager for the Troubadour club had told **John Boylan**, producer for **Linda Ronstadt** and **Rick Nelson**, that Meisner had quit. "When Rick heard I was leaving, John Boylan, his producer, asked if I wanted to put a band together with Rick," Meisner told **Sheree Homer** in her book *Rick Nelson: Rock 'n' Roll Pioneer*. He agreed and soon Boylan had Meisner playing bass behind Nelson as **The Stone Canyon Band**, and he tapped his former bandmates from **The Poor** to join him. [463, 1199, 1269]

Walsh, James Gang Release *James Gang Rides Again*

Just more than a year after **James Gang** released their first LP, they were in the studio again in the winter of 1970 with producer **Bill Szymczyk** to begin work on their second album, *James Gang Rides Again*.

Their first LP, *Yer' Album*, was a modest success, climbing into the lower reaches *Billboard's* Hot 100. That success caused a shuffle at the label, and the band was lifted to the Bluesway's parent, ABC Records, which hoped for a strong follow-up effort. The band didn't disappoint.

Rides Again got strong reviews when it was released in July 1970, led by *Funk #49*, a song co-written by the entire James Gang band—**Jim Fox**, **Dale Peters**, and Joe Walsh.

Though the song was a group effort, the nearly four-minute, lyrically light song about a wild girlfriend is largely driven by Walsh's signature guitar lick and Fox's thumping percussion (and a thematically well-placed cow bell). Walsh told the *BBC* in 1983 that he came up with the basic guitar lick, and even though he didn't believe the lyrics were that intellectual, they worked well for the song.

"The only thing we really added was the percussion middle part, which the three of us actually played," Walsh said. "Putting some parts on top of the drums, but that's the three-piece James Gang, and that's the energy and kind of the symmetry we were all about."

The song followed a naming formula from their first album, which featured a mild hit, *Funk #48*. The band told *Record World* during a promotional visit to their New York office in July 1970 that fans shouldn't expect a *Funk #50*, and that there was no specific significance to the name. That proved untrue years later when Walsh recorded *Funk 50* for his *Analog Man* album in 2012, and invited former James Gang bandmates Peters and Fox to record it with him.

The follow-up to *Funk #48*, which was predictably *Funk #49*, became the band's first real hit, climbing to #59 on *Billboard's* Hot 100 chart. Meanwhile the album, *Rides Again*, debuted at #164 on *Billboard's* Top LP chart, and by October 31, it had peaked at #20. Walsh was prolific on the album, with writing credits on every song except the

Bolero and **Vince Gurauldi** segments of the album's medley, *The Bomber*. **Poco**'s **Rusty Young** was invited into the studio to help with steel guitar and the well-traveled **Jack Nitzsche** helped the band and Szymczyk with the arrangements. [135, 363, 375, 762, 763, 770]

Amos Releases Longbranch/Pennywhistle's Debut Album

When **J.D. Souther** and Glenn Frey walked into T.T.G. Studios in Los Angeles to record their first album as **Longbranch/Pennywhistle**, they weren't quite songwriters yet. By their own estimation, they were still finding their way in the singer-songwriter world in the fall of 1969.

Once in T.T.G.'s large studio on Sunset Boulevard and Highland Avenue, they recorded nine original country-rock songs. Amos Records released *Rebecca*, *Jubilee Ann*, and *Bring Back Funky Women* as singles from December 1969 through February 1970, but they couldn't get airplay, not even locally in L.A.

The album's failure had more to do with unpolished material and threadbare experience than with musicianship. Amos Records President **Jimmy Bowen** and Producer **Tom Thacker** brought in first-rate session musicians to punch up the quality. Rock and Roll Hall of Fame inductee guitarist **James Burton**, slide guitar virtuoso **Ry Cooder**, and steel pedal guitar master **Buddy Emmons** were all contributing in the session. Wrecking Crew veterans **Larry Knechtel** (piano) and **Joe Osborn** (bass guitar) sat in, as did former **Derek and the Dominos** drummer **Jim Gordon** and master Cajun fiddle player **Doug Kershaw**. The album's instrumentation was crisp with thoughtful guitar phrasing throughout, but the songs weren't really radio-ready.

Souther would put a revised version of *Kite Woman* on his debut solo album three years later, but he said the songs were lacking. "I listen to it now and think, 'That's not very good,'" Souther told the *Chicago Tribune* in 2016. "I think [it lacks] the maturity to know what to leave out, and what's the appropriate investment for a song of any particular topic … It just sounds immature to me. I'd only been writing for a couple years, and that was the first bunch of even decent songs."

Geffen Records reissued the album in 2018, two years after Frey's death. In a statement with the reissue, Souther credited Frey as his roommate, best friend, and first songwriting partner in Los Angeles. "Quite honestly, we were just trying to do our best work in a very competitive environment," he said. "If in doing that we evolved a new architecture of some sort, fine, but remember we were all listening carefully to each other and to the giants before and among us.

"We listened to **Miles [Davis]**, **Hank Williams**, **Laura Nyro**, **Joni Mitchell**, **[John] Coltrane**, **Bach**, **Cole Porter**, **Tim Hardin**, **Bob Dylan**, **James Taylor**, and **Carole King** to name a few. We always said that if you want to make great music you should listen to great music. This album was our freshman project." [247, 325, 1217]

LONGBRANCH PENNYWHISTLE
Longbranch Pennywhistle
Amos Records, January 1970

When producer **Jimmy Bowen** brought Glenn Frey and **J.D. Souther** into his Amos Records studio in the fall of 1969, he thought they had the talent to become stars. Their songs were in the country-folk-rock groove that was so popular at the time, so he surrounded them with an all-star cast of musicians including rockabilly guitarist **James Burton**, **Ry Cooder** on slide guitar, **Buddy Emmons** on pedal steel, **Larry Knechtel** on piano, **Joe Osbourne** on bass and the irrepressible Cajun **Doug Kershaw** on fiddle. The result was a strong studio performance backing middling material. Amos released Frey's *Rebecca* as the first single. It dripped with potential, had meaningful lyrics, poignant guitar phrasing from Burton and a great hook leading into the chorus. But Amos couldn't get it on the radio. Souther's **Allman Brothers**-esque *Jubilee Ann* followed as a bluesy second single, but it didn't catch on either. Amos went with a thumper next in *Bring Back Funky Women*, co-written by Frey and Souther. The song's vibe harkened to **Dusty Springfield**'s *Son of a Preacher Man*, but it didn't get played either. Geffen Records re-released the album in 2018 after Glenn Frey's passing. Souther, looking back, said "We were just trying to do our best work in a competitive environment ... this album was our freshman project."

....

Cashbox
December 20, 1969

An energetic vocal duo, Longbranch Pennywhistle come across as fine performers and writers on this entertaining package. Sturdy arrangements build a country-folk-rock sound, and the lyrics are appropriately down to earth. Possibilities for Top 40 as well as underground exposure and sales.

Record World
January 10, 1970

Longbranch Pennywhistle on Amos LP looks great, a perfect example of ease and quality. Longbranch is straight-ahead country mod-funk. All the cuts are playable for their freshness – lyric content is spectacularly free of cliches, not to mention melodically.
– *Kal Rudman*

Kingsport (Tenn.) Times
April 23, 1977

This is an old, rather bad album featuring Glenn Frey, of Eagles fame, and **John David Souther**. Released many years ago, it's now unavailable except from companies that specialize in cut-outs and the price is ridiculous. The only reason I brought it up was because this has been such a slow week. Sorry. B-
–*Michael Clark*

PATHWAY ALBUM | RANDY MEISNER

RICK NELSON & THE STONE CANYON BAND
In Concert, The Troubadour, 1969
Decca Records, January 1970

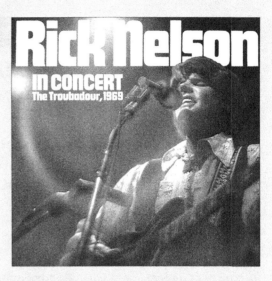

Rick Nelson, the teenage heartthrob from the 1950s television show *Ozzie and Harriet*, was mounting a comeback in 1968. Inspired by the music of **Bob Dylan**, he decided to build a musical comeback around country-infused rock and roll. He recruited former **Poco** bassist Randy Meisner, who, in turn, helped form Nelson's backing group, the **Stone Canyon Band**. They rehearsed, toured and made televised appearances as they gelled as a band and then launched the comeback with his concert LP, which was recorded at **Doug Weston**'s Troubadour club in West Hollywood. Meisner played bass, sang his trademark high vocals, and even helped produce the record. Opening with his own song, *Come on In*, it set the tone and he followed with *Hello Mary Lou*. Dylan's *She Belongs to Me* was a huge success, running Nelson into *Billboard*'s top 40 for the first time since 1964.

Record World
January 31, 1970

Rick Nelson in Concert is a driving, change-of-pace outing for the usually placid guy. Easy to Be Free is a highlight and its among the three tracks he penned himself. His Dylan cover *I Shall Be Released* will be a hit. He shows off his country-rock chops with *Who Cares About Tomorrow-Promises*, a sincere song that is played so well by that band of his, and they show off some great steel guitar work. Nelson is showing off some impressive songwriting skills.

Boston Globe
March 20, 1970

This is no revival effort. It's Ricky trying to catch up, primarily by singing songs by people like **Bob Dylan**, **Eric Anderson** and **Tim Hardin**. Wisely he has surrounded himself with capable musicians whose backup vocals give off a latter-day **Jefferson Airplane** sound. But after all these years Rick's singing is still stiff and stilted. This is an uninspiring record, and even the whooping berries in L.A.'s Troubadour can't make a case for it.
– Nathan Cobb

Rolling Stone
April 2, 1970

This album is an unmitigated delight, a strong set of authentic American music. Clearly now, the dude who can sing songs like *Hello Mary Lou* is also a member of that great company which includes the likes of **Bob Dylan** and **Buffalo Springfield**. Somehow Rick's music seems more authentic, as if he and his band had been hiding out on Okie bars all these years paying dues and assimilating the pure draft beer ethos of this music.
– Lester Bangs

Prior to First Single Release, Shiloh Suffers Tragedy

Don Henley's band, **Shiloh**, had finished recording their first single when band member **Jerry Surratt** was tragically killed in an automobile accident while friends and family anxiously waited for the tapes of their song, *Jennifer (O' My Lady)*, to be delivered.

The band had a chance encounter with rising country singer **Kenny Rogers** in Dallas earlier in the year. Surratt, the band's keyboard player, eagerly invited him to one of their shows and Rogers was impressed with the band. Pretty soon he was talking the group up to his partner, **Jimmy Bowen**, a record producer and owner of Amos Records. Bowen agreed to give the Linden, Texas, band a chance.

The group went to Los Angeles in February 1970 and spent two weeks living in Rogers' house and recorded *Jennifer*, a song co-written by Don Henley and Surratt. While they were in Los Angeles they also changed their name to the more southern-styled **Shiloh**; they had been known more recently as **Felicity**.

Band leader **Richard Bowden** said they hoped the name change would give the band a more genuine feel. "When we went out to California, we needed something a little more Southern sounding," Bowden told the *Texarkana Gazette* in 2014. "We were proud of our heritage. Shiloh was a community nearby. It was in the Bible and Civil War, too." The group had a unique sound that other bands in Texas had trouble duplicating, and they refined it over their three years together. Bowden likened the group's sound to "Eagles in rehearsal."

After the single was cut, Amos took a few months to get it distributed. Rogers, who was acting as a producer for the first time, was playing in nearby Texarkana, Texas, and wanted to pay the band a visit.

"There were lots of people there, maybe 40 to 50, to see Kenny Rogers," Bowden said. "He was bringing a tape of our song *Jennifer*. **Elvis Presley**'s music arranger, **Glen D. Hardin**, had written string music for the background, and it was beautiful. We were on cloud nine. We thought we'd hit the big time. Jerry's family was there, too."

But tragedy struck on April 10, 1970. Surratt, who so boldly struck up the conversation with Rogers in Dallas that got them discovered, was killed when his motorcycle was struck by an oncoming car.

Bowden said Surratt struck the oncoming car, driven by a friend, at about 60 miles per hour. "He was killed instantly as everyone was there watching it, Kenny and his group and the rest of us, which was horrible. It just threw him like a rag doll.

"We were devastated. Jerry was the heart of the band. He didn't have the voice that Henley had, but he had great energy on stage and was a great performer."

Surratt's passing sent the band reeling. "That threw a wrench in everybody's plans," Henley said, "and we sat in shock for a month. But we decided we had gone too far to go back." Bowden told the *Texarkana Gazette* in 2014 that the band believed Surratt

The Woodstock-like concert near Kickapoo Creek in Heyworth, Illinois in spring 1970 drew more than 60,000 fans to see bands like Canned Heatand Ted Nugent. It created a stir among residents and brought then-booking agent and future Eagles manager Irving Azoff into court.

KICKAPOO BAN: AZOFF RECASTS CONCERT AS COW AUCTION

SPRING 1970 – By the summer of 1970, future Eagles manager **Irving Azoff**, just 22 years old, was a key player in one of the most lucrative concert booking operations in the Midwest. Working for Chicago-based talent powerhouse Blytham Limited, Azoff was a young, powerful agent from Danville who directed more than 70 acts to clubs, festivals, college halls, and arenas from Ohio to Wisconsin. In the spring of 1970, Blytham was approached by **L. David Lewis**, an eccentric farm owner in Heyworth, Illinois, to provide acts for his own personal Woodstock festival on Memorial Day 1970.

Lewis came from an influential Illinois family, and inherited a 200-acre farm a little more than a mile outside of Heyworth, adjacent to Kickapoo Creek. Lewis had cash and was looking for bands to book. Blytham's **Bob Nutt** and Azoff virtually owned the market for booking talent in the Midwest and began arranging a Memorial Day festival that Lewis hoped would rival the legendary Woodstock festival that happened in New York just nine months earlier. The principle difference? Woodstock's admission was free, and Lewis' Kickapoo festival would charge a fee. Ads were placed in the local paper appealing to concert fans: "Let's come together in peace Memorial Day 1970." It was no small feat, and it was expensive. Stages were built and, at a cost of about $20,000, Lewis plowed under his corn around the stages and replaced it with sodded grass. He hired a motorcycle gang to provide security for the event and paid local businesses roughly $48,000 to promote the event, and they likely welcomed the surge in business that the concert would bring.

But local residents were not thrilled and filed a lawsuit to prevent the event; the State's Attorney General joined it in March. But by then, the wheels of the festival machine were already turning hard. Just days before the event, Illinois District Court Judge **Robert J. Immel** of Watesaka, Illinois, ruled that using the property for the festival was an illegal use of land zoned for agriculture. But by the morning of Thursday, May 28, more than 3,000 concert-goers had already begun camping out at the site and more than 30 bands had been contracted to play, including acts such as **B.B. King**, **Ted Nugent and the Amboy Dukes**, Azoff's good friend **Dan Fogelberg**, the **Butterfield Blues Band**, **Delaney and Bonnie**, **Canned Heat**, **Country Joe and the Fish**, and **The Finchley Boys**.

"We have to go on with the festival," Azoff told the *Chicago Tribune* on May 28. "There is too much involved not to. More than 30 bands are en route, fencing has been built, and food, sanitation and camping facilities installed. There are already more than a thousand people at the site, and thousands of tickets have been sold. This suit has been in the court since March 13. Why did they wait until now to enjoin us?" Defiant in the face of the legal obstacle, Lewis, Nutt, and Azoff took a different, tongue-in-cheek tack. Azoff told the *Associated Press* that the festival "would be billed as a cow auction and animals would be sold with accompanying music." Lewis told the press it was a political rally with music, adding that it would also be a giant 73rd birthday party for his mother, Lucille.

The day before the event, the court's posture changed a little, and the state police agreed not to block entry to the farm. The festival went on as planned and was a rousing success with more than 60,000 attending and earning more than $215,000. The state's attorney filed contempt charges against Lewis and a warrant was issued for his arrest, but police never found him. He disappeared into the night with his 18-year-old secretary and two sleeping bags filled with cash. An honorable scoundrel, Lewis paid the performing bands in cash the day of the event. He also paid Bob Nutt $20,737, and **John Baruck**, an agent who worked for Blytham $1,300 and then fled to Canada.

The concert was over but the legal issues were not. More than a month after the event, Nutt and Azoff were called as witnesses in an Illinois District Court hearing. Blytham's role as a booking agent—not a promoter—ensured they had avoided charges, but the State pressed the two men for details. Azoff explained that the bands were paid in cash, and that some proceeds had still, a month later, not been accounted for. He also comically explained how they evaded authorities during the concert, even going so far as to use nicknames over walkie-talkies to avoid identification since they feared the conversations were being recorded. Azoff said his alias was *Marvin Jones*, while Lewis was called *Chief Little Fox*, and Nutt was *Chief White Feather*. Azoff's devilish demeanor and jokester wit that were on display during the Kickapoo concert and hearings would become well known in the music industry, especially when he became manager with the Eagles and also with a performer whom he would meet for the first time just three months later, Joe Walsh. [8, 1345, 1346, 1347, 1348, 1349, 1388]

> We have to go on with the festival. There's too much involved not to. More than 30 bands are en route, fencing has been built, and food, sanitation and camping facilities installed. There are already more than 1,000 people at the site, and thousands of tickets have been sold.
> — *Irving Azoff, Blytham Limited booking agent*

PATHWAY ALBUM | DON FELDER

FLOW
Flow
CTI Records, January 1970

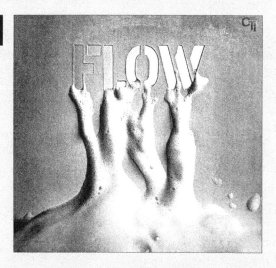

After playing in bands around Gainesville, Florida circuit for the better part of a decade, Don Felder connected with a group of Ocola, Florida musicians who, with Felder in tow, moved to New York and became the progressive rock-jazz group **Flow**. They passed an audition at the Fillmore East in Manhattan in front of famed jazz producer **Creed Taylor**, who signed them and got them to work on their debut self-titled album. The final product was a mixed bag of rock and jazz, which wasn't totally surprising given the lack of guidance offered by Taylor and producer **Rudy Van Gelder**. Felder and the multi-talented **John Winter** were the best things about the LP. Felder's melodic phrasing, especially on *Mr. Invisible* and *Summer's Gone*, showed promise and depth. Winter's piano, flute and saxophone stood out as well. Perhaps the best cut on the album was their cover of **Leadbelly**'s *Line 'Em*, which had an unusual arrangement and an enthusiastic performance. But lead singer **Chuck Newcomb**, who wrote four of the album's nine tracks, chose to put a spotlight on his vocals where his range was far too limited. Taylor chose to release *Mr. Invisible* as the debut single, and it got airplay in New York, but was far too jazzy for nationwide AM radio, whose audiences didn't have the patience or desire for extended jazz solos. The album failed and a few months later the group disbanded.

Record World
April 11, 1970

Two tracks stand out on this debut LP from **Flow**, a prog rock jazz hybrid band who are newcomers on **Creed Taylor**'s just-launched label, CTI Records. Check out *Daddy* and *Mr. Invisible*. The first is a very pretty recollection, and the latter is a bubbling rocker with lots of groovy changes.

Twin Falls Times-News
July 10, 1970

There's some very good musical moments in this album. The music is all original and shows sparks of true inventive genius. It's all very polished, very professional and varies from eclectic rock to almost jazz. The best tunes are *Winter's Gone*, which has some fine flute work, and *Arlene*, a soft ballad. Three stars.

Asbury Park Press
August 2, 1970

This rock group contains some good musicians, particularly **John Winter** and Don Felder. Lead singer **Chuck Newcomb** has some horrendous vocals that spoil the good effect **Flow** achieves. The arrangements, heavily tainted with jazz, are first rate. *Summer's Gone* is a great cut. But oh those vocals!
–Don Lass

would have wanted them to continue. By the summer of 1970, the single starting arriving at record stores. It was a regional hit in Texas, but it wasn't getting played nationally. It was still early though, and the trade press was offering favorable reviews.

"New group with a soft, almost Beatle-like approach will have impact," *Record World* reported, along with four stars, in its July 25, 1970 issue. A month later, *Cashbox* agreed, adding that *Jennifer* was a "finely styled ballad … that is brought into teen focus by a startling vocal. Could gain AM & FM exposure as a lead to chart status."

But even with those favorable nods, the single still couldn't get airplay. Years later, Henley was honest in his assessment. "It was an immediate flop," he told the *Longview (Texas) News-Journal* in December 1976. "One, because we were green and weren't very good songwriters, and two, the company was an honorable, but small-time record maker."

Although disappointed with radio's lack of national interest, they knew they would have another chance to make an impression. Bowen and Amos Records still planned on releasing a full album, so they impatiently waited for Rogers to call again. That call finally came and during May and June 1970, the band, with a couple new members, including Henley's college pal and future Eagles strings arranger, **Jim Ed Norman**, would head into the studio to record their debut. [1145, 1186, 1366]

SPRING 1970

 RELEASES
▶ **Shiloh**, with Don Henley, *Shiloh* (album)
▶ **The Flying Burrito Brothers**, with Bernie Leadon, *Burrito Deluxe* (album)
▶ **The Flying Burrito Brothers**, with Bernie Leadon, *Older Guys* (single)
▶ **Shiloh**, with Don Henley, *Simple Little Down Home Rock & Roll Love Song for Rosie* (single)
▶ **Poco**, with Timothy B. Schmit, *Poco* (album)

 COLLABORATIONS
▶ **Bernie Leadon** played resonator and acoustic guitar on **Hedge & Donna Caper**'s album *Special Circumstances*.

 ON SCREEN
▶ **Rick Nelson's Stone Canyon Band**, with Randy Meisner, appeared on the ABC TV show *Get It Together*. Performed *She Belongs to Me*, and *Easy to Be Free*. Also appeared with the band Illusion, and Ringo Starr (via videotape).

 ON THE ROAD WITH …
▶ **The Flying Burrito Brothers**, with Bernie Leadon: Linda Ronstadt, Longbranch/Pennywhistle, Savoy Brown, White Lightning, Smith, Joe Cocker, Cat Mother, Steel Image
▶ **Longbranch/Pennywhistle**, with Glenn Frey: Wendy Waldman, The Flying Burrito Brothers, Hamilton Camp
▶ **James Gang**, with Joe Walsh: The Sioux, Ralph Romano
▶ **Poco**, with Timothy B. Schmit: Turley Richards, The Moody Blues, Steve Miller Band, Spirit, Gypsy

PATHWAY ALBUM | TIMOTHY B. SCHMIT

POCO
Poco
Epic Records, May 1970

Poco more comfortably inhabited the space between country music and rock and roll than any other band in the early 1970s. Its second self-titled album found them hitting their stride where their intricate harmonies and precision picking were well represented in cuts like *Hurry Up, Keep On Believin'* (co-written by **Richie Furay** and Timothy B. Schmit) and the bluesy *Nobody's Fool*. And, to a limited extent, radio began to notice. **Jim Messina**'s *You Better Think Twice* gave the band it's first top 70 single and the group showed songwriting growth and a willingness to take some musical risks. Peaking at #58 on *Billboard*'s Album chart *Poco* rose higher than the band's debut album, *Pickin' Up the Pieces*. To continue climbing they would need to become more commercially relevant, so they cast an eye toward a band strength for their next album: their revered live shows.

Daily Utah Chronicle
May 26, 1970

As a rule a good group is either superb instrumentally or vocally superb, but not both. Here is the exception. **Poco** is to date, the only really viable blend of rock with country music. The group was put together by **Richie Furay** and **Jim Messina** of **Buffalo Springfield**. They've added Tim Schmit, a sensational bass player, since their first album. Country music turns me off, but I could listen to Poco all night. This album is great.
– Steve Poulson

Minneapolis Star-Tribune
July 26, 1970

Poco is an album that **Buffalo Springfield** might well have made if it were in existence today. It is vaguely country-oriented folk rock. It rocks somewhat harder than the Springfield, but no less precisely. And **Poco**'s singing is almost identical in harmony to that of the Springfield, much more so than **Crosby, Stills, Nash and Young**, the other band that shares two ex Springfield members (**Stephen Stills** and **Neil Young**).
–Mike Jahn

Chicago Sun-Times
July 11, 1970

Poco improved upon their first album, *Pickin' Up the Pieces*, with their latest self-titled LP. it's improved because the group is now comfortable in its new area and stretches out without worrying about authenticity. The new songs are all excellent, except for some bad vocal mixing here and there, which is a shame because the wonderful harmony is one of the best things about Poco. Their cut *Good Time* just about sums up the whole album.
– Al Rudis

Zacharia: Walsh Makes First Foray into Feature Films

Through the late 1960s, **James Gang** had made their mark on music as a three-piece power band covering the club circuit from New York to Michigan. Their stature grew one winter night in Pittsburgh in 1969 when they opened for **The Who**, and **Pete Townshend** and **Keith Moon** took a liking to the devilishly irreverent Joe Walsh. The band joined The Who on their European tour and their new-found presence began earning them top billing in larger arenas. It also opened some new doors.

The producer for their first album, **Bill Szymczyk**, had been tapped by ABC Pic-

tures to be the musical director for *Zacharia*, a surrealist, homoerotic Old West dramady loosely based on the **Herman Hesse** novel *Siddharta* and was billed as the "first electric Western."

Szymczyk invited them to lay down some tracks for the movie's soundtrack and to appear in the film. Szymczyk found himself with the project after recording James Gang's *Yer' Album*. After finishing the album, he was shipped off to Los Angeles when his ABC-Dunhill label was merged with its parent, ABC Records. "It was all very weird, very weird," Szymczyk says. "It was the perfect way to get introduced to Hollywood."

Along with James Gang, the movie featured the music of **Country Joe and the Fish**, **Doug Kershaw**, and the **New York Rock and Roll Ensemble** (featuring the late **Michael Kamen** as its lead singer). It was a decidedly low-budget picture for ABC. In the early 1970s, some low-dollar niche movies were considered "midnight movies." These late-night films played at theaters catering to the *Rocky Horror Picture Show*-type crowds and were akin to direct-to-video movies in the 1990s and 2000s. Zacharia certainly fit that bill, though it did star some recognizable actors such as *Miami Vice*'s **Don Johnson** (in his second-ever screen role), Tony Award winner **John Rubenstein**, and *Eight is Enough* character actor **Dick Van Patten**.

The studio sent the group to the production set in Mexico in March 1970 amid some band discontent. James Gang founder **Jim Fox** had convinced the band to add a fourth member, singer **Kenny Weiss**, and they recorded two songs for the soundtrack with Weiss singing lead. But Walsh and band manager **Mike Belkin** had misgivings about expanding to four, and just before the band left for Mexico, Weiss was unceremoniously cut.

Szymczyk put two of the band's songs on the soundtrack. The first, an instrumental called *Laguna Salada*, pays homage to The Who's *Pinball Wizard*, and onscreen Walsh even employs Townshend's signature windmill move as he strikes his chords against an unremarkable desert backdrop. The band also performs *Country Fever* onscreen as a saloon band, complete with writhing go-go dancers and a brief intermission for a shlocky gunfight.

The dustup between Fox, Walsh, and Belkin over adding Weiss foreshadowed some of the tensions that were emerging within the band. They would record two more albums and continue touring aggressively, but nearly all of the creative and songwriting responsibilities were falling to Walsh. The pressure of being the principal songwriter would force a breakup by the winter of 1971. [387, 759, 760, 1370, 1371, 1372, 1373]

Burritos, Leadon Release Second Album, *Burrito Deluxe*

There was something unique about **Gram Parsons** crooning the chorus to **The Rolling Stones**' *Wild Horses* on **The Flying Burrito Brothers**' second album *Burrito Deluxe*. At the time, The Rolling Stones had not even released the **Mick Jagger**- and **Keith**

Richards-penned ballad yet, so it was a musical coup for Parsons, who begged and convinced his good friend Richards to let the Burritos record the song. Parsons had helped lend a country flavor to the Stones' *Let It Bleed* album, including an uncredited arrangement assist on *Country Honk*, in the summer of 1969, so Richards acceded. The Burritos released their second album in April 1970, but it didn't have the commercial impact they had hoped.

The Burritos' label, A&M Records, never released *Wild Horses* as a single, but perhaps should have. In his review of the album for *Rolling Stone*, **Gary Von Tersch** called the Burritos' rendition "brilliant," while only offering lukewarm praise for the remaining 10 tracks. Perhaps there was an unspoken agreement between the Stones and the Burritos not to release it as a single, but a year later, the Stones did and their version soared to #28 on the *Billboard* Hot 100 chart. In all, A&M released four singles from *Burrito Deluxe* and none of them charted. The Burritos' first album, *The Gilded Palace of Sin*, was a critical success, but it too was a commercial failure. With more rock influences that its country-oriented predecessor, Deluxe didn't get much critical acclaim this time around.

The album was guitarist Bernie Leadon's first with the band. Leadon had just left a dysfunctional **Dillard & Clark**, and he hoped the new group with an established big label recording contract would offer him some stability. But the Burritos were already having their own internal issues. Parsons, the

PATHWAY ALBUM | BERNIE LEADON

THE FLYING BURRITO BROTHERS
Burrito Deluxe
A&M Records, April 1970

Frontman Gram Parsons put his own stellar mark on the **Flying Burrito Brothers** debut album, the *Gilded Palace of Sin*, in 1969, but the flamboyant singer dialed back his approach in the band's sophomore effort, *Burrito Deluxe*. Parsons earned writing credits on seven songs, but his level of effort here was less compelling. Parsons was already falling out with band leader **Chris Hillman**, but he bonded with new guitarist **Bernie Leadon**, and co-wrote *Man in The Fog* with him. Leadon, versatile as always, put his personality in the album and brought a legit country-rock feel on guitar and dobro, especially on *Older Guys*. But apart from Parson's emotional delivery of the **Rolling Stones**' as-yet-unreleased *Wild Horses* – which the Burritos didn't release as a single – his contributions fell short. The Burrito's technical work was superior, but the source material wasn't as good. Moreover, Parsons seemed disinterested. The music industry press gave the album solid marks, but the LP had little

....

Los Angeles Times
June 28, 1970

Though this album is a retreat from the daring excellence of the **Burrito**'s first album, *The Gilded Palace of Sin*, it does contain a few first-rate country-rock selections, particularly *High Fashion Queen*, *Lazy Days*, and *If You Gotta Go*, that makes it worthwhile. Its weakness is that it fails to extend the creative blend of traditional country music and contemporary rock outlook that was contained in the first album.
– Robert Hilburn

Oakland Tribune
July 18, 1970

This country-rock group includes three ex-members of the **Byrds** and each is a fine musician. Unless you can distinguish between their undistinguishable sound, the **Burrito Brothers** may leave you munching your sleeve (or review) in frustration. The group does get it together with the Richards-Jagger *Wild Horses* song. If you're still interested, there's a Dylan song too.
– Craig Modderno

Hackensack Record
July 19, 1970

The **Flying Burrito Brothers** have released their second album for A&M–*Burrito Deluxe*. It's their amalgam of tongue-in-cheek rock and country, perhaps a bit less of the country this time around, and done in high humor. The tunes that grabbed me the most were *Lazy Days*, *Man in the Fog* and *High Fashion Queen*. This may not be everybody's bag, but it's easy to see why they're so hot on the concert circuit these days.
–Allan Macaulay

group's enigmatic front man, was frequently drunk or stoned and was already far less productive in the studio than he had been with *Gilded Palace*.

Although he co-wrote most of the songs on *Burritos Deluxe*, Leadon told **John Einarson** in his book *Hot Burritos: The True Story of the Flying Burrito Brothers* that the album's songs weren't very good. "Gram just didn't show up with anything," he said. Leadon had three songwriting credits on the album, including *Man in the Fog*, *Older Guys*, and *God's Own Singer*, which eventually came to be associated with Parsons. At the end of a disastrous gig at the Brass Ring Club in Los Angeles in June 1970, Parsons performed drunk and out of time with the band and was fired by **Chris Hillman**.

Parsons, a trust fund kid, tried to recruit Leadon to leave the band, but couldn't. The Burritos would recruit **Rick Roberts** to become their new lead singer, but the commercial fortunes of the band weren't changing much. Within a year, Leadon would join yet another band, but this one would give him the commercial success that had avoided him over the last three years. [739, 1254]

Meisner Quits Stone Canyon Band, Returns to Nebraska

Coming off a grueling tour of U.S. military installations in Germany and Spain, Randy Meisner told his band leader, **Rick Nelson**, that he was quitting the **Stone Canyon Band** in the spring of 1970.

Meisner said artistic expression and money were the root causes for his departure,

but the band's reception overseas may have played a role as well. Meisner had joined Nelson's band just the year before, which he helped stock using band members from his previous L.A. band, **The Poor**.

Things had gone well for Nelson and the band over the year. They played to sold-out shows in California and appeared in television shows hosted by **Glenn Campbell** and **Joey Bishop** that raised the band's visibility. And although Nelson's album sales did not equal his sales from his heyday, they did better than many others in the nascent country-rock world. But after a year of off-and-mostly-on-nagain touring, the European trip came at a difficult time for Meisner, who hadn't been home to see his family in close to a year. Nelson's aggressive tour schedule put the jet-lagged band on stage every night for a month, with just a single night off. Concert-goers were not what they were used to either. With the Vietnam War still raging in Southeast Asia and on television screens, and anti-war protests on television screens at home and abroad, it was a difficult time for long-haired rock bands to be entertaining troops.

"We played a couple of places for the non-enlisted men, and those were great," Nelson said. "We'd then mainly play for the career soldiers. There were a couple of people that we were involved with who were very nice, but they were few and far between. We'd get guys with big cigars that would sit the whole show in the front row and turn their back on us. They could care less that we were playing. It never got beyond the point of talking about our hair, which wasn't even that long at the time. It's a long way to come from California, and to have that kind of reception. It was really a terrible experience. The end result was Randy Meisner quitting music for a year and going back to Nebraska."

Meisner left **Poco** because **Richie Furay** wouldn't let him have input in the band's final album mixes. Now, he felt like Nelson was exerting too much control, and the band wasn't getting paid. "I quit because I didn't feel I was getting a chance to express myself," Meisner said. "Rick always consulted us and we all made suggestions, but even so I wasn't happy with the music. I wasn't making any money, and I had been away from my family a long time, so I told Rick I can't handle this anymore."

Meisner returned to Nebraska to repair his marriage, and to get away from music. He started working with a friend at a John Deere dealership and settled in for a more easy-going life with fewer distractions. It wouldn't be long before he began missing the life of a Los Angeles musician. [67, 781, 1214]

Walsh on Hand for Tragedy at Kent State University

In perhaps the most consequential moment for Vietnam War protestors in 1970, four college students were slain at Kent State University in Kent, Ohio, May 4, 1970, when National Guardsmen opened fire on anti-war protesters. On-again, off-again student Joe Walsh was nearby as the events unfolded.

Walsh told the *San Diego Union Tribune* in 2012 that the reason he dropped out of the small Ohio university wasn't academic, it was because he was there when the infamous shootings took place on the Kent State campus. "When the shooting happened, they closed the university because the FBI was investigating," Walsh told *iHeartRadio*'s **Andrew Magnotta**.

"Everybody went home and all the places to play closed. And the townspeople didn't like us anymore, and Ohio didn't like us anymore because Nixon represented us as dirty, hippie, communists who were a danger to America. We weren't; we were just kids. So there was nothing there. Literally, Kent died."

Walsh said that "after that, I didn't look at college the same. [Then] the **James Gang** started to gather momentum and I decided I'd try pursuing music as a profession. Being at the shootings really affected me profoundly. I decided that maybe I don't need a degree that bad."

In 1988, Walsh began lobbying for a memorial for the slain students. "I knew **Jeffrey** [**Miller**] and I knew **Allison** [**Krause**], two of the people who were killed," Walsh explained to the *Associated Press*. "Those of us who were there will never forget it." Twenty years after the slayings, on May 4, 1990, Kent State University unveiled a monument on University Commons commemorating the tragedy; it later relented under pressure to include the names of the four students who were killed on a nearby marker. [7, 21, 22, 23, 223]

SUMMER 1970

 RELEASES
- ▶ **The Flying Burrito Brothers**, with Bernie Leadon, *Man in the Fog* (single)
- ▶ **James Gang**, with Joe Walsh, *James Gang Rides Again* (album)
- ▶ **Poco**, with Timothy B. Schmit, *You Better Think Twice* (single)
- ▶ **The Flying Burrito Brothers**, with Bernie Leadon, *If You Gotta Go* (single)

 COLLABORATIONS
- ▶ **Randy Meisner** played bass guitar on **Compton & Batteau**'s album *In California*.

 ON SCREEN
- ▶ **Linda Ronstadt with the Corvettes**, with Bernie Leadon, appeared on the Playboy Productions syndicated TV show *Playboy After Dark*. Episode 2.20 was hosted by Hugh Hefner. Ronstadt, with the Corvettes, appeared with Country Joe and the Fish and Nanci Roberts.

 ON THE ROAD WITH ...
- ▶ **The Flying Burrito Brothers**, with Bernie Leadon: The Guess Who, Brownsville Station, John Drake, John Sebatian, MC5, SRC, The Litter, The New York Rock and Roll Ensemble, The Stooges, The Third Power
- ▶ **Longbranch/Pennywhistle**, with Glenn Frey: The Dillards, Peter Evans, Doug Kershaw, Tim Weisberg, Danny Cox, Craig Hunley Trio
- ▶ **James Gang**, with Joe Walsh: The Who, The Flock, Frost, Jethro Tull, Savage Grace, Bob Seger, Suite Charity, Teegarden, Van Winkle, James Taylor, Big Brother & The Holding Company, Creedence Clearwater Revival, John Sebastian, Johnny Winter, Miles Davis, Paul Simon, Poco, Richie Havens, Sha Na Na, Three Dog Night, Hip Pocket, Cactus, The Youngbloods

- ▶ **Poco**, with Timothy B. Schmit: Brewer & Shipley, Captain Beefheart & His Magic Band, Goose Creek Symphony, John Sebastian, Mountain, Savage Grace, The Allman Brothers Band, Peter, Paul & Mary

Longbranch/Pennywhistle Open Troubadour in San Francisco

Glenn Frey and J.D. Souther and their label, Amos Records, had finished recording the debut album of **Longbranch/Pennywhistle** in January 1970.

Their first single, a Frey-penned song called *Rebecca*, was released in November 1969, but radio stations barely noticed. Amos followed that up by releasing a Souther tune, *Jubilee Ann*, in December, but it also didn't catch on. Amos finally pushed out the entire album in February with little, if any, marketing, and unsurprisingly, it didn't sell either. Frey and Souther had been working gigs all over Los Angeles since May of 1969, including sets with **Poco** and the **Flying Burrito Brothers** at the Troubadour club in Los Angeles, to try to lift the album locally. But apart from a strong following of friends and Troubadour acquaintances, there was scant awareness of it.

Their manager, **Doug Weston**, who owned the Troubadour, had them on hand for opening night at his new Troubadour club in San Francisco on August 15, 1970, where they served as the backing band for **Doug Kershaw**, a Louisiana fiddle player known widely as the Ragin' Cajun. Kershaw, who Frey and Souther knew since

PATHWAY ALBUM | JOE WALSH**

THE JAMES GANG
James Gang Rides Again
ABC Records, July 1970

Joe Walsh and the **James Gang** developed a loyal
following in Ohio by playing hard rock, and playing
it loud. So when Walsh and his bandmates got into
the studio with production whiz **Bill Szymczyk**
for their second album, they made a drastic change
and began experimenting. They introduced to their
work the piano, organ, orchestrated strings and
even some country-rock pedal steel guitar courtesy of **Poco**'s **Rusty Young**. It was different, but
under Szymczyk's guidance the strange brew worked, and worked well. Experimentation aside,
the band remembered to stay true to its roots. Walsh, **Dale Peters** and **Jim Fox** collaborated on
Funk #49, a song that tells the tale of a girlfriend wild enough to even give the often unruly Walsh
anxiety. It soared to #59 on *Billboard*'s Top Singles chart to give the band a solid hit. *The Bomber* was
the album's long jam, but the decision to include an uncredited Ravel's *Bolero* in the mid-portion
of the song brought legal threats from the composer's estate (and a subsequent scrub of later
pressings). Overall it was a strong, evolutionary effort from Ohio's power trio.

Cashbox
July 18, 1970

And suddenly the **James Gang** is
a group to make you sit up and
take notice. Side 1 is straight
rock cuts with a fine instrument
melody at the end. The quiet,
thoughtful *Ashes the Rain and I*
is a proper culmination of the
set. Excellently arranged strings
combine with tasteful acoustic
guitar to evoke sad images of
rainy days. Deck was imagina-
tively produced by **Bill Szymcyk**
who is fast becoming one of our
best men behind the boards.

Cincinnati Enquirer
August 2, 1970

The **James Gang** plays the
blues – the blues that churn
your adrenaline that gets you
excited. Big names in Cincinnati,
their music is meant to be played
loud. if you do it right, **Bugsley
Peters**' bass can vibrate your
entire life. Joe Walsh's keyboards
and guitars can drown your body
in funk. **Jim Fox**'s drums can
restructure your heartbeat. The
whole album sounds pretty good,
though it may overwhelm you at
first. Try it anyway.

York (Pa.) Daily Record
August 4, 1970

The **James Gang** is not just another rock band. Besides having
the most promising guitarist in
the world, Joe Walsh, they have
grown up a lot too. Side 1 of
Rides Again is reminiscent of **Led
Zeppelin**. Walsh's playing may
even worry Page a bit. He's even
great on piano and organ. *Tend
My Garden* and *There I Go Again*
are my favorites. A steel guitar in
rock music is so strange, but it's
got to be one of the nicest things
around. Give *Funk #49* a listen.

he sat in on the Longbranch/Pennywhistle recording sessions, brought star quality to Weston's event. He felt comfortable crossing over between country and rock. Warner Brothers had just released Kershaw's new album *The Cajun Way* months earlier to strong reviews. He had appeared on **Johnny Cash**'s television variety show, and had logged high-profile guest appearances on albums by **Bob Dylan**, **Arlo Guthrie**, and **Grand Funk Railroad**.

But the night of the grand opening, Kershaw didn't have a backing band, and he chose to prepare a setlist of relentlessly upbeat Cajun and rockabilly songs, the *Chicago Sun-Times* reported. Clearly, it wasn't a great musical fit for Frey and Souther, who were still finding their way instrumentally and whose craft was primarily focused on songwriting and singing.

Souther, comfortable with a guitar, could handle multiple instruments, and even played drums for **Bo Diddley**. Frey was a solid guitarist, and improving. But Weston did not appear to set them up for success that night. The duo marshaled on through the difficult set and "struggled vainly" to keep up as a rhythm section, the *Star-Times* reported. Worse, Kershaw seemed to know they were struggling and "played rather merciless games with them throughout the set."

Weston's San Francisco venture didn't last long, but the Los Angeles Troubadour brand remained untarnished. Kershaw continued to do well with his brand of Cajun, country, and rock, and released 11 albums for Warner through the 1970s. Nearly a year after Amos released their unsuccessful debut album, Souther and Frey wanted to change the formula to ensure better success with their second album, and wanted to release another album of original material. **Jimmy Bowen** and the cash-poor Amos Records had other ideas. There was an impasse brewing, and more frustrations were ahead for Frey and Souther. [1217, 1249]

Azoff, Joe Walsh Meet at Wisconsin's Majestic Hills

In the summer of 1970, rock venues across the Midwest were largely being booked as they had been for the last four years: through the concert machine known as Blytham Limited, and under the watchful eyes of **Bob Nutt** and Irving Azoff.

One of the more popular venues they booked was near Lake Geneva, Wisconsin, at the Majestic Hills Theater. The venue, just 20 minutes outside Chicago, played to upper crust patrons in the 1940s and 1950s, but by the early 1970s, it had become a shell of its former self. It had two side-by-side stages with a huge tree growing between them. It also housed a large metal structure used to store boats in the winter. There were no seats, so concert-goers were forced to stand for the entire show. If there was an opening act, they would set up bands on both stages so no between-show teardown and setup was required.

It was here that Azoff told then-*Rolling Stone* contributing editor **Cameron Crowe** in 1978 that he saw **The Who** perform live at the Majestic. It was either August 1968 or June 1969—Azoff didn't specify—but the show certainly had an impact on him. In August 1970, Azoff was back at Lake Geneva with **REO Speedwagon** when he met Joe Walsh for the first time.

Walsh was there with the **James Gang**, and Azoff decided to share. "I told Walsh, 'You know **Pete Townshend** was here and jumped off that tree. The guy was fuckin' crazy.' Middle of the set that night, Walsh got up in the tree, jumped off, fell down and nearly broke his fuckin' leg. He comes limping over to me afterward and says, 'Anything Pete Townshend can do, I can do.' It was wonderful."

Shows would continue at the Majestic through 1988, when a fire burned the uninsured hall to the ground. It was never rebuilt and became yet another lost rock legend. A year later, both Walsh and Azoff made pivotal moves in their careers. Azoff, looking for new adventures, would head to Los Angeles and meet the Eagles. Walsh dabbled in movies while he and his producer, **Bill Szymczyk**, recorded the soundtrack for an "electric western," but soon after Walsh would leave James Gang and head to Colorado and form a new band, **Barnstorm**. [481, 1323, 1342]

FALL 1970

 RELEASES
- ▶ **Rick Nelson's Stone Canyon Band**, with Randy Meisner, *Rick Nelson Sings* (album)

 COLLABORATIONS
- ▶ **Bernie Leadon** played guitar on **Odetta Sings**'s album *Odetta Sings*.
- ▶ **Joe Walsh** played rhythm guitar on **B.B. King**'s singles, *Ask Me No Questions*, *King's Special* and *Hummingbird* on King's album *Indianola Mississippi Seeds*.

 ON THE ROAD WITH ...
- ▶ **The Flying Burrito Brothers**, with Bernie Leadon: The Byrds, The New York Rock and Roll Ensemble, Albert King, James Gang
- ▶ **Longbranch/Pennywhistle**, with Glenn Frey: Sky
- ▶ **James Gang**, with Joe Walsh: Steppenwolf, The Moody Blues, The Who, Cactus, Love/Arthur Lee, Black Sabbath, Steve Miller Band, The Flying Burrito Brothers, The Youngbloods, Procol Harum, Faces, Van Morrison, Mungo Jerry

Staredown: Longbranch/ Pennywhistle's 2nd Album Nixed

Fresh off the humbling experience of watching their debut album flop, **J.D. Souther** and his **Longbranch/Pennywhistle** partner, Glenn Frey, tried to figure out what to do next in the fall of 1970. They had spent the last year playing across Los Angeles to gain attention for themselves and their album, but their efforts didn't move the needle. **Jimmy Bowen**, owner of Amos Records, who eagerly signed the pair a year earlier, was struggling too. "If our spirits at Amos stayed high throughout the year, our chart positions did not," Bowen said in his autobiography *Rough Mix*. "Neither Longbranch/Pennywhistle, nor **Shiloh** [another band Amos signed that included future Eagle Don Henley] got much airplay for Amos Records,"

Amos gave the duo freedom in the studio to create a debut album the way they saw fit, and gave them enviable studio support too. Bowen, who had resurrected the careers of **Frank Sinatra** and **Dean Martin**, and his producer, **Tom Thacker**, brought in seasoned hired guns to work the Longbranch/Penny-whistle sessions, including **James Burton**, **Ry Cooder**, **Doug Kershaw**, **Buddy Emmons**, and two members of the **Wrecking Crew**, **Larry Knechtel** and **Joe Osbourn**.

It was a hall of fame session team. But in the plodding months after its release, the duo's debut album fizzled. Frey and Souther had been getting close to **David Briggs**, the engineer who produced **Neil Young**'s debut album, *Everyone Knows This Is Nowhere*. The two visited Briggs' studio and played the original works for their planned second album, and he put his spin on them. Souther told **Debbie Kruger** in 1997 that the mix of songs was "really funky and it just wasn't sonically rounded off the way pop records were." It sounded more like Neil Young's album, and he and Frey liked that.

So, when it came time to record the second album, Souther and Frey took the record-ings from the Briggs' session to Amos Re-cords and played them. Bowen and Thacker shrugged. They didn't get it.

"Which is not to say that we were brilliant and they were stupid," Souther said. "It's just that they just didn't hear it." Bowen had nev-er heard of Briggs, had only a vague knowl-edge of Neil Young, and he had never heard of Young's partners in music, **Crazy Horse**. Bowen suggested they try recording other artists' songs, and that idea fell flat.

"It wasn't really their world," Souther said. "They were still trying to encourage us to re-cord songs that were well known. The fact is, we weren't writing spectacular songs—we were just starting—but I wasn't about to do anybody else's songs. I thought I was doing something unique. And my job, at whatever stumbling pace, was to embrace that artistry, not look for a way to get on the charts."

Frey recounted the impasse during a 1975 interview with *Rolling Stone*'s **Cameron Crowe**: "Then one day J.D. and I got in a fight with our record company and sudden-ly we couldn't make any more records," he said. "Every day we'd go to the office, ask if we could get released from our contracts and they'd say no, so we'd go down to the Troubadour bar and get drunk."

The true end to the Amos fiasco would only come after Frey met **David Geffen**, who saw both Frey's and Souther's poten-tial clearly. Geffen and his upstart label, Asylum Records, had the money and sav-vy to elevate both artists to heights even they had not foreseen. After the Eagles had formed in late 1971 and Souther was on his way to a solo career, Geffen reclaimed the Longbranch/Pennywhistle publishing rights from Bowen and the by-then-defunct Amos Records. [88, 790, 1217, 1247, 1363]

Nelson Lures Meisner Back To the Studio for *Rudy the Fifth*

Rick Nelson understood when Randy Meisner decided to quit his **Stone Canyon Band** in the spring of 1970. The touring and the poor reception they received in Germany and Spain, coupled with being away from his family for so long had worn Meisner down.

But Nelson also wanted Meisner's crystal high vocals in his music. When Meisner left Los Angeles for Scottsbluff, Nebraska, Nelson replaced him **Tim Cetera** (brother of **Chicago** singer **Peter Cetera**), who was a capable bassist, but could not match Meisner's vocal prowess. Nelson had recorded his next album, *Rick Sings Nelson*, without Meisner, and it was a solid, yet unremarkable effort. Nelson, who would be inducted into the Rock and Roll Hall of Fame in 1987, let it be known that there was a position open for Meisner if he wanted it.

Before Meisner mulled that return, he briefly flirted with starting another band to give him a steady source of income. But the band, **Goldrush**, ended nearly as quickly as it began. Soon after, **Allen Kemp**, who joined Nelson's band along with Meisner from the **Soul Survivors** and **The Poor**, called Meisner and told him the job was open again. Working for a friend at the John Deere dealership in Scottsbluff by day and playing in local bars by night didn't match the excitement of the music world in Los Angeles, so Meisner agreed to return. "One day I just thought, hell what am I doing playing rock 'n roll in Scotts Bluff, Nebraska?"

Meisner brought his steady bass playing and high vocals back to the Stone Canyon Band, and Nelson's next album, *Rudy the Fifth*, got decent reviews. Rock critics consider it a disappointingly overlooked album, and it had some importance to the overall ascendance of the country-rock movement that Nelson helped develop. Meisner played bass on all tracks except *Life*, and his high backing vocals shone on cuts like *Sing Me a Song* and the fine, unappreciated rocker *Gypsy Pilot*. The album had a more inspirational meaning for Nelson.

"That was when my dad had given up all attachments to the outcome," said Nelson's son, **Gunnar Nelson**, in 2014. "He had banished the critic that we all have sitting on our shoulder and just allowed himself to be completely, boldly creative, and I can hear the freedom in those grooves."

A free as the album made Nelson feel, it was less so for Meisner. He and Nelson remained friends, and Meisner helped him with other projects in the years ahead, but he felt like a hired gun in the Stone Canyon Band. Then one day in the spring of 1971 in San Jose, with Nelson scheduled on the same bill with **Linda Ronstadt**, Meisner found himself performing with Ronstadt's backing band, who included Glenn Frey and Don Henley. "This sounds pretty good, we ought to get a group together," Meisner recounted to *Westword* in 1995. "And Glenn kind of said, 'Yeah, we should.'" Months later, that suggestion took on a life of its own. [67, 781, 1379, 1380, 1381]

Ronstadt, Boylan Recruit Frey, Henley for Summer Tour

Linda Ronstadt was spreading her wings musically when she released her *Silk Purse* album in the spring of 1970. Her earlier work with the **Stoney Poneys** and her debut album, *Hand Sown ... Home Grown*, was more folk- and pop-oriented. With *Silk Purse*, the songs she chose were more country than folk—a trend others, including the Eagles, would capitalize on in the next five to six years. She convinced Capitol Records to let her include **Gary White**'s *Long, Long Time* and it paid off handsomely, with her first solo Top 25 record and a Grammy nomination.

Buoyed by the album's strong reception, she prepared for a tour to support it. Ronstadt said it was hard to find musicians in Los Angeles in the early 1970s. "First of all, nobody had any money in those days, so we couldn't pay them a lot," she told *Goldmine* in 2014. "Because of that, you couldn't hire those really good studio players to go on the road with you." She added that sometimes the best session players weren't necessarily appropriate to her music. "A guy like **Ricky Nelson** or **Elvis Presley** could afford to hire **James Burton**," she said. "I couldn't afford to hire someone like that. So I was always looking for a drummer that wouldn't just roll over me, that wouldn't just play right on through the feeling and dynamics."

She and her manager, **John Boylan**, had a vision of pulling together a supergroup of the best country-rock musicians available. They began assembling a backing band for the tour that included bass player **Casey Van Beek** and pedal steel guitarist **Kenny Bloom**. Ronstadt wanted Bernie Leadon to back her up, as he had done occasionally in the two years prior, but Leadon had already joined the **Flying Burrito Brothers** and couldn't go on the road. She was aware of Glenn Frey from his performances at the Troubadour with her current boyfriend, **J.D. Souther**, so she decided to ask him. Boylan offered Frey $250 a week to back Ronstadt.

"It was like, if I can't get Bernie, let me ask Glenn," Ronstadt said. "I didn't think Glenn was necessarily the right guy, but I knew he would make it more rock and roll. I liked his playing, and I thought he would be good, but he wouldn't be the same as Bernie, because he didn't know how to play all those bendy licks, and he didn't need to learn them, as it turned out." As she suspected, Frey was a great fit in her backing band and Ronstadt even gave him the stage during the tour to perform some solo numbers. But before they could hit the road, they needed a drummer. Boylan continued his search, but Frey already had ideas about how to fill a void.

"It was two days before rehearsal was supposed to start and [Linda's band] still hadn't found a drummer," Frey said. "And here was Henley, just standing right in the Troubadour. So, I struck up a conversation with him. I told him my whole trip was just stalled. I had all these songs and couldn't make a record and I wanted to put together a band, but I was going on the road with Linda. Henley said that he was fucked up

PATHWAY ALBUM | TIMOTHY B. SCHMIT

POCO
Deliverin'
Epic Records, January 1971

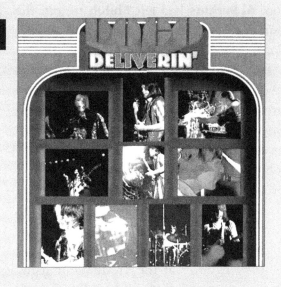

Richie Furay had been looking for a way to break **Poco** into the mainstream for three years. The band's strength was always in its tight live performances, so with its third album they decided to play to that strength. Nearly all the songs were new and original, save for **Jim Messina**'s *You Better Think Twice*. The group recorded the album in the Boston Music Hall and New York's Felt Forum.

Future Eagle Timothy B. Schmit's cuts *Hear That Music* and *Hard Luck* were strong contributions, and Furay's own *I Guess You Made It* and *C'Mon* helped round out a strong third album. *C'Mon* was just commercial enough to get airplay, rising all the way to #69 on *Billboard*'s Hot 100 singles chart. *Deliverin'* did just that for Epic Records, which had been patiently waiting for Poco to become commercially viable. The album was a success rising to #26 on the *Billboard* albums chart. It was the last Poco album for Messina, who would join ABC Records staff songwriter **Kenny Loggins** to form **Loggins & Messina** later in 1971.

Moline (Ill.) Dispatch
February 6, 1971

Poco fans will be delighted to hear that *Deliverin'*, on Epic, is out – and it's live. Poco, the goodtime cheery country-rock group, is here with lovely vocals, fantastic instrumental ability and five brand new hits. *I Guess You Made It* and *C'Mon* are all-new **Richie Furay** tunes. Tim Schmit is working out fine on bass and he's come up with *Hear That Music* and *Hard Luck*. *Kind Woman* is a Furay-penned pleasant surprise from the Buffalo Springfield era.

San Bernardino Sun
March 30, 1971

A sound and style all its own keeps **Poco** going. Made up of some more **Buffalo Springfield** alumni, Poco's happy country and western musical sound is combined here again with the usual fine harmonic vocals. The album was recorded at the Boston Music Hall and the Felt Forum in New York. *I Guess You Made It* nicely establishes the groups's style. *C'Mon* is also a fine cut with great rhythms.

The Ottawa Citizen
May 14, 1971

Poco live must be something. Even for a live LP (most of which are poor representations) *Deliverin'* comes full of life. It starts with some beautiful vocal harmony on a rocking electric number, *I Guess You Made It*. The album goes through a couple of lively country electric numbers and then into *Kind Woman*, a slow ballad written by **Richie Furay**. **Rusty Young**'s artistic steel guitar moves in intricate patterns.

too. **Al Perkins** had left **Shiloh** to join the Burritos and ... we were both at impasses. So, he joined Linda's group too."

The reasoning for recruiting Henley was two-pronged. Although Frey famously approached him in the Troubadour, Henley, Boylan, and Ronstadt were already well aware of each other. Henley had sent Shiloh's debut album to Boylan in the weeks prior and hoped that he might recommend the songs to Ronstadt to record. Boylan and Ronstadt also fondly remembered watching Shiloh perform her *Silver Threads and Golden Needles* at the Troubadour using the exact arrangement she used on her album version. Boylan auditioned Henley in Ronstadt's house in Laurel Canyon.

With the tour start date bearing down on them, Boylan made the same $250 per week offer to Henley that he had made with Frey. He accepted. And because the tour budget was tight, Frey and Henley ended up sharing hotel rooms as they traveled. "The first night of our tour, we decided to start a band," Frey said.

Ronstadt enjoyed a successful tour, but after the fall gigs ended, she still had a handful of shows to do, and the fall backup band would become scattered. Once again, Boylan would need to start looking for help. Two musicians he would choose would become the other half of the Eagles. [88, 340, 534, 790, 1156, 1186]

WINTER 1970-71

 RELEASES
- ▶ **Poco**, with Timothy B. Schmit, *Cmon'* (single)
- ▶ **Poco**, with Timothy B. Schmit, *Devliverin'* (album)

 COLLABORATIONS
- ▶ **Bernie Leadon** was a "musician" on **Bob Gibson**'s album *Bob Gibson*.
- ▶ **Bernie Leadon** was a "performer" on **Paul Seibel**'s album *Jack-Knife Gypsy*.

 ON THE ROAD WITH ...
- ▶ **The Flying Burrito Brothers**, with Bernie Leadon: Fanny, Longbranch/Pennywhistle, Poco
- ▶ **Linda Ronstadt**, with Glenn Frey and Don Henley: Quicksilver Messenger Service
- ▶ **Longbranch/Pennywhistle**, with Glenn Frey: The Flying Burrito Brothers
- ▶ **James Gang**, with Joe Walsh: The Byrds, Ten Years After, Cactus, Sha Na Na, Rare Earth, Chilliwack, Johnny Winter, Poco, Simon Craine
- ▶ **Poco**, with Timothy B. Schmit: Jo Mama, Savoy Brown, Gypsy, Don McLean, Bart Sommer, The Byrds

SPRING 1971

 RELEASES
- ▶ **James Gang**, with Joe Walsh, *Walk Away* (single)
- ▶ **Flow**, with Don Felder, *Mr. Invisible* (single)
- ▶ **James Gang**, with Joe Walsh, *Thirds* (album)

PATHWAY ALBUM | DON HENLEY

SHILOH
Shiloh
Amos Records, March 1970

Tragedy befell the East Texas band **Shiloh** before its debut album was ever pressed. **Jerry Surratt**, one of the band's leaders and a gifted songwriter, died in an automobile accident just before they were scheduled to record their debut album. After a period of mourning, the band, led by **Richard Bowden** and Don Henley, went to Los Angeles to record the album with Amos Records. It was an imperfect, but solid first effort. The best single wasn't an original, but **Michael McGinnis**'s *Simple Little Down Home Rock & Roll Love Song For Rosie* was catchy and Amos exec **Jimmy Bowen** made it the first single. It got scant airplay, which was predictable given the anemic marketing effort that was made. But the album had moments that showed real promise. Henley's *Same Old Story* was well-crafted ballad that should have easily found a home on country radio. Bowden's *I'm Gone* had an infectious Allman Brothers feel, **Al Perkins**' arrangement of the *Railroad Song* turned the traditional song into a fun-time thumper, and **Jim Ed Norman**, who would arrange music for the Eagles, wrote and arranged *Du Raison*, a dramatic instrumental that allowed Perkins and Bowden to show off. But the promise was never realized. Shiloh was still green at songwriting, and their label couldn't propel them to the next level.

Cashbox
August 15, 1970

NOTE - Amos Records distributed the single 'Jennifer' prior to the death of Jerry Surratt. Neither it nor its flipside made it onto the final cut of Shiloh's debut album.

Jennifer (O' My Lady) - A finely styled ballad side that is brought vividly into teen focus by a startling vocal. Could gain AM & FM exposure as a lead to chart status.

Record World
July 25, 1970

NOTE - Amos Records distributed the single 'Jennifer' prior to the death of Jerry Surratt. Neither it nor its flipside made it onto the final cut of Shiloh's debut album.

Jennifer (O' My Lady) - New group with a soft almost Beatle-like approach will have an impact. **Kenny Rogers** produced. Four stars.

Billboard
July 3, 1971

Kenny Rogers of the **First Edition** turns producer with a strong new group, four from Texas and one from the Florida area, with a heavy folk-rock sound. Best cuts for Top 40 include, *Simple Little Down Home Rock and Roll Love Song for Rosie*, and their own material, *Same Old Story*, and *I'm Gone*. Smooth group offers lots of chart potential.

ON THE ROAD WITH ...
▶ **Linda Ronstadt**, with Glenn Frey and Don Henley: Poco, Kenny Rogers, The Beach Boys, Charles Mingus, Elephant's Memory, Mitch Ryder, Mother Earth, NRBQ, Phil Ochs
▶ **James Gang**, with Joe Walsh: Emerson, Lake & Palmer, Steel River
▶ **Poco**, with Timothy B. Schmit: Linda Ronstadt, The Seigel-Schwall Band, Wishbone Ash, The Ides of March, Boz Scaggs, Gordon Lightfoot, Laura Nyro, Sha Na Na, Emerson, Lake & Palmer, John Mayall, Elliott Randall

Amos Records Releases Shiloh's Debut Album

When Don Henley, **Richard Bowden**, and the rest of their band, **Shiloh**, finally made their way into Quantum Studios in Torrance, California, to record their debut album, their producer, **Kenny Rogers**, was expecting great things. The band had original songs, they were well rehearsed, and they hoped that their strong live shows would translate in the studio. They had already been to Los Angeles once, recorded their first single, and wowed the Troubadour club in West Hollywood with a rousing performance.

"On Hoot Night at the Troubadour they had a cattle call to get up and play," Shiloh's bass player, **Mike Bowden**, said. "Maybe 15 or 20 acts would get up and see what the crowd reaction was. We went over really well. One of the songs we did was a cover of **Linda Ronstadt**'s *Silver Threads and Golden Needles*. Linda happened to be there. She really liked us and liked Henley because

he had a strong voice." After their performance, Ronstadt's manager, John Boylan, offered a contract on the spot. But the band was ensconced with their producer, Rogers, and they had a solid promise for an album from Amos Records, so they declined.

Amos pressed their first single, *Jennifer (O' My Lady)*, in January 1970, and had already started marketing it in the music trade magazines. But tragedy would derail the single. **Jerry Surratt**, one of the band's founding members, was killed suddenly in a car accident. They knew replacing his talent and spirit would be tough. The band had already managed a few changes since it formed in 1963. **Joey Brown** replaced original guitarist **Fred Neese** in 1965. And when Brown left in 1969, Bowden moved over from bass to lead guitar and his cousin, Mike, joined as the band's new bass player. With Surratt's passing, another change was at hand. **Jim Ed Norman**, a college buddy of Henley's, picked up the keyboard duties. Another Rogers discovery, **Al Perkins**, who was an award-winning steel pedal guitar player, joined to give the band a country twang they didn't have before. They continued rehearsing and fine tuning their original songs in Texas while waiting for Rogers's call to record their album.

They liked their material and had doggedly rehearsed three nights a week in a vacant Linden church that they rented for $25 a month. Henley wrote three of the album's tracks including *I'm Gone*, *Same Old Story*, and *God Is Where You Find Him*. Bowden chipped in with two country songs, *It's*

THE JAMES GANG
Thirds
ABC Records, April 1971

By the summer of 1971 the **James Gang** was nearing the end of its race. After completing a successful tour with **The Who** in Europe and fresh off filming a campy segment in the schlocky Western *Zacharia*, the band settled in with producer **Bill Szymczyck** to produce their third album, appropriately titled *Thirds*. The band continued experimenting musically, and but, perhaps, tried too hard. *White Man/Black Man* was a noble attempt the bridge the racial divide – they brought in **The Sweet Inspirations** (including **Whitney Houston**'s mother, **Cissy Houston**) for backing vocals – but it came across as hollow and over-produced. Walsh still brought the goods with *Walk Away*, which became a staple for the relentlessly touring James Gang, rose to #29 on Cashbox's singles chart. *Midnight Man* crept up to #80 on *Billboard*'s singles chart, but the promise that the group seemed to hold coming off their second album faded. Frontman Walsh had begun to outgrow the band and complained of studio "wonderfulness" and overdubs that were increasingly difficult to reproduce on stage. It would be his last studio album with the band.

Boston Globe
June 11, 1971

The **James Gang** combines mass appeal with musical excellence. The album's nine original cuts provide a mixed bag range from mellow to instrumental. The standout is *White Man/Black Man*, where vocalist-bassist **Dale Peters** lays down a plaintive blues line and explodes into a piercing guitar solo by Joe Walsh, while the **Sweet Inspirations** chant hauntingly ad infinitum. The James Gang is for everyone, *Yadig?*

Hackensack Record
June 13, 1971

James Gang doesn't come on like a blockbuster, but this crew is easy to live with. Composed of keyboards, guitars, drums and vibes, the album gets good backing from **Tom Baker**'s horn section on *White Man/Black Man*. The cuts run from thoughtful (*Things I Could Be*) to lively (*Midnight Man*, *Walk Away*). It hits you slowly, but their unwillingness to clobber you the first time around makes this one of the better understated albums of the season.

Carlisle (Pa.) Sentinel
June 19, 1971

The multi-faceted sounds of the **James Gang** roll out beautifully on their new album, *Thirds*. It opens with the hard, but tender *Walk Away*, which is destined for hit status. It has one of the finest recorded vibe sets in the cerebral *Yadig?* And then there's, unbelievably, the country funky tune *Dreamin' In the Country*. It staggers the imagination that a group can be hard rock, then jazz, then country with such equal excellence.

The Flying Burrito Brothers interview after a show in Amsterdam, Netherlands in 1971. (from left to right, Sneaky Pete Kleinlow, Rick Roberts, Chris Hillman, Michael Clarke and Bernie Leadon)

ROBERTS JOINS BURRITO BROTHERS; LEADON EYES HIS EXIT

SPRING 1971 – It was a tumultuous year for **Chris Hillman** and his band, the **Flying Burrito Brothers**. The band's second album was a commercial flop, and he was forced to oust his enigmatic frontman, **Gram Parsons**. There were positives in that time. The steady, workmanlike demeanor of **Bernie Leadon** brought a level of maturity to the band, and his guitar and banjo picking talents were unquestionable. But the Burritos still found themselves at a pivotal crossroads. With two commercially unsuccessful albums completed and work yet to start their third LP, Hillman wanted to change the formula.

The Burritos first album, *The Gilded Palace of Sin*, was a critic favorite and is often seen as a signature album in the country-rock movement in the late 1960s and early 1970s. Some found it a natural progression from Hillman and Parsons's last album with **The Byrds**, *Sweetheart of the Rodeo*. Lauded as it was, *Gilded* failed to find a wider audience. With their second album, *Burrito Deluxe*, the group brought an edgier country-rock sound with excellent execution, but the songs were subpar and, again, they couldn't get played regularly on AM radio. It was the same problem. They were too rock for country, and too country for rock. With Parsons gone, Hillman and the rest of the group considered breaking up, but opted to try again.

Hillman and the Burritos manager, **Ed Tickner**, were scouting for a new lead singer. Hillman wanted someone who would complement the Burrito's style and could write songs. Tickner found **Rick Roberts**, just 20 years old and a fresh face in Los Angeles, searching for session work at Columbia Records. Hillman was interested because he could play rhythm guitar well and could sing harmony. Moreover, he brought with him more than 25 songs canned and ready. Hillman invited him, and a change in the Burritos' style was clear immediately. Roberts didn't come from a traditional country or bluegrass background, but his songwriting path lent itself more toward pop-oriented country rock than the Burritos had ever played. Indeed, after he left the Burritos in 1974, Roberts went on to form **Firefall** and cut softer, radio-friendly hits like *You Are the Woman* and *Just Remember I Love You*.

The Burritos cut their eponymous third album, *The Flying Burrito Brothers*, in 1971 to strong critical reviews. The LP came to be known simply as the "blue album" to the band and their fans. Roberts' contributions were instantly impactful. He wrote seven of the 10 songs on the LP, with Hillman earning writing credits on three. The band also cut **Merle Haggard**'s *White Line Fever* and **Bob Dylan**'s *To Ramona*.

But all was not well with the Burritos. Hillman pushed for more commercial appeal, and his decision to reduce the steel guitar sound was partly responsible for **Sneaky Pete Kleinlow** leaving the band. Meanwhile, Hillman was having drug- and alcohol-related issues with drummer **Michael Clarke**, and even considered replacing him, Hillman told **John Einarson** in his book *Hot Burritos: The True Story of the Flying Burrito Brothers*.

"At one point when Michael Clarke was acting up we considered approaching Don Henley," Hillman said, "because Don had worked with [current Burrito] **Al Perkins** in **Shiloh** and Don was out of work at the time. We could have probably gotten him, too. But I don't think he would have stayed that long."

> At one point when Michael Clarke was acting up we considered approaching Don Henley, because Don had worked with Al Perkins in Shiloh and Don was out of work at the time. We could have probably gotten him, too. But I don't think he would have stayed that long.
>
> *— Chris Hillman, leader of the Flying Burrito Brothers*

The changes that Hillman was orchestrating, particularly the arrival of Roberts, was a sign for Leadon, who did not earn a writing credit on the blue album. Roberts brought more of a softer rock vibe to the group, which he would amplify in later Burritos albums. "But soft-rock was certainly not where I wanted to go," Leadon said. "The writing was on the wall for me when Rick showed up."

Leadon left the Burritos after their third album and found himself back in the familiar orbit of **Linda Ronstadt**. Her manager, **John Boylan**, was looking for musicians to back her up on an upcoming summer tour. Now available, he was a natural choice since he had already played alongside her in-between **Hearts and Flowers** and the Burritos. Boylan would soon reach out to Leadon for the job, and he would also soon add two promising young musicians to back her up: Glenn Frey and Don Henley. [739, 1375]

About Time and *Down on the Farm*. Norman added *Swamp River Country* and *Du Raison*, which included string work that he arranged and credited to the "Linden Philharmonic Orchestra" in a cheeky nod to Henley and Bowden's hometown.

Perkins put a funky new spin on the old traditional *Railroad Song*. The track with the most potential wasn't actually written by the band. *Simple Little Down Home Rock & Roll Love Song for Rosie* was written by **Michael McGinnis** and was the second single released by Shiloh. Their first single, *Jennifer*, which was co-written by Henley and Surratt, was left off the LP.

Even if the first single didn't sell, the band still had reason for optimism. Henley's *I'm Gone* had a southern rock vibe even though it didn't quite exist yet, that was magnified with Perkins' steel pedal licks and Mike Bowden's subtle, thumping bass. Henley showed his ability to shift gears by crafting a traditional country song, *Same Old Story*, that had vocal intonations that became his signature in later Eagles compositions. The song was genuine country and could have easily turned up on a traditional country AM radio. Richard Bowden's *Down on the Farm* was a frolicking, sod-busting, day-in-the-life piece that wasn't selected for release, but was undoubtedly true to the whimsical country direction that he followed later in his career, including his tongue-in-cheek work with **Pinkard & Bowden**.

Rogers and the band hoped for a strong marketing push from Amos that would get them radio airtime. But there were prob-lems bubbling up they couldn't see. Amos's owner, **Jimmy Bowen**, was in a bad position after he started Amos's expansion into his into pricey recording technology ventures. He had also become the distributor for other small labels, including **Lee Hazlewood**'s new LHI label. His eagerness to expand Amos had created a catch-22. They clearly could find talent, but the company was stretched so thin that if any of its acts had an even a modest hit, it lacked the capital needed to ensure its success. Bowen's eagerness to expand his business had ensured its failure.

But Rogers still had faith, and in the summer of 1971, he would use his influence to get Shiloh into the spotlight once more, **Dick Clark** style. [6, 26, 343, 1145, 1365, 1366]

Browne Leads: Geffen Signs Souther, Gives Frey a Mission

David Geffen knew he had something special when he signed singer-songwriter **Jackson Browne**. He and his partner, **Elliot Roberts**, had a small stable of stars that could write and sing their own songs, and they began to look for more that fit that bill. The divining rod that usually led them to those artists was Browne. **Doug Weston**'s Troubadour club in West Hollywood was a friendly place for Browne, who played there frequently on "Hoot Night" Mondays. He had opened there for **Linda Ronstadt** and had the tutelage of many performers there, including **Larry Murray**, co-owner of the Blue Guitar shop and a co-founder of the country-rock group **Hearts and Flowers**.

THE FLYING BURRITO BROTHERS
The Flying Burrito Brothers
A&M Records, June 1971

Shortly after the **Flying Burrito Brothers**' second album, *Burrito Deluxe*, rolled out band leader **Chris Hillman** fired the band's enigmatic frontman **Gram Parsons**. In his place, he invited a talented, but inexperienced **Rick Roberts** to join, and he brought a more commercial musical style. Roberts, who later became the frontman for **Firefall** was author to songs like *Strange Way* and *You Are the Woman*, wrote his well-received song *Colorado* for the band's new self-titled album, which became known simply as the "blue album." Hillman wanted a more mainstream sound, but that change would come with a price. **Sneaky Pete Kleinlow** was the first to leave, disgruntled over the album's sparse use of pedal steel guitar. Bernie Leadon felt pinched by Roberts' presence too; he didn't write any songs for the LP, though he did earn banjo, and lead electric and acoustic guitar credits. Hillman and Roberts dominated the album, writing or co-writing seven of the 10 songs. The country-rock sound was there, but the country vibe was gone. Only **Merle Haggard**'s *White Line Fever* was a true country song. The LP never cracked the *Billboard* charts. And Bernie Leadon? He found Glenn Frey and Don Henley shortly after a fortuitous visit to McCabe's Guitar Shop, and his decision to leave was proven sound.

Cashbox
May 22, 1971

The Burritos keep turning out one great album after another, and sooner or later, the people will pick up on them. Blending country music with their soft melodic style, they have come up with their best album yet. It includes **Merle Haggard**'s *White Line Fever* and **Dylan**'s *Ramona*. Pick it up. You might find you like the group after all.

Philadelphia Daily News
May 28, 1971

Perhaps this is the **Flying Burrito Brothers**' best record yet overall. Mostly they sing us a sad song in a low-key way, but the band has tightened up on records and they sound good. The Burritos play some solid country-flavored rock, though a big audience has yet to appear.
– Rich Aregood

Moline (Ill.) Dispatch
June 19, 1971

The Burritos have their third album out on A&M and it's a beauty from beginning to end. **Rick Roberts** has replaced **Gram Parsons** and fits in well with the rest. They do a good job on **Merle Haggard**'s *White Line Fever* and **Gene Clark**'s *Tried So Hard*. Roberts wrote *Colorado* and it's fantastic. Get this one. It's great.
– Dink Lorance

EAGLES: BEFORE THE BAND

who had also been a fellow Capitol Records recording artist. He also got to know many of the regular patrons and performers at the club, and he had a particularly discriminating eye for talent.

Browne had a discerning eye for talent, and Geffen soon came to depend on those skills. One day in the spring of 1971, Browne began talking up **J.D. Souther**, a Detroit-born, Amarillo, Texas-raised singer-songwriter who, along with his band partner Glenn Frey, lived in the same Echo Park apartment complex as Browne. Both Souther and Frey, a duo known as Longbranch/Pennywhistle, were biding time waiting to either record an album of new material or to be released from their Amos Records recording contract. Geffen met Souther and, encouraged by what he

heard, signed him to a solo contract.

But Browne wasn't done. He also recommended **Ned Doheny**, another artist who had become part of a posse of singers he had bonded with. Geffen signed him too. Finally, Browne introduced Geffen to Frey. While it was clear Souther would be comfortable as a solo artist, Geffen thought Frey would be better off as part of a group. "**David Crosby** is in a band," Geffen told Frey. "You should be in a band." Frey was initially disappointed by the assessment, but would soon take those words as a mission. He had already had some initial discussions with Ronstadt's manager, **John Boylan**, about playing in her summer tour. She was also looking for a drummer, and Frey already had someone in mind. [1, 6, 247, 790, 1217]

MEET THE EAGLES

All four original Eagles arrived in David Geffen's Asylum Records office in the Spring of 1971 eager and looking for a chance. They got it. They hoped they might make a couple albums, but fate had bigger plans for them.

SUMMER 1971

 RELEASES
▶ **The Flying Burrito Brothers**, with Bernie Leadon, *The Flying Burrito Brothers* (album)
▶ **The Flying Burrito Brothers**, with Bernie Leadon, *White Line Fever* (single)
▶ **James Gang**, with Joe Walsh, *Midnight Man* (single)

 COLLABORATIONS
▶ **Bernie Leadon** played guitar on **Russ Giguere**'s album *Hexagram 16*.

 ON SCREEN
▶ **Shiloh**, with Don Henley, appeared on the ABC TV show *American Bandstand*, Episode #14.42. **Kenny Rogers** headlined the show. Shiloh appeared twice, and played *Down on the Farm* and *Simple Little Down Home Rock and Roll Love Song for Rosie*.

 ON THE ROAD WITH …
▶ **Linda Ronstadt**, with Glenn Frey and Don Henley: Steve Martin
▶ **James Gang**, with Joe Walsh: Edgar Winter's White Trash, Steel River, Rory Gallagher
▶ **Poco**, with Timothy B. Schmit: Gunhill Road, Jerry Riopelle, The Allman Brothers Band, It's a Beautiful Day, Little Richard, Long John Baldry, Redeye, Joy of Cooking

Rogers Brings Shiloh, Henley Along to American Bandstand

Three months after the release of **Shiloh**'s debut album, the group hadn't gotten the attention they hoped for. The first single released off their new album, *Simple Little Down Home Rock and Roll Love Song for Rosie*, wasn't getting played on the radio.

The band's producer, **Kenny Rogers**, had discovered them at a boutique clothes store in Dallas, and was, himself, becoming an emerging crossover star in country and pop music. Rogers was scheduled to make a return appearance on ABC's *American Bandstand* with **Dick Clark** in June.

Shiloh needed a boost, and since Rogers was making an appearance on the nationally syndicated program, his friend Clark slotted the band in as the episode's second act. Shiloh's label, Amos Records, prepped the band for television by booking an appearance for them on *Box City*, a lesser-known West Coast knockoff of Bandstand, and then readied the group for the show on June 16, 1971. Back in Texas, the *Marshall News Messenger* trumpeted the group's upcoming appearance and barely mentioned Rogers' headliner status. Rogers opened with *For the Good Times*, a cover of **Kris Kristofferson**'s recent hit. Shiloh then played two songs off their album, *Down on the Farm* with music and lyrics by **Richard Bowden** and … *Love Song for Rosie* with vocals by Don Henley.

The contrast in songs played on the show were indicative of where below-the-surface differences existed in the group. Bowden's *Down on the Farm* was pure country and might have been a tough sell to Bandstand viewers and nationwide rock and pop record buyers. *Love Song for Rosie* was more mainstream and more in line with the rock music Henley wanted to record. If the band had found success, they may have found a way to bridge the gap in musical direction, but the absence of album sales—and the inability of their label to properly market them—only made the differences more glaring.

Soon after their national television appearance, they began meandering. Amos Records began shutting down its operations by the fall of 1971. Perkins left to join another country-rock band, **The Flying Burrito Brothers**, and the remaining pieces of Shiloh stayed in Los Angeles and looked for places where they could exercise their musical talents. Henley had made the Troubadour bar his personal haunting ground. It was in that dark bar that he soon met his future songwriting partner, Glenn Frey. [27, 1369]

Ronstadt Adds Meisner, Leadon; Disneyland Band is All Eagles

Linda Ronstadt started her road show as planned in the fall of 1970 with a gig at the Cellar Door in Washington, D.C. Her backing band that night included bass player **Casey Van Beek**, pedal steel guitarist **Kenny Bloom**, and Glenn Frey and Don Henley on rhythm guitar and drums, respectively. The tour lasted through the end of the year and when it ended, the band scattered. But Ronstadt still had a handful of shows and needed a backing band. Frey and Henley were still in Los Angeles and were agreeable, so Ronstadt's manager, **John Boylan**, only needed to find a lead guitar player and a bassist.

Boylan was also the manager for **Rick Nelson** at that time, and he knew when Randy Meisner quit **Poco**. Meisner had great bona fides as a bass player and an added dimension of having a high vocal range that made him even more valuable. Boylan jumped at the opportunity to place him with Nelson. Now Ronstadt needed a bass player to fill in for some gigs, so Boylan reached out to Meisner again. He was already familiar with Frey and Henley after Ronstadt and Nelson were co-booked for some dates. Meisner and Frey even joked about forming a band earlier. Both Henley and Frey were happy Boylan was able to land Meisner, who had impressive experience with Nelson and Poco.

With Meisner signed on, that left just a lead guitar player position to fill for Boylan. Ronstadt knew who to pursue. Bernie Leadon was well acquainted with her music and style and had impressive skills and versatility. He had backed her with his band, the **Corvettes**, on and off over the previous two years, so he would be a natural fit. The grapevine had informed Boylan that he was unhappy with the **Flying Burrito Brothers** and was available. While Boylan had an eye on him, Leadon was casting an eye toward them as well.

Leadon had learned that Boylan was putting together a new band with Frey and Henley. He knew of Frey from **Longbranch/ Pennywhistle**'s sets at the Troubadour, and he had heard good things about Henley from the Burritos' **Al Perkins**, who was a bandmate with Henley in Shiloh. Leadon took the initiative and called Boylan and told him he was interested in joining. Boylan said, "Great, I'll talk to the guys." By then, Meisner had already joined and Boylan set up an audition at SIR (Studio Instrument Rentals) on Sunset Boulevard.

"I remember the day I went down to that audition because the **Jackson Five** were rehearsing in the next room," Leadon said. "We saw all their wardrobe cases in the hallway. The four of us basically just played songs together and liked each other so we made a commitment that day."

With the band assembled the group gathered at Disneyland on a stage near what was then Tomorrowland, right next to Space Mountain. "We played a grad night gig at Disneyland in 1971, we had to do four shows a night," Ronstadt said. "You'd play a 20-minute set, then be off for three or four hours, then play another 20 minutes—there was a lot of time to kill between sets." The group killed time between sets playing poker with **Smokey Robinson**, who was also booked there that day.

Over the course of that afternoon and the week that followed, the group congealed. They liked each other, appreciated that they had four musicians who were also all singers and songwriters, and believed they could be band of their own. Within two weeks, they would be thanking Ronstadt for the opportunity and visiting **David Geffen** in search of a recording contract. Boylan hoped he might manage them, but Geffen would have other ideas. In the meantime, they got together and jammed for about a week and built up the courage to visit Asylum Records. [79, 88, 231, 236, 739]

Sanctuary: Geffen, Roberts Form Asylum Records

Fresh off forming Geffen-Roberts Management and quitting Creative Management Associates, **David Geffen** set to work in creating his next project, forming a new record label. **Ahmet Ertegun**, the president of Atlantic Records, set him on the path by agreeing to handle distribution and manufacturing for the new organization. Geffen and his partner, **Elliot Roberts**, decided they would continue to manage artists, but they would keep that side of the business separate from the new label. Roberts would handle the management side of the partnership, and Geffen would lead the label.

They named the new label Asylum Records. Geffen believed that the Laurel Canyon enclave where many of his artists resided was a bit of an "insane asylum." But he also wanted it to be a safe harbor for these performers, whom he genuinely felt needed a safe place to create and grow. "Asylum" would be both. At first they agreed to terms with artists with no contracts, a handshake practice that made artists feel empowered. The label became popular fast. "**Linda** [**Ronstadt**]'s manager, **John Boylan**, helped us a lot in the beginning," Glenn Frey told *New Musical Express* in 1973. "He's the one who suggested we go with (David) Geffen. Geffen was the best guy to be with 'cause he's the richest and youngest too. And on top of that, he was handing out the most artistic freedom."

PATHWAY ALBUM | TIMOTHY B. SCHMIT

POCO
From the Inside
Epic Records, September 1971

In just nine short months **Poco** had become a different band. The core was basically the same, with **Richie Furay** as leader, but **Jim Messina**'s departure left a void at producer. Epic Records' execs suggested **Steve Cropper**, the famed Memphis blues guitarist, and Furay hesitantly went along. Cropper and the band produced a tight album in his Memphis studio, but something was missing. Furay believed Cropper's R&B approach wasn't well suited to Poco's country-rock style. The addition of **Paul Cotton** gave the band an even harder rock edge, and while some of that shown through, it still didn't translate commercially. The band chose Timothy B. Schmit's cut *From the Inside* as the album's name because, Furay said, it described their way of making music and it also let Schmit know he was a full Poco member, not just a sideman. Inwardly, Furay was also upset over Epic's threadbare support for the band. *Just For You and Me* was a promising single, but it was never pushed by the label. A year later the band would try a more hard-edged approach.

Record World
September 18, 1971

They may not have rocketed to supergroupdom as quickly as some groups, but **Poco** has steadily and deservedly built a following. This album provides all the country-rock reasons why. Try *Hoedown* and *Ol' Forgiver*. **Paul Cotton**'s *Railroad Days* rocks just a little bit harder than Poco's usual singles, and this could be the one that breaks the Top 40. **Richie Furay**'s *Just For Me and You* can become Top 10 in a snap of fingers.

Washington Post
October 24, 1971

Poco is spirited country-rock band built around **Richie Furay**. Their new album, *From the Inside*, was produced by **Steve Cropper** and it is heavily country in feel and atitude. *Hoedown* is a great country introduction, and **Paul Cotton**'s *Bad Weather* is getting lots of airplay. But it's more style than substance. Poco doesn't dig far enough beneath the surface. It has the musicianship, but doesn't convince you it's important to come back.

San Mateo Times
November 6, 1971

Poco is quite successful in their latest album, *From the Inside*, but most of the good material is found on one side. The opening track, *Hoedown*, is a Poco classic in the tradition of *Hear That Music*. *Bad Weather* is a good track too, but it demonstrates Poco's lyrical limitations. The real strength of the band is their excellent harmonial abilities. This is a well-performed album and will certainly please any Poco fan, and also any fan of country-rock.

By September of 1971, Atlantic Records had announced the launching of Asylum under Geffen. Ertegun hailed Geffen's more than eight million records sold over the last three years in the trade publications *Billboard*, *Cashbox*, and *Record World*. "With the talent on its roster, Asylum is a major label from its inception," he said. He was right. **Joni Mitchell**'s contract with Reprise Records ended in June 1971, and she was immediately signed by Geffen. Ronstadt and her expiring Capital Records contract came the following year. Asylum set out a schedule for albums to roll out through the winter of 1972, including LPs from **Judee Sill**, **Jo Jo Gunne**, **David Blue**, and **Jackson Browne**. [1, 36, 693, 1383, 1384]

Azoff, Fogelberg Leave Illinois, Head to Los Angeles

Irving Azoff had been developing a Midwest artist booking and management empire since high school. The future media mogul had gone from representing one Danville, Illinois, band in 1968 to partnering with **Bob Nutt** and his company, Blytham Limited, as the booking agent and manager for nearly 90 bands across six Midwestern states by the summer of 1971.

Together, they made important connections with nightclubs, halls, and arenas. Just 24, Azoff was already in a position where he could make or break a band by deciding whether to put them on his circuit, and the bands he booked were making far more money than bands managed by others. Azoff took his job beyond booking bands

and gravitated into managing them too. He, along with partner **John Baruck**, handled the then-virtually unknown Champaign, Illinois-based **REO Speedwagon**, and his close friend, **Dan Fogelberg**, a denizen of Danville coffeehouses whom he discovered in a nightclub audition.

While he had developed his business in the Midwest, Azoff read *Rolling Stone* and other music trade magazines and kept tabs on the exploits of people like Asylum Records' **David Geffen** and **Bill Graham**, the famed promoter and owner of the Filmore East and West. The just-launched Asylum was stocking its artist stable with country- and folk-rock artists, so Azoff thought Fogelberg would be a good fit there. He sent a demo tape to Geffen and hoped to secure a record deal. Working with a skeleton crew of himself, **Elliot Roberts**, and a handful of secretaries and assistants, Geffen was multitasking when Azoff called to find out whether he had listened to Folgelberg's demo. "I heard the tape and I liked it," Geffen told Azoff. "I played the tape for **Jackson Browne** and he liked it too. If you wait a year or so for us to get up and running, then I will sign him."

Azoff was eager to meet Geffen, so he took a vacation to Los Angeles to discuss Fogelberg and to get a closer look at what had become the epicenter of the music business in 1970. When they met, Geffen reaffirmed his interest in Fogelberg, but said he couldn't sign him at that juncture. Disappointed, Azoff said he was going to pursue deals with other labels. Though he left with-

Steve Martin was one of many artists who, along with the members of the Eagles, were repeat performers at the Troubadour club in the West Hollywood. Martin blended music into his comedy routines, which were honed there before he found fame in motion pictures.

THE NAME GAME: *THE* EAGLES? ... HOPI OR GANG CULTURE?

SUMMER 1971 – **Steve Martin** was a Troubadour habitué. The now-world-renowned comedian got his start taking the stage at the West Hollywood club and running through his routines that would become familiar to *Saturday Night Live* and late-night talk show aficionados. He dated **Linda Ronstadt** and was a contemporary of the Eagles, who, like him, were searching for a break that would put them on the map.

In his 2007 book *Born Standing Up*, Martin recalled an encounter with Eagles co-founder Glenn Frey one night at the Troubadour, just before the Eagles signed a recording contract with **David Geffen**'s Asylum Records. Martin had found Glenn Frey lingering at the Troubadour bar, just after he had left **Longbranch/Pennywhistle**, and Frey offered that he was considering a name for his new band.

"What is it?" Martin asked. "Eagles," Frey replied. "You mean, *THE* Eagles," Martin retorted. "No," Frey said, "Eagles." "You mean, *THE* Eagles." "No, I mean Eagles." And, Martin concluded, the name of the group remains "Eagles."

The origin story of the Eagles name isn't entirely clear. Frey, a Detroit native, is said to have been enamored of the name because it reminded him of a street gang. Don Henley and Bernie Leadon both attributed some credit to the books they had been reading in 1971 on the Hopi Indian culture. "We were all reading books about the Hopis, and in the Hopi mythology the eagle is the most sacred animal with the most spiritual meaning," Leadon said, adding that the group wanted to have a name with mythological connotations. "The eagle flies closest to the sun and will carry out messages to the father, it symbolizes all the highest spirituality and morals. High morals. The best a man can be. I think it's a beautiful symbol."

Perhaps the earliest recorded instance of the band playing under the "Eagles" moniker was in Aspen, Colorado, in October 1971. The band had just been signed by David Geffen and was sent to Aspen to hone their act. They played at The Gallery club at the base of Aspen Mountain, and records there show that band playing under "Eagle," according to **G. Brown**, author of *Colorado Rocks*. [160, 231, 1163, 1186, 1393]

out a deal, the trip proved inspirational for him, and he started making plans to move west.

He got a nudge in that direction soon after he returned to the Midwest. An **REO Speedwagon** concert he booked in the sleepy town of Lake Geneva, Wisconsin, was raided by 400 policemen, state troopers, and Wisconsin National Guardsmen. **Alan Gratzer**, drummer for REO Speedwagon, told *Time Passages* that the police presence was intense that night. Authorities rushed in and shut the show down. The band then went back to Champaign. When the dust settled that night, 35 arrests were made, and the next morning, Azoff found himself in front of the district attorney and the town's sheriff.

Azoff told *Rolling Stone*'s **Cameron Crowe** in 1975 that the sheriff and D.A. offered him a deal: don't reopen the Majestic Hills club for another concert and they would not arrest him. "I said, 'Absolutely, man, we are closed.' I got across the Wisconsin state line, picked up a telephone, called WLS [WLS-AM 890 in Chicago] and had them put on the news that we would be open next week as usual ... with **Black Sabbath**, **Jethro Tull**, and **Mountain** on three consecutive nights." "And?" the curious Crowe quizzed Azoff. "They enjoined me and I moved to California," Azoff said.

Azoff was set to depart and gave his roommate, folk singer **Dan Fogelberg**, $200 and told him to meet him in Los Angeles and start making contacts. Fogelberg took the money and headed west, but had burned all that money by the time he reached Denver, which ended up being a beneficial unexpected week-long layover as Colorado became the inspiration for many of his future songs. Meanwhile, Azoff arrived in Los Angeles and began working for the Heller-Fischel Agency as a talent agent. Azoff had a connection there, having coordinated a **Lee Michaels** show in Des Moines from **Jerry Heller** in 1971. Not long after his former partner, **Bob Nutt**, also headed to Los Angeles, but didn't find the same level of success and was back in Illinois a few short years later.

On a new road, Azoff began finding and working for clients, and getting a feel for how the music game in Los Angeles worked. He started by getting a demo tape of Fogelberg to **Clive Davis** at Columbia Records, and then ironed out an agreement with him for a contract. Fogelberg would stay with Columbia for most of his career. Geffen and Azoff's first-ever spat was over the Columbia signing, with a livid Geffen shouting at Azoff, "That's my artist! You have to give him to me!" It was an appropriate welcoming to L.A. for Azoff. He was able to secure a deal for one of his artists, and one night at the famed Whiskey a Go Go, he stumbled upon another: a now-down-and-out **Joe Walsh**, who had left **James Gang**, formed a new band, **Barnstorm**, and cut an album that flopped. Now, he was looking for direction. Azoff had a compass. [1, 481, 1289, 1320, 1323, 1328, 1352, 1395]

LEADON LEADS: GEFFEN SIGNS EAGLES TO RECORDING DEAL

FALL 1971 – **John Boylan** had assembled an impressive backing band to support **Linda Ronstadt**'s summer tour of 1971, which included rhythm guitar player Glenn Frey and drummer Don Henley. The tour ended in the fall, but Ronstadt had more dates to be played, so Boylan added recently available bass player Randy Meisner and, at least for one show at Disneyland, lead guitarist Bernie Leadon.

Behind the scenes during the tour, Frey and Henley had engaged with Boylan to assemble their own band, complete with Ronstadt's knowledge and consent. Collectively, they just wanted to put the right pieces together. Playing together at grad night at Disneyland supporting Ronstadt, the four future Eagles realized they had found the right mix of talent and personalities.

The linchpin in the creation of the as-yet unnamed group was **David Geffen**, the founder of Asylum Records. Geffen had already signed **Jackson Browne**, and was playing a patient, eventually successful waiting game for Ronstadt and the one album she had remaining on her Capitol Records contract. At Browne's behest, Geffen brought Frey and his bandmate, **J.D. Souther**, into the Asylum stable by acquiring **Longbranch/ Pennywhistle**'s Amos Records contract from **Jimmy Bowen** for $15,000. He recognized Souther's lone wolf ways and pronounced him a solo act, though that decision didn't become final for a few weeks. Frey, he estimated, was better suited for a band. Henley, who was also attached to an Amos contract, might be a good fit in such a band too. So, Geffen also bought out Shiloh's contract for $12,000 and freed up Henley. Now, with two of the four primary components of Frey's new band in place, and Meisner and Leadon content to join, the band descended upon Geffen in his Sunset Boulevard office.

There was angst leading up to the meeting because the band and Geffen had not reached an agreement on royalties. Geffen had also not agreed on the final composition of the band. Poker-faced, Frey decided to give him a take-it-or-leave-it offer. Leadon and Meisner were the most experienced of the bunch, but Leadon's no-

nonsense demeanor was such that the group chose him to be the at-that-moment spokesperson to deliver an ultimatum.

"Geffen had no idea what we sounded like," Henley said, and indeed, the band had not even brought a demo tape to give him. "And here comes Bernie [Leadon] walking in saying, 'Okay, here we are. Do you want us or not?' It was a great moment. Geffen kinda said, 'Well ... yeah.'"

Indeed, Geffen had never heard the band play. The group had the strong and influential backing of Browne, Ronstadt, and Boylan, but Geffen was still risking signing the band sight unseen. The issue was resolved when he, **Elliot Roberts**, and **John Hartmann**, another manager with Asylum, visited a small hall in the San Fernando Valley where the band was rehearsing. They didn't want to be seen, so they watched the band over a stack of cardboard boxes in the middle of the room. What they heard was fresh, tight sounds from a well-rehearsed group. "We knew and committed to them right then," Hartmann said. "It was nothing to believe in the Eagles."

The pieces started to come together for the band quickly after Geffen agreed. But even Leadon and Meisner, who had far more experience in dealing with artist management and labels, may not have noticed the subtle differences Asylum was applying and how they differed from traditional artist contract norms.

Geffen managed the "label" side of Asylum, which include the nuts and bolts of getting albums made, distribution, marketing and promotion, and publicity. Meanwhile, Roberts handled the traditional tasks associated with artist management, such as booking tours, providing career advice and attending to a litany of sometimes-obscure artist requests.

> **Geffen had no idea what we sounded like. And here comes Bernie [Leadon] walking in saying, 'Okay, here we are. Do you want us or not?' It was a great moment. Geffen kinda said, 'Well ... yeah.'**
>
> *— Don Henley, Eagles co-founder*

A typical artist manager would also be responsible for negotiating contracts and fees, and that's where the lines between label and manager blurred somewhat for the two-in-one Asylum model. Those blurred lines would come back to haunt Geffen and Roberts later. But at the outset, it wasn't all bad for the group. Where most labels, like Amos Records, generally kept 100 percent of the publishing from the bands they signed, Geffen and Roberts took just 50 percent.

The legalities of the business aside, Geffen was encouraged by the band's tight musicianship and strong harmonies. But he also knew they weren't yet ready to be thrust under the bright lights. They would need to truly become a band first, and he absolutely didn't want that to happen in Los Angeles, where bright lights, distractions and, moreover, prying eyes might interfere with his chemistry experiment. So, he decided to send them to the mountains of Colorado. [1, 6, 88, 790, 1214]

Geffen Considers Fifth Eagle, But Souther Opts Out

With the negotiations the still-unnamed Eagles completed, **David Geffen** wasn't finished experimenting. He had already signed **Jackson Browne**, **Judi Sill**, and a host of others to his new Asylum Records label, but he was still looking for the right places for his varied pieces. He had decided early that **J.D. Souther**, Glenn Frey's partner in the duo **Longbranch/Pennywhistle**, should be a solo act. But he was having second thoughts.

"Geffen had the idea that maybe five writers and singers were better than four. We all rolled our eyes, but said, 'All right, David's always had pretty good ideas,'" Souther told the *Chicago Tribune*. "We rehearsed and played a set one afternoon at the Troubadour for David and **Elliot Roberts**, and I remember looking down the front line at the guys and saying, 'I don't see that they need me. I think the band is perfect the way it is.' Don and Glenn and I were going to keep writing songs together. That's the best possible outcome, we stay friends and co-writers. They had worked very hard, and they were ready. They didn't need me."

Randy Meisner had his concerns. He knew both Souther and Frey from their days with Longbranch/Pennywhistle, and worried about what dynamic the pairing of those two in this new band would do to the new group's organically evolved chemistry. He expressed his reservations to his bandmates, but it wouldn't matter, Souther had already decided against it.

Souther told **Marc Eliot** in his book *Take It to the Limit: The Untold Story of the Eagles* that his report card from school always said the same thing ... "Does not work well with others." He said the band considered the move, but knew it would never work. "I was clearly the fifth wheel. When Glenn and I split [from Longbranch/Pennywhistle], part of the reason was because he wanted to add more players, to put a band together, while I wanted to go home and write songs and be with **Linda** [**Ronstadt**]."

So, the band would move forward with the original four: Frey, Meisner, Don Henley, and Bernie Leadon. It wouldn't be the last time that Geffen considered moving Souther into a band though. And in 1973, he revisited the idea, and then joined him with former Byrd **Chris Hillman** and former **Poco** leader **Richie Furay** to form the **Souther-Hillman-Furay Band**. [6, 1147, 1207, 1248]

FALL 1971

RELEASES
▶ **James Gang**, with Joe Walsh, *Live in Concert* (album)
▶ **Poco**, with Timothy B. Schmit, *Just For Me and You* (single)
▶ **Poco**, with Timothy B. Schmit, *From the Inside* (album)

MILESTONES
James Gang with Joe Walsh: *James Gang Rides Again* (album) certified GOLD, RIAA.

COLLABORATIONS
Randy Meisner played bass guitar and provided backing vocals on **Rick Nelson**'s album *Rudy the Fifth*.

ON SCREEN
▶ **Linda Ronstadt** appeared on the CTV TV show *Nashville North* (aka *The Ian Tyson Show*). Ronstadt performed **Patsy Cline**'s *I Fall to Pieces* with Glenn Frey and Don Henley backing her. **John Hammond** and **Glen Sherley** also appeared.

ON THE ROAD WITH …
▶ **James Gang**, with Joe Walsh: SRC, REO Speedwagon, Five Man Electrical Band, Paul Butterfield Blues Band, John Mayall
▶ **Poco**, with Timothy B. Schmit: James Cotton Blues Band, England Dan and John Ford Coley, Doug Kershaw, Livingston Taylor

Judee Sill, David Blue Are Asylum's First Releases

A little more than a month after **David Geffen** and **Elliot Roberts** decided to form Asylum Records, the nascent company was planning album releases for the acts they signed.

The lightly staffed organization lined up its first three artists for planned release September 15, 1971, including folk singer **Judee Sill**, **David Blue**, and the **Jay Ferguson**-led band **Jo Jo Gunne**. Production issues held up the Jo Jo Gunne release until January 1972, roughly the same time Asylum released **Jackson Browne**'s self-titled (often referred to as the *Saturate Before Using*) debut album. Sill's album, the first

out of the gate for Geffen and Asylum, was released on time, but it couldn't find an audience. Geffen convinced **Graham Nash** to produce Sill's lead single on the album, *Jesus Was a Cross Maker*, a non-religious song about a heartbreaking relationship. But even with the Nash's well-known name attached to the album, neither the song nor LP could find an audience.

Blue was a Rhode Island-born singer-songwriter who had connections to **Bob Dylan** from his Greenwich Village days. A Troubadour loiterer, he came to the aid of Geffen one night when the producer was physically attacked in front of the club.

Blue had already released three albums, *David Blue* with Elektra, *These 23 Days in September*, and *Me* with Reprise, but none were commercially successful. Geffen thought he might turn that around. Blue did pen *Outlaw Man*, which would become a single on the Eagles' *Desperado* LP, but Blue's initial Asylum album, *Stories*, did not chart.

Geffen pushed all four acts in the trade press and also began teasing a new mystery band that he planned to send to London to record. *Cashbox* reported that the group included former **Longbranch/Pennywhistle** guitarist "Glen Frey," (sic) **Poco** bassist "Randy Mizner" (sic) former **Flying Burrito Brother** Bernie Leadon, along with Don Henley. The band would be produced by famed **Rolling Stones** producer Glyn Johns. [1, 696, 1383, 1396, 1397]

TAKE IT EASY: THE LEGEND OF WINSLOW, ARIZONA

SUMMER 1971 – **Jackson Browne** was in the process of completing his self-titled debut album in 1972 when he decided to take a road trip through small towns in Arizona and Utah in search of inspiration. While driving through Arizona he found it curious that many women were driving around in pickup trucks, which he never saw in Los Angeles. One day in Sedona, Arizona, as he was loitering on a street corner near the center of town, he saw a beautiful woman in a Toyota pickup drive by slowly and give him the once-over; he knew right then that she would be in the second verse of a song he was writing.

When he returned to Los Angeles, Browne focused on finishing his album at Crystal Sound Studios. He knew the song wasn't going to be on his current album, and he was getting frustrated over the second verse, so he shelved it. Meanwhile his friend and neighbor, Glenn Frey, was scouting for songs for the newly formed Eagles' debut album. Browne told him about the song and sang him the first verse. "That's cool. Is it done?" Frey asked. Browne said no, and Frey asked him to let him know when it was—the Eagles would like to record it.

Frey took the song back to the other members of the Eagles and they instantly liked it. Short on tracks for their album, the group encouraged Frey to approach Browne again. Frey got on the phone and pestered him about it, and asked if he could finish it. Browne, intently focused on finishing his album, agreed. Frey took it home and came up with the verse about the woman Browne told him about. He swapped out the Toyota for a flatbed Ford, which blended wonderfully with the verse about the small town of Winslow, where Browne had, indeed, broken down in his car on that fateful trip. The verse, "*It's a girl my lord in a flatbed Ford / slowin' down to take a look at me,*" was Frey's lyrical contribution to the song, but, more importantly, he also revised the chorus and the arrangement.

When Frey played his friend the completed song, Browne was delighted, especially with how the arrangement was modified to accentuate the chorus. In an interview with KNX-FM in Los Angeles, Browne told the DJ, "The way I was singing the verse and the chorus, there was almost no chorus. It took Glenn to go 'Take it eeeeeeeasyyyy.' I probably sang something like 'Take it ea-sy.' It took an arrangement."

It was a lesson in collaboration for Browne, who said that as the Eagles version flooded the airwaves, he was convinced that Frey's approach was right. "I learned it [the Eagles] way." [1, 1109, 1152, 1394]

❝❝ Take It Easy

On *Take It Easy*, I got Bernie [Leadon] to play double-time banjo; they all thought it was a bonkers idea but it worked. It was already a great song, but that one little thing made it different.
Eagles producer Glyn Johns, Uncut, February 2014

The Eagles' *Take It Easy* is simply the best sounding rock single to come out so far this year. The first time through, you could tell it had everything: danceable rhythm, catchy, winding melody, intelligent, affirmative lyrics, a progressively powerful arrangement mixing electric guitar and banjo, and a crisp vocal, with vibrant four-part harmony at just the right moments for maximum dramatic effect. To top it off, *Take It Easy* was co-written by **Jackson Browne** and Eagle Glenn Frey, whose vocal on the record fell somewhere between Browne and **Rick Nelson**.
– *Bud Scoppa, Rolling Stone, June 1972*

Take It Easy is a fine example of the things [the Eagles] are capable of doing with energy and motion. [It has] a toughness that doesn't back down in the face of their sweet harmony overlay. A disconcerting proportion [of the songs on their debut album] just don't demand to be played again and again, as was the case the first few days I had the *Take It Easy* single.
– *Ben Edmonds, Creem, September 1972*

Take It Easy, [the Eagles'] first 45 turned out to be *THE* summer song of last year, and in every state you can think of hips were slowly struttin' to the carefree rhythm. This was especially true in California, the group's home territory, where *Take It Easy* became a part of the summer alongside the mainstays: Coppertone, Coca-Cola, bikinis and the blue Pacific.
– *Danny Holloway, New Musical Express, March 1973*

I remember hearing it for the first time and it was amazing. I lived in an apartment in Studio City. I had the manager at my apartment and some of my friends had heard the *Take It Easy* single and they all played it and said, "That's never gonna make it." Now every time I see those people they say, "You were right! You were right!" It was great, I never could have believed then that the Eagles were gonna make it (laughs). It was great to hear it and to be able to send it to your parents. I love the way **Glyn Johns** mixes. It's so clean and nice. It sounded so good.
– *Randy Meisner, San Francisco Weekly, April 1998*

I knew Glenn Frey from playing these clubs – we kept showing up at the same clubs and singing on the open-mic nights. Glenn happened to come by to say 'hi,' and to hang around when I was in the studio, and I showed him the beginnings of that song, and he asked if I was going to put it on my record and I said it wouldn't be ready in time. He said 'well, we'll put it on, we'll do it,' 'cause he liked it. But it wasn't finished, and he kept after me to finish it, and finally offered to finish it himself. And after a couple of times when I declined to have him finish my song, I said, "all right." I finally thought, "This is ridiculous. Go ahead and finish it. Do it." And he finished it in *spectacular* fashion. And, what's more, arranged it in a way that was far superior to what I had written.
– *Jackson Browne, Unidentified audio interview, August 2005*

[*Take It Easy*]'s primary appeal, I think, is that it evokes a sense of motion, both musically and lyrically. The romance of the open road. The lure of adventure and possibility – Route 66, the Blue Ridge Parkway, Pacific Coast Highway. Great American writers from Thomas Wolfe to Jack Kerouac to Wallace Stegner have addressed this theme of the restlessness of the American spirit, of our need to keep moving, especially from east to west, in search of freedom, identity, fortune and this illusive thing we call "home."
– *Don Henley, Rolling Stone, June 2016*

After Glenn moved to L.A., I didn't hear from him for about two or three years. He was pursuing his own course out there. Then 1972 came along and I heard *Take It Easy*. And I said, "Oh, my God, what a great-sounding record! He did it!"
– *Bob Seger, Guitar Player, January 2016*

PATHWAY ALBUM | RANDY MEISNER

RICK NELSON
Rudy the Fifth

Decca Records, November 1971

When **Rick Nelson** cut his live album at the famed Troubadour club in West Hollywood in January 1970, the former teenage TV heartthrob was on the comeback trail. Bassist **Randy Meisner** quit Nelson's band after a grueling European USO tour in 1970, but by the time Nelson returned to the studio in mid-1971 he needed Meisner's high vocals again. Then working in a Nebraska John Deere dealership, Meisner was lured back to Los Angeles and played on every *Rudy the Fifth* track except *Life*. Critics gave the album fair reviews, but the record-buying public was skeptical of a shaggy-haired Nelson singing **Rolling Stones** songs. The album never charted despite Decca's heavy push of two singles, *Life* and *Gypsy Pilot*. Nelson would return to the charts a tear later with *Garden Party*, but Meisner had joined the Eagles by that time.

Detroit Free Press
October 17, 1971

Rick Nelson (nee Little Ricky Nelson) has a style that lies somewhere to the right of **Bobby Sherman** and **Tommy Roe**. His newest album is a chamber of musical horrors. If anything serves to kill it off, it's his rendition of Jagger's *Honky Tonk Woman*. So blatantly sexual, the song is delivered by Nelson with the guttiness of an eighth-grader groping his way through a kiddie matinee of Walt Disney's *Scandalous John*. If you must listen to this kind of stuff, do it in a closet.

Abilene Reporter-News
October 24, 1971

Ever since **Rick Nelson** released **Bob Dylan**'s *She Belongs to Me* he's been heading toward a beautifully entertaining album, *Rudy the Fifth*. Rick blends seven original songs with a few by Dylan, **Mick Jagger** and **Shirley** and **Leonard Lee**. Rick's own *Life* is great and typifies the mood of the album. Dylan's *Just Like a Woman* and *Love Minus Zero* fit right in. If there's any doubt in your mind that Nelson has changed with the times, listen. You can almost hear *Travelin' Man* echoing in the background.

Arizona Republic
December 5, 1971

Rick Nelson has emerged from his TV days with a very good album, with a new **Rick Nelson** sound. *Rudy the Fifth* brings together Nelson and a new group, the **Stone Canyon Band**, which includes Randy Meisner, **Tom Brumley**, **Pat Shanahan**, **Allen Kemp** and **Steve Love**. Songs include seven originals by Nelson, plus cuts from Dylan and Shirley and Lee. The new sound Nelson brings would have to be described as country-rock, with an accent on the former. Try it, you'll like it.

Geffen Sends 'Teen King & The Emergencies' to Aspen

It had been a busy summer and fall for **David Geffen** in 1971. He had signed a bevy of acts to his new Asylum Records label including **Judee Sill**, **David Blue**, **Jackson Browne**, and, most recently, four country-rock musicians who would eventually become the Eagles.

The group was excited about getting a recording contract, but Geffen knew they weren't ready to record yet. He wanted them to become a band outside of the bright lights of L.A., so he sent them to the relative solitude of Colorado.

Geffen told the band, "You need to go write some songs, you're not really ready to record yet," Don Henley said. "So, they packed us off to Aspen. You know, it could have been worse. There were people there who were way higher than we've ever been. We played at a club up there called The Gallery, which was at the foot of Aspen Mountain. We didn't have a big catalog of our own tunes at that point. We were just getting started. We needed to learn how to play together as a band. And we did."

The Gallery had begun to make a name for itself for country-rock acts by hosting regular appearances by the **Nitty Gritty Dirt Band**. In October 1971, the group, playfully billed as **Teen King and the Emergencies** by Frey, started their month-long residency in Aspen.

"I remember the first night, there were 40 people for the first set, then 80 people for the second set. By the fourth show of the night, it was packed. The word spread pretty quickly," Frey said. The group played several weeks of gigs at the club, and would return a month later for another round, all at $500 a week split between the four band members. "It was a good way to get started," Frey added. "Out from under the Hollywood microscope. We were able to play a bunch of songs over and over, get to know each other. It was a total experience, something I'll always look at fondly."

The following month the band played five nights a week, from December 11 to 15, 1971, at the since-shuttered Tulagi club on Boulder's University Hill.

The gig, which was arranged between Geffen and former University of Colorado student and current elite concert promoter **Chuck Morris**. "I got a call from their manager at the time, David Geffen," Morris told the *Daily Camera* in 2003. "He said, 'I've got this new band I'm putting together. They're on their way to England to record their first record. They're going to be huge. I'd like them to play for five days, just work out their material. Their producer's going to fly in.'"

Indeed, Geffen had arranged to have famed producer **Glyn Johns** sit in on their sets in Colorado. Johns, an engineer that Frey coveted, had produced records for heavyweights of rock like **The Who**, **Led Zeppelin** and **The Rolling Stones**. Geffen wanted him to produce their first record. But Johns, with a track record for working with bad boy English bands, would need to be convinced to take on an easy-going country rock band. He would get his first taste of them at Tulagi's. And the "audition" did not go well. [1, 460, 461, 462, 586, 1152, 1391, 1392]

WINTER 1971-72

COLLABORATIONS
▶ **Joe Walsh** played lead guitar and provided backing vocals for singles *Medley*, *Jessica Stone* and *California Fairy Tale* on **Jimmie Haskill**'s album *California '99*.
▶ **Glenn Frey** (guitar, backing vocals), **Don Henley** (drums, backing vocals), **Bernie Leadon** (guitar, backing vocals) and **Randy Meisner** (bass guitar, backing vocals) provided musical support on **Linda Ronstadt**'s album *Linda Ronstadt*.
▶ **Glenn Frey** played guitar, piano and provided backing vocals on **J.D. Souther**'s album *John David Souther*.

ON THE ROAD WITH ...
▶ **James Gang**, with Joe Walsh: Jake Jones, Julia
▶ **Poco**, with Timothy B. Schmit: Jerry Riopelle, Dr. John, Humble Pie, Alice Cooper

Walsh Leaves James Gang, Forms Barnstorm in Colorado

When Joe Walsh joined **James Gang** in April 1969, he was immediately thrust into the role of frontman, lead guitarist, and rhythm guitarist as well. The band played across the Midwest and had developed a name for themselves, fighting their up way from opening support band to becoming headliners in large clubs and arenas.

They were picked by **The Who** to join them on their European tour to support

their concept album, *Tommy*. Along the way, the band welcomed producer **Bill Szymczyk**, who found them in a small Ohio club, signed them, and produced three albums, including two that went gold.

But Walsh was getting tired and felt musically unfulfilled. Through three albums, Walsh had written or co-written a majority of the songs and nearly all of the charting singles. Musically, other things were bothering Walsh. The group was becoming more complex in the studio where a reliance on overdubs had grown to the point where duplicating the sound on stage was challenging. Further, Walsh was growing as a writer and wanted to start incorporating piano, rhythm guitars, and harmonies, which wasn't possible as a three-piece band.

"I was really frustrated with the James Gang," Walsh said. "I wanted to expand the group and add some more people to it. I was beginning to get keyboard ideas. But I couldn't get the others to go along with me. They didn't want to change. Things got worse and worse. Finally, I had to leave. The money was good, but it got to the point that the money didn't matter anymore."

Another issue was that Walsh thought he was being typecast as a heavy guitarist. There was more to him than that, he felt, and he feared becoming synonymous with **Blue Cheer**, one of the first heavy metal bands known more for being loud than being talented. "I was scared I might have that label for life," Walsh said. "I didn't want to be a heavy metal flash lead guitar player. I didn't want to be known for that,

I wanted to be known to the public and to my peers as more of a songwriter, more of a musician, so at some point, I decided not to express myself in a three-piece very loud group anymore."

Walsh planned his break from the group and planned to form another, but didn't execute the plan immediately. Szymczyk, his James Gang producer and confidant, had moved out to Los Angeles when ABC Records absorbed Dunhill Records and he took over their West Coast operations. But he moved again to Denver in early 1971 to form his own label, Tumbleweed Records, with his partner **Larry Ray**. With a new group and a new album on his mind, he decided to go where his producer had set up a studio.

Walsh reached out to **Joe Vitale**, a veteran club circuit drummer he had befriended in Ohio, and asked him if he was interested in joining his new band. Vitale had just landed steady work touring in the summer and fall with **Ted Nugent**, but wanted to work with Walsh. He approached Nugent and explained, and he happily agreed, but asked Vitale to finish the tour, which he did. Then it was just a matter of waiting for Walsh to call to set things up.

Weeks passed and Vitale, who by then had no job, didn't get a call. His girlfriend drove by Walsh's house, and was surprised to find it empty. Walsh had already moved, and left no word or message for Vitale. Around Kent, Ohio, there was an expression called "Pulling a Walsh," which happened when someone did something with no notice or explanation. Vitale said he was living it.

In January 1972, Walsh finally called and asked Vitale if he was ready to come, and Vitale joined him in Colorado. [135, 358, 1307, 1326, 1344]

Walsh Turns Down Offer To Join Humble Pie

Joe Walsh was weary from life as the frontman for **James Gang**. He was writing all the songs, and there was no interest among the other band members in growing musically. He had a growing sense that the band was being pigeonholed as a heavy metal act, which he wanted no part of. So, he quit James Gang.

About that time, a well-known English band, **Humble Pie**, was losing it's lead singer, **Peter Frampton**. The loss of Frampton came at an inopportune time for the band, which had released a new album in the spring of 1971 with Frampton as its frontman, *Rock On*, that surged to #21 on *Billboard*'s Hot 100 chart. A&M Records was releasing a live album, *Rockin' the Fillmore*, and both were getting strong reviews.

Band leader **Steve Marriott** reached out to Walsh to recruit him to the band. Walsh's reputation had grown after James Gang was asked to open for **The Who** on their *Tommy* tour across Europe. It was a move that Walsh wanted to make too, but other commitments got in the way.

"That was something I really wanted to do, but I think the problem was that I had definite commitments, if not to the James Gang, at least to my management and to my record company." Walsh said that those

FREY LANDS TEMPCHIN'S *PEACEFUL, EASY FEELING* FOR DEBUT

FALL 1971 – In the early, grueling days when Glenn Frey and **J.D. Souther**, performing as **Longbranch/ Pennywhistle**, were carrying their instruments from their cars to coffeehouses, auditoriums, and local halls, they were resolute about paying their dues to make a living in music. In those coffeehouse days, there was circle of singer-songwriters who played these venues that the duo befriended. One such friend was **Jack Tempchin**, an Ohio-born, San Diego-raised singer-songwriter and self-professed hippie, who they met during a shared a gig at a local club in San Diego.

But one spring day in 1971, a little more than a week after **David Geffen** signing the as-yet-unnamed Eagles to their first recording contract, Tempchin found himself strumming guitar strings in **Jackson Browne**'s house in Los Angeles. "Glenn came in, and he heard me playing my new song, and he recorded it on a cassette tape. He said, 'Jack, I've just put a new band together, and we're going to play for all the record companies. Do you mind if we work up the song?'" Tempchin gave Frey the go-ahead to work on the arrangement for Tempchin's song, *Peaceful Easy Feeling.*

The song, he said, was written for a waitress he met while playing at a coffeehouse gig in El Centro, California. "The waitress said I could go home with her later," Tempchin told *Rolling Stone* in 1978. "Then she just disappeared," he said laughing. He said he had already told his friends to leave—he was going with her— and he ended up sleeping on a linoleum floor of the mini-mall coffeehouse he performed at, and that's where he started the song. "I started writing the lyrics on the back of a poster [advertising my show]. The poster is in the Rock and Roll Hall of Fame now. I wrote some really stupid lyrics and then I kept writing and all of sudden I noticed I had written the phrase 'peaceful easy feeling.'"

Tempchin integrated more women he had met into the song, but said the real magic happened when Frey took the song and rearranged it in just one day. "Glenn ... took the song and put just the right musical arrangement, just the right attitude. He recorded it in an amazing way so you feel like you are out in the desert. So, he came back the next day, and played me a cassette of the [the band] playing [it]. Then a week later, Glenn got three giant record execs to come into this tiny rehearsal studio [to hear the Eagles' songs], and they got signed and that was it." [582, 1295, 1389, 1390]

people weren't friendly to the idea of moving to England and joining Humble Pie.

"I very much wanted to—I've always had a high amount of respect for Steve Marriott and Frampton," Walsh told the *BBC*, and that was something that I really wanted to do, but I just couldn't." [135]

Eagles Blow Boulder Audition; Glyn Johns Declines to Produce

A few weeks into their introduction to the rock world, the as-yet-unnamed Eagles were playing to sparse-but-growing crowds in Aspen, Colorado, to tune-up prior to recording their first album. Their manager, **David Geffen**, hoped to land **Glyn Johns** as their producer, but Johns, who famously worked with **The Rolling Stones** and **Led Zeppelin**, would need to be convinced.

Geffen booked the band for a week of gigs in Boulder at Tulagi's on Boulder University Hill in mid-December and arranged to have Johns flown in for what would be, in essence, an audition for the band. But Geffen's choice of venues and timing for the performance was awful. The band's preferred venue in Aspen, The Gallery, had become dependably packed for the band and were always a supportive crowd. The band hadn't yet played in Boulder, which was nearly four hours away, and they certainly didn't have a following there. To make matters worse, the University of Colorado at Boulder had final exams scheduled for that week, so crowds would be light, if non-existent.

"Why they chose Tulagi's in Boulder on a snowy December night is still a mystery to me," Don Henley told the *Denver Post* in 2015. "But Johns duly arrived at the Denver airport and I picked him up in a rental car and drove him to the club in Boulder. The roads were icy and snow was falling." Henley said there were about six or seven people in the club, and the band played a "lackluster set, with which Mr. Johns was not impressed."

Henley said the entire plan was wrong from the outset—the place, the timing, everything. "I know that the circumstances and the atmosphere in general were bleak," he said. "Our managers just didn't have a clue what they were doing and neither did we. The simple fact is that, no matter where we had performed that showcase, it was premature; we simply weren't ready to make an album. We didn't have enough original material or enough experience playing together as a band."

"[They] were at least playing with a few members of the public along," Johns said. "They were not that impressive. They played a selection of covers. **Chuck Berry** rock and roll kind of thing." The dynamic between Bernie Leadon, who Johns called a "great country picker" and Frey, an "average rock and roll guitar player" was confusing, and they pulled bass player Randy Meisner in two different directions. "I didn't see what all of the fuss was about at all."

Johns added that the sound was not great, and that, combined with a fairly bland, somewhat awkward stage presence, convinced him that "they were not worth pursuing, and I returned to London."

JACK TEMPCHIN

Glenn Frey and **J.D. Souther** were working the clubs and coffeehouses across Southern California while they tried to find success as the duo **Longbranch/Pennywhistle**. They met and became friends with another aspiring singer-songwriter working the same circuit, **Jack Tempchin**. After Frey joined the Eagles in 1971 he was hunting for singles to include on the band's debut album and asked Tempchin if they could rearrange and record one of his songs, *Peaceful Easy Feeling*. Tempchin gave the OK, and the song became the third hit single off the Eagles' debut album.

Tempchin was born in Ohio, and was raised in San Diego. He taught himself to play guitar when he was 18 and he began playing blues in local coffeehouses in the late 1960s. He met country singer **Hoyt Axton** in a San Diego coffeehouse and Axton decided to use one of his songs, *Circle Ties That Bind*, in his sets. That was the affirmation that Tempchin needed to keep pursing a career in music.

Tempchin wandered California in the early 1970s looking to be discovered. In L.A. Frey introduced him to former Epic Records executive **Clive Davis**, who signed his band, the **Funky Kings** to his Arista label. They released an album in 1976 including his song *Slow Dancin'*, which crested at #106 on *Record World*'s singles chart. A year later **Johnny Rivers** would score a Top 10 hit with the song, which was good for Tempchin, but not for the Funky Kings who broke up shortly after.

Though he didn't find commercial success as a performing artist, his skills as a songwriter were unquestionable. His songs have been recorded by **Randy Meisner**, **George Jones**, **Patty Loveless**, **Glen Campbell**, **Tom Rush**, **Tanya Tucker** and **Olivia Newton-John**. After the Eagles broke up in 1980, Frey reached out to Tempchin and asked him to collaborate, and they began a songwriting partnership that spanned decades. They co-wrote more than 30 songs, including *The One You Love*, *You Belong To The City*, *Part of You, Part of Me*, *True Love*, and *Smuggler's Blues*.

Between 1994 and 2017 Tempchin released 10 more solo albums. He was inducted into the Songwriter's Hall of Fame in 2019. [335, 336, 582, 860, 1295, 1391]

It was a dispiriting turn of events. Years later, Leadon said in exasperation, "God damn. It's not what we expected."

Discouraging as it was, Geffen was not ready to give up on Johns. After their gigs in Boulder, the band returned to L.A. and continued to rehearse. Geffen would ask a reluctant Johns to give the group another try, and he eventually relented. And this time he heard something he had not heard before. [19, 36, 79, 83, 1152, 1391, 1393]

Ronstadt Releases Third Album Backed by Four Future Eagles

Linda Ronstadt's star was beginning to rise in the winter of 1972. She made a name for herself with her first group, the **Stone Poneys**, and reached #13 on the *Billboard* Top 100 chart with *Different Drum* in 1966. She became a solo act in 1969 and became the first female "alternative country" act in America (a term that eventually gave way to country-rock) and her first album *Hand Sown ... Home Grown* was warmly received by critics.

Her second album *Silk Purse* elevated her higher and garnered a Grammy nomination for Best Contemporary Vocal Performance/ Female for her single, *Long, Long Time*, which was a Top 25 single. She was getting regular spots on television specials as well. After spending the better part of a year touring, it was time for Ronstadt to begin work on her third album, *Linda Ronstadt*.

She picked a backing band for the record from an impressive collection of strong session musicians like legendary steel pedal

guitar players **Buddy Emmons** and **Sneaky Pete Kleinow**, along with fiddle player **Gib Guilbeau**. She also tapped players who she had grown recently familiar with, including **J.D. Souther**, **Richard Bowden**, and the four original Eagles. Glenn Frey, Don Henley, and Bernie Leadon were already well acquainted with her musical style, with each having accompanied her on tour at some point over the previous two years. Randy Meisner, too, had joined her for a few sets at her week-long Disneyland gig in the summer of 1971. So she naturally invited them to the studio to record what would be her last LP on Capitol Records.

Early on, the record was envisioned as a live album, and while two live cuts did make the final product, producer **John Boylan** brought the remaining eight cuts into the studio. The album was an eclectic mix of country-rock, and included songs written by **Johnny Cash**, **Jackson Browne**, **Neil Young**, and **Livingston Taylor**. Ronstadt led off the LP with the Browne's *Rock Me on the Water*, which offered a more up-tempo arrangement than the original courtesy of "lone arranger" Glenn Frey, who also played electric guitar on the cut. Frey also provided guitar and backing vocal support for *Birds*, *I Fall to Pieces*, *Faithful*, and *Rescue Me*.

In his review of her album for *Creem* in April 1972, **Ben Edmunds** credits *I Fall to Pieces*, *Birds*, and *Rescue Me* as the albums strongest cuts. Each song was recorded live, he wrote, and her backing band makes her performance more forceful. "Her supporting group on these three cuts contained most (or all) of a damn fine band called the Eagles," he said, "which you'll undoubtedly be hearing more of the next time you turn around."

Indisputably, the Eagles made their presence felt on the album. Henley appeared on six of the 10 tracks, playing drums and providing backing vocals, while Leadon and Meisner appeared on three tracks each. While all four Eagles did perform on the album, they did not appear as a single unit on any of them, although Frey, Henley, and Meisner all participated in *Birds* and *Rescue Me*. Ronstadt valued Meisner's high backing vocals, but wasn't fond of his bass playing, so she relied on Henley's former **Shiloh** bandmate, **Mike Bowden**, for those duties, though he did work the four-strings in *In My Reply*.

Even with the all-star cast, the album wasn't earth shaking for Ronstadt. Her fourth album, which was her first with **David Geffen**'s Asylum Records, became her true breakthrough album in 1973. In a bit of cross marketing, Capitol even released a second issue of the album in 1971 rebranding the album *Linda Ronstadt and Friends*, and giving top billing to the Eagles among those also appearing with her on the album on the cover. [55, 1398, 1399]

Glyn Johns Do-Over: Eagles' Harmonies Change His Mind

When Glyn Johns left Boulder, Colorado, in December 1971, the Eagles were flummoxed. Johns, who had produced rock heavyweights like **The Who** and **Led Zeppelin**, had traveled halfway across the world at **David Geffen**'s enthusiastic behest to watch the Eagles perform live in a freezing cold club in front of an uninspiring crowd of just eight. Johns, unabashedly honest, said he was not impressed with their musicianship, calling them "confused," and offered that he "didn't know what the fuss was all about."

Don Henley would explain to the *Denver Post* in 2015 that he thought the performance, and Johns' subsequent rejection, would have happened regardless of the venue because the band wasn't ready to cut an album yet. The group didn't know what it was doing, and neither did its management. But Geffen was not ready to give in. Johns was scheduled to be in Los Angeles in March 1972 to produce **Rita Coolidge** and **David Anderle** at Elektra Studios, so Geffen made another entreaty.

"Geffen would not let it go," Johns said, "insisting that I had not seen the Eagles in the best circumstances. He pestered me until I agreed to go back to L.A. and see the band in rehearsal, and thank God he did."

Johns said that he arrived in L.A. and spent the morning in a rehearsal hall and the band played through the set he had already seen in Boulder. The result, he said, was "pretty much the same." Unmoved, Johns and everyone in the hall decided to break for lunch when someone suggested they play Johns one more song, a Randy Meisner cut called *Take the Devil*. Frey and Bernie Leadon grabbed acoustic guitars and

GLYN JOHNS

Eventual Eagles producer Glyn Johns (right) at the sound board with Mick Jagger at Olympic Recording Studios in London in 1967.

Glyn Johns was already a legend in the music industry when then-Eagles manager David Geffen convinced the famed sound engineer and producer to sit in on a session with the not-quite-ready-for-prime-time Eagles on a cold winter night in Denver, Colorado, in 1971. Though the Denver "audition" did not go well for the band, the relationship between Johns and the group did not end there, mostly due to Geffen's relentless efforts.

When Johns was 17 he was an occasional singer and part-time manager for a band called **The Presidents**. He took a low-level engineer job at IBC Studios in London, where he was responsible for setting up and tearing down the equipment before and after recording sessions. As his skills and credibility grew, so did his reputation among rising artists in England. He was the engineer for **The Kinks**' debut album in 1964 and by the mid-1960s, he was go-to producer for the **Rolling Stones** (*Out of Our Heads*, *December's Children*, *Their Satanic Majesty's Request*, *Let It Bleed*), **The Small Faces**, **Traffic**, **Procol Harum**, and the **Steve Miller Band**. He took a huge leap forward professionally when he recorded **The Beatles**' *Let It Be* in 1969 and **The Who**'s *Who's Next* in 1971. Johns' work in the 1960s made him a legendary manager and producer, and when **David Geffen** started Asylum Records and signed the Eagles, he had just one producer in mind to record them: Johns.

It took some convincing—and two auditions—but the band's soaring harmonies sold him and he guided the group through two and a half albums, including back-to-back gold records and the band's first chart-topping single, *Best of My Love*. The band's musical tastes were expanding in 1973, and they felt they needed someone who let them express themselves more in the studio, so they parted with the English producer. Johns continued producing, and helped **Eric Clapton** finish his *Slowhand* album. In the 1980s, his work slowed, but he still managed to help engineer albums by **Midnight Oil**, **Nanci Griffith**, and **Belly**. He was inducted into the Rock and Roll Hall of Fame in 2012 and his autobiography, *Sound Man*, was released in 2014. [19, 133, 482, 1408]

Glenn Frey (left), Bernie Leadon and Don Henely take a break during a press conference in Amsterdam in 1972. Leadon and Henley teamed up on wrtiing Witchy Woman for the band's debut album. The song rose to #9 on Billboard's Hot 100 singles chart.

LEADON, HENLEY TEAM UP FOR MINOR-KEY *WITCHY WOMAN*

FALL 1971 – Not long after the soon-to-be Eagles inked their contracts with **David Geffen** and Asylum Records, they started searching for songs and writing new materials. Glenn Frey was turning over rocks and found two gems that his friends **Jackson Browne** and **Jack Tempchin** had developed, which ended up being *Take It Easy* and *Peaceful Easy Feeling*, respectively. Frey had also written two songs, the anthem to barflies *Chug All Night* and the introspective ballad with four-part harmonies that initially caught Glyn Johns' attention, *Most of Us Are Sad*. The most veteran of the band's musicians, Randy Meisner, was working on two songs, *Take the Devil*, and *Tryin'*, and was developing another with Bernie Leadon, *Earlybird*.

Leadon offered *Train Leaves Here This Morning*, a track he had co-written with former **Dillard & Clark** bandmate **Gene Clark**, that had been sadly overlooked on their *Great Expedition* album four years earlier. Relatively quiet as the band was developing songs was drummer Don Henley, whose father had taken ill during this period. Henley had written three songs for his former band, **Shiloh**, on their debut album a year earlier, but would only earn one writing credit on the Eagles debut album, *Witchy Woman*, a song that he co-wrote with Bernie Leadon. Still, it ended up in the *Billboard*'s Top 10.

Witchy Woman was developed from an Eastern Asian-influenced instrumental that Leadon had developed and played for Henley at his house in Topanga Canyon. "[Bernie] came over one day and started playing this strange, minor key riff that sounded like a Hollywood movie version of Indian music—you know, the kind of stuff they play when the Indians ride up on the ridge while the wagon train passes below," Henley said. "It had a haunting quality, and I thought it was interesting, so we put a rough version of it down on a cassette tape."

Henley said that shortly after he came down with the flu, contracted a high fever, and was semi-delirious at times. When the fever subsided, he returned to reading a book on the relentlessly spirited **Zelda Fitzgerald**, who, along with an amalgam of women he said he met at the Whiskey a Go Go and the Troubadour, became muses for his lyrics. Girls he knew in the early 1970s who had curiously played with Ouija boards and attended séances and palm readings also affected his writing, he said.

Years later, Leadon flatly explained the song's origin's to KSHE-95 in Crestwood, Missouri. "I don't know, it's sorta Chinese [sounding]," he said. "And then Henley put that tom-tom beat to it. I conceived all the sections of *Witchy Woman* as a guitar instrumental—and then Henley wrote the words to it."

Once Henley returned with the lyrics and the arrangement, the band started rehearsing and developing the song's harmonies.

"One day they needed a place to rehearse their vocal parts," **Linda Ronstadt** said in her autobiography *Simple Dreams*. "**John David [Souther]** offered the living room of our little house on Camrose Place. The room wasn't very big, so we went out to the movies to give them some space. When we walked in a few hours later, they sounded fantastic. They had worked out a four-part harmony arrangement of a song that Bernie and Don wrote and had spent time getting their vocal blend just right. In that small room, with only acoustic guitars and four really powerful voices, the sound was huge and rich. They called the new song *Witchy Woman*. I was sure it was going to be a hit." And it was, as the second song released off the band's debut album, it rose to #9 on *Billboard*'s Hot 100 chart.

> **[Bernie] came over one day and started playing this strange minor-key riff that sounded like Hollywood version of Indian music — you know, the kind of stuff they play when the Indians ride up on the ridge while the wagon train passes below. It had a haunting quality.**
>
> **— *Don Henley, Eagles co-founder***

"As soon as they saw that *Witchy Woman* worked as well as it did, they thought they could play a little bit harder, funkier stuff," Souther told *Guitar Player* in 2016. "Glenn was always up for playing stuff with some tempo. As it went on, they wanted to play rock and roll."

Now, with a grouping of songs they thought would fill their album, Geffen wanted them to begin playing the new music in front of an audience. But he wanted to avoid the glaring eyes of the Troubadour and Whiskey crowds, so he decided to send them someplace quieter. Some country-rock bands like the **Nitty Gritty Dirt Band** had found an out-of-the-way spot to work out new material in Colorado, so Geffen gave the band enough money to buy a van and live on, and set up a month of gigs in Aspen. It was time for them to become a band. [15, 208, 209, 534]

they sang the song around the piano without bass or drums.

"All of us were standing in a group near the door of the building, and there it was," Johns said. "The harmony blend from heaven. It knocked me clean off my feet. In effect, the band had four great lead singers all with completely different voices. When they sang together it created the most wonderful sound." At that instant, lunch was scrapped and Johns had changed his mind about producing the band. They spent the rest of the day reviewing the material the band had compiled and he begun to realize they were a much better combination of musicians than he had given them credit for.

"The contrast of Bernie's and Glenn's guitars was refreshing, with Randy and Don providing a solid and versatile rhythm section for it to all sit on. Their writing was fairly obvious, and I liked them as people," Johns said, "which was the main thing that made me go back, and it wasn't until I saw them in rehearsal, without a PA and without all the bad sound, that I realized their quality."

Johns said he was converted and excited to make the record, and was even sheepish in admitting that he hadn't spotted their potential earlier. He stayed with them for a few more days, helping them iron out tracks for the album, and then headed back to London the next day to begin recording their debut album. [19, 133, 1391]

Eagles, Johns Record Group's Debut Album in London

The soon-to-be-Eagles had convinced **Glyn Johns** that they were worth producing, so they packed up their gear and headed for England. Frey especially was excited, because he had wanted to record with Johns.

"[When] we were ready to record ... Glyn was our favorite producer in reputation," **Bernie Leadon** said, "because he can work in both capacities as engineer and producer, so he was a really good choice."

Frey, perhaps the producer's strongest advocate when the band was trying to choose someone to provide the musical direction, was enamored of Johns' approach. "Each one of us has a lot of respect for various engineers, but Glyn controls the sound like one of us would play our instrument," Frey said. "We were also looking for a guy who was super-experienced and could help direct all of us. A really important factor was that Glyn was an engineer and producer too. There's only a few people like that. He's one of the hardest-working people I've ever met in my life. When we record, he's like a fifth member of the group."

The band settled into a small apartment in London and took practically no time for anything else but recording. "[They] picked us up, took us to the studio, and then we'd go back to this little place and drink ourselves to sleep," Don Henley said. "Next day, we'd get up and do it all again."

Johns commanded the studio and stretched the band in areas they might not have gone otherwise. His first move was to focus the band on the vocal blends that he was so taken with in Los Angeles. He also wanted to concentrate on a more acoustic approach. "On *Take It Easy*, I got Bernie [Leadon] to play double-time banjo; they all thought it was a bonkers idea but it worked. It was already a great song, but that one little thing made it different."

"We learned tons and tons from Glyn," Henley said about their time in the studio with Johns. "How to cut through a lot of bullshit in arranging songs and how to shape them up real fast in the studio. He helped us take professional attitudes and mold them into professional recording artistry. He also taught me a lot about myself."

Johns said that he had a tough time discerning enthusiasm from the band. He had a clear idea of the sound he wanted to get with them, but they didn't like it much at the time. "They didn't seem to be over-enamored of what was going on," he said. "I couldn't even get them excited on playback—we finished the record and played it back, and they still weren't jumping up and down, which I put down to them being insecure, which they were then."

Insecure or not, the band came back from London after a two-week recording session, but Geffen still wasn't completely happy. The distribution of songs and writing credits was even, and the selection of songs was good, but Henley was the lead singer on just one cut: *Witchy Woman*. Frey had called Henley's voice "golden" and Geffen wanted him to have more of a presence. Neither Geffen nor the band was hap-

py with the London studio cut of **Jackson Browne**'s *Nightingale*, so Johns returned to Los Angeles and the band re-recorded it. Once that track was laid down, Geffen and his partner, **Elliot Roberts**, set to work to promote it. Full-page ads were taken out in *Billboard*, *Cashbox*, and *Record World* to generate buzz. They planned to unleash the Eagles on the music world in May 1972. [19, 36, 66, 133, 482]

SPRING 1972

RELEASES
- **Eagles**, *Take It Easy* (single)
- **Rick Nelson's Stone Canyon Band**, with Randy Meisner, *I Wanna Be With You* (single)

ON THE ROAD WITH ...
- **Eagles**: Joe Cocker, Joni Mitchell, Jackson Browne, Ned Doheny, Cass Elliott
- **Poco**, with Timothy B. Schmit: John Hammond

Eagles Visit Joshua Tree for Debut Cover Art Photoshoot

Fresh off recording their debut album in London, the Eagles returned to Los Angeles with just one task remaining before the LP could be released: get the album cover designed. **Crosby, Stills, & Nash** had tapped the creative fountain of **Gary Burden** and his photographer partner **Henry Diltz**, and they suggested the Eagles use them too.

Burden and Diltz had produced covers for CSN, **Mama Cass**, all **Neil Young**'s solo work, and **The Doors**. The covers Burden and Diltz created had become epochal in the late 1960s and early 1970s. **The Mamas and Papas**' *If You Can Believe Your Eyes and Ears* album cover with **Denny Doheny**, **Cass Elliot**, and **John** and **Michele Phillips** in a bathtub became iconic. So too did Crosby, Stills & Nash's eponymous album with the three singers sitting on a battered red couch in front of an abandoned house, and The Doors' *Morrison Hotel* album cover, where the band illicitly posed inside the uncooperative hotel's front window.

Having the selective Burden and Diltz handling a band's cover design was an impressive sign of stature in the rock music community, and Geffen and the Eagles wanted them. Moreover, after meeting, there was a genuine feel of camaraderie between Burden, Diltz, and the band. Bernie Leadon considered them the "cool guys" to have work on an album.

When the time came to get started, there wasn't much of a plan. Leadon described the concept as "go to the Troubadour and stay there until closing, and then we would drive to Joshua Tree." The band packed for the trip with a bag of peyote buttons, trail mix, bottles of tequila, water, and blankets. They headed to the desert and would shoot photos of what happened there. Leadon brought his banjo, and once the Troubadour closed, they headed out. Frey openly wondered how they found the campsite in the dark, but they arrived at 4:30 in the morning, each of them popped a peyote button in their mouths and started brewing some peyote tea. As the sun was rising, the band

spotted an eagle flying above, which proved inspirational to Frey.

Burden said his process for developing the covers always involved a collaboration with the artist. "I listen to them, I listen to the music and generally informs me what it wants to look like and say, visually," Burden told *Figment News* in 2013. "As I often say; I have never made *my* album cover. I lend my expertise to a project in service to the artists and the music. It's always about the music." He said he liked to take bands out of their comfort zone, as well, by taking trips that would get them away from their girlfriends, telephones, or anything that would interfere with his artistic direction.

On the trip to Joshua Tree with the Eagles, he employed another tool. Peyote was a key component of the trip, Burden admits. "I hasten to add, no one was hog tied and force fed anything," he said almost defensively. "It is my belief that if you are in the desert you should be in the desert. It was a mutual agreement and what came of that commitment has certainly served the band well. No? The images of the first album cover I think really set the tone for visually what Eagles are."

Artistically, the Joshua Tree trip was a success for Burden and Diltz. All the Eagles sales and marketing materials for the debut album emerged from the shots on that trip. Pictures of the band sitting atop boulders, unsmiling with brooding, smoldering visages, made their way onto full-page ads in *Billboard*, *Record World*, and *Cashbox*. The album cover itself would become a

ME

ET THE EAGLES

bone of contention between **David Geffen** and Burden and Diltz.

Burden had taken wonderfully gritty photos of the band around the campfire. He also captured a shot of the eagle Frey found so inspiring with its wings spread wide against a peerless blue sky. When he returned to his studio, he merged the photos into an album cover that folded out into a poster with the campfire photo at the bottom of the poster that visually ascended to the shot of the eagle at the top. It was an inspired approach and relatively unique to cover design at the time. That creativity was crushed, however, by Geffen, who didn't get it and chose economy over art.

Diltz said that Geffen, without consulting with him, Burden, or the band, had the cover glued shut, which eliminated the poster and "didn't make sense to anyone."

"The inside spread was upside down when you opened the cover," Burden added.

The album art hit its mark and conveyed the image that the band wanted. Now it was up to Geffen and Roberts to get the album onto the airwaves. It started slow, but by the summer of 1972, everyone was happy with the results. [1152, 1401, 1402, 1403, 1404]

SUMMER 1972

RELEASES
▶ **Eagles**, *Eagles* (album)
▶ **Eagles**, *Witchy Woman* (single)

MILESTONES
▶ **James Gang** with Joe Walsh: *Live in Concert* (album) certified GOLD, RIAA.
▶ **James Gang** with Joe Walsh: *Thirds* (album) certified GOLD, RIAA.

COLLABORATIONS
Timothy B. Schmit played bass guitar on **Redwing**'s album *What This Country Needs*.

ON THE ROAD WITH ...
▶ **Eagles**: Yes, The Edgar Winter Group, Neil Young, Procol Harum, Asule, Jo Jo Gunne, Mahavishnu Orchestra, Uriah Heep, Humble Pie, Black Oak Arkansas, Jethro Tull
▶ **Poco**, with Timothy B. Schmit: Leon Russell, J.J. Cale, Cornelius Brothers & Sister Rose, Blood, Sweat & Tears, Alice Cooper, Black Oak Arkansas, Bloodrock, Faces, Fleetwood Mac, James Gang, The Dillards, Three Dog Night, Tower of Power, Wishbone Ash

Asylum Records Releases Eagles Debut Album

Although the Eagles completed their self-titled album at the end of January 1972, it wasn't actually released until early that summer. Asylum Records founder **David Geffen** understood the value of building anticipation and began priming the pump for the album's release that spring.

He began dropping hints in the trade press that his new band had completed its work with **Glyn Johns** and their debut single was ready to drop.

Geffen started his assault on the trade press in May, and secured a front-page story in *Cashbox* about all of Asylum's new acts. **Linda Ronstadt**, **David Blue**, **Joni**

ALBUM | EAGLES

EAGLES
Eagles
Asylum Records, June 1972

The four members of the Eagles were not ebullient when producer **Glyn Johns** rolled the playback for their just-completed debut album. London was a drag for the Eagles and they wanted to go back to Los Angeles. But Johns' two weeks of studio work – at a bargain price of about $125,000 – produced a well-received debut. The band handled all their instrumentation on their own, and even though their approach was country-rock, there was no steel guitar. Glenn Frey, Randy Meisner and Bernie Leadon each got three writing credits apiece, while Don Henley shared a writing credit with Leadon. *Take It Easy* and *Nightingale* were contributed by **Jackson Browne**, and *Peaceful Easy Feeling* came from Frey's friend **Jack Tempchin**. The album's harmonic blend was made for radio. By August it had peaked at #22 nationally, and three songs, *Take It Easy*, *Peaceful Easy Feeling* and *Witchy Woman* had all cracked the top 25. The Eagles had arrived.

....

Chicago Daily Herald
June 30, 1972

Each year new groups cut albums, and most aren't worth a listen. But the Eagles are remarkable. They have a very distinctive sound when harmonizing. By the end of side 1 you could identify any song of theirs you ever hear. The music is real tight, a controlled fury on faster numbers like *Chug All Night* and some soft sounds on *Most of Us Are Sad* and *Train Leaves Here This Morning*. It is a great first album, and one of the best this year.

Rolling Stone
June 22, 1972

It's a girl my lord, in a flatbed Ford/ Slowin' down to take a look at me ... Each time I listen to *Take It Easy* it unfurls new pleasures. The rest of the songs – and a major part of the album – are as good as those lines. And get the single too – it has a side that isn't on the LP. Eagles is right behind **Jackson Browne**'s record as the best first album this year. And I could be persuaded to remove the word 'first' from that statement.
– *Bud Scoppa*

Ore. Statesman-Journal
June 25, 1972

From out of the Western skies comes Eagles. On the strength of the single *Take It Easy* and experience with other top L.A. bands, the group's first album shows promise. They come from **Poco**, **Flying Burrito Brothers**, **Dillard & Clark** and **Linda Ronstadt** bands. Eagles combine rhythm, catchy melody and creative lyrics to produce a soothing sounds. *Peaceful Easy Feeling* and *Nightingale* are good tunes dealing with simple love.

Mitchell, **Jackson Browne**, **Steve Ferguson**, **Ned Doheny**, **J.D. Souther**, **Judee Sill**, **Jo Jo Gunne**, and, of course, the Eagles, all adorned the cover of the trade magazine. To reach the music-buying public Geffen needed to convince radio stations and disc jockeys to embrace Asylum's artists, so he expended capital, monetary and otherwise, to elevate his stable. And he paid particular attention to lifting the Eagles.

In *Billboard*'s April 1, 1972 edition Geffen boasted expectations that Asylum would cross over $3 million in sales that year, and gushed over the recently released albums from Jo Jo Gunne, Browne and Sill. And he emphasized that the Eagles album would be released soon and they would be touring with **Neil Young** to start the summer.

The album's first single, *Take It Easy*, was released May 1, 1972, nearly two months ahead of the album and gradually began getting heavy airplay across the United States.

Record World reported that Atlantic Records CEO **Ahmet Ertegun**, who backed Geffen's Asylum label play, predicted that the Eagles debut would be #1 in six weeks, "which makes David Geffen's heart go pitter-patter."

While the band's debut never reach Ertegun's lofty projection, it made its presence felt on the radio. By the time the album was released June 17 *Take It Easy* was already in the Top 40. It cracked into the *Record World* top 100 at #84 on May 27. It landed on *Cashbox*'s top 100 at #96 on May 20, and on June 3 it entered the *Billboard* Hot 100 at #79.

"This record is a home run," *Record World*'s **Kal Rudman** wrote in his *Money Music* column June 3. "Many compare them to **Creedence Clearwater [Revival]** at their height. David Geffen, like **Wes Ferrell**, has become a legend in the business."

By June it was clear Asylum had a runaway hit on its hands. Geffen took the time to thank music directors across the country for their indulgence in a letter to *Record World*'s Rudman.

"Thank you and the many program directors and major top 40 stations who didn't 'wait and see' on the Eagles," Geffen wrote in the June 10, 1972 issue, "but went on it right away and really established an important group and important record from the very beginning. Since Asylum Records and I are new to the radio business, it is very encouraging to know that so many people give new things a chance. I am sincerely grateful."

By July 1 *Take It Easy* was breaking in every major and secondary Top 40 radio station in the country. It peaked at #6 on the *Record World* charts on August 5, and peaked at #12 on the *Billboard* Hot 100 chart on July 22. The critically acclaimed debut eventually produced two more Top 25 singles: *Witchy Woman* and *Peaceful Easy Feeling.*

For four frustrated, struggling musicians who couldn't buy a break just one year earlier, it was a quite a turnaround. Up ahead in the distance more struggles awaited, but for now the band began living the rock and roll dream. [10, 12, 14, 20, 36, 202, 588]

UP AHEAD IN THE DISTANCE

With the delivery of their debut album in June 1972, the Eagles achieved something that many of their country-rock brethren struggled with: commercial success. California bands like the Byrds, the Mamas and Papas, and Buffalo Springfield began to scratch the surface of commercial success, but they could not sustain. In the late 1960s Los Angeles-based bands like Poco, Dillard & Clark and the Flying Burrito Brothers began changing their formulas and made inroads, but like their predecessors could not find that final radio-pleasing ingredient. Although their musical skills were masterful, and their performances impressively tight, that element of commercial appeal remained elusive.

But the Eagles cracked the code on commercial success. Glenn Frey, affectionately known by his bandmates as *The Lone Arranger*, had an innate ability to take an average song and make it quite good. Further, he could make a good song great. And, has he did throughout the life, he could take a great song and make it legendary. Likewise, Don Henley's ability to conjure insightful, intimate lyrics and weave them into lilting harmonies with complex instrumentation evolved into his own master class in meaningful songwriting. Randy Meisner and Bernie Leadon had already spent time with high-performing bands and they brought precision playing and vocals, along with a country-rock credibility that was critical for that period in rock music.

David Geffen and his business acumen and marketing skills put the Eagles in a position to succeed, though it was their talent that ultimately drove their success. Collectively they advanced the genre of country-rock to another level. Even though the band would come to eschew that country-rock label, the Eagles' songs and performances in their debut and follow-up album, *Desperado*, pushed the music industry toward more commercial country-and-western infused rock. It created opportunities for new bands who used their formula.

The unexpected success of the band's first album created higher expectations for themselves, their fans and, to an uncomfortable degree, their label. They would run headlong into those expectations the following year. Extreme highs and lows were to come, but their evolution into a superband had begun. Book two in this series, *Up Ahead in the Distance*, will follow those changes.

– *Rik Forgo*

Index

Johnny Silver and the Silver Beatles 100
Johns, Glyn 48, 94, 122, 187, 189, 193, 196, 197, 198, 204
Johnson, Don 151
Jo Jo Gunne 179, 185, 203
Jones, George 19, 194
Jones, Quincy 122, 139
Jones, Rickie Lee 37
Joplin, Janis 53, 103
Jourard, Marty 89
Judy Garland Show, The 45, 61

K

Kaleidoscope 93
Kamen, Michael 151
Kasem, Casey 17
Katzenberg, Jeffrey 48
Kaufmann, Clayton "Doc" 21
Keisker, Marion 25
Kelcourse, Paul 80
Kelly, Walt 101, 114
Kemp, Allen 86, 124, 161, 188
Kennedy, John F. 61
Kent State University 64, 155
Kerouac, Jack 67, 187
Kershaw, Doug 142, 143, 151, 156, 160, 185
K&F Manufacturing 21
Kimmel, Robert 37
Kincaid, Jesse Lee 92
King, B.B. 16, 122, 123, 130, 140, 147, 159
King, Carol 122
King, Tom 41, 95, 108
Kingston Trio, The 16, 89
Kinks, The 82, 133, 197
Kitchen Cinq 116
Knechtel, Larry 142, 143
Knob Hill Singers, The 53
Knowing You, Loving You 93
Kriss, Tom 121
Kristofferson, Kris 175
Kruger, Debbie 160
KWKH 19
KXOA 68

L

Lamont, Joe 23

LaPiere, Cherilyn 47
Larson, Nicolette 37
Last Heard, The 44
Laughlon, Tom 85, 102
Laughton, Charles 32
Lawyers in Love 75
Leadbelly 148
Leadon, Bernie 15, 22, 35, 39, 40, 49, 50, 53, 55, 56, 62, 77, 79, 85, 87, 89, 92, 93, 94, 96, 97, 98, 99, 101, 113, 115, 116, 119, 120, 127, 131, 132, 133, 136, 139, 140, 149, 152, 153, 156, 159, 162, 164, 168, 171, 175, 176, 180, 182, 184, 185, 190, 193, 195, 196, 198, 200, 202, 204, 206
Led Zeppelin 55, 65, 94, 127, 133, 157, 189, 193, 196
Leiberson, Goddard 135
Lennon, John 15, 17, 33, 47, 48, 91, 100
Leo, Andy 102, 138
Leone, Dave 67, 68, 80
Lester, Richard 91
Let's Play Make Believe 99
Levine, Joey 76
Lewis, Jerry Lee 29
Lewis, L. David 146
Life in the Fast Lane 24
Lifeson, Alex 22
Lightfoot, Gordon 89, 120, 124, 166
Lime, The 109
Lind, Bob 87, 113
Lindley, David 37, 109
LiPuma, Tommy 128
LiveNation 70
Lives for No One 103
Loggins, Kenny 163
Loggins & Messina 163
Loma Records 83, 86
Lonely One, The 39
Lonely Teardrops 33
Longbranch/Pennywhistle 37, 55, 56, 66, 74, 77, 78, 116, 117, 120, 127, 132, 133, 134, 140, 142, 149, 156, 158, 159, 160, 164, 172, 176, 180, 182, 184, 185, 192, 194
Louisiana Hayride, The 15, 19, 25, 52
Love, Mike 43
Love Amy 116

Bibliography

[1] King, T. (2000). The Operator, New York, NY: Broadway Books

[2] Holson, L.M. (Feb 20, 2016). The Boy from Brooklyn: David Geffen Comes Home, with Cash to Spare, New York Times

[3] Singular, S. (1997). The Rise and Rise of David Geffen, Secaucus, NJ: Birch Lane Press

[4] Rudman, K. (Jun 10, 1972). A Letter from David Geffen, Record World, 27(1303), 16.

[5] Geddy, P.A. (Oct 28, 2015). Don Henley: Return to Cass County, County Line Magazine

[6] Eliot, M. (2005). To the Limit: The Untold Story of the Eagles, Cambridge, MA: Da Capo Press

[7] Varga, J. (May 4, 1970). Fact or fiction? With Joe Walsh, you never know, San Diego Union Tribune

[8] Associated Press (May 28, 1970). Festival will go on despite ban by court, Alton (Ill.) Evening Telegraph

[9] Magnotta, A. (Aug 17, 2018). State Shooting, iHeartRadio

[10] Recording Industry Assn. of America, Gold Certification, James Gang, James Gang Rides Again, (Oct 26, 1971).

[11] Gibson, J. (May 5, 1972). The Coast, Record World, 26(1298), 14.

[12] Rudman, K. (May 13, 1972). Money Music, Record World, 26(1299), 18.

[13] Rudman, K. (May 27, 1972). Money Music, Record World, 27(1301), 18.

[14] Record World. (Jun 17, 1972). Hits of the Week, 27(1304), 1.

[15] Browne, D. (Jun 10, 2016). Eagles Complete Discography: Don Henley Looks Back, Rolling Stone

[16] Recording Industry Assn. of America, Gold Certification, James Gang, Thirds, (June 26, 1972).

[17] Recording Industry Assn. of America, Gold Certification, Eagles, (Jan 22, 1974).

[18] Recording Industry Assn. of America, , (Mar 22, 1974).

[19] Johns, G. (2014). Glyn Johns: Sound Man, New York, NY: Plume/Penguin-Randon House

[20] Clemons, J. (Jul 2, 1972). You Can't Ignore Eagles Album, Salina (Kan.) Journal

[21] The Atlanta Constitution. (Feb 8, 1988). Singer Walsh wants Kent State Memorial, The Atlanta Constitution.

[22] The Central New Jersey Home News. (Apr 24, 1990). Kent State Memorial Shrouded in Controversy, The Central New Jersey Home News.

[23] Wisconsin State Journal. (Apr 28, 1990). Kent State memorial to add victims' names, Wisconsin State Journal.

[24] Valentine, P. (Feb 5, 1972). David Geffen: David's Talented Asylum, Sounds

[25] Prufer, J. (Dec 29, 2014). Joe Walsh's Measles on the Kent State Commons Back in 1966, DrRockandroll.

blogspot.com. Retrieved from http://drrockandroll.blogspot.com/2014/10/joe-walshs-measles-on-kent-state.html

[26] The Marshall (Texas) News Messenger. (Mar 21, 1971). Shiloh Record Released.

[27] The Marshall (Texas) News Messenger. (Jun 16, 1971). Group to Perform on National TV.

[28] Duncan, Z. (Oct 20, 1979). Blue Steel Plotting Fun Rock Revolution, The Indianapolis News

[29] Oermann, R. (Sep 28, 1983). 'New Kid in Town' is Jim Ed Norman, The Tennessean

[30] McCollum, B. (Feb 19, 2016). Glenn Frey remembered in sign ceremony in Royal Oak, Detroit Free Press

[31] Seger, B. (1978). Album Credits: Stranger in Town

[32] Marsh, D. (May 15, 1980). Bob Segar's 'Wind' is mostly hot air, Rolling Stone

[33] Hurst, J. (Feb 26, 1984). When these two country writers finally met, something funny started, Chicago Tribune

[34] Nicks, S. (1981). Album Credits: Bella Donna

[35] Taylor, J. (1976). Album Credits: Sweet Baby James

[36] Holloway, D. (Mar 10, 1973). The Eagles: Takin' It Easy, New Musical Express

[37] Walker, J. (Jun 1, 1973). Tom Waits: Thursday Afternoon, Sober as a Judge, Music World

[38] Rensin, D. (Jan 1, 1974). Jackson Browne: Such a Clever Innocence, Crawdaddy!

[39] Crowe, C. (May 18, 1975). America Starts to Rediscover Itself, Los Angeles Times

[40] Soeder, J. (Mar 18, 2009). With Eagles ready to land at The Q, Don Henley sounds off on the band's new album, musicians' rights and misinterpreted lyrics, The Cleveland Plain Dealer

[41] Charlesworth, C. (Dec 11, 1976). Eagles: Where Eagles Dare, Melody Maker

[42] Poet, J. (Jun 7, 1974). Sarah Kernochan: House of Pain; Tom Waits: Closing Time; Eagles: On The Border, Berkely Barb

[43] Burgess, S. (Jan 1, 1977). Echoes: An Interview with Gene Clark, Dark Star

[44] Charone, B. (Jan 8, 1977). The Eagles: Life in the Fast Lane, Sounds

[45] Silverton, P. (May 14, 1977). Frankie Miller: Be Good To Yourself, Sounds

[46] Gans, D. (Jan 1, 1980). The Eagles' Don Felder" A Short Run To the Top, Axe Magazine

[47] Thomas, M. (1981). Album Credits: Alive Alone

[48] Zimmer, D. (Nov 7, 1980). Randy Meisner: Ex-Eagle Flies High Solo, BAM

[49] Meisner, R. (1980). Album Credits: One More Song

[50] Seger, B. (1969). Album Credits: Ramblin' Gamblin' Man
[51] Seger, B. (1980). Album Credits: Against the Wind
[52] Seger, B. (1982). Album Credits: The Distance
[53] Seger, B. (1986). Album Credits: Like a Rock
[54] Seger, B. (1991). Album Credits: The Fire Inside
[55] Ronstadt, L. (1972). Album Credits: Linda Ronstadt
[56] Ronstadt, L. (1973). Album Credits: Don't Cry Now
[57] Ronstadt, L. (1974). Album Credits: Heart Like a Wheel
[58] Ronstadt, L. (1976). Album Credits: Hasten Down the Wind
[59] Ronstadt, L. (1977). Album Credits: Simple Dreams
[60] Ronstadt, L. (1998). Album Credits: We Ran
[61] Smyth, P. (1992). Album Credits: Patty Smyth
[62] Nicks, S. (1983). Album Credits: The Wild Heart
[63] Nicks, S. (1994). Album Credits: Street Angel
[64] Nelson, R. (1971). Album Credits: Rudy the Fifth
[65] Nelson, R. (1970). Album Credits: In Concert at the Troubadour, 1969
[66] Rensin, D. (Jul 1, 1974). The Eagles Have Stopped Takin' It Easy, Crawdaddy!
[67] Charone, B. (Jan 1, 1975). The Eagles, Hit Parader
[68] Rensin, D. (Jan 2, 1975). Tom Rush's Circle: Joni, James & Cows, Rolling Stone
[69] Rensin, D. (Mar 13, 1975). Dan Fogelberg: Home Free At Last, Rolling Stone
[70] Fogelberg, D. (1974). Album Credits: Souvenirs
[71] Fogelberg, D. (1977). Album Credits: Nether Lands
[72] Fogelberg, D. (1981). Album Credits: The Innocent Age
[73] Fogelberg, D. (1984). Album Credits: Windows and Walls
[74] Fogelberg, D. (1990). Album Credits: The Wild Places
[75] Scoppa, B. (Jun 1, 1975). The Eagles: One Of These Nights, Phonograph Record
[76] Rosen, S. (Dec 1, 1975). Fishing With the Eagles for the Universal Trout, Circus Raves
[77] Charone, B. (Mar 27, 1976). The Eagles: Desperados in Blue Jeans and Sneakers, Sounds
[78] Gilbert, J. (Oct 1, 1972). Flying Burrito Brothers: After the Burritos, Let It Rock
[79] Gilbert, J. (Mar 10, 1973). Eagles Make It Easy, Sounds
[80] Tobler, J. (May 1, 1973). Jac Holzman: Then and Now, ZigZag
[81] Charlesworth, C. (Apr 12, 1975). The Eagles: Eagle Eyed, Melody Maker
[82] Uhelszki, J. (Jun 1, 1975). Joe Walsh: Lonely in the Spotlight, Creem
[83] Nolan, T. (Jun 1, 1975). The Eagles: California Dreamin', Phonograph Record
[84] Case, B. (Jul 26, 1975). Billy Cobham: When This Man Plays Drums, He Thinks of a Box Trying to Roll, New Musical Express
[85] Gambaccini, P. (Jul 31, 1975). Elton & Company Seduce Wembley, Rolling Stone
[86] Gambaccini, P. (Aug 28, 1975). Eagles Fly High with Disco "Nights", Rolling Stone
[87] Goldstein, P. (1993). The Rolling Stone Interviews, New York, NY: Back Bay Books/Little, Brown & Co.
[88] Crowe, C. (Sep 25, 1975). Eagles: Chips Off the Old Buffalo, Rolling Stone
[89] Rosen, S. (Sep 27, 1975). Eagles: The Earthpeople's Band, Sounds
[90] Partridge, R. (Nov 1, 1975). Tanya Tucker: Country Girl, Melody Maker
[91] Woffinden, B. (Jan 10, 1976). A Cat Stevens Spiritual Tours Vacation, New Musical Express
[92] Brown, M. (Jan 24, 1976). The Soulful Return of Gene Clark, Sounds
[93] Brown, M. (Feb 21, 1976). You Don't Buck the Rules on the Bus: Buck Owens, Street Life
[94] Charone, B. (Feb 28, 1976). The Eagles: Their Greatest Hits 1971-1975 (Asylum), Sounds
[95] Uhelszki, J. (Mar 1, 1976). Lynyrd Skynyrd: Fifths and Fists for the Common Man, Creem
[96] Charone, B. (Mar 6, 1976). Bill Wyman: Lone Stone, Sounds
[97] Bell, M. (May 8, 1976). Steely Dan: The Royal Scam, New Musical Express
[98] Charlesworth, C. (May 15, 1976). Boz Scaggs: Scaggs in Silk, Melody Maker
[99] Deller, F. (Jun 5, 1976). Tom Waits: Would you say this man was attempting to convey an impression of sordid Bohemianism?, New Musical Express
[100] Brown, M. (Jun 12, 1976). Tom Waits: Warm Beer, Cold Women, Sounds
[101] Connolly, K. (Jul 1, 2013). Richard Thompson, BOMB
[102] Charone, B. (Sep 4, 1976). Linda Ronstadt: Hand Sewn Home Grown, Sounds
[103] Bangs, L. (Oct 1, 1976). How The Eagles Cleaned Up the Wild West, Music Gig
[104] Goldman, V. (Oct 30, 1976). Fleetwood Mac: John and Christine and Stevie and Lindsay and Mick..., Sounds
[105] Cohen, M. (Nov 1, 1976). Jackson Browne, Winning, Phonograph Record
[106] Farren, M. (Nov 13, 1976). Nashville, New Musical Express
[107] Charone, B. (Nov 20, 1976). Linda Ronstadt: Hey, Mister That's Me Up On The Jukebox, Sounds
[108] Kent, N. (Dec 18, 1976). The Eagles: Hotel California (Asylum), New Musical Express
[109] Hancock, D. (Feb 5, 1977). Eagles Get The Bird, National RockStar
[110] Demorest, S. (Mar 17, 1977). The Eagles: Hotel California (Asylum), Circus
[111] Whitall, S. (May 1, 1977). Rock Stars Talk Back, Creem
[112] Shapiro, S. (May 14, 1977). Bob Seger: Rock 'n' Roll's Mr Nice Guy, Sounds
[113] Cromelin, R. (Jun 1, 1977). Steely Dan: Excerpts from a Teenage Opera, Phonograph Record
[114] Makowski, P. (Jun 25, 1977). There'll Always Be A Rainbow As Long As Ritchie's Here, Sounds
[115] Morthland, J. (Jul 1, 1977). Bob Seger Conquers The World (And About Time!),
[116] Snowden, D. (Jul 12, 1977). Little Feat: The Rock and Roll Doctors, Rock Around the World
[117] Bell, M. (Jan 14, 1978). Boz Scaggs: Portrait of The Image as a Reality, New Musical Express
[118] Swenson, J. (Oct 5, 1978). REO Speedwagon Makes Its

Own Way, Rolling Stone

[119] Robins, W. (Dec 10, 1978). Steely Dan's Greatest-Hits & Quips, Los Angeles Times

[120] Leviton, M. (Mar 2, 1979). McGuinn Clark and Hillman: Flight From The Past, BAM

[121] Bell, M. (May 19, 1979). J. Geils Band: Return Of The Hard-Drivin' Man, New Musical Express

[122] Williams, M. (Sep 29, 1979). The Eagles: The Long Run (Asylum),

[123] Kent, N. (Sep 29, 1979). The Eagles: The Long Run (Asylum), New Musical Express

[124] Aronowitz, A. (Nov 14, 1979). Fleetwood Mac's Tusk and The Eagles' The Long Run, Washington Post

[125] Rambali, P. (Dec 8, 1979). Standing Up For The Small Man,

[126] Zimmer, D. (Feb 1, 1980). Graham Nash: The Winds Of Change, BAM

[127] Leviton, M. (Mar 7, 1980). More Hot Burritos: the Flying Burrito Brothers, BAM

[128] Robertson, S. (Mar 15, 1980). Warren Zevon: Bad Luck Streak In Dancing School (Asylum) and Wanted Dead Or Alive (Pickwick),

[129] Bell, M. (Mar 15, 1980). Call Tom Petty The New Springsteen And He'll Cut You!, New Musical Express

[130] Cooper, M. (Mar 22, 1980). The Eagles: Oakland Coliseum, Record Mirror

[131] Marsh, D. (Jun 1, 1980). Father-Figure Knows Best: Rock managers from Elvis to Elvis, Trouser Press

[132] Tobler, J. (Jan 1, 1982). Bill Szymczyk, The Record Producers

[133] Tobler, J. (Jan 1, 1982). Glyn Johns, The Record Producers

[134] Rensin, D. (Jul 1, 1982). 20 Questions: Stevie Nicks, Playboy

[135] Tobler, J. (1983). The Guitar Greats - The 1982 BBC Interviews, Buckinghamshire, UK: Northdown Publishing Ltd.

[136] Zimmer, D. (Mar 1, 1983). Danny Kortchmar: The Standup Rocker, Record

[137] Holdship, B. (May 1, 1983). Bob Seger: Big Victories, Creem

[138] Cook, R. (Feb 23, 1985). Don Henley, New Musical Express

[139] Tannenbaum, R. (Oct 1, 1985). Pino Palladino Doesn't Fret, Musician

[140] Scoppa, B. (Jan 1, 1986). Don Henley in Conversation, Record

[141] Simmons, S. (Oct 1, 1986). I Confronted Metallica On Their Own Terms!, Creem

[142] Sweeting, A. (Oct 1, 1987). The Jesus & Mary Chain: Ah, Showbusiness.., Q

[143] Rowland, M. (Dec 1, 1988). If Guns N' Roses are Outlawed, only Outlaws will have Guns N' Roses, Musician

[144] Zimmer, D. (Dec 2, 1988). The Desert Rose Band: Chris Hillman's Hot Burrito #3, BAM

[145] Walker, C. (Jan 1, 1990). Guy Clark: Cold Dog Soup, Steve Young: Primal Young, Conway Savage: Nothing Broken, Bap Kennedy: Lonely Street, HQ

[146] Maconie, S. (Feb 2, 1991). Motorhead: Don't Lemmy Be

Misunderstood, New Musical Express

[147] Tannenbaum, R. (Apr 16, 1992). Country's New Gold Rush, Rolling Stone

[148] Bradley, L. (Jul 2, 1992). Glenn Frey: Life After The Eagles, Independent

[149] DeCurtis, A. (Apr 1, 1993). Garth Brooks: Ropin' The Wind, Rolling Stone

[150] Simmons, S. (Jan 1, 1994). Sheryl Crow, Rolling Stone

[151] Eggar, R. (Jan 23, 1994). Garth Brooks, The Sunday Times

[152] DiMartino, D. (Aug 1, 1994). The Eagles: Irvine Meadows Amphitheatre, California, MOJO

[153] Hoskyns, B. (Sep 1, 1994). Neil Young: A Conversation with Elliot Roberts, MOJO

[154] Wheeler, S.P. (Sep 1, 1994). Bob Seger: Turning The Page, Music Connection

[155] DeYoung, B. (Jan 6, 1995). Willie Nelson: Funny How Time Slips Away, Goldmine

[156] Selvin, J. (Mar 19, 1995). Ronstadt Proves She Can Go Home Again, San Francisco Chronicle

[157] Weizmann, D. (Apr 7, 1995). Techno Queen of Melrose Place: Traci Lords, Los Angeles Reader

[158] Roeser, S. (Aug 18, 1995). Warren Zevon: Left Jabs and Roundhouse Rights, Goldmine

[159] Hutton, J. (Jan 1, 1996). L.A. Confidential: Life In The Fast Lane With Redd Kross's Jeffrey & Steven McDonald, Bucketful of Brains

[160] Hibbert, T. (Aug 1, 1996). 'We're the F***in' Eagles. Kiss My Ass!', Q

[161] Associated Press (Mar 21, 1980). 'Desperate trucker' frees hostage for a song, Fort Myers News-Press

[162] Hoskyns, B. (Dec 1, 1996). Ed Sanders and the Fugs, MOJO

[163] Zolo, P. (Jan 1, 1997). Portrait - The Music of Dan Fogelberg from 1972-1997, Columbia Legacy

[164] Black, J. (Jan 1, 1997). The Troubadour Club: A History, Troubadour

[165] Simmons, S. (Jul 1, 1997). Crazy Horse: Ralph, Billy, Poncho... and Neil, MOJO

[166] DiMartino, D. (Sep 1, 1997). Fleetwood Mac: The Way We Were, MOJO

[167] Kruger, D. (Jun 17, 1998). The Linda Ronstadt Interview, DebbieKruger.com/writer/freelance/ronstadt.html + DebbieKruger.com/writer

[168] Hoskyns, B. (Jul 1, 1998). Gram Parsons: The Good Ol' Boy, MOJO

[169] Himmelsbach, E. (Jul 12, 1998). Brian Wilson: The Last Brother, Los Angeles Times

[170] O'Hagan, S. (Sep 12, 1998). Gram Parsons: Another Country, Guardian

[171] Kruger, D. (Oct 9, 1998). J D Souther, Goldmine

[172] Lynskey, D. (Nov 1, 1998). Pras: Playa For Today, Face

[173] Hoskyns, B. (Apr 1, 1999). What's He Building In There? An Interview with Tom Waits, MOJO

[174] George-Warren, H. (Jul 1, 1999). The Long Way Around: Gram Parsons, No Depression

[175] Cameron, K. (Sep 11, 1999). Leftfield: "We Waited. That's What We Did.", New Musical Express

[176] Himmelsbach, E. (Mar 3, 2000). Sons of The Pioneers:

Beachwood Sparks, LA Weekly

[177] George-Warren, H. (Jul 15, 2000). Southern Gallery: Tom Petty, Oxford American

[178] Hardy, P. (2001). The Faber Companion to 20th Century Popular Music: The Eagles, London, UK: Faber & Faber

[179] Hoskyns, B. (Jan 1, 2001). Hotel Roberto, Rock's Backpages

[180] Hoskyns, B. (Jan 26, 2001). Almost Infamous, Rock's Backpages

[181] Bennettt, M. (Aug 19, 1972). A fine singing band, but elusive, The Brandon (Manitoba, Canada) Sun

[182] Weller, D. (May 24, 1973). Eagles Soar Into Diversity, Honolulu Star-Bulletin

[183] Hilburn, R. (Apr 14, 1974). The Eagles: Hatched in a Bar-room, Los Angeles Times

[184] Garfield, K. (Jun 2, 1974). Eagles Waiting to Fly Higher, The (Nashville) Tennessean

[185] McDonough, J. (Jul 29, 1973). Eagles With a Tale of Young Man in the West, San Francisco Examiner

[186] Isenberg, B. (Jun 27, 1976). Putting Stars in Their Places, Los Angeles Times

[187] Arar, Y. (Dec 24, 1980). Randy Meisner: A Former Eagle Wings It Alone, Washington (Pa.) Observer-Reporter

[188] Martin, G. (Jan 1, 2003). Rings Around Cardiff: Super Furry Animals, Daily Mirror

[189] Mack, J. (1982). Album Credits: Jack Mack and the Heart Attack: Cardiac Party

[190] Campbell, M. (Aug 2, 1988). Little River Band is back and has Shorrock singing, Fon Du Lac Commonwealth Reporter

[191] Campbell, M. (Aug 25, 1988). Little River Band hopes Eagle combination flies, Richmond (Ind.) Palladium-Item

[192] Waterloo (Iowa) Courier. (Jul 24, 1988). Little River Band back with Shorrock.

[193] Footman, T. (Nov 1, 2003). Gathering Moss: The Fossilisation of Rolling Stone, Rock's Backpages

[194] Sutcliffe, P. (Dec 1, 2003). Fleetwood Mac: Take it to the Limit, MOJO

[195] Willman, C. (Oct 11, 2018). Lindsey Buckingham's Fleetwood Mac Attack: 21 Things We Learned From His Lawsuit, Variety

[196] Wood, M. (Jul 17, 2017). Why I felt betrayed by Fleetwood Mac at Classic West, Los Angeles Times

[197] Wood, M. (Jul 16, 2017). The Eagles fly again at the Classic West, Los Angeles Times

[198] Gans, D. (Sep 1, 1982). Fleetwood Mac: Where's Stevie?, The Record

[199] Reckard, E.S. (Sep 5, 1989). Azoff Quits as Chairman of MCA's Music Unit,

[200] Grein, P. (May 7, 1983). Azoff Looking Beyond Records, Billboard

[201] Billboard. (Jan 25, 2018). No. 4: Irving Azoff | Power 100, Billboard.

[202] Billboard. (Jun 17, 1972). Eagles - Asylum SD 5054 (Atlantic), Billboard.

[203] Billboard. (Jul 1, 1972). Hot Chart Action, Billboard.

[204] Freedland, N. (Jul 8, 1972). Two Neophyte Labels Compare Early Notes, Billboard

[205] Billboard. (Jul 22, 1972). Young Bloods Lend Zest to Management, Agency Fields, Billboard.

[206] Billboard. (Jul 22, 1972). Being Involved with the Music is the Key to Running a Successful Night Club, Billboard.

[207] Greene, A. (Feb 7, 2013). Flashback: All the Eagles Unite for Rock and Roll Hall of Fame Induction, Rolling Stone

[208] K-SHE-95 - Real Rock Radio. (Jun 6, 2016). Don Henley reveals the inspiration to 'Witchy Woman'.

[209] Crowe, C. (Aug 1, 2003). Eagles: Very Best Of - Conversations with Don Henley and Glenn Frey, Retrieved from http://www.theuncool.com/journalism/the-very-best-of-the-eagles/

[210] Ragland, J. (Aug 24, 2000). Channel Island Now is Public Property, Los Angeles Times

[211] Eagles. (2003). Album Credits: The Very Best Of

[212] Kuntzman, G. (Jan 19, 2016). Glenn Frey's death is sad, but the Eagles were a horrific band, New York Daily News

[213] Christgau, R. (Jun 1, 1972). Trying to Understand the Eagles, Newsday

[214] Klosterman, C. (2013). I Wear the Black Hat: Grappling with Villains (Real and Imagined), New York, NY: Scribner

[215] Deusner, S. (Aug 9, 2013). Quit defending the Eagles! They're simply terrible, Salon

[216] Willman, C. (Jan 20, 2016). Why Are the Eagles So Hated? An Explainer on the Immensely Popular Yet Divisive Rock Band, Billboard

[217] Fanelli, D. (Sep 21, 2017). Don Felder Talks Eagles Gear, "Hotel California" and His Slide Guitar Influences, Guitar World

[218] Felder, D. (2008). Heaven and Hell : My Life in the Eagles, Hoboken, NJ: John Wiley & Sons

[220] Liberty, J. (Sep 7, 2014). Kalamazoo DJ to meet the Eagles almost 4 decades after helping band get No. 1 hit, Retrieved from https://www.mlive.com/entertainment/kalamazoo/index.ssf/2014/09/longtime_kalamazoo_dj_to_meet.html

[221] Craker, L. (Sep 9, 2014). The Eagles' energetic encore tops nostalgic night (Review, photo gallery), Retrieved from https://localspins.com/eagles-energetic-encore-tops/

[222] Bacher, D. (Oct 8, 2012). Joe Walsh's Long Run, Retrieved from https://www.interviewmagazine.com/music/joe-walsh-analog-man

[223] Clary, M. (May 4, 1975). The return of Joe Walsh, Akron (Ohio) Beacon Journal

[224] Taylor, C. (Oct 24, 2010). Emma's fountain lives long after rock 'n' roll tragedy, Boulder (Colo.) Daily Camera

[225] Beinstock, R. (May 19, 2016). Joe Walsh: My Life in 15 Songs, Rolling Stone

[226] Kiefer, P. (Nov 1, 2018). Irving Azoff, Hollywood A-listers Team to Save Legendary Deli Nate 'n Al, The Hollywood Reporter

[227] Aswad, J. (Jul 10, 2018). Mega-Manager Irving Azoff Grows Business With Diverse Portfolio, Variety

[228] Carson, C. (Aug 13, 1977). Friends together for 'Progres-

sions', Binghamton (N.Y.) Press and Sun-Bulletin

[229] Laughton, T. (Aug 1, 2016). Tom Laughton - The Maudy Quintet, Retrieved from http://www.gainesvillerockhistory.com/MaundyQuintet.htm

[230] George-Warren, H. (Jul 15, 2000). Southern Gallery: Tom Petty, Oxford American

[231] Einarson, J. (2001). Desperados: The Roots of Country Rock, New York, NY: Cooper Square Press

[232] Gullboy Music Review (Mar 25, 2003). Hearts and Flowers, Gullboy Music Review. Retrieved from http://gullbuy.com/buy/2003/3_25/heartsflo.php

[233] Lewis, R. (Jul 17, 2015). Disneyland at 60: Five great musical moments at the Magic Kingdom, Los Angeles Times

[234] Broeske, P. (Feb 12, 1989). A 'Wiseguy' Who's Really a Regular Guy : TV's Ken Wahl, a star who shuns the star label, relishes his real-life role as an 'anti-celebrity', Los Angeles Times

[235] Oermann, R.K. (Sep 15, 1985). Fabulous McGuire Sisters Revive Sweet Trio Harmony, The (Nashville) Tennessean

[236] Lewis, R. (Jan 19, 2016). Linda Ronstadt, whose backing band was the hub for the Eagles, remembers Glenn Frey, Los Angeles Times

[237] The Madison Square Garden Company. (Oct 8, 2018). Azoff Music Management Reaches Agreement to Acquire The Madison Square Garden Company's 50 Percent Interest, The Madison Square Garden Company.

[238] Green, S. (Sep 11, 2013). Irving Azoff Teams Up Again With James Dolan At The Madison Square Garden, Jewish Business News

[239] Aswad, J. (Oct 8, 2018). Azoff Management to Buy Out MSG's Interest in Azoff-MSG Entertainment for $125 Million, Variety

[240] Begley, S. (Mar 7, 2016). Eagles Co-Founder's Wife Lana Ray Meisner Dies in Accidental Shooting, Time

[241] Walker, T. (Mar 7, 2016). Eagles founder Randy Meisner's wife Lana Rae Meisner dies at couple's home after accidental gunshot to the head, Independent

[242] Smith, E. (Jan 1, 2013). Live Nation Chairman Azoff Resigns, Wall Street Journal

[243] Live Nation Entertainment. (Dec 31, 2012). Irving Azoff Resigns As Live Nation Entertainment Chairman and Front Line CEO, Live Nation Entertainment.

[244] Ellis, R. (Nov 10, 2018). California wildfire burns film set used in HBO's 'Westworld,' other TV shows and movies, CNN

[245] Cacciola, S. (Mar 24, 2014). The Man in the Middle, New York Times

[246] Smith, E. (Feb 21, 2009). Can He Save Rock 'n' Roll?, Wall Street Journal

[247] Hoskyns, B. (2006). Hotel California, Hoboken, NJ: Joihn Wiley & Sons

[248] Reid, G. (Feb 25, 2006). Stevie Nicks, New Zealand Herald

[249] Sutcliffe, P. (Jan 1, 2006). David Gilmour: And This Is Me.., MOJO

[250] Cameron, K. (Apr 1, 2007). The Stooges: Return To The Fun House, MOJO

[251] Brown, M. (Sep 8, 2007). Stevie Nicks: A Survivor's Story, Telegraph Magazine

[252] Simmons, S. (May 1, 2008). The Q Interview: Stevie Nicks, Q

[253] Snow, M. (Oct 1, 2009). Tom Petty, MOJO

[254] Fogerty, J. (2009). Album Credits: The Blue Ridge Rangers Ride Again

[255] Hoskyns, B. (Mar 1, 2013). Heartaches and Hangovers: Gram Parsons' GP, MOJO

[256] Butcher, S. (Feb 1, 2018). Boyd Elder Is the Most Famous Artist You've Never Heard Of, Texas Monthly

[257] Fauerso, N. (Oct 8, 2018). Boyd Elder Dies at 74, Glassfire

[258] Bloch, M. (Sep 27, 1978). The West is Won!, The Palm Beach (Fla.) Post

[259] Kruger, D. (Jun 1, 2013). The Eagles: Birds Of Pray, Rhythms

[260] Sutcliffe, P. (Jun 1, 2013). The Eagles: History Of The Eagles: The Story Of An American Band, MOJO

[261] Martin, G. (Nov 17, 2014). Charles Manson and the Death of the Californian Dream, Sabotage Times

[262] Peeples, S.K. (Mar 1, 1978). Boyd Elder: Encounters of the Southwestern Kind, Rocky Mountain Musical Express

[263] Hoskyns, B. (Jan 28, 2016). Glenn Frey, 1948-2016, Billboard

[264] San Diego Reader. (May 10, 2007). Scottsville Squirrel Barkers.

[265] Patterson, J. (Aug 16, 1992). "Common Thread" raising money for Walden Woods, Indiana (Pa.) Gazette

[266] Spevak, J. (Jun 6, 1993). Ex-Eagles in concert: Frey glided, Walsh soared, Rochester (N.Y.) Democrat and Chronicle

[267] Graff, G. (Jun 7, 1993). 2 Old Birds Still Fly, Detroit Free Press

[268] Knight-Ridder News Service. (Jul 24, 1993). Musician segues into own TV series, .

[269] Ciliberti, D.F. (Aug 27, 1993). "Glenn Frey Live" Laces with 1970s Eagles hits, Morristown (N.J.) Daily Record

[270] Bobbin, J. (Oct 23, 1993). Former Eagle Glenn Frey moves to TV, Tribune Media Service

[271] Goldstein, P. (Sep 29, 1985). Frey continues to spread his wings, Los Angeles Times

[272] Vare, E.A. (Dec 15, 1985). Musician Frey enters filmland, Hattiesburg (Miss.) American

[273] Shriver Jr, J. (May 20, 1990). New record companies scour the globe in hopes of swinging on a star, Los Angeles Times

[274] Scapelliti, C. (May 20, 2017). Did Jethro Tull Inspire the Eagles' "Hotel California?", Guitar Player

[275] Aspden, P. (Apr 3, 2017). Why Hotel California marked a watershed for rock, Financial Times

[276] Asgar, R. (Jun 25, 2014). Theft By Led Zeppelin And Apple? No, Just Innovation, Forbes

[277] Billboard. (Jun 11, 2001). Eagles Drop Suit Against Eagle Group.

[278] Reckard, E.S. (Sep 5, 1989). Azoff Quits as Chairman of MCA's Music Unit, Associated Press

[279] Los Angeles Times. (Sep 6, 1989). Azoff Resigns as Head

of MCA Music Unit to Form Own Firm.

[280] Grow, K. (Nov 15, 2014). Joe Walsh on His 'Sonic High-ways' Appearance: 'I'm an Honorary Foo Fighter', Rolling Stone

[281] Baltin, S. (May 14, 2014). Joe Walsh Records With Foo Fighters, Talks Eagles & Blues Album, Billboard

[282] Chapel Hill (N.C.) Daily Tar Heel. (Jun 1, 1978). Randy Meisner: Randy Meisner.

[283] Meisner, R. (1978). Album Credits: Randy Meisner

[284] Meisner, R. (1982). Album Credits: Randy Meisner: Randy Meisner

[285] Williams, J. (Feb 22, 1980). Souther - Co-Founder of California Rock, The Gaffney (S.C.) Ledger

[286] Kishbaugh, J. (Nov 14, 1980). Meisner Learns from His Early Mistakes, Wilkes-Barre (Pa.) Citizens' Voice

[287] Arar, Y. (Nov 27, 1980). Ex-Eagle's solo flight seems to be soaring after flying the coop, Fort Meyers (Fla.) News-Press

[288] Kowalski, J. (Aug 26, 1984). "The Allnighter" by Frey has "flashes", Fon Du Lac (Wis.) Commonwealth Reporter

[289] Ferguson, R. (Dec 22, 1984). Alone, Timothy B.'s a crowd, Mattoon (Ill.) Journal Gazette

[290] Hilburn, R. (May 23, 1982). The Eagles - The Long Run is Over, Los Angeles Times

[291] Jones, P. (Jul 12, 1975). British Boxoffice Receipts Sizzling, Billboard

[292] Recording Industry Assn. of America, RIAA Gold Record Winners, (Jul 12, 1975).

[293] Recording Industry Assn. of America, One of These Nights, (Aug 2, 1975).

[294] Hilburn, R. (Dec 13, 1975). One of Eagles Leaves the Nest, Los Angeles Times

[295] Palmer, R. (Mar 26, 1981). Rock tycoon's musical domain keeps him busy and successful, New York Times

[296] Bream, J. (Feb 21, 1995). The Egos Have Landed, Minne-apolis Star Tribune

[297] Reynolds, L. (Aug 11, 1982). Secret messages in music?, Mount Carmel (Ill.) Daily Republican-Register

[298] U.S. House of Representatives, H.R.6363 - Phonograph Record Backward Masking Labeling Act of 1982, (May 12, 1982).

[299] Recording Industry Assn. of America, Eagles: Lyin' Eyes, Asylum, (Nov 8, 1975).

[300] Snopes.com (Apr 24, 2014). The Eagles song "Hotel California" is about Satanism, Snopes.com. Retrieved from https://www.snopes.com/fact-check/hotel-cal-ifornia/

[301] Selvin, J. (Nov 26, 1995). Q&A with Don Henley, San Francisco Examiner

[302] Richey, R. (Feb 5, 1984). Catering to Satan, Muncie (Ind.) Star Press

[303] Marsh, D. (Jul 3, 1975). 'One of These Nights' Lacks Sense of Unity - Eagles have done better, Rolling Stone

[304] Greene, A. (Jul 16, 2015). Flashback: The Eagles Play 'Take It to the Limit' in 1977, Rolling Stone

[305] Gallagher, B. (Jun 9, 2017). Final Cars 3 Trailer Pushes Lightning McQueen to the Limit, Retrieved from https://movieweb.com/cars-3-trailer-final/

[306] Sullivan, P. (Oct 25, 1973). Gram Parsons: The Mysterious Death – and Aftermath, Rolling Stone

[307] Los Angeles Times. (Sep 20, 1973). Gram Parsons Dies; Country, Rock Musicisn.

[308] New York Times. (Nov 7, 1973). 2 Plead in Theft and Burn-ing of Coffin with Rock Singer, New York Times.

[309] Billboard. (Feb 12, 2001). Fired Eagles Guitarist Felder Sues Henley, Frey.

[310] Kennedy, M. (Jan 19, 2018). Eagles v. Hotel California: After Lawsuit, Band Reaches A Settlement, Re-trieved from https://www.npr.org/sections/thet-wo-way/2018/01/19/579145980/eagles-v-hotel-cali-fornia-after-lawsuit-band-reaches-a-settlement

[311] Stempel, J. (Jan 16, 2018). Widow of Eagles guitarist Frey sues NYC hospital for wrongful death, Reuters

[312] Itzkoff, D. (Feb 12, 2013). The Long, Long Run: Glenn Frey and Don Henley Reflect on 'History of the Eagles', New York Times

[313] Edgers, G. (Nov 28, 2016). Don Henley says the Eagles are done. It was always Glenn Frey's band, Washing-ton Post

[314] Scoppa, B. (Mar 9, 2013). Don Felder Gives 'History of the Eagles' a Mixed Review, The Hollywood Reporter

[315] Collins, J. (Jun 1, 2017). Welcome To The Hotel California (Trademark), Forbes

[316] Variety. (Jan 10, 2018). Joe Walsh Signs With Sony/ATV Music Publishing.

[317] Treleven, E. (Apr 17, 2015). Don Henley and Duluth Trad-ing settle lawsuit, apology issued, Wisconsin State Journal

[318] Michaels, S. (Jun 4, 2014). The Eagles' Don Henley accuses Frank Ocean and Okkervil River of song theft, Guardian

[319] Brooks, D. (Oct 3, 2016). Irving Azoff says the "Pirates" at YouTube are "Really Evil", Retrieved from http://www.ampthemag.com/the-real/irving-azoff-says-pirates-youtube-really-evil/

[320] Associated Press. (Oct 15, 2000). Henley sued by long-time fan, Associated Press.

[321] Brown, H. (Oct 10, 2016). Bad Vibrations: where did it all go wrong for the Beach Boys?, The Telegraph

[322] Halperin, S. (Sep 17, 2018). Paul McCartney, Don Henley, Katy Perry, More Pen Letter to SiriusXM: 'We Will Boycott', Variety

[323] New York Daily News. (Nov 20, 2017). Glenn Frey's son Deacon joins Eagles as the band eyes a new tour.

[324] Tunis, W. (Apr 5, 2018). Don Henley on the Eagles carry-ing on: "We wanted everybody to be all in.", Lexington (Ky.) Herald-Leader

[325] (Aug 7, 2018). Pre-Eagles Glenn Frey & J.D. Souther album set for reissue, Retrieved from https://www.kshe95.com/real-rock-news/pre-eagles-glenn-frey-j-d-souther-album-set-for-reissue/

[326] Waddell, R. (Oct 12, 2007). The Billboard Q&A: The Eagles' Glenn Frey, Billboard

[327] Edgers, G. (Jan 18, 2016). Glenn Frey, 'the one who start-ed it all' with the Eagles, Washington Post

[328] Graff, G. (Oct 11, 2018). Deacon Frey flies like an Eagle in

his father's old band, The Oakland Press

[329] Atkinson, K. (Sep 26, 2018). Eagles Announce 'Legacy' CD & LP Box Sets, Billboard

[330] Eau Claire (Wis.) Leader-Telegram. (Mar 24, 1994). Hell hath frozen over for the Eagles.

[331] Billboard (Mar 16, 1985). Chart History: Glenn Frey, Billboard. Retrieved from https://www.billboard.com/music/glenn-frey/chart-history

[332] Berry, W. (Mar 22, 1980). Everything's coming up mega-bucks for Frey, Associated Press

[333] Picozzi, M. (Nov 6, 2018). And he had a part in the show too!, Retrieved from http://www.1029thewhale.com/2018/11/06/and-he-had-a-part-in-the-show-too/

[334] Dretzka, G. (Apr 23, 2014). Down and Dangerous, Retrieved from http://moviecitynews.com/author/gary-dretzka../page/13/

[335] (Jan 14, 2019). Eagles Songwriter Jack Tempchin To Be Inducted Into The Songwriters Hall of Fame, Retrieved from https://www.broadwayworld.com/bwwmusic/article/Eagles-Songwriter-Jack-Tempchin-To-Be-Inducted-Into-The-Songwriters-Hall-of-Fame-20190114

[336] Kawashima, D. (Jun 28, 2017). Interview with Jack Tempchin, Singer/Songwriter and Hit Songwriter For The Eagles ("Peaceful Easy Feeling," "Already Gone") and Glenn Frey, Songwriter Universe

[337] Graff, G. (Jun 29, 1992). Ex-Eagle Flies Solo, Detroit Free Press

[338] Hilburn, R. (Jun 5, 1994). Hotel California: Back in business, The Age (Melbourne, Victoria, Australia)

[339] Skiba, K. (Dec 6, 2016). Staples, Eagles get Kennedy Center Honors, Chicago Tribune

[340] Graff, G. (Jan 18, 2016). How Glenn Frey & Don Henley Became the Eagles, As Told by Linda Ronstadt, Billboard

[341] Epting, C. (Jun 4, 2013). Ten Places the Eagles Took Flight, Rock Cellar Magazine

[342] Edgers, G. (Dec 4, 2016). Eagles: Hell has really frozen over, Washington Post

[343] Young, C.M. (Nov 29, 1979). The Eagles: Hell if for Heroes, Rolling Stone

[344] McConnell, M. (Jan 19, 2016). Glenn Frey's musical sojourn started at his Royal Oak high school with an $18 gig, The Oakland Press

[345] Johnson, G. (Jan 1, 2009). MRRL Hall of Fame: GLENN FREY, Michigan Rock and Roll Hall of Fame. Retrieved from https://www.michiganrockandrolllegends.com/mrrl-hall-of-fame/105-glenn-frey

[346] Hilburn, R. (Aug 12, 1972). Souther album rewarding, The Honolulu Advertiser

[347] James, J. (Aug 21, 1966). Animals in Action - One Teenager's View, Santa Rosa (Ca.) Press Democrat

[348] James, J. (Feb 12, 1967). Spotlight - The New Breed, Santa Rosa (Ca.) Press Democrat

[349] Steele, G. (Apr 21, 1967). Washington High School - Benefit for Adopted Son, The Argus (Fremont, Ca.)

[350] Santa Rosa (Ca.) Press Democrat. (Dec 16, 1968). Glad!.

[351] San Francisco Examiner. (Apr 27, 1986). The New Breed:

Want Ad Reader.

[352] Schmit, T.B. (2009). Album Credits: Expando

[353] Schmit, T.B. (2001). Album Credits: Feed the Fire

[354] Schmit, T.B. (1990). Album Credits: Tell Me the Truth

[355] Schmit, T.B. (1987). Album Credits: Timothy B

[356] Schmit, T.B. (1984). Album Credits: Playin' It Cool

[357] Schmit, T.B. (2016). Album Credits: Leap of Faith

[358] Dayton Daily News. (Sep 24, 1972). Ex-Gangster Joe Walsh Man of Many Talents.

[359] Walsh, J. (1973). Album Credits: The Smoker You Drink, the Player You Get

[360] Williams, R. (Sep 1, 1973). Joe Walsh: The Smoker You Drink, The Player You Get, Melody Maker

[361] Charlesworth, C. (Sep 29, 1973). Joe Walsh: Barnstorming the USA, Melody Maker

[362] Rosen, S. (Nov 1, 1974). R.E.O. Speedwagon: The Band That Flies Together, Circus Raves

[363] Crowe, C. (Feb 1, 1975). Joe Walsh Tends His Garden, Rolling Stone

[364] Larkin, C. (2011). The Encyclopedia of Popular Music, London, UK: Omnibus Press

[365] Heath, C. (Sep 15, 2019). Creating While Clean, GQ

[366] James Gang. (1969). Album Credits: Yer' Album

[367] World United Music. (Sep 24, 2015). Legends of Rock: Joe Walsh.

[368] Goldstein, P. (Jul 15, 1990). Atlantic Bites Back with Free-Speech Album, Los Angeles Times

[369] St. Louis Post-Dispatch. (Nov 25, 1980). People: Don Henley.

[370] Lansing State Journal. (Jan 15, 1981). Rights Waived.

[371] Loder, K. (Jan 16, 1981). Stiffs have rough time on tour, The Greensville (S.C.) News

[372] Dayton Daily News. (Jan 29, 1981). Henley asks for drug diversion help.

[373] Chicago Tribune. (Feb 26, 1981). Eagles rock star fined in teen-girl drug case.

[374] DemocraticUnderground.com. (Nov 21, 2017). Don Henley, on this day 1980, DemocraticUnderground.com.

[375] James Gang. (1970). Album Credits: James Gang Rides Again

[376] Olszewski, M. (2003). Radio Daze: Stories from the Front in Cleveland's FM Air Wars, Kent, OH: The Kent State University Press

[377] Recording Industry Assn. of America, James Gang Rides Again, (Oct 26, 1971).

[378] Recording Industry Assn. of America, James Gang: Live In Concert, (Jun 26, 1972).

[379] Recording Industry Assn. of America, James Gang: Thirds, (Jul 12, 1972).

[380] Recording Industry Assn. of America, Joe Walsh: The Smoker You Drink, The Player You Get, (Nov 2, 1973).

[381] Recording Industry Assn. of America, Joe Walsh: So What, (Jan 14, 1975).

[382] Recording Industry Assn. of America, Joe Walsh: But Seriously Folks, (Aug 7, 1978).

[383] Recording Industry Assn. of America, Glenn Frey: No Fun Aloud, (Dec 8, 1982).

[384] Recording Industry Assn. of America, Glenn Frey: The

Allnighter, (Aug 6, 1985).

[385] Recording Industry Assn. of America, Joe Walsh: But Seriously Folks, (May 31, 1978).

[386] Associated Press (Jul 12, 1985). In contrast to songs, Glenn Frey has a lot going right for him, Minneapolis Star Tribune

[387] Cedrone, L. (May 25, 1971). Very Different Western, Baltimore Evening Sun

[388] Bishop, P. (Sep 5, 1985). Joe Walsh keeps it lean and gritty, The Pittsburgh Press

[389] Heldenfels, R.D. (Aug 22, 2001). Drew Carey: Sitcom aiming for more laughs this season, Akron Beacon Journal

[390] Associated Press, Rocker Joe Walsh joins Drew Carey's band, (Aug 25, 1998).

[391] Righi, L. (Aug 10, 2007). Joe Walsh will do more than fly like an Eagle, The Morning Call (Allentown, Pa.)

[392] McCollum, B. (Jan 19, 2016). Glenn Frey details Detroit days in Free Press interview, Detroit Free Press

[393] Gilbert, M. (Nov 20, 2012). 'American Masters' profiles mogul David Geffen, Boston Globe

[394] The Star Press (Muncie, Ind.). (Jul 6, 1985). Why has rock star Don Henley taken on the plight of the American farmer as his champion cause?.

[395] IMDB.com, Just Shoot Me! (TV Series) -- A&E Biography: Nina Van Horn (parody), (May 9, 2000).

[396] U.S. Senate, Media Ownership: Hearing before the Committee on Commerce, Science and Transportation, United States Senate, One-Hundred Eighth Congress, First Session, Jan 30, 2003; Testimony of Don Henley, (Jan 30, 2003).

[397] Scribd. (Apr 30, 2016). Don Henley's Runaway Tours Appearance.

[398] Barton, D. (Jul 15, 1990). Henley crusades to alert fans to environmental decay, The San Bernardino County Sun

[399] Connelly, C. (Apr 24, 1985). The former Eagle has landed, Arizona Republic

[400] Hilburn, R. (Aug 8, 1982). Henley rises after the fall of 1980, Los Angeles Times

[401] (Jan 16, 2019). Don Henley, Retrieved from https://live.wdrv.com/listen/artist/b2c2d4fe-8c1e-44ec-8be6-ff500e105a90

[402] Unterberger, A. (Jul 30, 2017). Eagles Are Their Own Special Guests at Day One of Classic East Festival, Billboard

[403] Hall, R. (May 1, 2017). Timothy B. Schmit of the Eagles: An Intimate Chat, Retrieved from https://bestclassic-bands.com/timothy-b-schmit-interview-5-17-17/

[404] Willman, C. (Jul 17, 2017). Concert Review: 'Yesterday's Gone,' but the Music Lives on for Fleetwood Mac, Journey, Classic West Crowd, Variety

[405] Grammy Awards, 16th Annual GRAMMY Awards (1973), (Mar 14, 2015).

[406] Grammy Awards, 18th Annual Grammy Awards, (Feb 28, 1976).

[407] Rock and Roll Hall of Fame, Eagles - 1998, (Jan 12, 1998).

[408] Grammy Awards, 20th Annual Grammy Awards, (Feb 23, 1978).

[409] Hilburn, R. (Jan 12, 1998). The Long Run, Los Angeles Times

[410] Hinckley, D. (Jun 15, 2000). Songwriters take measures, New York Daily News

[411] Songwriters Hall of Fame, Glenn Frey: Eagles co-founder and lead vocalist, (Jun 15, 2000).

[412] Songwriters Hall of Fame, Don Henley: Eagles lead vocalist, lyricist, producer, (Jun 15, 2000).

[413] Pareles, J. (Jun 17, 2000). Humming the Way Into the Hall of Fame, New York Times

[414] Francischine, T. (Feb 21, 2017). Don Felder to be inducted into Florida Artists Hall of Fame, Gainesville (Fla.) Sun

[415] Talbot, C. (Feb 23, 2013). Tyler, Perry lead 2013 class for Songwriters Hall of Fame, The Jackson (Tenn.) Sun

[416] Songwriters Hall of Fame, Jackson Browne, (Jun 1, 2007).

[417] Art of the Song Coffeehouse. (Jan 1, 2012). Glenn Frey Interview: A Tribute.

[418] Ferrara, L. (Nov 15, 2012). Eagles' Glenn Frey teaches songwriting; talks tour, The Washington Times

[419] Fricke, D. (Sep 21, 2015). Cass County, Rolling Stone

[420] Cashbox. (Jun 21, 1986). If Anybody Had a Heart, Cashbox.

[421] Newman, M. (Jan 9, 2012). Bob Seger moves new fans with classic songs, Daily Press (Newport News, Va.)

[422] Bream, J. (Mar 13, 2004). A devoted dad, Seger still finds time to write and sing, Minneapolis Star Tribune

[423] The Windsor Star (Windsor, Ontario, Canada). (Dec 20, 2016). Glenn Frey, 67.

[424] Campbell, M. (Jan 12, 1984). Don Felder enjoys creating the music, Lancaster (Ohio) Eagle-Gazette

[425] Maza, M. (Feb 7, 1984). Fractured friendships, Arizona Republic

[426] Tampa Tribune. (Aug 17, 1984). Lou Ann Barton - Old Enough.

[427] (Mar 5, 1982). Lou Ann Barton's 'Old Enough', Washington Post

[428] Associated Press. (Feb 7, 1985). Henley wants to show down isn't out, Associated Press.

[429] Facebook: Don Henley, He was like a brother to me, (Jan 19, 2016).

[430] Powers, B. (Jan 14, 2019). The Late Glenn Frey's Wife Continues Negligence Case Against Doctor, Radio.com 98.7 KLUV

[431] Lynch, J. (Jan 19, 2016). Eagles Manager Says Glenn Frey's Death Caused Partly By Medications, Billboard

[432] Seemayer, Z. (Jan 18, 206). Glenn Frey Dies at 67: Travis Tritt, Niall Horan, Sheryl Crow and Other Celebs Share Touching Tributes, ETOnline.com

[433] Aswad, J. (Oct 13, 2017). Bob Seger Dedicates New Album, 'I Knew You When,' to the Eagles' Glenn Frey, Variety

[434] Lockett, D. (Jan 18, 2017). Bob Seger Wrote a Tribute Song to His Old Friend Glenn Frey for the First Anniversary of Frey's Death, Vulture

[435] Edgers, G. (Nov 4, 2015). Eagles founder Glenn Frey facing surgery; band to put off Kennedy Center Honor, Washington Post

[436] Whitaker, S. (Jan 23, 2016). Bob Seger Recounts Glenn

Frey's Last Days, Taste of Country

[437] Graff, G. (Jan 18, 2016). Bob Seger remembers Glenn Frey as "brilliant," "titanic" talent, The Oakland Press

[438] McCollum, B. (Apr 20, 1997). Unity is the theme for the Detroit Music Awards, Detroit Free Press

[439] Graff, G. (Dec 5, 2016). Bob Seger performs for Glenn Frey, Eagles at Kennedy Center Honors, The Oakland Press

[440] Appleford, S. (Jan 10, 1993). Learning From a Pro : Glenn Frey takes slight detour from his post-Eagles career to teach the craft of songwriting at UCLA Extension, Los Angeles Times

[441] Felder, D. (1981). Album Credits: Heavy Metal soundtrack: Heavy Metal (Takin' A Ride)

[442] Mettler, M. (Apr 4, 2014). QA: Don Felder on The Soundtrack of Summer and the secret to the Eagles' greatest hits, Fox News Live

[443] Teverbaugh, K. (Aug 16, 1981). 'Heavy Metal' album sounds good by itself, Muncie (Ind.) Star Press

[444] Latrobe (Pa.) Bulletin. (Sep 18, 1991). Nicks explains song on album, Latrobe (Pa.) Bulletin.

[445] Salem (Ore.) Statesman Journal. (Jul 6, 1992). Buffett-Speak: Changes in attitudes.

[446] Graff, G. (Jul 21, 1994). Buffett embraces Florida, Daily Record (Morristown, N.J.)

[447] Island Jay Islander Blog. (Feb 22, 2014). What is a Parrothead?.

[448] Palmer, R. (Aug 7, 1982). Former Eagles' solo LP debut distinctive, The Indianapolis Star

[449] Henley, D. (1982). Album Credits: I Can't Stand Still

[450] Hilburn, R. (May 30, 1982). Henley, Frey discuss the Eagles, the breakup, Los Angeles Times

[451] McNally, J. (Jun 25, 1982). Eagle Glenn Frey cuts loose with raw rhythm and blues, The Petaluma (Ca.) Argus-Courier

[452] Frey, G. (1982). Album Credits: No Fun Aloud

[453] Van Matre, L. (Oct 15, 1982). Eagles' breakup was no near-miss, Tallahassee Democrat

[454] Beebe, G. (Nov 30, 1984). Henley builds perfect beast, Santa Cruz (Ca.) Sentinal

[455] Hilburn, R. (Jan 20, 1985). Don Henley more at home out of the Eagles' nest, Los Angeles Times

[456] Campbell, M. (Feb 5, 1985). Ex-Eagle Don Henley proves he's not finished with rock 'n roll, The Paducah (Ky.) Sun

[457] Rosenberg, H. (Sep 1, 1982). Vengeful song turns rock musician into television critic, Los Angeles Times

[458] Teverbaugh, K. (Sep 5, 1982). Can't Stand Still: Multi-talented Don Henley is one high-flying ex-Eagle, The Star Press (Muncie, Ind.)

[459] Tucker, K. (Sep 15, 1982). 3 Eagles make solo flights, Austin American-Statesman

[460] Condon, S. (Jan 21, 2016). Frey had strong ties to Aspen 'partytown', The Aspen Times

[461] Oksenhorn, S. (Sep 3, 2010). The long run is not over for Eagles' Frey, The Aspen Times

[462] San Francisco Weekly. (Apr 29, 1998). Fake It to the Limit.

[463] Sharp, K. (Nov 10, 2016). Catching Up with Eagles and Poco Co-Founder Randy Meisner (Interview), Rock Cellar Magazine

[464] Bowden, J. (Jun 11, 2017). Randy Meisner Remembers Fist Fight With Glenn Frey & Other Eagles Regrets, Retrieved from https://www.youtube.com/watch?v=ZEUElqyN5CM

[465] Dillon, N. (Jan 19, 2016). Eagles bassist Randy Meisner sad he and the late Glenn Frey can't 'Take It to the Limit' one more time, New York Daily News

[466] Sheff, D. (Jan 12, 1981). Bassist-Composer Randy Meisner Courageously Bailed Out of the Eagles So That He Could Rock His Own Boat, People

[467] Young, C. (Aug 9, 1977). 2 Eagles get into altercation, Mansfield (Oh.) News-Journal

[468] Newman, M. (Jun 19, 2015). Don Henley Talks Solo Album: 'I Do Not Want to Spend the Rest of My Life Being a Jukebox', Billboard

[469] Mansfield, B. (Sep 23, 2015). Don Henley: Music 'keeps me from going nuts', USA Today

[470] Gilbert, C. (Sep 30, 2015). Don Henley: The CMT.com Interview, CMT.com

[471] The Marshall (Texas) News Messenger. (Oct 29, 1963). The Four Speeds perform at the Corral Club.

[472] Graff, G. (Jan 18, 2016). Glenn Frey, the Lone Arranger, Spark Plug, Man with the Plan: An Appreciation of the Eagles Leader, Billboard

[473] Journal and Courier (Lafayette, Ind.). (Jun 29, 1963). The Dillards - "Back Porch Bluegrass".

[474] Van Matre, L. (Mar 20, 1985). Ex-members of Eagles talking again, but reunion not near, The Des Moines Register

[475] Knopper, S. (Jan 20, 2016). How the Eagles' 'Greatest Hits' Invented a New Kind of Blockbuster, Rolling Stone

[476] Salem (Ore.) Statesman Journal. (Dec 9, 1999). The Eagles claim record title.

[477] Horgan, R. (Jan 20, 2016). A Desperado Absconded With Journalist's Eagles Softball Souvenir, AdWeek

[478] Greene, A. (May 11, 2017). Rolling Stone at 50: When the Editors Took on the Eagles in Softball, Rolling Stone

[479] Crowe, C. (Jan 21, 2016). Remembering Glenn Frey: Cameron Crowe on Eagles' Teen King, Rolling Stone

[480] Crowe, C. (Aug 17, 2015). Cameron Crowe Looks Back on His 1975 Eagles Cover Story, Rolling Stone

[481] Crowe, C. (Jul 15, 1978). They call him Big Shorty, Rolling Stone

[482] Uncut. (Feb 14, 2014). Glyn Johns – Album By Album.

[483] Anderson, T. (Mar 1, 1998). Montana artist sculpts a tribute to musical Eagles, Great Falls (Montana) Tribune

[484] Sweitzer, P. (Sep 12, 1999). Rain doesn't dampen Winslow corner dedication, Arizona Daily Sun (Flagstaff, Arizona)

[485] The Republic (Columbus, Indiana). (Jan 25, 2000). Fans 'take it easy' at Winslow corner, The Republic (Columbus, Indiana).

[486] Nebraska Music Hall of Fame Foundation, Biography: Randy Meisner, (Jan 1, 2000).

[487] Hurst, J. (Sep 21, 1980). Johnny Lee cons his way to country stardom , Chicago Tribune

[488] Los Angeles Times. (Oct 5, 1980). Irv Azoff's Front Line Management is taking over the mansgement chores for Chicago.

[489] Palmer, R. (Mar 18, 1981). The Pop Life: How a Rock Tycoon Made it to the Top, New York Times

[490] Rockwell, J. (May 21, 1978). When the Soundtrack Makes the Film, New York Times

[491] Maslin, J. (Sep 3, 1982). 'Ridgement High', New York Times

[492] New York Times. (Apr 27, 1983). MCA hires Irving Azoff.

[493] Fabrikant, G. (Oct 20, 1985). A Movie Giant's Unfinished Script, New York Times

[494] Holden, S. (Mar 1, 1987). "Starlight Express" rolls to market with a rock beat, New York Times

[495] Fabrikant, G. (Sep 6, 1989). MCA Music Group Names New Chairman, New York Times

[496] Fabrikant, G. (Oct 31, 1989). Ex-Head of MCA Unit Talks to Time Warner, New York Times

[497] Fabrikant, G. (Oct 22, 1990). New Products Help to Bolster Music Sales, New York Times

[498] Lev, M. (Jan 5, 1992). Can All Those Upstart Record Labels Survive?, New York Times

[499] Goodman, F. (May 10, 1992). Vanity Labels: Good Business Or an Ego Boost?, New York Times

[500] Holden, S. (Apr 22, 1994). Review/Film; Young, Black and Confused In the Complicated 1970's, New York Times

[501] Smith, T.W. (Apr 28, 1997). Foreman Looking for Who's Next, New York Times

[502] Strauss, N. (Apr 29, 1998). The Pop Life; Mike Tyson Faces the Music, New York Times

[503] Meier, B. (May 24, 1998). Big Money, Big Fallout For Tyson; The Ex-Champion Blames the Promoter for Financial Problems, New York Times

[504] Maslin, J. (Dec 11, 1998). Dad's a Snowman. (Is Mom Santa?), New York Times

[505] Hirschorn, M. (Mar 26, 2000). Up From the Mailroom, New York Times

[506] Gelt, J. (Oct 4, 2017). David Geffen pledges $150 million for new LACMA building, Los Angeles Times

[507] James, M. (Feb 7, 2018). Billionaire Patrick Soon-Shiong reaches deal to buy L.A. Times and San Diego Union-Tribune, Los Angeles Times

[508] (Apr 2, 2014). David Geffen, Retrieved from https://www.biography.com/people/david-geffen-9542656

[509] Sisario, B. (Feb 11, 2016). A Word With: Irving Azoff, a Hard-Charging Artists' Manager, New York Times

[510] Holson, L. (Jan 10, 2002). Importance of Being Important, With Music, New York Times

[511] Strauss, N. (Aug 18, 2002). The Lost Boys: How a Pop Sensation Came Undone, New York Times

[512] Leeds, J. (Jan 6, 2005). Talent Managing Business to Reunite Industry Figures, New York Times

[513] Leeds, J. (Nov 8, 2007). A Trade Publication Alters a Rule, Lifting an Eagles Album to No. 1, New York Times

[514] Levine, R. (Jun 9, 2008). For Some Music, It Has to Be Wal-Mart and Nowhere Else, New York Times

[515] New York Times. (Oct 23, 2008). Ticketmaster to Buy Front Line, Report Says.

[516] New York Times. (Nov 12, 2008). Ticketmaster Reduces Fees for Eagles Tickets.

[517] New York Times. (Feb 5, 2009). Springsteen: This Merger Isn't Born to Run.

[518] Sorkin, A.R. (Feb 8, 2009). Merger Expected of Ticketmaster and Live Nation, New York Times

[519] New York Times. (Feb 11, 2009). Live Nation and Ticketmaster Defend Merger.

[520] Bloomberg. (Feb 25, 2010). Eagles put the squeeze on scalpers.

[521] Chmielewski, D.C. (Jan 26, 2010). Ticketmaster-Live Nation merger gets US approval, Los Angeles Times

[522] Segal, D. (Apr 24, 2010). Calling Almost Everyone's Tune, New York Times

[523] Sisario, B. (Sep 4, 2013). Irving Azoff Starts New Entertainment Business, New York Times

[524] Iannazzone, A. (Mar 19, 2014). Jackson Returns to 'Glory Days', Hartford Courant

[525] Cacciola, S. (Mar 18, 2014). Full-Court Press Wooed Jackson to Knicks, New York Times

[526] Sisario, B. (Oct 29, 2014). New Venture Seeks Higher Royalties for Songwriters, New York Times

[527] Ross, P. (Jan 9, 1977). Dark Songs by California's Eagles, New York Times

[528] MTV.com. (Sep 13, 1985). 1985 MTV Video Music Awards.

[529] Los Angeles Times. (Dec 17, 1968). Comic Larry Hankin Opens at Troubadour.

[530] Gorrell, J. (Jan 17, 1964). Linda Ronstadt signs contract, Arizona Daily Star

[531] Pavillard, D. (Nov 25, 1966). 2 Tusconians leave home and become Stone Poneys, Tuscon Daily Citizen

[532] Los Angeles Times. (Feb 12, 1967). Latest group to emerge in the lucrative folk field.

[533] Boston Globe. (May 7, 1967). Revere Raiders Rock.

[534] Ronstadt, L. (2013). Linda Ronstadt: Simple Dreams, New York, NY: Simon & Schuster

[535] Hartford Courant. (Feb 21, 1997). Frey reunited with Don Johnson on Nash Bridges.

[536] Penrose, N. (Sep 14, 2016). Fred Armisen & Bill Hader Explain How 'Documentary Now!' Cast Irving Azoff & His Son in Eagles Spoof, Billboard

[537] Callahan, M. (Sep 28, 2000). Full Moon Records, Retrieved from https://www.bsnpubs.com/elektra/fullmoon.html

[538] Oliver, M. (Feb 15, 1999). Doug Weston, Troubadour Founder, Dies, Los Angeles Times

[539] Los Angeles Times. (Apr 17, 1951). Arnold Antiques.

[540] PBS: American Masters. (Nov 1, 2012). Timeline: Year by Year, how David Geffen Invented Himself, PBS: American Masters.

[541] Coolidge, R. (1972). Album Credits: The Lady's Not for Sale

[542] Souther, J.D. (1972). Album Credits: John David Souther

[543] Betts, S.L. (Mar 15, 2016). Flashback: The Byrds Flip the Opry Script, Rolling Stone

[544] Fong-Torres, B. (Sep 22, 1991). Gram Parsons: The Father of Country Rock, San Francisco Chronicle

[545] Rocky Mount (N.C.) Telegram. (May 5, 1974). Sunday Highlights.

[546] Beck, M. (Sep 17, 1973). TV Rock Producer, The Orlando Sentinal

[547] Everett, T. (Nov 29, 1975). Tom Waits: Not So Much a Poet, More a Purveyor of Improvisational Travelogue, New Musical Express

[548] Jarvis, E. (Jun 24, 1977). Eagles Soar to Success, Pensacola News Journal

[549] Kilday, G. (Aug 22, 1977). Rock Goes to the Movies in 'FM', Los Angeles Times

[550] Ivans, M. (Aug 17, 1977). Elvis Presley Dies; Rock Singer was 42; Heart Failure Is Cited by Coroner—Acclaim Followed Early Scorn', New York Times

[551] Selway, J. (Sep 26, 2015). Don Henley: My voice won't last much longer. But I'm lucky to have had an amazing career, The Daily Express

[552] Fricke, D. (Nov 21, 2017). Don Henley Talks 'Hotel California' Reissue, Eagles' Future, Rolling Stone

[553] Lewis, R. (Oct 15, 2017). Hotel California gets a 40th anniversary release, Los Angeles Times

[554] Azoff, I. (May 9, 2016). Dear YouTube: An open letter from Irving Azoff, Recode

[555] Twitter. (Jul 25, 2013). #EaglesonSpotify.

[556] Gartner, E. (Nov 12, 2014). Irving Azoff Threatens to Yank 20,000 Songs From YouTube , The Hollywood Reporter

[557] Shaw, L. (Nov 18, 2014). Irving Azoff Demands YouTube Remove Pharrell, the Eagles, Bloomberg

[558] Owsinski, B. (Sep 9, 2013). Irving Azoff Reinvents The Major Record Label, Forbes

[559] Knopper, S. (Dec 12, 2016). Irving Azoff, Top Radio Group Sue Each Other Over Songwriter Rates, Rolling Stone

[560] (Oct 13, 2018). 'A Conscious Uncoupling': What's Next After the MSG-Azoff Split?, Billboard

[561] (Nov 3, 2014). For Don Henley, a Beatles star remains his primary influence: 'I loved what he stood for, what he believed in', Retrieved from http://somethingelsereviews.com/2014/11/03/don-henley-john-lennon/

[562] Baltin, S. (Dec 28, 2018). Why John Lennon Remains The Ultimate Rock Star, Forbes

[563] Fricke, D. (Dec 27, 2001). 'Imagine': The Anthem of 2001, Rolling Stone

[564] Newman, M. (Jun 11, 2012). Before the Fast Lane, New Jersey Monthly

[565] Briggs, A. (Feb 11, 1966). Impresario for Big Beat Generation, Los Angeles Times

[566] Hilburn, R. (Aug 2, 1970). Atmosphere, Talent key to Club's Success, Los Angeles Times

[567] Cromelin, R. (Mar 4, 1979). Whiz kid returns to active duty, Los Angeles Times

[568] Hilburn, R. (Mar 25, 1972). Jackson Browne: Acclaim at Last, Los Angeles Times

[569] Hilburn, R. (Sep 2, 1972). David Geffen: From mailroom boy to head of record company, Los Angeles Times

[570] Chicago Daily News. (Aug 1, 1974). American dream molded in vinyl.

[571] Bate, M. (Aug 23, 1974). Paul does it his way, The Ottowa Journal (Ottowa, Ontario, Canada)

[572] Young, C.M. (Jun 5, 1977). Eagles file suit against Warner, Rolling Stone

[573] Schruers, F. (May 19, 1978). Rolling Stone notes, Poughkeepsie Journal

[574] Allen, J. (Feb 25, 1981). What makes David Geffen, New York Daily News

[575] Klinger, J. (Feb 22, 1980). JD Souther feels like a singer for the first time with Top 10 disc, Fort Lauderdale News

[576] Campbell, M. (Dec 31, 1976). Eagles become an American band, Tampa Tribune

[577] Nordyke, K. (Feb 15, 2016). Grammys: Eagles' Glenn Frey Honored With "Take It Easy" Performance, The Hollywood Reporter

[578] Webster, A. (Dec 18, 2008). The Eagles land in Guitar Hero: World Tour, ARS Technica

[579] Nisbet, C. (Jan 27, 2016). Machine Head's Flynn on his love of the Eagles, Louder

[580] Lefsetz, B. (Jan 18, 2016). Op Ed: Glenn Frey – Bob Lefsetz, Encore

[581] Carson, C. (Sep 25, 1976). Kings like Eagles, Press and Sun-Bulletin (Binghampton, N.Y.)

[582] Holden, S. (Dec 7, 1978). Jack Tempchin Lacks that Peaceful Easy L.A. Feeling, Rolling Stone

[583] Frolick, J. (Feb 12, 1979). Jules, Polar Bears melt skepticism with new LP, Austin American-Statesman

[584] MacIntosh, D. (Dec 8, 2011). Songwriter Interviews: J.D. Souther, SongFacts.com

[585] Ledbetter, L. (Dec 9, 1980). John Lennon of Beatles Is Killed; Suspect Held in Shooting at Dakota, New York Times

[586] Cashbox. (May 13, 1972). Eagles Ink Asylum Deal.

[587] Cashbox. (May 27, 1972). Ronstadt signs with Asylum.

[588] Everett, T. (Jun 10, 1972). Insights & Sounds, Cashbox

[589] Cashbox. (Nov 25, 1972). Warner Comm. Buys Asylum; Geffen 7 Yr Deal.

[590] Cashbox. (May 5, 1973). Desperado - Eagles - Asylum SD 5068.

[591] Cashbox. (Jun 2, 1973). The Promotional Stage.

[592] Cashbox. (Aug 18, 1973). Flying High.

[593] Cashbox. (Aug 25, 1973). Geffen Chairs Elektra-Asylum.

[594] Cashbox. (Apr 6, 1974). On the Border - Eagles - Asylum 7E-1004.

[595] Cashbox. (Apr 6, 1974). High Flying Jam.

[596] Kelly, D. (Jun 7, 1974). 200,000 struggle through the Jam, The San Bernadino County Sun

[597] Cashbox. (Apr 20, 1974). Irv Azoff Sets Mgmt..

[598] Cashbox. (May 4, 1974). Eagles (Asylum 11036) - Already Gone.

[599] Cashbox. (Jun 22, 1974). Souther Hillman & Furay Asylum LP As Tour Is Set.

[600] Cashbox. (Jul 6, 1974). The Eagles have reportedly embarked on a venture.

[601] Cashbox. (Jul 27, 1974). Epic Prod. Deal w/ Full Moon Co..

[602] Cashbox. (Aug 24, 1974). Eagles (Asylum 45202) - James Dean.

[603] Cashbox. (Aug 24, 1974). Eagles Re-Sign with Asylum.

[604] Cashbox. (Sep 14, 1974). Eagles cancel European tour.
[605] Dougherty, P. (Jun 19, 1981). Music Channel on Cable TV, New York Times
[606] Cashbox. (Sep 14, 1974). New ATI Acts.
[607] Cashbox. (Sep 21, 1974). NAIF Benefit Scores $105,000.
[608] Cashbox. (Sep 21, 1974). Ladies Love Outlaws - Tom Rush - Columbia KC-330054.
[609] Cashbox. (Nov 16, 1974). Eagles (Asylum 45218) - The Best of My Love.
[610] Cashbox. (Dec 7, 1974). Kellman to Front Line; Brings Ripperton In.
[611] Cashbox. (Jan 11, 1975). Points West, East Coastings.
[612] Breschard, J. (Jan 11, 1975). Talent on Stage: Eagles, Dan Fogelberg, Cashbox
[613] Cashbox. (Nov 22, 1975). Front Line Files Countersuit in Walsh Battle.
[614] Cashbox. (Mar 22, 1975). Don Kirshner's Rock Concert.
[615] O'Keefe, D. (1975). Album Credits: So Long Harry Truman
[616] Cashbox. (Apr 26, 1975). Eagles, Fogelberg Top U.S. Package.
[617] Cashbox. (May 31, 1975). Eagles (Asylum E-45257) One of These Nights.
[618] Cashbox. (Jun 7, 1975). 4th Eagles LP to Receive Special Attention from EA.
[619] Cashbox. (Jun 21, 1975). One of These Nights - Eagles - Asylum 7E-1039.
[620] Cashbox. (Aug 2, 1975). Breaks from Bob in New York.
[621] Cashbox. (Aug 16, 1975). Epic Pacts Azoff's Full Moon Records.
[622] Cashbox. (Aug 23, 1975). Columbia, Epic Dominate First Annual Rock Music Awards Show.
[623] Cashbox. (Aug 30, 1975). Eagles Go Platinum 2nd Time This Year.
[624] Cashbox. (Sep 6, 1975). Station breaks.
[625] Cashbox. (Sep 13, 1975). Picks of the week: Lyin' Eyes.
[626] Cashbox. (Oct 11, 1975). Points West.
[627] Cashbox. (Nov 8, 1975). Joni Mitchell, Jackson Browne Re-Sign with Asylum Records.
[628] Comanor, J. (1976). Album Credits: A Rumor In His Own Time
[629] Cashbox. (Dec 13, 1975). For the Record.
[630] Cashbox. (Dec 20, 1975). Points West.
[631] Cashbox. (Dec 20, 1975). Picks of the Week.
[632] Cashbox. (Jan 10, 1976). Million Midnight.
[633] Cashbox. (Jan 17, 1976). Post-Christmas Release Falloff Hurts Retailers.
[634] Cohen, G. (Jan 17, 1976). Rock Shows Debut on Cable TV, Cashbox
[635] Cashbox. (Jan 24, 1976). Ian, Eagles Receive Most 1976 Grammy Nominations.
[636] Cashbox. (Jan 24, 1976). Arista Pacts with Azoff's Morning Sky.
[637] Cashbox. (Feb 14, 1976). Eagles 'Greatest' Keys E/A/N LPs.
[638] Cashbox. (Mar 6, 1976). Eagles Greatest Hits First RIAA Platinum.
[639] Cashbox. (Mar 6, 1976). Go East, Young Man.
[640] Cashbox. (Mar 20, 1976). Scaggs Signs with Azoff's Front Line.
[641] Cashbox. (Apr 10, 1976). Eagles' Hits Remain in #1 Spot By Wide Margin, But Perhaps Not For Long.
[642] Carmicle, J.B. (May 1, 1976). The Artists: Music and Lyrics, Cashbox
[643] Cashbox. (May 22, 1976). For the Record.
[644] Cashbox. (Jun 26, 1976). Leber-Krebs.
[645] DiMauro, P. (Aug 7, 1976). For the Record, Cashbox
[646] Cashbox. (Aug 28, 1976). Turntable Go-Round.
[647] Cashbox. (Sep 11, 1976). Hooked on Lunacy.
[648] Cashbox. (Oct 2, 1976). For the Record.
[649] Cashbox. (Oct 16, 1976). Funky Kings (Arista AS 0209) Slow Dancing.
[650] Doheny, N. (1976). Album Credits: Hard Candy
[651] Cashbox. (Oct 30, 1976). Eagles Play Sold Out Forum, 3 New Songs.
[652] Cashbox. (Oct 30, 1976). Eagles Celebrate.
[653] Carmicle, J.B. (Nov 27, 1976). RKO's Abrupt Eagles' Airing Forces E/A Into Rush Release, Cashbox
[654] Cashbox. (Dec 12, 1976). Hotel California - Eagles.
[655] Cashbox. (Dec 12, 1976). Eagles (Asylum 45373) New Kid in Town.
[656] Cashbox. (Dec 25, 1976). Eagles Earn Platinum.
[657] Cashbox. (Mar 5, 1977). Modell's Advertises Eagles Album for $2.
[658] Cashbox. (Mar 12, 1977). Eagles (Asylum 45386) (Dist. Elektra) Hotel California.
[659] Cashbox. (Mar 12, 1977). Eagles 2X Platinum.
[660] Cashbox. (Apr 2, 1977). East Coastings.
[661] Terry, K. (Apr 9, 1977). Eagles at the Garden, Cashbox
[662] Cashbox. (May 14, 1977). Eagles (Elektra/Asylum 45386) Life in the Fast Lane.
[663] Weber, J. (May 21, 1977). The Eagles Sue David Geffen, WB Music, in Publ. Dispute, Cashbox
[664] Cashbox. (May 21, 1977). East Coastings, Points West.
[665] DiMauro, P. (May 28, 1977). "Beatlemania" Points to Broadway Despite Possible Legal Problems, Cashbox
[666] Cashbox. (Jun 11, 1977). East Coastings, Points West.
[667] Cashbox. (Jul 2, 1977). East Coastings, Points West.
[668] Cashbox. (Jul 2, 1977). Country Roundup.
[669] Cashbox. (Jul 30, 1977). East Coastings, Points West: Eyes of Texas on Eagles.
[670] Cashbox. (Aug 27, 1977). East Coastings, Points West: Jeans On.
[671] Cashbox. (Sep 24, 1977). The Bernie Leadon/Michael Georgiades Band (Elecktra/Asylum 45433).
[672] Cashbox. (Oct 1, 1977). Soft-Rock Stations Providing Early Exposure for New Acts.
[673] Fulton, D. (Oct 8, 1977). Talent On Stage: Linda Ronstadt/Leadon-Michael Georgiades Band, Cashbox
[674] Cashbox. (Oct 15, 1977). East Coastings, Points West: As the Eagle Flies.
[675] Cashbox. (Oct 22, 1977). East Coastings, Points West: Life in the Solo Lane.
[676] Cashbox. (Oct 22, 1977). East Coastings, Points West: Who Were Those Guys?.
[677] Lewis, R. (Nov 12, 1977). Punk Rock in England: There's More to It Than Meets the Ear, Strangler's Mgr. Says,

Cashbox

[678] Cashbox. (Nov 19, 1977). East Coasting, points West: International Gold.

[679] Cashbox. (Nov 26, 1977). Glenda Griffith.

[680] Hilburn, R. (Jan 22, 1977). Beyond the Gold and Platinum, Los Angeles Times

[681] Kilday, G. (Aug 22, 1977). Rock Goes the the Movies in "FM", Los Angeles Times

[682] Young, C.M. (Sep 11, 1977). Jaggers still together, despite constant rumors, Rolling Stone

[683] Cashbox. (Dec 31, 1977). East Coastings, points West: Life in the Film Lane.

[684] Associated Press. (Dec 4, 1977). Singer Linda Ronstadt joins list of movie stars, Associated Press.

[685] Kleiner, D. (Mar 30, 1978). 'FM' ... a movie about DJs trying to maintain dignity, Chambersburg (Pa.) Public Opinion

[686] Fort Lauderdale News. (Mar 3, 1978). Stones put touches on their new album.

[687] The Daily Utah Chronicle. (May 3, 1978). What price integrity?.

[688] Knoedelseder Jr, W.K. (Apr 16, 1978). A Rock/Film Honeymoon in Splitsville: The Makers of 'FM' Aren't Speaking to Each Other, Los Angeles Times

[689] Baltake, J. (Aug 13, 1978). Film feud: Culture vs. hard cash, Chicago Tribune

[690] Kilday, G. (Nov 8, 1978). Film Clips: The Western Spurred On, Los Angeles Times

[691] Serril, T. (May 10, 1978). 'FM' called a pleasant surprise, The Central New Jersey Home News

[692] McGuinn, R. (1991). Album Credits: Back from Rio

[693] Record World. (Sep 11, 1971). Asylum to Atlantic.

[694] Lawrence, T. (Jul 31, 1971). New Asylum Label Readies First Product, Record World

[695] Record World. (Oct 7, 1971). Geffen-Roberts to WB.

[696] Record World. (Dec 11, 1971). Production Pacts Big Atlantic Factor.

[697] Ross, R. (Aug 7, 1971). Burritoes, Lomas Crowd Pleasers, Record World

[698] Ovens, D. (Jul 1, 1972). Billboard Pick Singles: hot Chart Action, Billboard

[699] Billboard. (Aug 4, 1973). Geffen & Roberts Splitting Asylum Reins; Build Staff.

[700] Billboard. (Aug 11, 1973). Inside Track.

[701] Billboard. (Nov 17, 1973). DJ Assn Issues Drug-Abuse Spots.

[702] Rogers, K. (1982). Album Credits: Love Will Turn You Around

[703] Cashbox. (Apr 24, 1982). East Coasting, Points West.

[704] Cashbox. (Jun 12, 1982). Airplay: Station to Station.

[705] Cashbox. (Jun 19, 1982). No Fun Aloud - Glenn Frey.

[706] Cashbox. (Aug 14, 1982). Ravyns (Full Moon/Asylum) Raised on Radio.

[707] Cashbox. (Aug 21, 1982). Glenn Frey, The One You Love.

[708] Cashbox. (Aug 21, 1982). Don Henley, Johnny Can't Read.

[709] Cashbox. (Aug 28, 1982). Don Henley, I Can't Stand Still.

[710] Albert, M. (Aug 13, 1982). Merchandising: Top 200 Albums, Cashbox

[711] (Jan 5, 1980). Eagles Come Home for Christmas, Cashbox

[712] Cashbox. (Jan 19, 1980). International Dateline.

[713] Cashbox. (Jan 25, 1980). East Coastings: The Music of Business.

[714] Zevon, W. (1980). Album Credits: Bad Luck Streak in Dancing School

[715] Cashbox. (Jan 26, 1980). Air Play: Network News.

[716] Cashbox. (Feb 9, 1980). Artist Development is being Redfined by Record Labels.

[717] Cashbox. (Feb 16, 1980). Solters Appointed VP, Front Line Management Co..

[718] Cashbox. (Feb 16, 1980). Eagles, I Can't Tell You Why.

[719] Cashbox. (Feb 23, 1980). The Long Run for Real.

[720] Cashbox. (Mar 8, 1980). East Coastings.

[721] Cashbox. (Mar 8, 1980). Station to Station.

[722] Cashbox. (Mar 29, 1980). East Coastings, Points West.

[723] Cross, C. (1979). Album Credits: Christopher Cross

[724] Cashbox. (May 3, 1980). Urban Cowboy, Sountrack.

[725] Cashbox. (Jun 21, 1980). Points West.

[726] Hilbun, J.D. (Feb 15, 2015). Desperado, Setlist.fm. Retrieved from https://www.setlist.fm/setlist/ea-gles/1974/fant-ewing-coliseum-monroe-la-23ca54db.html

[727] Morse, S. (Apr 26, 1990). A night of rock nirvana at the Centrum, Boston Globe

[728] Tampa Tribune. (Jan 29, 2014). All-stars honor Beatles, Tampa Tribune.

[729] Bauder, D. (Mar 16, 2010). Genesis, ABBA inducted into Rock Hall of Fame, Associated Press

[730] Weisman, J. (Jul 10, 1972). Pine Knob Cancels Rock Con-certs, Detroit Free Press

[731] Lewis, R. (Jan 23, 2016). Linda Ronstadt remembers Glenn Frey, Los Angeles Times

[732] Calgary Herald. (Jul 31, 1990). Singer switches tracks: J.D. Souther makes his name in film.

[733] Rodgers, L. (Mar 15, 2009). J.D. takes Souther-ly route back to the stage, Arizona Republic

[734] Lipton, L. (Sep 29, 1990). Troubadour JD Souther Found acting an offer he couldn't refuse, Los Angeles Times

[735] Rodman, S. (Nov 11, 2008). He feels like a new kid again, Boston Globe

[736] Lewis, R. (Sep 27, 2008). The ballad of a classic guitar shop, Los Angeles Times

[737] Brown, M. (Nov 21, 2017). 'Hotel California' Producer on the Making of the LP, Retrieved from https://bestclas-sicbands.com/bill-szymczyk-interview-11-21-17/

[738] Sexton, P. (Jun 21, 2018). Beach Boys Triumph At Elton John's Wembley Extravaganza, UDiscovermusic.com

[739] Einarson, J. (2008). Hot Burritos: The True Story of the Flying Burrito Brothers, London, UK: Jawbone Press

[740] Tom, L. (Jan 21, 2010). None Other: Gene Clark & the Rise of Country Rock, Retrieved from http://popcul-turepress.blogspot.com/

[741] Creamer, J. (Oct 9, 1987). The Nitty Gritty Dirt Band: After 21 Years, Band Hopes American Sound Defies Classifi-cation, The Montgomery (Ala.) Advertiser

[742] Parlin, G. (Aug 1, 1987). Nitty Gritty Dirt Band: Still Together, La Crosse (Wis.) Tribune

[743] Meehan, J. (Sep 21, 1977). Music Notes, The Newspaper (Park City, Utah)
[744] Creighton, J. (May 3, 1987). New Nitty Gritty Dirt Band Dazzles Fans at Westport, St. Louis Post-Dispatch
[745] Brodeur, N. (Dec 9, 2016). Rocker Joe Walsh gets MoPOP Founders Award, joined by Ringo Starr, Dave Grohl in Seattle, Seattle Times
[746] Irving, C. (May 15, 1976). High-riding Carter turns to party rifts, San Francisco Examiner
[747] Butkiewicz, J. (Jan 31, 1986). From many bands they came to form the group Black Tie, The Times Leader (Wilkes-Barre, Pa.)
[748] Devault, R. (Feb 8, 1986). Black Tie: Pedigreed Rock, The Atlanta Constitution
[749] Surkamp, D. (Feb 6, 1986). Black Tie is a star-studded act, St. Louis Post-Dispatch
[750] Fleming, M. (May 25, 2007). The Scottsville Squirrel Barkers - From Blue Guitar to Country Rock, Northern Georgia Bluegrass Chronicles
[751] Wiser, C. (Nov 15, 2003). Songwriter Interviews: Mike Campbell, Songfacts.com
[752] Devenish, C. (Mar 19, 2002). Henley Fires Back at RIAA, Rolling Stone
[753] Andrews, T.M. (Aug 20, 2018). The Eagles once again have the all-time best-selling album in the U.S, up-staging Michael Jackson, Washington Post
[754] Detroit Free Press. (Aug 11, 1981). 'Heavy Metal' can't find right track.
[755] Associated Press. (Dec 19, 1983). Guitarist says creating is best part of music, Associated Press.
[756] Graff, G. (Jan 5, 1984). Taking flight - Don Felder's solo career soars after Eagles call it quits, Austin American-Statesman
[757] Yearwood, T. (1992). Album Credits: Hearts in Armor
[758] Duffey, M. (Apr 22, 1978). Stones' tour to begin in Jun, Rolling Stone
[759] Cashbox. (Feb 14, 1970). Film Role Set for Ensemble.
[760] Cashbox. (Feb 21, 1970). Hollywood: Meanwhile, back at the ranch ....
[761] Cashbox. (May 9, 1970). Producer Profile: Bill Szymczyk.
[762] Cashbox. (Jul 18, 1970). ABC/Dunhill Gives Ray and James Big Push.
[763] Cashbox. (Jul 18, 1970). James Gang Rides Again - James Gang.
[764] Cashbox. (Jul 18, 1970). James Gang - Funk #49.
[765] Cashbox. (Oct 31, 1970). James Gang ends European tour.
[766] Billboard. (Dec 19, 1970). How WNCR-FM Became a Showcase 'By Accident'.
[767] Record World. (Jul 25, 1970). James Gang Rides Again.
[768] Record World. (Jul 25, 1970). James Gang - Funk #49.
[769] Sigman, M. (Aug 15, 1970). Kooper Joins James Gang for Record World Visit, Record World
[770] Record World. (Nov 28, 1970). James Gang Takes Over.
[771] Cashbox. (Sep 14, 1974). The Kids & Me - Billy Preston.
[772] Starr, R. (1983). Album Credits: Old Wave
[773] Horowitz, J. (Jul 17, 1980). Nights of Sounds and Music, Minneapolis Star Tribune
[775] Carrack, P. (2009). Album Credits: I Know That Name
[776] Patterson, J. (Nov 30, 1993). 'Thread' Exudes Legacy of Eagles, Associated Press
[777] Marsh, D. (Feb 4, 2015). The Grammys in 1976: Was the Captain & Tennille really better than Jefferson Starship?, The Guardian
[778] (Feb 15, 2016). Eagles Get Presented Grammy for "Hotel California" That They Didn't Accept in 1977, Billboard
[779] Oppel, P. (Apr 19, 1980). Where Eagles Dare, Los Angeles Times
[780] Johnson, G. (Oct 15, 2018). Rick Nelson: Rockabilly Ricky, The Pop Years & The Crash, Retrieved from https://www.michiganrockandrolllegends.com/dr-js-blog/278-rick-nelson-pt-1-rockabilly-ricky
[781] Homer, S. (2012). Rick Nelson, Rock 'n' Roll Pioneer, Jefferson, NC: McFarland & Company, Inc.
[782] Tiegel, E. (Jan 4, 1981). 'Aces' unlucky for producers, Billboard
[783] Abbott, J. (Sep 10, 1989). Paul Shaffer, Coast to Coast, The Orlando Sentinal
[784] Arizona Republic. (Dec 14, 1990). 'Blues' a big hit for 'Simpsons'.
[785] The Honolulu Advertiser. (Oct 3, 1990). The jam is on tonight.
[786] Antczak, J. (Jan 8, 1991). Starr intent on getting beyond Beatle days; releases new CD, Fon Du Lac Commonwealth Reporter
[787] The Newark (Ohio) Advocate. (Apr 13, 1993). Ringo is going home.
[788] Gunderson, E. (Feb 9, 1994). Whitney and baby stole the show, The Honolulu Advertiser
[789] CMT.com. (Jun 22, 2012). Joe Walsh and Friends Meet at CMT Crossroads.
[790] Goodman, F. (1998). The Mansion on the Hill, New York, NY: Vintage Books
[791] Eng, S. (1996). Jimmy Buffett: The Man from Margaritaville Revealed, New York, NY: St. Martin's Griffin
[792] Firefall. (1977). Album Credits: Luna Sea
[793] Henley, D. (1995). Album Credits: Actual Miles: Don Henley's Greatest Hits
[794] Roberts, R. (1972). Album Credits: Windmills
[795] Roberts, R. (1973). Album Credits: She Is a Song
[796] Browne, J. (1973). Album Credits: For Everyman
[797] Browne, J. (1974). Album Credits: Late for the Sky
[798] Newman, R. (1974). Album Credits: Good Old Boys
[799] Walsh, J. (1974). Album Credits: So What
[800] The Souther–Hillman–Furay Band. (1974). Album Credits: The Souther–Hillman–Furay Band
[801] Browne, J. (1976). Album Credits: The Pretender
[802] Souther, J.D. (1974). Album Credits: You're Only Lonely
[803] Souther, J.D. (1976). Album Credits: Black Rose
[804] Barton, L. (1982). Album Credits: Old Enough
[805] Souther, J.D. (1984). Album Credits: Home By Dawn
[806] Zevon, W. (1976). Album Credits: Warren Zevon
[807] Zevon, W. (1982). Album Credits: The Envoy
[808] Zevon, W. (1987). Album Credits: Sentimental Hygiene
[809] Zevon, W. (2003). Album Credits: The Wind
[810] Zevon, W. (2006). Album Credits: Reconsider Me: The Love Songs

[811] Boylan, T. (Dec 1, 1978). The L-Ps (Terence Boylan - Don't Hang Up Those Dancin' Shoes), The (Saskatchewan) Leader-Post

[812] Newman, R. (1977). Album Credits: Little Criminals

[813] Newman, R. (1983). Album Credits: Trouble in Paradise

[814] Newman, R. (1995). Album Credits: Randy Newman's Faust

[815] The Stone Poneys. (1967). Album Credits: Evergreen, Volume 2

[816] Ronstadt, L. (1999). Album Credits: Western Wall: The Tucson Sessions

[817] Ronstadt, L. (2014). Album Credits: Duets

[818] Fogelberg, D. (1978). Album Credits: Twin Sons of Different Mothers

[819] Walsh, J. (1976). Album Credits: You Can't Argue with a Sick Mind

[820] Walsh, J. (1978). Album Credits: But Seriously, Folks...

[821] Walsh, J. (1981). Album Credits: There Goes the Neighborhood

[822] Walsh, J. (1983). Album Credits: You Bought It – You Name It

[823] Walsh, J. (1985). Album Credits: The Confessor

[824] Bonoff, K. (1977). Album Credits: Karla Bonoff

[825] Bonoff, K. (1979). Album Credits: Restless Nights

[826] Bonoff, K. (1982). Album Credits: Wild Heart of the Young

[827] Cross, C. (1983). Album Credits: Another Page

[828] Goffin, L. (1979). Album Credits: Kid Blue

[829] Boylan, T. (1980). Album Credits: Suzy

[830] John, E. (1980). Album Credits: 21 at 33

[831] Manchester, M. (1980). Album Credits: For the Working Girl

[832] Burnett, B. (Feb 1, 1981). On Music: Blue Steel, Jackson (Miss.) Clarion-Ledger

[833] Nicks, S. (1998). Album Credits: Enchanted

[834] Various Artists. (1982). Album Credits: Fast Times at Ridgemont High - sountrack

[835] Mitchell, J. (1977). Album Credits: Don Juan's Reckless Daughter

[836] Mitchell, J. (1985). Album Credits: Dog Eat Dog

[837] Mitchell, J. (1988). Album Credits: Chalk Mark in a Rain Storm

[838] Taylor, J. (1985). Album Credits: That's Why I'm Here

[839] Walsh, J. (1992). Album Credits: Songs for a Dying Planet

[840] Aerosmith. (1993). Album Credits: Get a Grip

[841] Browne, J. (1993). Album Credits: I'm Alive

[842] John, E. (1993). Album Credits: Duets

[843] Webb, J. (1993). Album Credits: Suspending Disbelief

[844] Storyville. (1993). Album Credits: Bluest Eyes

[845] Donohue, D. (1992). Album Credits: Dane Donohue

[846] Lawrence, K. (Jan 11, 2002). Musicians battling record labels over copyright for songs, Owensboro (Ky.) Messenger-Inquirer

[847] Carla Olson & The Textones. (1984). Album Credits: Midnight Mission

[848] Carla Olson & The Textones. (1995). Album Credits: Wave of the Hand: The Best of Carla Olson

[849] Bue, D. (1973). Album Credits: Nice Baby and the Angel

[850] Blue, D. (1975). Album Credits: Com'n Back for More

[851] Prine, J. (1975). Album Credits: Common Sense

[852] Fool's Gold. (1976). Album Credits: Fool's Gold

[853] Simon, C. (1976). Album Credits: Another Passenger

[854] Scaggs, B. (1980). Album Credits: Hits!

[855] Scaggs, B. (1988). Album Credits: Other Roads

[856] Buffett, J. (1985). Album Credits: Last Mango in Paris

[857] Buffett, J. (1988). Album Credits: Hot Water

[858] Buffett, J. (1989). Album Credits: Off to See the Lizard

[859] Little River Band. (1994). Album Credits: Reminiscing: The Twentieth Anniversary Collection

[860] Tempchin, J. (1978). Album Credits: Jack Tempchin

[861] Nelson, R. (1963). Album Credits: A Long Vacation

[862] Gayden, M. (1976). Album Credits: Hymn To The Seeker

[863] Welch, B. (1990). Album Credits: Man Overboard

[864] Souther-Hillman-Furay Band. (1975). Album Credits: Trouble in Paradise

[865] Furay, R. (2006). Album Credits: Heartbeat of Love

[866] Stills, S. (1984). Album Credits: Right By You

[867] Manassas. (1973). Album Credits: Down the Road

[868] Crosby, Stills & Nash. (1982). Album Credits: Daylight Again

[869] Furay, R. (1979). Album Credits: I Still Have Dreams

[870] Marx, R. (1987). Album Credits: Richard Marx

[871] Marx, R. (1994). Album Credits: Paid Vacation

[872] Compton & Batteau. (1970). Album Credits: In California

[873] Dillard, D. (1970). Album Credits: The Banjo Album

[874] Nitty Gritty Dirt Band. (1968). Album Credits: Rare Junk

[875] Brooks, D. (1969). Album Credits: Denny Brooks

[876] Clifford, B. (1969). Album Credits: See Your Way Clear

[877] Hedge & Donna Capers. (1970). Album Credits: Special Circumstances

[878] Sings, O. (1970). Album Credits: Odetta Sings

[879] Giguere, R. (1971). Album Credits: Hexagram 16

[880] Gibson, B. (1971). Album Credits: Bob Gibson

[881] Taylor, K. (1971). Album Credits: Sister Kate

[882] Siebel, P. (1971). Album Credits: Jack-Knife Gypsy

[883] Barry McGuire & the Doctor. (1971). Album Credits: Barry McGuire & The Doctor

[884] Lind, B. (1971). Album Credits: Since There Were Circles

[885] Parrish, M. (1972). Album Credits: It's A Cinch To Give Legs To Old Hard-Boiled Eggs

[886] Parsons, G. (1974). Album Credits: Grievous Angel

[887] David Bromberg Band. (1975). Album Credits: Midnight On The Water

[888] Fairweather-Low, A. (1975). Album Credits: La Booga Rooga

[889] Harris, E. (1976). Album Credits: Elite Hotel

[890] Harris, E. (1975). Album Credits: Pieces Of The Sky

[891] Fairweather-Low, A. (1976). Album Credits: Be Bop 'N' Holla

[892] Toto. (1986). Album Credits: Fahrenheit

[893] Hillman, C. (1976). Album Credits: Slippin' Away

[894] Reddy, H. (1977). Album Credits: Ear Candy

[895] McCorison, D. (1977). Album Credits: Dan McCorison

[896] Various Artists. (1978). Album Credits: White Mansions - A Tale From The American Civil War 1861-1865

[897] Woodstock Mountains Revue. (1978). Album Credits: Pretty Lucky

[898] Nuttycombe, C. (1978). Album Credits: It's Just a Lifetime

[899] Various Artists. (1980). Album Credits: The Legend Of Jesse James

[900] Various Artists. (1981). Album Credits: God Loves Country Music

[901] Coltrane, C. (1981). Album Credits: Silk & Steel

[902] Hillman, C. (1983). Album Credits: Morning Sky

[903] Harry Browning and Laury Boone. (1983). Album Credits: Sweet Harmony

[904] Down Home Praise. (1983). Album Credits: Down Home Praise

[905] Denver, J. (1984). Album Credits: John Denver's Greatest Hits, Volume 3

[906] Francisco, D. (1984). Album Credits: Holiness

[907] Hillman, C. (1984). Album Credits: Desert Rose

[908] Clark, G. (1986). Album Credits: Roadmaster

[909] Watson, H. (1987). Album Credits: Blue Slipper

[910] Durham, B. (1987). Album Credits: Where I Grew Up

[911] Watson, H. (1987). Album Credits: Helen Watson

[912] Hiatt, J. (1988). Album Credits: Slow Turning

[913] Alabama. (1988). Album Credits: Southern Star

[914] Neuwirth, B. (1988). Album Credits: Back To The Front

[915] Nitty Gritty Dirt Band. (1989). Album Credits: Will The Circle Be Unbroken (Volume Two)

[916] Watson, H. (1989). Album Credits: The Weather Inside

[917] Green on Red. (1989). Album Credits: This Time Around

[918] Griffith, N. (1989). Album Credits: Storms

[919] Berg, M. (1990). Album Credits: Lying to the Moon

[920] Rogers, K. (1990). Album Credits: Love Is Strange

[921] Foster & Lloyd. (1990). Album Credits: Version of the Truth

[922] Bashung. (1991). Album Credits: Osez Joséphine

[923] Tritt, T. (1991). Album Credits: It's All About to Change

[924] Astor, T. (1991). Album Credits: Voll Aus Dem Leben

[925] Malloy, M. (1992). Album Credits: Nobody Wins in This War

[926] Alabama. (1992). Album Credits: American Pride

[927] Restless Heart. (1992). Album Credits: Big Iron Horses

[928] Rivière, V. (1992). Album Credits: Mojave

[929] Shocked, M. (1992). Album Credits: Arkansas Traveler

[930] Reeves, R. (1992). Album Credits: The More I Learn

[931] Reeves, R. (1993). Album Credits: What Comes Naturally

[932] Bashung. (1993). Album Credits: J'écume

[933] Crosby, D. (1993). Album Credits: Thousand Roads

[934] Berg, M. (1994). Album Credits: The Speed of Grace

[935] Malloy, M. (1994). Album Credits: Ceilings and Walls

[936] The Amazing Rhythm Aces. (1996). Album Credits: Ride Again - Volume 1

[937] Woodruff, B. (1994). Album Credits: Dreams & Saturday Nights

[938] Neuwirth, B. (1996). Album Credits: Look Up

[939] Groovegrass. (1998). Album Credits: GrooveGrass 101

[940] McCaslin, M. (1999). Album Credits: Rain: The Lost Album

[941] Hart, T.L. (1999). Album Credits: Tara Lyn Hart

[942] Harris, E. (2001). Album Credits: Anthology (The Warner | Reprise Years)

[943] The Jayhawks. (2003). Album Credits: Rainy Day Music

[944] Harris, E. (2003). Album Credits: Stumble Into Grace

[945] Eagles. (2003). Album Credits: The Very Best of the Eagles

[946] Cowan, J. (2014). Album Credits: Sixty

[947] Crow, S. (2002). Album Credits: C'Mon C'Mon

[948] Cash, J. (2002). Album Credits: American IV: The Man Comes Around

[949] Barris, S. (2016). Album Credits: The Road in Me

[950] Dana, V. (1970). Album Credits: If I Never Knew Your Name

[951] Eve. (1970). Album Credits: You Go Your Way

[952] Browne, J. (1977). Album Credits: Running on Empty

[953] Larson, N. (1978). Album Credits: Nicolette Larson

[954] Carl, M. (1983). Album Credits: The Lonely Guy soundtrack

[955] Lee, J. (1984). Album Credits: 'Til The Bars Burn Down

[956] Farren, C. (1985). Album Credits: Girls Just Want to Have Fun soundtrack

[957] Tempchin, J. (1994). Album Credits: After the Rain

[958] King, B. (2005). Album Credits: B.B. King & Friends - 80

[959] Souther, J.D. (2007). Album Credits: Border Town - The Very Best Of J.D. Souther

[960] Salisbury, S. (2000). Album Credits: Falling to Pieces

[961] Mallory, L. (2002). Album Credits: That's The Way It's Gonna Be

[962] Salisbury, S. (2005). Album Credits: Sandy

[963] Dinner, M. (1974). Album Credits: The Great Pretender

[964] Pure Prairie League. (1975). Album Credits: Two Lane Highway

[965] Angelle. (1977). Album Credits: Angelle

[966] Gibb, A. (1978). Album Credits: Shadow Dancing

[967] Bee Gees. (1981). Album Credits: Paradise

[968] Vitale, J. (1981). Album Credits: Plantation Harbor

[969] Bee Gees. (1981). Album Credits: Living Eyes

[970] Shorrock, G. (1982). Album Credits: Villain of the Peace

[971] Felder, D. (1983). Album Credits: Airborne

[972] Ann, R. (1983). Album Credits: Hello It's Me

[973] Streisand, B. (1984). Album Credits: Emotion

[974] Ross, D. (1985). Album Credits: Eaten Alive

[975] Bon Jovi, J. (1992). Album Credits: A Very Special Christmas 2

[976] Zander, R. (1993). Album Credits: Robin Zander

[977] Nelson. (1995). Album Credits: Because They Can

[978] Henely, D. (2000). Album Credits: Inside Job

[979] Zevon, W. (2002). Album Credits: Genius: The Best Of Warren Zevon

[980] Bishop, S. (1984). Album Credits: Sleeping With Girls

[981] Styx. (2015). Album Credits: Live At The Orleans Arena Las Vegas

[982] king, b. (1970). Album Credits: Indianola Mississippi Seeds

[983] Haskell, J. (1971). Album Credits: California '99

[984] Witherspoon, J. (1971). Album Credits: Handbags and Gladrags

[985] King, B. (1972). Album Credits: L.A. Midnight

[986] America. (1973). Album Credits: Hat Trick

[987] The Fabulous Rhinestones. (1973). Album Credits: Freewheelin'

[988] REO Speedwagon. (1973). Album Credits: Ridin' The Storm Out
[989] Stanley, M. (1973). Album Credits: Michael Stanley
[990] Derringer, R. (1973). Album Credits: All American Boy
[991] King, B. (1973). Album Credits: The Best of B.B. King
[992] Vitale, J. (1975). Album Credits: Roller Coaster Weekend
[993] Manzarek, R. (1975). Album Credits: The Whole Thing Started With Rock & Roll Now It's Out Of Control
[994] Moon, K. (1975). Album Credits: Two Sides of the Moon
[995] Ferguson, J. (1976). Album Credits: All Alone In The End Zone
[996] Kooper, A. (1976). Album Credits: Act Like Nothing's Wrong
[997] Stewart, R. (1976). Album Credits: A Night on the Town
[998] Talton, Stewart & Sandlin. (1976). Album Credits: Happy To Be Alive
[999] Wyman, B. (1976). Album Credits: Stand Alone
[1000] Ferguson, J. (1977). Album Credits: Thunder Island
[1001] Emerson, Lake & Palmer. (1977). Album Credits: Works (Volume 1)
[1002] Gibb, A. (1977). Album Credits: Flowing Rivers
[1003] Ferguson, J. (1978). Album Credits: Real Life Ain't This Way
[1004] The Beach Boys. (1980). Album Credits: Keepin' The Summer Alive
[1005] Entwistle, J. (1981). Album Credits: Too Late The Hero
[1006] Richie, L. (1982). Album Credits: Lionel Richie
[1007] Henely, D. (1982). Album Credits: I Can't Stand Still
[1008] Ferguson, J. (1981). Album Credits: White Noise
[1009] Quarterflash. (1982). Album Credits: Take Another Picture
[1010] Ross, D. (1983). Album Credits: Ross
[1011] The Party Boys. (1985). Album Credits: You Need Professional Help
[1012] McDonald, M. (1985). Album Credits: No Lookin' Back
[1013] Winwood, S. (1986). Album Credits: Back in the High Life
[1014] Dolby's Cube. (1986). Album Credits: Howard the Duck soundtrack
[1015] Jimmy Davis & Junction. (1987). Album Credits: Kick the Wall
[1016] The Oak Ridge Boys. (1987). Album Credits: Where the Fast Lane Ends
[1017] Bar-Kays. (1989). Album Credits: Animal
[1018] Staff, R. (1990). Album Credits: Live From The Pacific Amphitheatre
[1019] Starr, R. (1989). Album Credits: Starr Struck: Best of Ringo Starr, Vol. 2
[1020] Wilson Phillips. (1990). Album Credits: Wilson Phillips
[1021] Herbs. (1990). Album Credits: Homegrown
[1022] Gibb, A. (1991). Album Credits: Andy Gibb
[1023] King, A. (1991). Album Credits: Red House
[1024] Summer, H.L. (1991). Album Credits: Way Past Midnight
[1025] Kaye, T.J. (1992). Album Credits: Not Alone
[1026] Emmanuel, T. (1993). Album Credits: The Journey
[1027] Billy Bacon and the Forbidden Pigs. (1995). Album Credits: The Other White Meat
[1028] Starr, R. (1998). Album Credits: Ringo Starr - VH1 Storytellers
[1029] Nelson, W. (2004). Album Credits: Outlaws and Angels
[1030] May 4 Task Force. (2005). Album Credits: The Kent State May 4 CD Project
[1031] Chesney, K. (2007). Album Credits: Just Who I Am: Poets & Pirates
[1032] Various Artists. (2007). Album Credits: Dear Mr. Fantasy
[1033] JD & The Straight Shot. (2008). Album Credits: Right on Time
[1034] Voormann, K. (2010). Album Credits: A Sideman's Journey
[1035] Starr, R. (2010). Album Credits: Y Not
[1036] McCartney, P. (2012). Album Credits: iTunes Live From Capitol Studios
[1037] Starr, R. (2012). Album Credits: Ringo 2012
[1038] Brooks, K. (2012). Album Credits: New To This Town
[1039] The Coloradas. (2013). Album Credits: Big Empty
[1040] Campbell, M. (Feb 3, 1977). Record Industry Goes Platinum,
[1041] Moore, L. (Aug 16, 1979). Clamping down on gold records, San Francisco Examiner
[1042] Peck, A. (Mar 13, 1977). Diamond records suggested when gold, platinum too easy, Chicago Daily News
[1043] Kot, G. (Nov 3, 2013). Eminem rekindles the bad old days, Baltimore Sun
[1044] The Stanley Clark Band. (2014). Album Credits: Up
[1045] Foo Fighters. (2014). Album Credits: Sonic Highways
[1046] Hollywood Vampires. (2015). Album Credits: Hollywood Vampires
[1047] Starr, R. (2015). Album Credits: Postcards From Paradise
[1048] Mayall, J. (2017). Album Credits: Talk About That
[1049] Bolton, M. (2017). Album Credits: Songs of Cinema
[1050] Mahal, T. (2017). Album Credits: TajMo
[1051] Starr, R. (2017). Album Credits: Give More Love
[1052] Redwing. (1972). Album Credits: What This Country Needs
[1053] Neuwirth, B. (1974). Album Credits: Bob Neuwirth
[1054] Steely Dan. (1974). Album Credits: Pretzel Logic
[1055] Quarterflash. (1981). Album Credits: Quarterflash
[1056] Prism. (1983). Album Credits: Beat Street
[1057] Little America. (1987). Album Credits: Little America
[1058] The Jeff Healey Band. (1988). Album Credits: See the Light
[1059] Toto. (1990). Album Credits: Past To Present 1977-1990
[1060] Jordan, M. (1990). Album Credits: Cow
[1061] Buffett, J. (1992). Album Credits: Boats Beaches Bars & Ballads
[1062] Boel, H. (1992). Album Credits: My Kindred Spirit
[1063] Open Skyz. (1993). Album Credits: Open Skyz
[1064] Gaitsch, B. (2006). Album Credits: A Lyre in A Windstorm
[1065] Henley, D. (1997). Album Credits: The Bridge School Concerts Vol. One
[1066] Gaitsch, B. (2003). Album Credits: Aphasia
[1067] Fogelberg, D. (2000). Album Credits: Something Old,

[1068] Toto. (1983). Album Credits: IV
[1069] The Beach Boys. (1996). Album Credits: Stars and Stripes
[1070] Pack, D. (2005). Album Credits: The Secret of Movin' On
[1071] The Blind Boys of Alabama. (2009). Album Credits: Duets
[1072] Jordan, M. (2010). Album Credits: Crucifix In Dreamland
[1073] Colvin, S. (2015). Album Credits: Uncovered
[1074] Wynonna & The Big Noise. (2016). Album Credits: Wynonna & The Big Noise
[1075] Carrack, P. (2017). Album Credits: The Singles Collection
[1076] Harrison, G. (1992). Album Credits: George's Last Concert - The Royal Albert Hall
[1077] Kenny Wayne Shepherd Band. (2014). Album Credits: Goin' Home
[1078] Miller, F. (2016). Album Credits: Double Take
[1079] Rundgren, T. (2017). Album Credits: White Knight
[1080] David Bromberg Band. (1976). Album Credits: How Late'll Ya Play 'Til
[1081] Johns, E. (2015). Album Credits: Silver Liner
[1082] Bromberg, D. (1977). Album Credits: Out Of The Blues: The Best Of David Bromberg
[1083] Tiny Town. (1998). Album Credits: Tiny Town
[1084] Carnes, K. (2003). Album Credits: The Best of Kim Carnes
[1085] Newton, J. (2010). Album Credits: Duets: Friends & Memories
[1086] Marx, R. (1984). Album Credits: The Way She Loves Me
[1087] Nelson, R. (1972). Album Credits: Garden Party
[1088] Electric Range. (1996). Album Credits: Electric Range
[1089] Springsteen, B. (2003). Album Credits: Atlantic City (import)
[1090] Rogers, K. (2006). Album Credits: Water & Bridges
[1091] Travis, R. (2011). Album Credits: Anniversary Celebration
[1092] Paisley, B. (2011). Album Credits: This Is Country Music
[1093] Blind Pilot. (2014). Album Credits: Looking Into You - A Tribute To Jackson Browne
[1094] Gill, V. (2018). Album Credits: Restoration: Reimagining The Songs Of Elton John And Bernie Taupin
[1095] Bottle Company. (1968). Album Credits: Lives for No One
[1096] Jack Mack and The Heart Attack. (1982). Album Credits: True Lovin' Woman
[1097] The Daily Oklahoman. (Dec 23, 1984). Van Halen Grabs Most Heavy Metal: Platinum.
[1098] Richmond, D. (Dec 21, 1984). Spinoffs: Making Platinum, St. Louis Post-Dispatch
[1099] Gamboa, G. (Mar 15, 1999). Rock hall ceremonies keep everyone guessing, The Akron Beacon-Journal
[1100] Horn, J. (May 28, 1994). Eagles reunion plagued by legal questions, Associated Press
[1101] The Signal (Santa Clarita, Calif.). (Dec 19, 2001). Eagle Degree.
[1102] Billboard. (Oct 9, 2018). Joe Walsh Tells His Recovery Story at Facing Addiction/NCADD Gala, Billboard.
[1103] Hoad, J. (Dec 11, 2018). Ringo Starr Blackout Drunk, RecoveryBootCamp.com
[1104] Selvin, J. (Dec 18, 2006). Worst Christmas song ever? Father Guido Sarducci takes a shot, to the tune of '99 Bottles of Beer on the Wall.', San Francisco Chronicle
[1105] Thornton, B.B. (2003). Album Credits: The Edge of the World
[1106] last.fm. (Jan 28, 2008). Lacewing (The Measles).
[1107] Nebraska Music Hall of Fame Foundation. (Jan 1, 2001). Biography: The Drivin' Dynamics, Nebraska Music Hall of Fame Foundation.
[1109] Wiseman, R. (1982). Jackson Browne: The Story of a Hold Out, Garden City, NY: Doubleday Books
[1110] Rodman, S. (Sep 7, 2014). Back to the Woods, Boston Globe
[1111] Henry Diltz, H. (May 1, 2007). The Eagles, The Uncut
[1112] Campbell, M. (Dec 29, 1976). Eagles: The 'Song Band' Soars Still Higher, Associated Press
[1113] Helt, J. (Apr 24, 2015). Interview with Former Eagles Guitarist Don Felder, MusicRecallMagazine.com
[1114] Rochester (N.Y.) Democrat and Chronicle. (Dec 8, 1973). Dylan Forms Co..
[1115] Hilburn, R. (Sep 1, 1973). Showcase Goal of the New Roxy, Los Angeles Times
[1116] Arizona Republic. (May 8, 1985). Stick: A Review.
[1117] WCSX 94.7 - Detroit's Classic Rock. (Jan 18, 2019). WCSX Classic Cuts : Smuggler's Blues.
[1118] O'Neill, S. (1983). Album Credits: Foreign Affairs
[1119] Glynn, M. (May 7, 1983). Azoff Named As MCA Disc Group Head, Corporate VP, Cashbox
[1120] Cashbox. (Jan 8, 1983). Singles Out of the Box: Don Henley, "I Can't Stand Still".
[1121] Philips, C. (Apr 29, 1993). EMI Offer Intensifies Henley Feud With Geffen, Los Angeles Times
[1122] philips, C. (Sep 1, 1993). Henley Ups the Ante in Geffen Fight, Los Angeles Times
[1123] Wickham, P.J. (Jan 23, 1988). Sun Rhymthm Section Brings Back The Memphis Sound, Cashbox
[1124] Goldstein, P. (May 8, 1983). The Azoff Wars: High-Decibel Pop, Los Angeles Times
[1125] Shefchik, R. (Apr 4, 1985). Soundtrack LPs stage a strong comeback with aid of MTV stars, Muncie Evening Press
[1126] Cashbox. (Feb 23, 1985). East Coastings.
[1127] Heaton, M. (Jul 7, 2013). David Spero, artist-manager, talks about what went on behind the scenes with the Eagles, Cleveland.com
[1128] The Times (Shreveport, La.). (Mar 28, 1948). KWKH inaugurates new radio-stage show.
[1129] Wilson, E. (Feb 15, 1956). Rock & Roll Set Adores Elvis Presley, The Tennessean
[1130] Bonfiglio, J. (Dec 29, 2016). Don Felder content with life outside the fast lane, The Herald-Palladium (St. Joseph, Mich.)
[1131] Chula Vista Star News. (Sep 12, 1963). Hootenanny is set for Saturday night.
[1132] Goldsmith, T. (Feb 24, 1987). Musician gets down to the 'Nitty Gritty', The Tennessean
[1133] Associated Press. (Jul 22, 1978). Folks are different now

New, Borrowed, And Some Blues

that he's famous.

[1134] Associated Press. (Jun 16, 1994). Meisner, Leadon omitted from Eagles reunion tour.

[1135] The Journal Times (Racine, Wisc.). (Nov 28, 1994). Former Eagles bassist forms new band.

[1136] Frey, G. (2014). Glenn Frey pays homage to The Beach Boys, (Film/Video),

[1137] George-Warren, H. (2005). The Rolling Stone Encyclopedia of Rock & Roll, London, UK: Simon & Schuster

[1138] Taylor, M. (Jul 8, 2012). Glenn Frey - Interview Exclusive, Retrieved from https://www.uberrock.co.uk/interviews/58-Jul-interviews/5430-glenn-frey-interview-exclusive.html

[1139] Poco. (1984). Album Credits: Inamorata

[1140] Floegel, R. (Jan 1, 2011). Sacremento Rock & Radio Museum: The New Breed, Sacremento Rock & Radio Museum. Retrieved from http://www.sacrockmuseum.org/the-new-breed.html

[1141] Cannon, S. (Oct 7, 2018). Bob Seger's Rarest Records, Retrieved from https://blog.discogs.com/en/bob-seger-rarest-records/

[1142] Devault, R. (Dec 20, 1986). Bob Seger rolls like a rocker one last time, The Atlanta Constitution

[1143] Rich Jr, C. (Aug 14, 2004). Randy Meisner, CharlieRichJr.com

[1144] Corcoran, M. (Sep 17, 1994). Don Henley pleased with Eagles' reunion tour, Dallas Morning News

[1145] Abeles, N. (Jul 23, 2014). In the Beginning: The Four Speeds, Texarkana Gazette

[1146] Christensen, T. (Feb 10, 2007). A duet that began long ago, Dallas Morning News

[1147] Texarkana Gazette. (Jul 23, 2014). Band shows off instruments, outfits in photo.

[1148] Browne, D. (Oct 18, 2015). Songwriter J.D. Souther Stumbles Into His Role in 'Nashville', Rolling Stone

[1149] Greene, A. (Aug 28, 2012). The Dude Survives: Jeff Bridges on the Enduring "Big Lebowski", Rolling Stone

[1150] Bell, M. (Mar 27, 2015). Musician Jessie Bridges making her own way and her own name outside of her famous acting family, Calgary Herald

[1151] Leahy, A. (Dec 17, 2014). Flashback: See Feuding Eagles 'Take It Easy' With Travis Tritt, Rolling Stone

[1152] Ellwood, A. (2013). History of the Eagles: The Story of an American Band, (Film/Video), Jigsaw Productions

[1153] Klinger, J. (Feb 23, 1980). Souther making name on his own, Colorado Springs Gazette Telegraph

[1154] Murray, T. (Mar 10, 2012). Rebels with a musical cause, Edmonton Journal (Edmonton, Alberta, Canada)

[1155] Pensacola News Journal. (May 18, 2000). The Eagles sue Hotel California Grill.

[1156] Sharp, K. (Mar 8, 2014). Rock Hall-bound Linda Ronstadt reflects on her life, legacy and music, Goldmine

[1157] Einarson, J. (2005). Mr. Tambourine Man: The Life and Legacy of the Byrds' Gene Clark, New York, NY: Backbeat Books

[1158] Unterberger, R. (2002). All Music Guide to Rock, New York, NY: Backbeat Books

[1159] Los Angeles Times. (May 2, 1963). Hootenanny included in La Mirada Festival.

[1160] Palladium-Item (Wayne, Ind.). (Jul 26, 1949). 2 Air Force Pilots Killed in Plane Crash.

[1161] The Daily Oklahoman. (Feb 15, 1959). Danny Cuts a New Disc at City Recording Studio.

[1162] Plasketes, G. (2017). Warren Zevon: Desperado of Los Angeles, Lanham, MD: Rowman & Littlefield

[1163] Martin, S. (2007). Born Standing Up: A Comic's Life, New York, NY: Scribner

[1164] Public Broadcasting System. (Nov 1, 2012). Timeline: Year by Year, how David Geffen Invented Himself, .

[1165] Criscione, L. (Sep 10, 1966). Buffalo Springfield: Buffalo Herding Clancy, KRLA Beat

[1166] Gormley, M. (May 19, 1967). The Buffalo Springfield; For What They're Worth, The Ottowa Journal (Ottowa, Ontario, Canada)

[1167] Star-Gazette (Elmira, N.Y.). (May 27, 1967). What does "Buffalo Springfield" mean?.

[1168] Express and News (San Antonio, Tex.). (Aug 13, 1966). Pop group on TV.

[1169] Kening, D. (Jan 30, 1990). Poco and the pastor, Chicago Tribune

[1170] Campbell, M. (Sep 8, 1990). "Straight and Narrow" detours Poco tour, Associated Press

[1171] Browning, N.L. (Dec 17, 1966). A Golden Name Change, Detroit Free Press

[1172] The News Journal (Wilmington, Delaware). (May 15, 1998). What's Cool: Benefit concert for Tiger Woods Foundation.

[1173] Los Angeles Times. (Jun 17, 1998). Tiger Jam I.

[1174] Eder, B. (Jan 1, 2010). Valarie Mountain, Retrieved from https://www.allmusic.com/artist/valerie-mountain-mn0002312701/biography

[1175] (Mar 18, 2019). Cashbox, Retrieved from https://cashboxmagazine.com/

[1176] Kart, L. (Apr 25, 1982). Record World's demise a bad note for consumers, Chicago Tribune

[1177] Messenger, B. (Apr 24, 1979). Record World keys hits, Jackson (Miss.) Clarion-Ledger

[1178] Kazenoff, I. (Mar 1, 1998). Trivia Sign Language, AdAge

[1179] Traube, L. (May 25, 1946). The Billboard Presents .., Billboard

[1180] Tayler, P. (Sep 12, 2009). Forty Years After Woodstock, A Gentler Generation Gapiv. Rock's Rise, Pew Research Center, Social & Demographic Trends

[1181] Lufkin, L. (Mar 22, 1981). An Ex-Eagle's Flight from the Nest, San Francisco Examiner

[1182] Voger, M. (Nov 9, 2007). Loco for Poco, Asbury Park Press (N.J.)

[1183] Record World. (Mar 18, 1967). R&B Beat: The Poor: She's Got the Time.

[1184] Record World. (Mar 11, 1967). The Poor: She's Got the Time (She's Got the Changes).

[1185] Cashbox. (Feb 11, 1967). Green Stone Inks 5.

[1186] Einarson, J. (2001). Desperados: The Roots of Country Rock, New York, NY: Cooper Square Press

[1187] Cashbox. (Aug 5, 1967). 'Intimate' Disko in NY; Called 'Salvation'.

[1188] Cashbox. (Aug 12, 1967). Smash Rushes Track of "Hells Angels on Wheels".

[1189] Cashbox. (Feb 4, 1967). Capitol Markets New Album, Tape Product.

[1190] Fong-Torres, B. (2011). Eagles: Taking It to the Limit, Philadelphia, PA: Running Press Book Publishers

[1191] Connelly, C. (Aug 1, 1991). The Second Life of Don Henley, GQ

[1192] Wenner, J. (Nov 9, 1967). Letter from the Editor, Rolling Stone

[1193] Cohen, R. (Dec 1, 2017). The Rise and Fall of Rolling Stone, The Atlantic

[1194] Hagan, J. (2017). Sticky Fingers: The Life and Times of Jann Wenner and Rolling Stone Magazine, New York, NY: Vintage Books

[1195] Rock Cellar Magazine. (Apr 1, 2014). Linda Ronstadt: Long, long time Simple Dreams.

[1196] Finkle, D. (Mar 2, 1968). It's Where the Girls Are With 'Happening' Groups, Cashbox

[1197] Brown, J. (Sep 1, 2014). The Architect of 70's AOR: Bill Szymczyk on Recording Joe Walsh, B.B. King, & the Eagles, TapeOp

[1198] Smith, B. (Jun 25, 2004). A Mood That Flows, The Gainesville (Fla.) Sun

[1199] Crowe, C. (Apr 26, 1973). Poor Poco: They Were 'The Next Big Thing' Four Years Ago, Rolling Stone

[1200] Warburton, N. (Oct 1, 2009). Down In LA ~ The Brewer and Shipley interview, The Strange Brew Blog

[1201] (Apr 19, 2012). The Poor (1966-1968), Retrieved from http://musicofsixties.blogspot.com/2012/04/the-poor-poor-1966-1968.html

[1202] (Mar 12, 2018). Chronology, Retrieved from http://www.angelfire.com/rock3/deliverin/MEISNER/randy-concerts.htm

[1203] Hinson, M. (Jan 19, 2016). A beer run for Glenn Frey: A local remembrance, Tallahassee Democrat

[1204] Weschler, T. (2010). Travelin' Man: On the Road and Behind the Scenes with Bob Seger, Detroit, MI: Wayne State University Press

[1205] Graff, G. (Oct 31, 2017). Bob Seger: the legend of the Ramblin' Gamblin' Man, Louder

[1206] Graff, G. (Jan 18, 2016). Bob Seger on Glenn Frey: 'He Had a Drive, An Imagination & A Talent That Was Just Titanic', Billboard

[1207] Crowe, C. (May 23, 1974). A Child's Garden of Jackson Browne, Rolling Stone

[1208] Goldstein, R. (Feb 16, 1967). Los Angeles: The Vanishing Underground, Village Voice (Los Angeles, CA)

[1209] Johnson, P. (Nov 13, 1966). Youths on Strip Pelt Buses, Police, Los Angeles Times

[1210] Associated Press. (Nov 13, 1966). Tenn-Agers Riot On Sunset Strip, Set Bus on Fire, Associated Press.

[1211] Einarson, J. (1997). For What It's Worth: The Story of Buffalo Springfield, New York, NY: Cooper Square Press

[1212] Cashbox. (Jan 7, 1967). Pick of the Week: Buffalo Springfield, "For What It's Worth".

[1213] Greenfield, R. (2011). The Last Sultan: The Life and Times of Ahmet Ertegun, New York, NY: Simon & Schuster

[1214] Sims, J. (Aug 17, 1972). The Eagles Take It Easy & Soar, Rolling Stone

[1215] Sharp, K. (Mar 13, 2019). Bob Seger Recalls Opening for KISS in the 1970s and the Stories Behind His Most Celebrated Songs (The Interview), Rock Cellar Magazine

[1216] Long Beach (Calif.) Independent. (Jan 23, 1970). Far-out group for nearby concert.

[1217] Bowen, J. (1997). Rough Mix, New York, NY: Simon & Schuster

[1218] Millar, B. (Jan 1, 1972). Buddy Knox, Pye Records

[1219] Rumble, J. (Apr 12, 2014). Producer Playback: An Interview with Jimmy Bowen, Country Music Hall of Fame

[1220] Schone, M. (Oct 24, 1993). In Nashville, The Eagles' Pedestal Perch, Washington Post

[1221] Thodoris, A. (Apr 11, 2012). Interview: Bernie Leadon, Hit Channel

[1222] Cashbox. (Jun 17, 1967). Now Is the Time for Hearts and Flowers.

[1223] Hearts and Flowers. (2003). Album Credits: The Complete Hearts and Flowers Collection

[1224] Seger, B. (Jan 14, 2019). Glenn Frey fondly remembered by Bob Seger, In the Studio with Redbeard

[1225] Scapelliti, C. (Jan 21, 2016). Glenn Frey: 13 of His Greatest Recorded Moments, Guitar Player

[1226] Browne, D. (Jan 28, 2016). Glenn Frey: An Oral History, Rolling Stone

[1227] Aydlette, L. (Oct 19, 2013). Joan and Alex's sisterhood of song, The Palm Beach (Fla.) Post

[1228] Holiday Fitness Center. (Jul 3, 1989). Holiday Fitness Center Ad Campaign: Glenn Frey - Hard Rock, Rock Hard, .

[1229] Catlan, R. (Feb 16, 1989). Madonna, Glenn Frey sell out to corporate concerns, Hartford Courant

[1230] Baltin, S. (Oct 20, 2018). Jackson Browne Helps McCabe's Guitar Shop Turn 60 In Transcendent Night, Forbes

[1231] Everett, T. (Jan 30, 1982). McCabe's Hippie Spirit Celebrates Anniversary, Los Angeles Herald Examiner

[1232] The San Bernadino County Sun. (Jun 8, 1971). 'Date Nites' Conclude Saturday.

[1233] Ward, J. (Mar 1, 2005). The Honey Ltd. Story: Loud Harmonic Transcendence, Perfect Sound Forever magazine

[1234] Hoby, H. (Jul 27, 2013). Honey Ltd: 'After 45 years, we're finally going to get copies of our own record', The Guardian

[1235] Cashbox. (Mar 9, 1968). Newcomer Picks: Honey Ltd..

[1236] Forgo, R. (Apr 5, 2019). Interview with Alexandra Sliwin Collins, Time Passages

[1237] Cashbox. (Nov 9, 1968). Dillard & Clark: Out on the Side.

[1238] Record World. (Aug 24, 1968). A&M Signs Dillard & Clark.

[1239] Bickhart, J. (Feb 15, 1969). The Fantastic Expedition of Dillard & Clark, Rolling Stone

[1240] Cashbox. (Mar 23, 1968). Glad: Say What You Mean

[Egg, BMI-Floegel].

[1241] Cashbox. (Jul 20, 1968). Glad: A New Tomorrow.

[1242] Cashbox. (Dec 7, 1968). Glad: Johnny Silver's Ride.

[1243] Glad. (1968). Album Credits: Feeling Glad

[1244] Feenstra, P. (Sep 1, 2012). Interview: Don Felder, Retrieved from http://www.getreadytorock.com/rock_stars/don_felder.htm

[1245] DonFelder.com. (Jan 25, 2019). Don Felder to Release New Album | American Rock 'N' Roll Out Apr 5, .

[1246] Bennington, R. (Jun 22, 2013). JD Souther, American Songwriter, The Interrobang

[1247] Geffen Records. (Aug 6, 2016). Longbranch/Pennywhistle - The Legendary 1969 Collaboration Of Late Eagles Co-Founder Glenn Frey and Acclaimed Songwriter JD Souther To Be Released on CD and Vinyl on Sep 28 via Geffen/UMe, .

[1248] Stewart, A. (May 19, 2016). JD Souther has written everything, for everyone, Chicago Tribune

[1249] Orloff, K. (Aug 15, 1970). Now Sound of the Troubadour, Chicago Star-Times

[1250] Perkins, T. (Aug 30, 2013). J.D. Souther returns to touring with a little 'Nashville' on the side, St. Louis Post-Dispatch

[1251] Haber, J. (Mar 20, 1968). Honey Ltd. -- Just for the Record, Los Angeles Times

[1252] Boston Globe. (Feb 20, 1969). The Byrds, Flying Burrito Brothers Share Bill at Boston Tea Party.

[1253] San Francisco Examiner. (Nov 1, 1969). Flying Burrito Brothers Add Rhythm Guitarist Bernie Leadon.

[1254] Wahlquist, G. (Sep 6, 1970). Flying with the Burrito Brothers, The Sydney Morning Herald

[1255] Record World. (Oct 11, 1969). James Gang: Yer' Album.

[1256] Rock of Ages Interviews. (Mar 9, 2010). Bernie Leadon.

[1257] The Remingtons. (1993). Album Credits: Aim for the Heart

[1258] Leo, J. (1983). Album Credits: Rockin' on the 6th

[1259] Nitty Gritty Dirt Band. (1988). Album Credits: Workin' Band

[1260] Miller, J. (Nov 7, 2017). Interview: John McEuen, Retrieved from https://artscenterlive.org/2017/11/07/interview-john-mceuen/

[1261] Trussell, R. (Aug 6, 1987). The Revamped Dirt Band is Alive and Kicking Up Dust, Chicago Tribune

[1262] Dean, V. (Sep 27, 2016). John McEuen on making his new album 'Made in Brooklyn': interview, Sarasota Herald-Tribune

[1263] Beaudoin, J. (Nov 9, 2016). All Acoustic Instruments and Kitchen Utensils: Nitty Gritty Dirt Band History With Jeff Hanna, Pop Matters

[1264] Goldmine. (Mar 27, 2009). Backstage Pass: Chris Darrow – A brilliant disguise.

[1265] Jourard, M. (2016). Music Everywhere: The Rock and Roll Roots of a Southern Town, Gainesville, FL: University Press of Florida

[1266] Campbell, R. (Nov 19, 2008). Poco picked up the pieces and found magic in the music, Chron

[1267] Hilburn, R. (Dec 18, 1969). Poco Highlights Its Albums, Los Angeles Times

[1268] The Atlanta Constitution. (Oct 15, 1977). Quick cuts from the rock scene.

[1269] Furay, R. (2006). Pickin' Up the Pieces: The Heart and Soul of Country Rock Pioneer Richie Furay, Colorado Springs, CO: Waterbook Press

[1270] Rudis, A. (Jun 14, 1969). Buffalo Springfield Transformed, Chicago Sun-Times

[1271] Los Angeles Times. (Jan 2, 1965). McCabe's Guitar Shops.

[1272] The Californian (Salinas, Calif.). (Dec 8, 2008). Rock club co-founder Elmer Valentine dies, The Californian (Salinas, Calif.).

[1273] Tuck, M. (Dec 17, 1966). Chaos On The Sunset Strip: Teens Demonstrate For Dance Rights, KRLA Beat

[1274] WhiskeyaGoGo.com (Apr 14, 2019). Whiskey a Go Go: History, WhiskeyaGoGo.com. Retrieved from https://whiskyagogo.com/calendar/history/

[1275] Daley, D. (May 1, 2005). Greg Ladanyi: Jackson Browne, Don Henley & The SoCal Sound, Sound on Sound

[1276] McCabe's Guitar Shop. (Apr 13, 2019). Beware: History Happens, .

[1277] Riskin, B. (Aug 7, 2013). McCabe's Guitar Shop: Bob Riskin, National Assn. of Music Merchants

[1278] Simmons, M. (Sep 24, 2008). A Half-Century of McCabe's Guitar Shop, LA Weekly

[1279] Lewis, R. (Sep 27, 2008). The ballad of a classic guitar shop, Los Angeles Times

[1280] Basler, B. (Nov 5, 1969). Musical merger is a convincing paradox, The Indianapolis News

[1281] Houghton, M. (Sep 1, 1973). A Guide to Contemporary Country Groups, Let It Rock

[1282] Dillard & Clark. (1969). Album Credits: Through the Morning, Through the Night

[1283] Allen, J. (Mar 29, 1981). With new label bearing his name, record biz wiz has done it again, New York Daily News

[1284] Hoskyns, B. (Oct 16, 2005). Lady of the Canyon, The Guardian

[1285] Miller, S. (Dec 3, 2004). Artie Mogull, 77; A&R Man Signed Legendary Acts, New York Sun

[1286] Hilburn, R. (Sep 2, 1972). A Rise from Mailroom to Record Asylum, Los Angeles Times

[1287] Lacey, S. (2012). American Masters: Inventing David Geffen, (Film/Video), Public Broadcasting System

[1288] Hoskyns, B. (Nov 18, 2005). Sex, drugs and the billion-dollar rise of David Geffen, The Independent

[1289] Henke, J. (Jul 29, 1977). Dan Fogelberg Has Everything His Own Way, Rolling Stone

[1291] Associated Press. (Mar 16, 1976). Boz Scaggs: Columbia Records ordered nothing but the finest ....

[1292] Bego, M. (2005). Joni Mitchell, Lanham, MD: Taylor Trade Publishing

[1293] Kubernik, H. (2009). Canyon of Dreams: The Magic and the Music of Laurel Canyon, New York, NY: Sterling Publishing

[1294] Knipperberg, J. (Aug 2, 1970). King of Spanish Rock on New Disc, The Cincinnati Enquirer

[1295] Patterson, R. (May 10, 2018). Glenn Frey Collaborator

Jack Tempchin Talks Songs, BestClassicBands.com

[1296] Lass, D. (Aug 2, 1970). Record Previews: Flow (CTI), Asbury Park Press (N.J.)

[1297] Record World. (Aug 2, 1981). Shell Shocked (Joe Walsh Promo).

[1298] Graham, S. (May 9, 1981). Elektra/Asylum Calls Out the Tanks To Push Joe Walsh's New Album, Record World

[1299] Record World. (Aug 15, 1981). Joe Walsh Is the Man for the Job.

[1300] Rolling Stone. (Jul 9, 1981). Eagles won't fly this year.

[1301] Good, D. (Jan 20, 2012). Joe Walsh: Saving the World, One Monk at a Time, San Diego Reader

[1302] Valentine, P. (Oct 17, 1970). The James Gang, Sounds

[1303] Guitar Player. (May 1, 1972). Pete Townshend.

[1304] Guitar Player. (May 1, 1982). Pete Towshend.

[1305] Rosen, S. (Apr 1, 1980). Townshend Talking, Sound International

[1306] Scoppa, B. (Apr 10, 1975). Joe Walsh - Forms and Textures of Rock Today, Rolling Stone

[1307] Hilburn, R. (Dec 1, 1973). Joe Walsh Will Wait and See, Los Angeles Times

[1308] Amendola, B. (Oct 1, 2015). Features: Joe Vitale, Modern Drummer

[1309] Konczak, H. (2014). Joe Vitale - Drummer for Joe Walsh, (Film/Video),

[1310] Kurtz, W. (Oct 24, 2017). The days of Joe Walsh's 'Barnstorm', Goldmine

[1311] Cashbox. (Feb 28, 1970). Creed Taylor Forms CTI Label, Operation Sets Indie Status.

[1312] Cashbox. (May 16, 1970). CTI Flows On.

[1313] Cashbox. (May 30, 1970). Insight & Sounds: Flow.

[1314] Record World. (May 16, 1970). Album Reviews: Flow (CTI 1003).

[1315] Record World. (Jun 6, 1970). Success Comes In No Easy Flow.

[1316] Billboard. (Apr 18, 1970). Flow-CTI CTI 1003 (S).

[1317] Craft, D. (Jul 27, 2006). Return to the '70s, The Pantagraph (Bloomington, Illinois)

[1318] Howie, M. (Feb 6, 2015). Whatever happened to: Irving Azoff, The News-Gazette (Champaign, Illinois)

[1319] Frazier, T. (Dec 1, 2004). The Shades Of Blue, Retrieved from http://home.unet.nl/kesteloo/shadesofblue.html

[1320] The Indianapolis Star. (Sep 11, 1971). Sherwood Sets Black Sabbath.

[1321] Fey, B. (2012). Backstage Past (Barry Fey), Los Angeles, CA: Lone Wolf Press

[1322] Record World. (Apr 20, 1974). Azoff Forms Front Line.

[1323] Harutunian, G. (Jul 17, 2015). Chasing ghosts at Lake Geneva's Majestic Hills Theater, The Beacon (Williams Bay, Wisconin)

[1324] (May 15, 2015). Pete Townshend, Eddie Vedder, Joe Walsh, Rick Nielsen, and Joan Jett rock Chicago cancer benefit, Retrieved from https://www.kshe95.com/real-rock-news/pete-townshend-eddie-vedder-joe-walsh-rick-nielsen-and-joan-jett-rock-chicago-cancer-benefit/

[1325] (Aug 3, 2016). Jethro Tull Setlist at Majestic Hills The-ater, Lake Geneva, WI, USA , Retrieved from https://www.setlist.fm/setlist/jethro-tull/1970/majestic-hills-theater-lake-geneva-wi-3c7996b.html

[1326] di Perna, A. (Jun 5, 2012). Joe Walsh Discusses His Career, Gear and New Album, 'Analog Man', Guitar World

[1327] Meyers, D. (Mar 2, 2016). The Glorious and Weird History of the Talk Box, Ocean 104.7

[1328] Billboard. (Sep 9, 2016). Irving Azoff Remembers Early N.W.A Manager Jerry Heller, His Former Boss.

[1329] Dannen, F. (1990). Hit Men, New York, NY: Straight Arrow Publishers (Random House)

[1330] Billboard. (Jan 27, 2012). Billboard Reveals 2012 Power 11.

[1331] Record World. (May 14, 1966). Dot Appoints Minor, Vescevo.

[1332] Henke, J. (Mar 19, 1981). REO Speedwagon's Big Breakout, Rolling Stone

[1333] BestClassicBands.com. (Sep 15, 2015). REO Speedwagon's A&R Exec Talks About Gary Richrath.

[1334] Amabile Angermiller, M. (Mar 24, 2017). Journey's True Believer: Manager John Baruck on How Synchs and Touring Helped the Band Reach the Rock Hall, Billboard

[1335] Sheff, D. (Mar 23, 1981). Now It's Cheat to the Beat, as REO Speedwagon Finally Arrives with 'Hi Infidelity', People

[1336] Downs, D. (May 2, 2019). REO Speedwagon - Biography, Amoeba Music

[1337] MusicianGuide.com. (Aug 20, 2008). REO Speedwagon Biography.

[1338] Forsythe, N. (Oct 7, 2016). The Red Lion Inn: 50 Years of a Campustown Rock Icon, SmilePolitely.com

[1339] Nooger, D. (May 9, 1981). Manager Profile: John Baruck Reaches the Top After 11 Years Guiding REO, Cashbox

[1340] Rettgen, G. (Apr 4, 1968). Fun and Night Life, The Capital Times (Madison, Wisc.)

[1341] Megan, G. (Mar 15, 2018). Jay B. Ross, 1942-2018: Attorney fought for the rights of musicians, Chicago Tribune

[1342] Sullivan, M. (Jun 8, 1985). They're playing our song: Remembering The Guild, One-Eyed Jacks, REO, The Pantagraph (Bloomington, Illinois)

[1343] Metro St. Louis Live Music Historical Society (Oct 16, 2018). Irving Azoff/Bob Nutt/Blytham Ltd, Metro St. Louis Live Music Historical Society. Retrieved from https://web.archive.org/web/20181016204650/http://www.stlmusicyesterdays.com/Irving%20Azoff.htm

[1344] Dey, J. (Nov 18, 2018). Jim Dey | 'I was comforted by the fact that Bob was so involved in the church', The News-Gazette (Champaign, Illinois)

[1345] Vitale, J. (2008). Joe Vitale: Backstage Pass, Ashland, OH: Hit Records LLC

[1346] Hatch, D. (Jun 3, 2010). Cue Card: This 1970 'Incident' full of memories, Peoria Journal-Star

[1347] Luciano, P. (Jun 3, 2010). Luciano: Remembering the Kickapoo Creek Rock Festival, 40 years later, Peoria Journal-Star

[1348] The Pantagraph (Bloomington, Illinois). (Jun 30, 1970). Bought LSD, Marijuana At Festival -- Policeman.

[1349] Gorner, P. (May 28, 1970). Rock Festival Forbidden, but …, Chicago Tribune

[1350] (May 29, 2017). Kickapoo Creek Film, National Public Radio

[1351] Roland, T. (Oct 14, 1998). Biography takes Eagles story 'To the Limit', The Tennessean

[1352] Hunter, A. (Aug 21, 2014). Indiana Beach Music Scene, Part 2, The Weekly View (Indianapolis, Indiana)

[1353] McGrady, P. (2017). Dan Fogelberg: Story in Song, Seattle, WA: Amazon Digital Services LLC

[1354] Lema, J. (Feb 15, 2014). Revisiting The Rec, The State-Journal Register (Springfield, Illinois)

[1355] McLane, B. (Jan 1, 1997). The One Eyed Jacks, Retrieved from https://www.benmclane.com/OneEyed.htm

[1356] Peterson, D. (Sep 17, 2012). The School of Rock, Retrieved from https://illinoisalumni.org/2012/09/17/the-school-of-rock/

[1357] Clarke, S. (Jan 1, 1975). A Certain Western Charisma, Melody Maker

[1358] Record World. (Mar 1, 1975). Azoff Countersuit.

[1359] Sekuler, E. (Apr 5, 1975). Irv Azoff: Manning the Front Line, Record World

[1360] Lake, D. (Oct 2, 2017). New Eagles Track Featured On Dan Fogelberg Tribute Album, 94.7 WLS - Chicago

[1361] Record World. (May 10, 1975). Walsh Heads for Wembley.

[1362] Record World. (Aug 2, 1975). Flying High.

[1363] Edmonds, B. (Dec 20, 1975). The Coast: Broken Wing, Record World

[1364] Kruger, D. (Oct 2, 1997). JD Souther interview, DebbieKruger.com/writer/freelance/jdsouther.html + DebbieKruger.com/writer

[1365] Vitale, J. (Aug 4, 2018). Joe Vitale/Joe Walsh Post, Retrieved from https://www.facebook.com/joe.vitale.395/posts/2113783515354681?__xts__[0]=68.ARAemvEBdex1tr7M5JZo-uteH943m1rU_D0FNbgB_iyTPOhPVFLlvA7oAl2x03YJ82dW-wE_AcWuodAn-sRLqUBnpr89Sf2zmzyuUVZkRf--DhTlK-WsXvT-18G7uILi8eXSBCK4LdDTOI4WfGwicBbF8NK-P9NMdtwq-DNkYAtDydhP6mzITaU8wbvHSMOw-395MQ6FHnnbSrtsu-pbJmW7wBYvZwJsORu0xw-FtD5LDD2Sx6e13fsT6HFzlHIaD-9FJW-Tv8k3803P-CUXkOAzZcqXn5GB3re5U0eaaWT7TgqwtAAU-if-uqm0s2ZJvNcNiSWOPvCFaZL5HYVjg5mm82r-JVR2cg&__tn__=C-R

[1366] Cashbox. (Aug 15, 1970). Shiloh (Amos 140).

[1367] Owens, T. (Dec 26, 1976). From East Texas to the Eagles: Henley returns for 'identity fix', Longview (Texas) News-Journal

[1368] Soundtrack. (2002). Album Credits: Disney's The Country Bears

[1369] Dunkerley, B. (Aug 21, 2014). Kenny Rogers on Working With Dolly, Dottie and Mall Cops, Rolling Stone

[1370] Cavuto, N. (Apr 18, 2012). Kenny Rogers Remembers Dick Clark, Fox News Live

[1371] MacKensie, B.S. (Dec 9, 2015). Joe Walsh's Power Trio Apotheosis, Medium

[1372] Kutner, R. (Aug 16, 2006). James Gang: Interview with Joe Walsh, The Aquarian

[1373] Daley, D. (Nov 1, 2004). Bill Szymczyk: Producer, Sound on Sound

[1374] , . (). LACM's Let's Talk Music Presents: Joe Walsh, (Film/Video),

[1375] Wilson, B. (2016). I Am Brian Wilson, New York, NY: Da Capo Press

[1376] Hilburn, R. (Jun 1, 1971). Burritos Switch to a Gentle Sound, Los Angeles Times

[1377] Hugg, J. (Aug 23, 1973). Eagles Set for Special on TV, Vidette-Messenger of Porter County (Valparaiso, Ind.)

[1378] Gannett News Service (Feb 13, 1990). Henley, his music makes hometown sing, St. Cloud (Minn.) Times

[1379] Hartmann, J. (Aug 24, 2009). Hartmann's Law - If It's Not Good Live Dump It, Retrieved from http://the-holodigm.blogspot.com/2009/08/hartmanns-law-if-its-not-good-live-dump.html

[1380] Fleysher, E. (Oct 11, 1971). A Hip Rick Nelson Has Changed His Image, New York Daily News

[1381] MaltShopCruise.com. (Jul 17, 2014). Featured Artists: Matthew and Gunnar Nelson.

[1382] Roberts, M. (Jan 11, 1995). Taken Past the Limit, Westword

[1383] Edwards-Rinkle, C. (Jun 22, 1986). Distance doesn't diminish pride for Hughlene Henley, The Marshall (Texas) News Messenger

[1384] Cashbox. (Sep 11, 1971). Geffen's Asylum Co. Teamed with Atlantic Label Family.

[1385] Billboard. (Sep 11, 1971). Full Talent Line-Up for Atl, Geffen Label.

[1386] Rook, J.H. (Sep 4, 2014). WLS Bound, JohnRook.com

[1387] Bashe, P. (1992). Teenage Idol, Travelin' Man: The Complete Biography of Ricky Nelson, New York, NY: Hyperion

[1388] Cole, J. (May 22, 2019). Interview: Jim Cole, Time Passages

[1389] Faber, G. (May 22, 2019). Interview: George Faber, Time Passages

[1390] Price, D.E. (Oct 27, 2016). Jack Tempchin on New Album, Glenn Frey Tribute and Eagles Classics, Rolling Stone

[1391] Zollo, P. (Mar 4, 2016). Jack Tempchin, Who Wrote "Peaceful Easy Feeling," Looks Back On His Partnership with Glenn Frey, American Songwriter

[1392] Wenzel, J. (Oct 11, 2015). Don Henley dishes on Colorado past, new album, state of country music, Denver Post

[1393] Sebastian, M. (Jan 19, 2016). Glenn Frey and the Eagles a storied part of Boulder's music history, The Daily Camera (Boulder, Colo.)

[1394] Brown, G. (2004). Colorado Rocks! A Helf-Century of Music in Colorado, Boulder, CO: Pruett Publishing Company

[1395] Engel, J. (1994). Jackson Browne: Going Home, (Film/Video),

[1396] Gratzer, A. (May 26, 2019). Interview: Alan Gratzer, Time Passages

[1397] Welch, C. (Oct 1, 1971). Judee Sill: Judee Sill (Asylum), Melody Maker

[1398] Welch, C. (Mar 25, 1972). Judee Sill: Lunch And Judee, Melody Maker

[1399] Cashbox. (Oct 9, 1971). Linda Ronstatdt: I Fall to Pieces (Capitol 3210).

[1400] Edmonds, B. (Apr 1, 1972). Linda Ronstadt: Linda Ronstadt, Creem

[1401] Record World. (Aug 19, 1972). Album Picks: John David Souther.

[1402] Carney, J. (Nov 19, 2013). Henry Diltz: The TVD Interview, The Vinyl District

[1403] James, G. (May 14, 2016). Interview With Rock Photographer Henry Diltz, ClassicBands.com

[1404] Jackson, L. (2005). The Eagles: Flying High, London, UK: Piatkus

[1405] (May 8, 2013). Embrace Collaboration: A Conversation with Gary Burden, Retrieved from http://figment. cc/2013/05/08/embrace-collaboration-a-conversation-with-gary-burden/

[1406] Segal, D. (Apr 24, 2010). Calling Almost Everyone's Tune, New York Times

[1407] Kurutz, S. (Aug 22, 2019). Bill Szymczyk, AllMusic

[1408] Walsh, J. (Oct 31, 2014). Glyn Johns interview: My 50 years of producing rock classics, The Independent

[1409] Morrison, J. (Oct 22, 2018). Country-rock Icon JD Souther Comes to Attucks, Veer

[1410] MPR. (Nov 28, 2016). The Song 'Reed Petite' Boosted Motown.

[1411] Brown, M. (Jan 23, 2016). Berry Gordy: The Man Who Built Motown, The Telegraph

[1412] Graham, A. (Jan 18, 2016). Eagles' Glenn Frey a 'soul guy in a country rock band', The Detroit News

[1413] McEuen, J. (Apr 1, 2018). John McEuen: The Life I've Picked,

[1414] Young, R. (Apr 11, 2017). Timothy B. Schmit On Going Solo, The Eagles And His Life In Music, WBUR 90.9 FM

[1415] Larsen, P. (Jan 4, 2017). Eagles' bassist Timothy B. Schmit is back on his own, Orange County Register

[1416] DeMasi, V. (Nov 15, 2017). Timothy B. Schmit Returns to His Roots on 'Leap of Faith', Guitar Player

[1417] Parks, J. (May 11, 2012). The EAGLES Timothy B. Schmit talks about The Long Run, his solo career and life as an Eagle, Legendary Rock Interviews

[1418] (Jun 1, 2009). Don Henley: Off the Record, Off the Record with Joe Benson

[1419] Harry, B. (Jan 1, 1992). The Ultimate Beatles Encyclopedia,

[1420] Cromelin, R. (Sep 1, 1973). Jackson Browne: in concert at McCabe's, Phonograph Record

[1421] Worrell, B. (Nov 23, 2015). The Gear of the Eagles Guitarists, Reverb

[1422] (Jan 24, 2006). The Earliest Days of the Electric Guitar, Retrieved from http://www.rickenbacker.com/history_early.asp

[1423] Burrows, T. (2013). 1001 Guitars To Dream of Playing Before You Die, London, UK: Universe Publishing

[1424] Wagner, D. (Apr 26, 1970). James Gang - Yer' Album, Green Bay (Wis.) Press-Gazette

[1425] Knippenberg, J. (Oct 12, 1969). Cultists Like James Gang, Cincinnati Enquirer

[1426] Johnson, J. (Jun 7, 1969). 'Who' Creates an Ambitious 75-Minute 'Pop, Rock Opera', Atlanta Journal-Constitution

[1427] Goodman, J. (Jul 4, 1948). Capsule Disc Will prove Boon to Lazy, Salt Lake Tribune

[1428] Tucker, G. (Mar 17, 1949). Disk Gets Us in an Old Groove Once More, Salem Statesman-Journal

[1429] St. Louis Post-Dispatch. (Feb 15, 1949). Rainbow Music.

[1430] Tampa Bay Times. (Sep 14, 1958). Stereo on Singles.

[1431] McCash, D. (Jun 21, 2018). The Eagles walked to New Orleans Wednesday and won our hearts, New Orleans Times-Picayune

[1432] Sublette, N. (2009). The Year Before the Flood: A Story of New Orleans, Chicago, IL: Chicago Review Press

[1433] Puschmann, K. (Mar 16, 2017). The Eagles' Don Henley reveals the secret to writing a classic song, New Zealand Herald

[1434] Martin, T. (Jul 10, 1987). 'Dirty' Song Coming To Town, The Gaffney (S.C.) Ledger

[1435] Gillette, C. (2011). The Sound of the City: The Rise of Rock and Roll, New York, NY: Da Capo Press

[1436] (Jun 13, 2013). Billy Ward and the Dominoes, Retrieved from http://www.soulwalking.co.uk/Billy%20 Ward%20&%20Dominoes.html

[1437] Van Matre, L. (Aug 9, 1989). Lone Eagle, Chicago Tribune

[1438] (Jan 1, 1986). Alan Freed: The Boundary Smashing, Trend-Setting Evangelist of Rock and Roll, Retrieved from https://www.rockhall.com/inductees/alan-freed

[1439] Sheerin, J. (Mar 21, 2012). How the world's first rock concert ended in chaos, BBC News

[1440] (Oct 17, 2017). Elvis Presley, Retrieved from https:// www.sunrecords.com/artists/elvis-presley

[1441] (Nov 6, 2019). Elvis Preseley, Retrieved from https:// www.rockhall.com/inductees/elvis-presley

[1442] Young, C.M. (May 29, 2008). Eagles: Peaceful, Uneasy Feeling, Rolling Stone

[1443] Owston, J. (Oct 26, 2013). Asylum Records: James Dean, Retrieved from http://zeegrooves.blogspot. com/2013/10/asylum-records-james-dean.html

[1444] Vozick-Levinson, S. (Mar 7, 2009). The Eagles get censored. Wait, what?, Entertainment Weekly

[1445] Iorio, P. (Dec 6, 2017). Don Henley's 'Goddamn' Problem, Huffington Post

[1446] National Coalition Against Censorship (Nov 28, 2014). Music Censorship in America; A Brief History, NCOC

[1447] Garside, S. (Feb 15, 1977). Rob Strandlund Promising, Paterson (N.J.) News

[1448] Applefeld Olson, C. (Jun 4, 2019). 2019 SHOF Inductee Jack Tempchin Tells the Tale Behind 'Peaceful Easy Feeling', Billboard

[1449] (Jul 25, 1969). Steve Young: Rock Salt and Nails, Calgary Herald

[1450] Mortiarity, E. (Mar 18, 1978). Steve Young: Worth the Wait, Johnson City (Tenn.) Press

[1451] McNally, J. (Dec 19, 1980). 'Eagles Live' is a passable album of some of the band's best songs, The Petaluma (Calif.) Argus-Courier

[1452] Betts, S. (Mar 18, 2016). 'Seven Bridges Road' Singer Steve Young Dead at 73, Rolling Stone

[1453] Freeland, D. (Sep 23, 2019). Behind the Song: The Eagles "Seven Bridges Road", American Songwriter

[1454] Elber, L. (May 1, 2002). 'American Bandstand' celebrates in style, Associated Press

[1455] Scranton (Pa.) Times-Tribune. (Aug 3, 1957). 'American Bandstand' makes debut Aug. 5.

[1456] Philadelphia Inquirer. (Jan 21, 1964). Taping of 'Bandstand' goes west in wake of Clark's departure.

[1457] Sacduto, A. (1974). Mick Jagger: Everybody's Lucifer, London, UK: Berkley Medallion

[1458] Cedrone Jr, L.R. (Jun 17, 1964). Hair Gets Longer and Longer, Baltimore Evening Sun

[1459] Gilmore, E. (Jun 1, 1964). Recovered from the Beatles? Rolling Stones Arrive Tuesday, Associated Press

[1460] (Jan 11, 2019). The Story Behind The Music: Seven Bridges Road, Retrieved from https://routepublishing.wordpress.com/2019/01/11/the-story-behind-the-music-seven-bridges-road/

[1461] Kazek, K. (Nov 8, 2018). Alabama is home to the real 'Seven Bridges Road', The Birmingham (Ala.) News

[1462] Redwing Online (Feb 24, 2003). Redwing? Glad? New Breed? Sorting it all out: A brief history, Redwing Online. Retrieved from http://www.desktop21.com/redwing/

[1463] Basler, B. (Nov 5, 1969). Musical merger is a convincing paradox, The Indianapolis News

[1464] Roberts, R. (2015). Lame Brain: My Journey Back to Real Life, Longmont, CO: Mount James Publishing

[1465] Segal, D. (Apr 24, 2010). Calling Almost Everyone's Tune, New York Times

[1466] Gibson.com (Jun 8, 2012). Joe Walsh Says Duane Allman Taught Him Slide Guitar, Gibson.com. Retrieved from http://es.gibson.com/News-Lifestyle/News/en-us/joe-walsh-says-duane-allman-0608-2012.aspx

[1467] Aledort, A. (Nov 20, 2018). Slidedog: The Slide Guitar Mastery of Duane Allman, Guitar World

[1468] Poe, R. (2006). Skydog: The Duane Allman Story, New York, NY: Backbeat Books

[1469] (Jan 8, 2019). A Taste of Rainmakers: Irving Azoff, Hits Daily Double

[1470] Greenhaw, W. (2001). My Heart Is in the Earth: True Stories of Alabama & Mexico, Montgomery, AL: River City Publishing

[1471] Malone, J. (Oct 11, 1996). Interview, Mike Nesmith, The Janice Malone Show

[1472] Matthews, I. (1993). Album Credits: The Soul of Many Places: The Elektra Years, 1972-1974

[1473] Davis, C. (2013). Clive Davis: The Soundtrack of My Life, New York, NY: Simon & Schuster

[1474] Kreps, D. (Mar 5, 2009). Eagles At Center of Goddamn "Fast Lane" Censorship Battle, Rolling Stone

[1475] Hamilton, A. (Nov 5, 2015). Celebrating Seniors - JD Souther Turns 70, Retrieved from https://50plusworld.com/celebrating-seniors-jd-souther-turns-70/

[1476] Scoppa, B. (Jun 22, 1972). The Flying Burrito Brothers : Last of the Red Hot Burritos, Rolling Stone

Photo Credits

Every effort has been made to identify copyright holders and obtain their permission for the use of copyrighted material. Images reproduced with permission appear below with page citation. Notification of any additions or corrections that should be incorporated in future reprints or editions of this book would be greatly appreciated.

Made in the USA
Monee, IL
15 February 2023

27835169R10136